International Law and Economics

The world has been experiencing a long period of globalization. At the same time, ever more international law has been created to deal with the many consequences of globalization such as problems of coordination, spillover effects across countries, the protection of foreign direct investment or the prosecution of crimes against humanity. To date, the economic analysis of international law has been lagging behind this development. This series aims at changing this by contributing to the understanding of international law. It strives to be a forum for contributions on all aspects of the economic analysis of international law ranging from the analysis of the genesis of international law, its ratification, its effects on government behavior, the means to monitor compliance to sanctions against actors not complying with the law.

Oliver Englisch

Automated Copyright Filters

A Law and Economics Analysis

Springer

Oliver Englisch
University of Hamburg
Hamburg, Germany

ISSN 2364-1851 ISSN 2364-186X (electronic)
International Law and Economics
ISBN 978-3-031-83160-7 ISBN 978-3-031-83161-4 (eBook)
https://doi.org/10.1007/978-3-031-83161-4

This Springer imprint is published by the registered company Springer Nature Switzerland AG
The registered company address is: Gewerbestrasse 11, 6330 Cham, Switzerland

Preface

Is it socially desirable to automate the enforcement of legal rules? This question initiated the journey that led me to write this book. It cannot be answered in general as the trade-offs involved vary significantly between different areas of law. Automated filters to enforce copyright law on user-uploaded content platforms are a logical starting point: They play a pioneering role, are applied on a large scale, and have received considerable attention in the academic and public discourse—especially in connection with the EU Copyright in the Digital Single Market Directive.

A review of the extensive literature on automated copyright filtering reveals a scarcity of research from a law and economics perspective. This research gap is unfortunate. An understanding of automated copyright filtering requires insights on strategic interactions between the various actors, efficient decision-making in the face of uncertainty, and discrepancies between privately and socially efficient incentives. Economic analysis is an excellent tool for shedding light on these issues.

As a lawyer who received a solid education in economics during his undergraduate studies, I saw myself well prepared to take on the challenge of contributing to closing the research gap. To be able to meet the standards of legal and economic research, I expanded my knowledge through various graduate-level courses on microeconomics, law and economics, and copyright law at the University of Hamburg and the University of Oxford. My working environment at the Institute of Law and Economics at the University of Hamburg was highly conducive to interdisciplinary research as it allowed me to engage in regular dialogue with researchers from both disciplines.

I was fortunate to receive invaluable support from my supervisor, Professor Georg von Wangenheim, to whom I am most grateful. He sparked my interest in the economic analysis of law during my undergraduate studies and provided support in my academic pursuits ever since. His advice, critical comments, and creative ideas played a major role in bringing this book to life. I am also indebted to my second supervisor, Professor Stefan Voigt, who provided crucial counsel on how to focus my research and offered great support with respect to its publication.

A research stay at the University of Oxford proved to be an extremely fruitful opportunity for advancing my research. I am most grateful to my academic advisor, Professor Dev Gangjee, for his guidance and for introducing me to scholars engaged in related fields. I would also like to thank Professor Graeme Dinwoodie as well as Professor Wolf-Georg Ringe for making the visit possible and the members of the Oxford Intellectual Property Research Centre for numerous thought-provoking discussions. My research further benefitted from the opportunity to use the outstanding library of the Max Planck Institute for Innovation and Competition, for which I am most thankful.

Several people read or listened to different versions of my research and provided support by making suggestions, pointing out weaknesses, as well as praising strengths. I would like to express my gratitude to Professor Anne van Aaken, Professor Paul Belleflamme, Professor Walter Blocher, Dr. Marek Endrich, Professor Christoph Engel, Linda Englisch, Professor Michèle Finck, Professor Henning Grosse Ruse-Khan, Dr. Dr. Oliver Hofmann, Dr. Michael Karas, Professor Annette Kur, Maximilian Mantei, Professor Viktor Mayer-Schönberger, Dr. Stephan Michel, Professor Giulia Priora, Professor Kristoff Ritlewski, and Dr. Antonia Sommerfeld. I am also thankful for numerous helpful comments by members of the graduate school 'The Economics of the Internationalisation of the Law' at the University of Hamburg as well as by participants of the Colloquium Recht & Ökonomie at the University of Kassel, of the Intellectual Property Discussion Group at the Oxford Intellectual Property Research Centre, and of the Young Scholars IP Lecture Series at Bucerius Law School.

I had the privilege of receiving a generous scholarship, financial assistance for my research stay, and a reimbursement of expenses for conferences as well as workshops from the German Research Foundation, for which I am most grateful. Moreover, I highly appreciate the excellent support provided by the team at Springer Nature in the publishing process.

Last but not least, I cannot thank my family, friends, and Antonia enough for their unwavering support during the journey.

The results of my research are presented in this book. They show how automated copyright filtering affects the goals of copyright policy, how errors can most efficiently be avoided, and how right holders' and platforms' incentives can best be aligned to social desirability. The book thereby offers a new perspective on crucial questions and helps to disentangle complex relationships as well as to scrutinise prevailing assumptions. At the same time, it points to several unresolved questions. It is my hope that it will not only enhance our understanding of automated copyright filtering but also serve as a starting point and source of inspiration for future law and economics research on this and related topics.

Hamburg, Germany | Oliver Englisch

Contents

Chapter 1
Introduction

Abstract Automated filtering has considerable potential to protect the interests of right holders; however, it also carries the risk of producing serious negative side effects. This introduction sets out the approach taken in this book to examine how a well-balanced design of automated filtering can be achieved. It further provides working definitions and explanations of key terms to clarify the scope of analysis.

'Thank you and congratulations to all of you for safeguarding video for years to come' (The Emmy Awards, 2018, 1:17:34). With these solemn words, the host of the 69th Annual Technology and Engineering Emmy Awards Ceremony concluded the honouring of providers of technology used to detect copyright-protected content. Not long after, thousands of infuriated protesters took to the streets across the EU to voice their opposition against the imminent adoption of the Copyright in the DSM Directive (2019) (Reuter, 2019), which obliges EU Member States to introduce a liability regime that effectively requires user-uploaded content platforms to automatically filter out copyright-infringing upload attempts. These diametrically opposed perceptions are indicative of a technology that has great potential to protect the interests of right holders but also carries the risk of producing serious negative side effects.

The main negative side effect is that automated filters block lawful upload attempts. The state-of-the-art technology fingerprinting estimates the likelihood of a copyright infringement by assessing the similarity between an upload attempt and a work in a reference database. It cannot emulate the standard-based and context-dependent legal analysis necessary to determine whether an upload attempt infringes copyright law. Automated filters therefore produce errors. This consideration is supported by empirical evidence.[1] It led some commentators to oppose filtering (Civil Liberties Union for Europe and others, 2017; Open Rights Group, 2016,

[1] For example, Erickson and Kretschmer (2018) observe the availability of 1,839 YouTube music video parodies between January 2012 and December 2016. They find that in December 2016, 32.9% of the parodies were taken down because of alleged copyright infringements. While it is unclear how many of these parodies were lawful, it is likely that many of them were indeed covered by a copyright exception. Jacques et al. (2018) use the same data set but report a higher percentage

O. Englisch, *Automated Copyright Filters*, International Law and Economics,
https://doi.org/10.1007/978-3-031-83161-4_1

paras. 10–11, 29–31; J. Reda, 2017). While the underlying concern regarding users' freedom of speech is justified, it is important to note that the use of an automated filter is not an either-or decision: Platforms make various design choices, and each choice influences the social costs and benefits of filtering.

This book investigates how a well-balanced design of automated filtering can be achieved. The remainder of this introduction outlines the course of analysis (Sect. 1.1) and provides working definitions as well as explanations of key terms to clarify the scope of analysis (Sect. 1.2).

1.1 Course of Analysis

To examine how a well-balanced design of automated filtering can be achieved, it is crucial to understand how filtering affects the goals copyright policy pursues. From an economic perspective, copyright policy seeks to incentivise content creation by increasing right holders' profits and to promote access to creative content. However, a review of the existing literature in Sect. 3.1 shows that the effects of automated filtering on these objectives have not yet been analysed when considering the competition between right holders and unlawful copiers. Chapter 3 therefore addresses the following research question:

Research Question 1[2]
How does automated filtering affect right holders' profits and the number of works uploaded to a user-uploaded content platform when right holders compete with unlawful copiers for views?

Chapter 3 inter alia finds that automated filters promote right holders' interests even if they do not block all unlawful uploads of a work, that is, produce errors in the form of false negatives. As the avoidance of false negatives requires investments in filtering or leads to a higher probability of false positives, this finding raises the question how filters should be designed to efficiently[3] avoid errors. However, a review of the extant literature in Sect. 4.1 shows that despite some relevant contributions, the design of automated filtering to best approach efficient error avoidance

of parodies taken down for alleged copyright infringements: 38.5%. In addition, they analyse the sources of takedowns and find that most parodies were taken down through YouTube's Content ID.

[2]The numbering serves to facilitate references to research questions. It does not rank the questions.

[3]In this book, efficiency refers to Kaldor–Hicks efficiency, that is, a state in which no reorganisation is possible that would yield benefits for 'winners' that are so high that 'losers' could be compensated while winners keep some of the benefits. The concept goes back to writings by Kaldor (1939, p. 550) and Hicks (1939, p. 706).

has not yet been analysed comprehensively. Chapter 4 therefore addresses the following research question:

> **Research Question 2**
> What design of automated filtering best approaches efficient error avoidance?

To approach the design of automated filtering sketched in Chap. 4, right holders and platforms must strive for efficiency from a social perspective. However, in the absence of regulation, neither right holders nor platforms have socially efficient incentives.[4] It is thus crucial to understand how their incentives can best be improved. While some measures to influence right holders' and platforms' incentives have been discussed, a review of the related literature in Sect. 5.1 shows that it has not yet been examined comprehensively how right holders' and platforms' incentives can best be steered towards efficiency. Chapter 5 therefore answers the following research question:

> **Research Question 3**
> How can a policymaker best steer right holders' and user-uploaded content platforms' incentives to design automated filtering towards efficiency?

Theoretical economic analysis is particularly well-suited to address these research questions: It offers methods and analytical frameworks to examine strategic decision-making as well as to identify and compare social costs and benefits. The research questions have different characteristics. To ensure that each question is addressed in the most feasible way, this book applies different approaches to each question. The approaches are explained and justified at the beginning of each chapter.

Before diving into the analysis, it is useful to outline the relevant economic, technical, and legal background. Chapter 2 performs this task. Finally, Chap. 6 concludes by summarising the main contributions to the literature and indicating starting points for future research.

1.2 Key Terms and Scope of Analysis

This section explains how key terms related to user-uploaded content platforms (Sect. 1.2.1), the lawfulness of uploads (Sect. 1.2.2), and automated filtering (Sect. 1.2.3) are understood in this book. It thereby also delimits the scope of analysis.

[4] For explanation, see Sect. 5.3.1 (right holders' incentives) and Sect. 5.4.1 (platforms' incentives).

1.2.1 User-Uploaded Content Platforms

In this book, the term user-uploaded content platforms refers to services to which users can upload music or videos in such a way that their uploads become directly available to other users. Prominent examples of such platforms are Dailymotion, Facebook, Instagram, Mixcloud, Soundcloud, Twitch, Veoh, Vimeo, and YouTube. The working definition points to two key characteristics. First, a user-uploaded content platform hosts music or videos. To keep the analysis focused, other types of copyright-protected subject matter (e.g. images, text, or software code) are not considered.[5] Second, users' uploads become directly available to other users. This excludes services that are not open to user uploads, for example, Amazon Prime, Apple Music, Deezer, Netflix, and Spotify. Automated filtering does not, of course, exclude platforms from the working definition.

Note that many alternative terms for user-uploaded content platforms exist, for example, hosting services, online content-sharing service providers, online platforms, online service providers, and user-generated content platforms. For the sake of clarity, this book consistently uses the term (user-uploaded content) platforms, except when the wording of a legal provision is relevant for the discussion. In the interest of readability, the addition 'user-uploaded content' is omitted unless useful for a distinction between user-uploaded content platforms and other types of platforms.

Three types of actors participate on platforms: viewers, uploaders, and advertisers. The term viewers refers to individuals who access content. It encompasses listeners of music. Uploaders include individuals who unlawfully upload content and individuals who lawfully upload content. A lawful uploader is either the right holder or a person who is otherwise permitted to upload, for example, because of a non-exclusive licence or a copyright exception. The term right holder refers to the copyright owner unless the copyright owner has granted an exclusive licence, in which case the exclusive licensee is the right holder.

Note that viewers and uploaders are not necessarily different people. The same person may at times be a viewer, at times an unlawful uploader, and at other times a lawful uploader. This multiplicity of roles is not relevant for the research interests of this book. For simplicity, viewers, unlawful uploaders, and lawful uploaders are thus treated as different people.

A distinction between viewers and uploaders is sometimes not needed. In such cases, the term users refers to both viewers and uploaders. Likewise, when a distinction between users and advertisers is not necessary, the term platform participants refers to users and advertisers.

[5]For an overview of the availability of filtering technology and reference databases for different types of subject matter, see Gann and Abecassis (2018, pp. 8–10).

1.2.2 Lawfulness of Uploads

The terms unlawful uploads and copyright-infringing uploads refer to uploads that infringe right holders' economic rights in music or videos.

Copyright law not only protects creative works but also related activities. Many countries and international conventions distinguish between authors' and neighbouring rights.[6] Authors' rights grant exclusive rights to authors of works. A neighbouring right protects a person whose non-authorial creation involves a work, for example, a performer or sound recording producer. This book considers infringements of both types of rights since automated filtering is arguably employed to remove content regardless of whether authors' or neighbouring rights are infringed.[7] In the interest of readability, the term copyright is used for authors' and neighbouring rights unless a distinction is needed.

Uploads can be illegal for other reasons, for example, if they contain hate speech or child abuse imagery. However, as each type of illegal content has unique characteristics, this book focuses on copyright infringements.

Uploads may further infringe right holders' moral rights.[8] Unlike economic rights, which relate to the commercial exploitation of content, moral rights protect the connection between authors or performers and their content as elements of their personalities. While automated detection of infringements of moral rights is conceivable,[9] it would be an entirely different task than filtering for infringements of

[6]These terms are translations of the French terms *droit d'auteur* and *droits voisins*. Frequently used synonyms are copyright and related rights, respectively. Some legal systems do not explicitly distinguish between authors' and neighbouring rights. However, conceptually, they can still be separated.

[7]For example, in the EU, Article 17(4) of the Copyright in the DSM Directive (2019) introduces liability of platforms for unauthorised uploads of 'copyright-protected works and other subject matter'.

[8]International copyright law contains two moral rights: right of attribution and right of integrity (for authors: Article 6bis(1) of the Berne Convention, 1886; for performers: Article 5(1) of the WIPO Performances and Phonograms Treaty, 1996). The right of attribution entitles authors or performers to have the authorship or performance recognised. Uploading content without a (correct) indication of the author or performer may infringe this right. The right of integrity enables authors and performers to prohibit alterations that hurt their honour or reputation. An upload of a modified version of a work may infringe this right. As a rule of thumb, at least explicit moral rights protection is stronger in civil law than in common law countries (see Goldstein & Hugenholtz, 2013, p. 358). Yet, even if copyright law does not grant a moral right, the essence of the right may still be protected by provisions outside copyright law (Hurt & Schuchman, 1966, p. 424).

[9]An automated evaluation of whether an upload attempt infringes the right of attribution would require an analysis of whether the author or performer is adequately indicated. If the reference database contains the correct author or performer and rules on how to attribute the author or performer are sufficiently precise, such an automated analysis appears possible. An evaluation of whether an upload attempt infringes the right of integrity requires an analysis of the extent to which it affects an author's or a performer's honour or reputation. Using state-of-the-art technology, it is hard to imagine how such an analysis could be automated.

economic rights. In the interest of a focused analysis, this book concentrates on economic rights.

Moreover, uploads of music or videos may infringe the rights of right holders of other subject matter, for example, if music features copyright-protected lyrics or if a video contains a copyright-protected image. Consistent with the focus on platforms that host music or videos, violations of right holders' economic rights in other subject matter than music or videos are left aside.

This book presumes that one correct answer to the question whether an upload attempt is lawful exists. The answer is not necessarily obvious. Indeed, the vagueness of legal doctrines creates uncertainty about the lawfulness of upload attempts. The challenges created by this vagueness feature prominently in the discussion of the design of automated filtering that best approaches efficient error avoidance in Chap. 4. Still, to be able to speak of lawful or unlawful upload attempts and of erroneous filtering decisions, it is crucial to presume that every upload attempt can be unambiguously characterised as either lawful or unlawful.[10]

When considering substantive copyright law and when reviewing the legal framework for automated filtering, this book reflects on the relevant rules under US and EU law, including, where insightful, laws of selected Member States. The first reason for this choice of legal orders is that US law and EU law diverge in many important aspects, providing valuable insights on various questions (see Kulk, 2018, pp. 6–7; Leistner, 2019, p. 472). Second, both legal orders are important for automated filtering. Possibly because many platforms originate from the US (Wilman, 2020, para. 1.16), the copyright policies of many platforms focus on US copyright law[11] and on the requirements for escaping liability under US law[12] (see Grosse Ruse-Khan, 2021, pp. 166–167). Furthermore, US law has been particularly influential in shaping liability provisions in other countries.[13] Recent legal acts in the EU, namely, the Copyright in the DSM Directive (2019) and the Digital Services Act (2022), can be expected to additionally direct platforms' attention to EU copyright law and the requirements for escaping liability under EU law. Moreover, they may

[10]The fact that an upload attempt may be lawful in one country but not in another does not conflict with this assumption. The lawfulness of an upload attempt may then diverge, for example, based on the copyright law of the countries from which the upload attempt can be accessed. However, the lawfulness can still unambiguously be defined based on each applicable law. The applicable law can be defined based on the applicable choice of law principle. For an overview of relevant choice of law principles, see Sect. 4.5.1.1.

[11]For example, YouTube's and Instagram's explanations of copyright exceptions centre around fair use. They do, however, mention that other copyright exceptions apply in other countries (Google, n.d., pt. Fair use on YouTube; Instagram, n.d., pt. What are fair use and other exceptions to copyright?).

[12]For example, YouTube's and Vimeo's counter notification procedures are clearly designed to comply with US law, namely, 17 U.S.C. § 512(g)(2) (Google, n.d., pt. Submit a copyright counter notification; Vimeo, 2022).

[13]US rules on liability have been included in preferential trade agreements between the US and various countries and have served as templates for others (Samuelson, 2021, pp. 307–308; Seng, 2014, pp. 373–374).

be trendsetting pieces of legislation (regarding the Copyright in the DSM Directive, 2019, see Hinze, 2019, p. 154; Husovec, 2019, p. 539).

1.2.3 Automated Filtering

The term automated filtering refers to the usage of fingerprinting technology to block upload attempts identified as copyright-infringing and encompasses a manual review of selected automated decisions. Three elements of this working definition deserve to be stressed. First, while different content recognition technologies exist, in the interest of a focused analysis, this book concentrates on fingerprinting, the state-of-the-art technology. Second, as an alternative or complement to screening upload attempts, platforms can screen content that has already been uploaded ('legacy scans'). This approach involves the same content recognition technology as screening upload attempts and is thus associated with qualitatively similar effects. For the sake of a focused analysis, this book concentrates on the screening of upload attempts. Third, platforms can attach different consequences to finding an infringement than blocking,[14] for example, precluding unlawful copiers from monetisation ('demonetising')[15] or assigning a lower rank to unlawful content ('downranking').[16] These consequences affect unlawful copiers' benefits from uploading qualitatively in the same way as blocking and thus produce qualitatively similar effects. To keep the analysis focused, this book concentrates on blocking.

In public statements, producers of filters take pride in the high levels of precision their filters allegedly achieve, claiming that they can match 'audio content with over 99.7% precision' (Dredge, 2016) and that '[w]ith identification rates at 99.99%, [...] content recognition technology produces virtually zero false positives' (Audible Magic Corporation, n.d.). Opponents of automated filtering, on the other hand, maintain that filters produce a substantial number of false positives (e.g. Angelopoulos et al., 2018, p. 3; Rendas, 2017, p. 44). The seeming contradiction between these positions can be resolved by noticing that the former refers to the precision of content recognition technology in identifying matches between two pieces of content, while the latter considers its precision in identifying copyright infringements. For the research interest of this book, the latter is the decisive understanding.

A filter is considered to produce an error if it blocks a lawful upload attempt ('false positive') or allows an unlawful upload ('false negative'). Given the assumption that existing copyright law is efficient (Sect. 2.1), false positives and false negatives create net social costs. The product of the probability and the net social

[14] For a taxonomy of remedies platforms employ, see Goldman (2021, pp. 24–39).

[15] For example, as an alternative to blocking, YouTube enables right holders to monetise upload attempts that unlawfully copy from their works (Google, n.d., pt. How Content ID works).

[16] For an example of downranking due to alleged copyright infringements, see Singhal (2012).

costs of blocking a lawful upload attempt is referred to as the expected net social costs of a false positive. The sum of the expected net social costs of a false positive for all lawful upload attempts made to a platform is termed aggregate expected net social costs of false positives. *Mutatis mutandis*, the same terms are used for false negatives. When convenient, the term aggregate expected net social costs of errors is used to refer to the sum of aggregate expected net social costs of false positives and false negatives. Reducing probabilities of errors is also costly. The term aggregate direct costs describes the costs of preventing errors, which include the costs of resolving deficiencies of the reference database, performing and advancing the automated analysis, and manually reviewing upload attempts.

References

17 U.S.C. § 101 et seq. (US). https://www.law.cornell.edu/uscode/text/17

Angelopoulos, C., Bently, L., van Gompel, S., Husovec, M., Kretschmer, M., Senftleben, M., & Stalla-Bourdillon, S. (2018, June 29). *The copyright directive: Misinformation and independent enquiry—Statement from European Academics to Members of the European Parliament in advance of the Plenary Vote on the Copyright Directive on 5 July 2018*. https://dare.uva.nl/search?identifier=b274883c-b7e9-475a-80cd-81c96e194841

Audible Magic Corporation. (n.d.). *Our core technology*. Retrieved July 2, 2024, from https://www.audiblemagic.com/technology/

Berne Convention. Berne Convention for the Protection of Literary and Artistic Works 1886, as revised at Paris in 1971 and amended in 1979 (adopted 28 September 1979, entered into force 19 November 1984), WIPO Lex No. TRT/BERNE/001 (1886). https://www.wipo.int/wipolex/en/text/283693

Civil Liberties Union for Europe and others. (2017, October 16). *Article 13: Monitoring and filtering of internet content is unacceptable—Open letter*. https://www.eff.org/files/2017/10/16/openletteroncopyrightdirective_final.pdf

Copyright in the DSM Directive (EU). Directive (EU) 2019/790 of the European Parliament and of the European Council of 17 April 2019 on copyright and related rights in the Digital Single Market and amending Directives 96/9/EC and 2001/29/EC, OJ L 130/92. (2019). https://eur-lex.europa.eu/legal-content/EN/TXT/PDF/?uri=CELEX:32019L0790

Digital Services Act (EU). Regulation (EU) 2022/2065 of the European Parliament and of the Council of 19 October 2022 on a Single Market For Digital Services and amending Directive 2000/31/EC, OJ L 277/1. (2022). https://eur-lex.europa.eu/legal-content/EN/TXT/PDF/?uri=CELEX:32022R2065

Dredge, S. (2016, April 25). *YouTube defends Content ID following music labels' criticism*. Music Ally. https://musically.com/2016/04/25/youtube-defends-content-id-following-music-labels-criticism/

Erickson, K., & Kretschmer, M. (2018). "This Video is Unavailable": Analyzing copyright takedown of user-generated content on Youtube. *Journal of Intellectual Property, Information Technology and Electronic Commerce Law, 9*(1), 75–89.

Gann, A., & Abecassis, D. (2018, June 6). *The impact of a content filtering mandate on online service providers*. https://www.analysysmason.com/consulting-redirect/reports/the-impact-of-a-content-filtering-june2018/

Goldman, E. (2021). Content moderation remedies. *Michigan Technology Law Review, 28*(1), 1–59.

Goldstein, P., & Hugenholtz, P. B. (2013). *International copyright: Principles, law, and practice* (3rd ed.). Oxford University Press.

Google. (n.d.). *Copyright and rights management*. YouTube Help. Retrieved July 17, 2024, from https://support.google.com/youtube/topic/2676339?hl=en-GB&ref_topic=6151248&sjid=7784574668489471573-EU

Grosse Ruse-Khan, H. (2021). Transition through automation. In N. Bruun, G. B. Dinwoodie, M. Levin, & A. Ohly (Eds.), *Transition and coherence in intellectual property law: Essays in honour of Annette Kur*. Cambridge University Press.

Hicks, J. R. (1939). The foundations of welfare economics. *The Economic Journal, 49*(196), 696–712.

Hinze, G. (2019). *A tale of two legal regimes: An empirical investigation into how copyright law shapes online service providers' practices and how online service providers navigate differences in U.S. and EU copyright liability standards*. UC Berkeley Electronic Theses and Dissertations. https://escholarship.org/uc/item/6xb3s3f6

Hurt, R. M., & Schuchman, R. M. (1966). The economic rationale of copyright. *The American Economic Review, 56*(1/2), 421–432.

Husovec, M. (2019). How Europe wants to redefine global online copyright enforcement. In T. E. Synodinou (Ed.), *Pluralism or universalism in international copyright law*. Kluwer Law International.

Instagram. (n.d.). *Copyright*. Help Centre. Retrieved August 27, 2024, from https://help.instagram.com/126382350847838?helpref=faq_content

Jacques, S., Garstka, K., Hviid, M., & Street, J. (2018). An empirical study of the use of automated anti-piracy systems and their consequences for cultural diversity. *SCRIPTed, 15*(2), 277–312.

Kaldor, N. (1939). Welfare propositions of economics and interpersonal comparisons of utility. *The Economic Journal, 49*(195), 549–552.

Kulk, S. (2018). *Internet intermediaries and copyright law: Towards a future-proof EU legal framework*. Ridderprint.

Leistner, M. (2019). Intermediary liability in a global world. In T. E. Synodinou (Ed.), *Pluralism or universalism in international copyright law*. Kluwer Law International.

Open Rights Group. (2016, December 6). *Modernising the European copyright frameworks*. https://www.openrightsgroup.org/app/uploads/2020/03/openrightsgroup_ipo_modernising_european_copyright_framework.pdf

Reda, J. (2017, September 28). *When filters fail: These cases show we can't trust algorithms to clean up the internet*. https://juliareda.eu/2017/09/when-filters-fail/

Rendas, T. (2017, September 6). *Form and substance in the value gap proposal*. Better regulation for copyright: Academics meet policy makers. https://felixreda.eu/wp-content/uploads/2017/09/2017-09-06_Better-Regulation-for-Copyright-Academics-meet-Policy-Makers_Proceedings.pdf

Reuter, M. (2019, March 25). *Protests against copyright directive: All cities, dates and numbers of participants across Europe*. https://netzpolitik.org/2019/protests-against-copyright-directive-all-cities-dates-and-numbers-of-participants-across-europe/

Samuelson, P. (2021). Pushing back on stricter copyright ISP liability rules. *Michigan Technology Law Review, 27*(2), 299–343.

Seng, D. (2014). The state of the discordant union: An empirical analysis of DMCA takedown notices. *Virginia Journal of Law & Technology, 18*(3), 369–473.

Singhal, A. (2012, August 10). *An update to our search algorithms*. Google Inside Search: The Official Google Search Blog. https://search.googleblog.com/2012/08/an-update-to-our-search-algorithms.html

The Emmy Awards. (2018, May 24). *The 69th Annual Technology & Engineering Emmy Awards ceremony*. YouTube. https://www.youtube.com/watch?v=z7ki_jOa_CQ

Vimeo. (2022, September 1). *Vimeo copyright policy*. https://vimeo.com/dmca

Wilman, F. (2020). *The responsibility of online intermediaries for illegal user content in the EU and the US*. Edward Elgar.

WIPO Performances and Phonograms Treaty (adopted 20 December 1996, entered into force 20 May 2002) 2186 UNTS 203. (1996). https://www.wipo.int/wipolex/en/text/295477

Chapter 2
Economic, Technical, and Legal Background

Abstract This book's analysis of how a well-balanced design of automated filtering can be achieved presupposes an understanding of the economic implications of the dual-use problem of user-uploaded content platforms, of technical features of the state-of-the-art technology fingerprinting, and of the legal framework. This chapter provides this understanding. The economic implications of the dual-use problem, that is, the problem that platforms can be used for lawful and copyright-infringing uploading, are identified with recourse to the economic rationale for copyright protection. A crucial takeaway is that by facilitating copyright-infringing uploads, platforms expand access to creative content but disincentivise content creation. The technical features of fingerprinting are explained by means of a comparison to other content recognition technologies. A key takeaway is that circumvention of fingerprinting-based filters is possible but requires alterations of the content concerned. With respect to the legal framework, US law and EU law are reviewed regarding the extent to which filtering helps platforms to escape liability for copyright-infringing uploads and regarding responsibilities to prevent blockings of lawful upload attempts. An important takeaway is that not only the targeted regulation of filtering under EU law, but also US law, which does not explicitly regulate filtering, shapes platforms' incentives regarding automated filtering.

Keywords User-uploaded content platforms · User-generated content platforms · Online content-sharing service providers · Automated filtering · Upload filters · Fingerprinting technology · Automated copyright enforcement · Copyright in the Digital Single Market · Digital Services Act · Digital Millennium Copyright Act

Rumour has it that the idea of YouTube's founders to build a video-sharing platform was inspired in part by the difficulties they encountered in searching for a video of Janet Jackson's infamous 'wardrobe malfunction' during the 2004 Super Bowl halftime show (Schiavenza, 2015). Ironically, an upload of a recording of the show may well have amounted to a copyright infringement. This anecdote illustrates the dual-use problem of platforms: A platform that is operated with a view to making content available to a broad audience may also be used to unlawfully disseminate copyright-protected content.

O. Englisch, *Automated Copyright Filters*, International Law and Economics,
https://doi.org/10.1007/978-3-031-83161-4_2

This chapter lays the groundwork for the analysis. It explains the economic implications of the dual-use problem (Sect. 2.1), the functioning of the technology that is used to tackle it (Sect. 2.2), and the US and EU legal frameworks relevant for using this technology (Sect. 2.3). Section 2.4 emphasises the main takeaways for the analysis.

2.1 Economic Implications of Dual-Use Problem

Platforms can display targeted content suggestions and advertisements by estimating viewers' preferences. Moreover, they enable viewers to conveniently search for content. The consequence is a reduction in transaction costs, notably search costs, in the relationships between uploaders and viewers, and between advertisers and viewers (see Evans & Schmalensee, 2007, pp. 158–159; OECD, 2010, p. 37). Thereby, platforms enable transactions that prohibitively high transaction costs would otherwise prevent. These reductions in transaction costs aid lawful and unlawful uploaders alike if copyright law is not enforced on a platform. Like a photocopier, a VCR, a peer-to-peer network, and other devices and architectures, a platform can thus be characterised as a dual-use technology.[1]

The social welfare implications of the dual-use problem of a platform can be described with recourse to the economic rationale for copyright protection. The starting point is the observation that producing creative content is costly, while reproducing it is cheap (Landes & Posner, 1989, p. 326; Shapiro & Varian, 1999, p. 3). Without copyright protection, competition between creators and unlawful copiers would drive prices for accessing works down, possibly to the marginal costs of reproduction. Too low prices prevent creators from recouping their sunk costs of production and thus disincentivise content creation (Landes & Posner, 1989, p. 326). Copyright protection provides creators with limited monopoly power over their creations. The prospect of earning monopoly profits once a work has been created increases the benefits of creating the work and thereby incentivises content creation.[2] The flip side is that the costs of prospective creators who seek to incorporate elements of previous works rise (Landes & Posner, 1989, pp. 332–333). This increase in the costs of creating works counteracts the incentivising effect of copyright protection. Moreover, since right holders increase prices to realise their monopoly profits, some consumers are prevented from accessing works, resulting in deadweight losses.[3]

---

[1] The term dual-use technology is employed by analogy to its use describing technology with both military and civilian functions (Lemley & Reese, 2004, n. 36).

[2] This incentive theory plays an important role in most countries (Dinwoodie, 2004, p. 164). For a formal discussion, see Landes and Posner (1989, pp. 333–336).

[3] For a formal discussion, see Landes and Posner (1989, pp. 336–341).

The social benefits resulting from the production and consumption of creative content are not limited to the benefits of creators and consumers. For instance, by creating content, the creator may develop new skills (Lessig, 2008, pp. 80–82), and by consuming content, the consumer may become more learned. Such educational effects benefit not only the person educated but also society at large as they may result in more innovation, improved social discourse, and economic and cultural growth (Fullerton, 1991, p. 75). Moreover, creative content forms an important part of culture and plays a social role (Elkin-Koren, 1997, p. 1198; Kaesling & Knapp, 2020, p. 816).

Copyright law balances the benefits against the costs of protection by determining the scope, duration, and depth of protection. If copyright law strikes the socially efficient balance, lawful uploads produce net social benefits and unlawful uploads net social costs. Whether existing copyright law approaches an efficient balance is debatable.[4] There are good reasons to expect inefficiencies. Inefficiencies may result from successful rent-seeking (see e.g. Litman, 2002, pp. 350–354; Patry, 1996, p. 141). For instance, it is often argued that the duration of copyright protection is not the result of striking a balance between social costs and benefits of protection but of one-sided pressure by right holders (e.g. Eger, 2015, pp. 29–31; Litman, 2017, pp. 12–13). Moreover, existing doctrines may inefficiently regulate new types of uses. For instance, image macros (i.e. a subcategory of Internet memes, comprising well-known pictures supplemented with a humorous caption; Bonetto, 2018, p. 990) are a habitual mode of online expression and arguably do not appreciably harm right holders (Matalon, 2019, pp. 419–420). They may nevertheless constitute copyright infringements.[5]

Notwithstanding potential inefficiencies, this book assumes that substantive copyright law is efficient. Put differently, it is presumed that lawful uploads are associated with net social benefits and unlawful uploads with net social costs. The efficiency of substantive copyright law is a common, albeit not always explicit, assumption when analysing the efficiency of measures to enforce copyright law (e.g. Gilbert & Katz, 2001, p. 967; Husovec, 2016, p. 9; Kaesling & Knapp, 2020, n. 32). For one thing, this assumption is out of necessity. The efficiency of substantive copyright law is not part of the research interest of this book. For another, it is based on the consideration that if tolerating some copyright infringements contributes to efficiency, changing the scope, duration, or depth of protection can achieve the same effect. Adjusting the balance through legislation or, where possible, court

[4] For an overview of some of the more fundamental criticism of copyright protection, see Frosio (2020, pp. 712–713).

[5] Based on EU copyright law, image macros are likely to infringe a right holder's exclusive rights and are often not covered by an exception (Bonetto, 2018, pp. 992–995). Based on US copyright law, image macros are in many cases likely to be covered by the fair use doctrine (Patel, 2013, pp. 251–255).

decisions appears preferable to somewhat arbitrary lax enforcement (Liebowitz, 2014, pp. 226–227).[6]

Note that the assumption that copyright law is efficient does not conflict with the possibility that an upload attempt is lawful in one country but not in another. Differences may be based on differences in the relevance and structure of domestic cultural and creative industries (see Elkin-Koren & Salzberger, 2013, pp. 244–245), differences in economic characteristics (see e.g. Watt, 2009, p. 89), and differences in preferences and values.[7] In other words, for different countries, different copyright laws can be efficient.

2.2 Content Recognition Technology

The availability of unlawful and lawful content on a platform, and thus the social costs and benefits of operating a platform, can be influenced by filtering upload attempts. This section explains how technologies to detect unlawful upload attempts function.

Content recognition technologies use reference databases that contain identifiers and information on works, for example, on copyright ownership and licensing arrangements. Content recognition technologies compare the identifiers of works in reference databases with identifiers of upload attempts to detect unlawful uploads. As noted above, this book focuses on fingerprinting, the state-of-the-art technology. Nevertheless, a tour d'horizon of the functioning, precision (i.e. the capability to only define content as matching that is in fact matching), and recall (i.e. the capability to define matching content as matching) of other technologies is useful to understand the relevant features of fingerprinting.[8]

---

[6] While legislation and court decisions are arguably expedient, albeit ponderous, channels for addressing inefficiencies resulting from new types of uses, it may be argued that right holders' pressure would continue to bar the way to eliminating inefficiencies caused by one-sided pressure by right holders. However, it is then questionable whether laxer enforcement is a realistic strategy since right holders could exert the same pressure on the entities entrusted with enforcement. Moreover, rent-seeking by right holders has become at least a less promising strategy due to changed power relations. For one thing, the tech lobby has become an increasingly powerful player (Lev-Aretz, 2013, pp. 227–229). For another, facilitated by new means of communication and organisation, notably social media, which significantly reduce the transaction costs of engaging in collective action, independent creators and consumers have become more influential (Lev-Aretz, 2013, pp. 229–234).

[7] Copyright law is an instrument of cultural and information policy (Austin, 2000, pp. 610–613; Dinwoodie, 2000, p. 471; Ginsburg, 2000, p. 267). Differences in national copyright laws may thus be the result of a pursuit of different policy objectives.

[8] Precision and recall are common measures to evaluate content recognition technology (e.g. Esmaeili et al., 2011, p. 220; Lu, 2009, p. 3; Sartor & Loreggia, 2020, p. 45). Precision is defined as the ratio of true positives to all positives. Recall is defined as the ratio of true positives to the sum of true positives and false negatives. Note that true/false positives in this section have a different meaning than in the rest of this book. Here, a true positive refers to an upload attempt

The simplest content recognition technologies are keyword and metadata matching. These technologies use indications in the titles, descriptions, or metadata of upload attempts (e.g. regarding titles of works or artists' names) or compare characteristics of upload attempts (e.g. file sizes or durations) with characteristics of works in the reference database. Keyword and metadata matching are rather imprecise as keywords may appear in the titles or descriptions of unrelated content (see Giblin-Chen & Davison, 2006, p. 65) and different types of content may have the same durations or file sizes. Moreover, keyword and metadata matching have a low recall as uploaders can choose titles and descriptions in ways that make detection unlikely, alter or remove metadata, and modify file sizes or durations (see Sartor & Loreggia, 2020, p. 40; Seidel, 2009, p. 1525).[9]

Watermarking is a more sophisticated content recognition technology. It relies on identifiers that are embedded directly into creative content ('watermarks').[10] The watermarks are technically recognisable but usually imperceptible to the human eye or ear. Content recognition technology screens for the watermarks. Watermarking is precise because watermarks are uniquely created for every work or even every copy of a work. However, the recall is low as copies of content from which watermarks have been removed, in which watermarks have been blurred, or which did not contain watermarks in the first place are not detectable.[11]

Content recognition technologies that extract identifiers from works rather than embed them therein overcome this challenge. Hash value matching follows this approach. An algorithm calculates a cryptographic hash value of files in the reference database (Gomes et al., 2003, p. 72). The same algorithm calculates a hash value of upload attempts. If the hash value of an upload attempt is identical to the hash value of a file in the reference database, a match is found. Hash value matching is precise as even a slight difference between a file in the reference database and an uploaded file results in different hash values.[12] The downside of this property is that files that are slightly altered cannot be detected (European Union Intellectual Property Office, 2020, p. 9; Raue & Steinebach, 2020, p. 358; Sartor & Loreggia, 2020, p. 38). Hash value based content recognition technologies can thus be circumvented with relative ease and without making modifications that are bothersome to viewers, resulting in a low recall.

---

correctly identified as containing parts of a work in the reference database. In the rest of this book, a true positive refers to an upload attempt correctly identified as a copyright infringement. To avoid confusion, this section does not use the terms true/false positives/negatives.

[9] Yet, obscure titles and descriptions and incorrect or no metadata make it harder to find content (Giblin-Chen & Davison, 2006, pp. 65–66). Despite the ease of circumvention, keyword matching and metadata matching thus render unlawful uploading less attractive.

[10] For a detailed explanation, see Gomes et al. (2003, pp. 66–68).

[11] For an overview of circumvention techniques, see European Union Intellectual Property Office (2020, p. 14).

[12] The exception is a 'hash collusion', that is, an assignment of the same hash value to distinct content (Gorwa et al., 2020, p. 4).

To get around this problem, the state-of-the-art content recognition technology fingerprinting uses an algorithm to extract characteristic features from works and generates unique fingerprints.[13] Relevant features may, for instance, include the loudness and pitch of songs (Gomes et al., 2003, p. 72), and the luminance and colour patterns of videos (Lu, 2009, pp. 4–6, 6–7; Raue & Steinebach, 2020, pp. 360–361). The same algorithm is used to generate fingerprints of content uploaded to a platform (Seidel, 2009, p. 1526). The fingerprints of upload attempts are compared with the fingerprints of (pre-selected)[14] works in the reference database. This comparison yields a similarity score for each pair of fingerprints (Lu, 2009, p. 3).

Fingerprinting is less precise than hash value matching as different works evincing similar features may produce similar fingerprints. At the same time, fingerprinting has a higher recall because it can detect copying uploads even if the content has been modified. To disguise content so that it can bypass fingerprinting technology, the relevant features must be altered. Disguising methods include pitch-shifting, colour-shifting, mirror-imaging, zooming-in, modifying the aspect ratio, inserting light effects, delaying or speeding up, and framing infringing videos in 'innocent' images (see Brøvig-Hanssen & Jones, 2021, p. 10; Google, 2024, pt. Our tools are cutting edge). Circumvention of this kind is costly for uploaders and can be bothersome for viewers (see Brøvig-Hanssen & Jones, 2021, p. 10). Several upload attempts may be needed to successfully bypass detection while keeping detriments to viewers low. The specification of the similarity score required for a match is associated with a trade-off between precision and recall (see European Union Intellectual Property Office, 2020, p. 20).

Fingerprinting technology is frequently used by right holders to find possible infringements of their works on platforms[15] and by platforms to filter upload attempts. Providers of fingerprinting-based filters for platforms include ACRCloud,[16] Audible Magic,[17] and INA-Signature.[18] Moreover, in-house fingerprinting-based filters, such as 'Content ID' used by YouTube (Google, n.d., pt. How Content ID works) and 'Rights Manager' used by Facebook and Instagram (Meta, 2024), exist.

[13] For more detailed explanations, see Gomes et al. (2003, pp. 70–72) or Haitsma and Kalker (2003, pp. 214–216). Fingerprinting is sometimes also referred to as 'perceptual hashing' (e.g. Gorwa et al., 2020, p. 4).

[14] For the necessity of and approaches to pre-selection, see Haitsma and Kalker (2003, pp. 217–220) or Lu (2009, pp. 7–8).

[15] Well-known providers of fingerprinting-based tools for right holders to identify uses of their works include Audible Magic, Pex, and Vobile.

[16] ACRCloud (2024) inter alia lists the platforms audiomack and likee and the company ByteDance, which inter alia owns the platform TikTok, as customers.

[17] Platforms using Audible Magic include Dailymotion, Soundcloud, Twitch, and Veoh (Audible Magic, n.d.).

[18] For example, in addition to Audible Magic, the platform Dailymotion uses INA-Signature (Dailymotion, 2024).

2.3 Legal Framework for Automated Filtering

Platforms choose whether and how they use content recognition technology to detect unlawful upload attempts, and (alleged) right holders decide whether they enter content into the reference database and what information they indicate. The legal framework influences platforms' and right holders' decisions. This section explains to what extent automated filtering helps platforms to escape liability for unlawful uploads (Sect. 2.3.1) and what responsibilities right holders and platforms have to prevent blockings of lawful upload attempts (Sect. 2.3.2).

2.3.1 Liability of Platforms for Unlawful Uploads

By uploading copyright-protected content to a platform, an uploader may infringe a right holder's exclusive rights.[19] Under certain circumstances, platforms are additionally liable for copyright-infringing uploads by their users. To what extent does automated filtering help platforms to escape liability? Sections 2.3.1.1 and 2.3.1.2 address this question for US and EU law, respectively.

Note that platforms can also escape liability by obtaining licences for the uploaded content. However, it is hard to predict what content will be uploaded. A platform would thus effectively have to obtain licences for all potentially relevant content. Collecting societies offer a possible route to obtain far-reaching licences, but even collecting societies do not represent all right holders (Senftleben, 2020, pp. 305–306). Due to high transaction costs and as right holders are not obliged to grant licences, obtaining licences from all potentially affected right holders is hardly feasible (Quintais, 2020, p. 38; Samuelson, 2021, p. 321).[20] Based on these considerations, this section presumes that comprehensive licensing is no viable alternative to automated filtering.

[19] International copyright law requires uploads to be included in right holders' rights (for authors: Article 8 of the WIPO Copyright Treaty, 1996; for performers: Article 10 of the WIPO Performances and Phonograms Treaty, 1996; for phonograms producers: Article 14 of the WIPO Performances and Phonograms Treaty, 1996; for audiovisual performers: Article 10 of the Beijing Treaty on Audiovisual Performances, 2012). In the US, the primarily applicable right is the right of public performance in 17 U.S.C. § 106(4), (6) if a platform does not offer downloads (US Copyright Office, 2016, pp. 36–47). Under EU law, the primarily relevant rights are the right of communication to the public of works in Article 3(1) of the InfoSoc Directive (2001) and the right of making available to the public of other subject matter in Article 3(2) of the InfoSoc Directive (2001).

[20] In *Poland v. Parliament and Council* (2022, para. 48), the CJEU noted that Article 17(4) of the Copyright in the DSM Directive (2019) is based on the premise that platforms 'are not necessarily able to obtain authorisation for all the protected content that may be uploaded' and pointed out that right holders are not obliged to grant licences.

2.3.1.1 US Law

To examine the extent to which automated filtering helps platforms to escape liability under US law, it is useful to first outline the conditions under which platforms are liable for unlawful uploads. Platforms are liable if the conditions for safe harbour protection are not met while the conditions for secondary liability are fulfilled.[21] This section therefore first explains these conditions. As a final step, it reflects on whether and how automated filtering helps platforms to qualify for safe harbour protection and to avoid secondary liability.

Note that in recent years, proposals have been made to change some of the relevant provisions (e.g. Tillis, 2020). Because these proposals have not yet been adopted, they are not considered in the following outline of the rules applicable under US law.

Safe Harbour Protection

17 U.S.C. § 512(c)[22] provides platforms with a qualified immunity ('safe harbour'), shielding them against liability for monetary relief and limiting the possibility of injunctive relief for copyright-infringing uploads.[23] The safe harbour applies if a platform has taken systemic precautions and meets several conditions with respect to specific copyright-infringing uploads.

Systemic precautions include the designation of an agent whom right holders can notify of claimed infringements, § 512(c)(2), the establishment of a policy under which repeat infringers' accounts are terminated, § 512(i)(1)(A), and the accommodation of and no interference with standard technical measures used by right holders to identify or protect their works, § 512(i)(1)(B) in conjunction with § 512(i)(2).[24] A platform does not need to filter upload attempts; see § 512(m).

Upload-specific conditions encompass a lack of actual knowledge of an infringing upload, § 512(c)(1)(A)(i), and a lack of awareness of 'facts or circumstances from which infringing activity is apparent' ('red flag knowledge'), § 512(c)(1)(A)(ii). If a platform obtains actual or red flag knowledge of an infringement, it must take the upload down expeditiously or else forfeits immunity with respect to that upload, § 512(c)(1)(A)(iii). Likewise, when a right holder sends a notification that complies

---

[21] One may also contemplate primary liability. Yet, since *Religious Tech. Center v. Netcom On-Line Comm.* (1995, pp. 1368–1370), courts require volitional conduct to affirm direct infringements by intermediaries. Platforms that do not select content but merely enable users to upload are unlikely to meet this condition. For an overview of the case law, see Kulk (2018, pp. 237–242).

[22] Unless indicated otherwise, all further references to statutory provisions in this and the following section refer to title 17 U.S.C.

[23] According to § 512(c)(1), it applies to infringements 'by reason of the storage at the direction of a user of material'. The forms of injunctive relief courts may grant even if safe harbour protection applies are defined in § 512(j)(1)(A).

[24] One could entertain the idea that by requiring that a platform 'accommodates [...] standard technical measures', safe harbour protection presupposes the employment of automated filtering. However, such a reading is hard to reconcile with the remainder of § 512 (Gallo, 2010, pp. 302–304).

with several conditions to the designated agent, the platform must remove the content expeditiously to preserve immunity ('notice-and-takedown'), § 512(c)(1)(C).[25] The notification must contain a statement that the sender subjectively (*Rossi*, 2004, pp. 1004–1005) has a good faith belief that the relevant content 'is not authorized by the copyright owner, its agent, or the law', § 512(c)(3)(A)(v). This condition requires right holders to consider whether an upload constitutes a fair use (*Lenz*, 2015, pp. 1131–1133).[26]

Even without actual or red flag knowledge of infringing activity, a platform may forfeit immunity with respect to uploads from which it receives a direct financial benefit if it has 'the right and ability to control' the infringing activity, § 512(c)(1)(B), which presupposes that the platform influences the infringement or participates in it (*Viacom v. YouTube*, 2013, p. 118). Existing case law suggests that a 'right and ability to control' infringing activity can generally not be affirmed for the types of platforms considered in this book, but the exact requirements are yet to be clarified. For YouTube, the US District Court for the Southern District of New York negated a 'right and ability to control' the infringing activity, inter alia as there was no evidence that YouTube induced users to upload infringing content, pre-screened uploads for quality, or steered users to infringing uploads (*Viacom v. YouTube*, 2013, pp. 121–122). The same court also negated a 'right and ability to control' the infringing activity for Vimeo (*Capitol Records, LLC v. Vimeo, LLC*, 2013, pp. 525–535).

Secondary Liability

A platform that does not meet the requirements for safe harbour protection may be held secondarily liable, so that remedies in the form of injunctions, § 502(a), or damages[27] may be awarded.[28] Secondary liability may arise based on the platform's position vis-à-vis the unlawful copier or based on the role the platform plays in the infringement.

Based on its position vis-à-vis the unlawful copier, a platform may be subject to vicarious liability if it receives a direct financial benefit from an infringing upload and has the right and ability to supervise the infringing activity (cf. *Shapiro, Bernstein & Co. v. HL Green Company*, 1963, p. 307).[29] The direct financial benefit prong has been construed broadly, including cases in which infringements 'enhance

[25] § 512(c)(3)(A) lists the elements that a notification must include to be effective. § 512(c)(3)(B)(ii) stipulates conditions under which an incompliant notification still triggers actual or red flag knowledge.

[26] For an explanation of the fair use doctrine, see Sect. 4.4.1.4.

[27] As compensation, right holders can either choose actual damages suffered due to the infringement and additional profits the platform earned due to the infringement, § 504(a)(1) in conjunction with § 504(b), or statutory damages, § 504(a)(2) in conjunction with § 504(c).

[28] In addition, courts can order a recovery of court costs and an attorney's fees to the prevailing party, § 505.

[29] Vicarious liability for copyright infringements is based on the common law doctrine of *respondeat superior*, which governs the liability of employers for their employees' behaviour.

the attractiveness' to potential viewers (*Fonovisa v. Cherry Auction*, 1996, p. 263). The supervision prong has been found to be satisfied by the file-sharing service Napster as it had the ability to identify infringing content using keyword searches and to terminate uploaders' access to the system (*Napster*, 2001, p. 1024). It remains to be seen what kind of monitoring courts expect from platforms to escape vicarious liability. It is important to note that despite the confusing linguistic overlap, the 'right and ability to control' detrimental to safe harbour protection is construed more narrowly than the 'right and ability to supervise' favourable to vicarious liability. The former requires 'something more' (*Viacom v. YouTube,* 2012, p. 38), that is, influence on or participation in the infringement (*Viacom v. YouTube*, 2013, p. 118).

Based on the role a platform plays in an infringement, it may further be subject to contributory liability if it 'induces, causes or materially contributes to the infringing conduct' with knowledge of the infringing activity (*Gershwin Publishing Corp. v. Columbia Artists Man., Inc.*, 1971, p. 1162).[30] Since 'material contribution' has been construed as encompassing the 'site and facilities' for direct infringement (*Fonovisa, Inc. v. Cherry Auction, Inc.*, 1996, p. 264), it is easily met by platforms. Regarding the knowledge prong, the US Supreme Court declined to impute knowledge if a device is 'capable of substantial noninfringing uses' (*Betamax*, 1984, p. 442).[31] In *Aimster* (2003, pp. 651–653), the 7th Circuit construed this principle more narrowly than a literal reading would suggest, arguing that to negate knowledge, a service must actually be used for non-infringing purposes. The Court argued in obiter dictum that the service 'must show that it would have been disproportionately costly [...] to eliminate or at least reduce substantially the infringing uses' (*Aimster*, 2003, p. 653). In its subsequent decision in *Grokster* (2005), the US Supreme Court did not endorse, but also not explicitly repudiate, this test (Samuelson, 2006, p. 28).

Instead, the Court developed the 'inducement rule' according to which secondary liability is affirmed if a device is distributed 'with the object of promoting its use to infringe copyright' (*Grokster*, 2005, p. 919). Under this rule, mere knowledge of potential or actual infringing activity does not establish liability, but 'purposeful, culpable expression and conduct' is required (*Grokster*, 2005, p. 937). The Court used the following indicators as evidence for inducement: advertisements that encourage infringements, targeting known infringers, failure to adopt filtering technology, and dependence of the commercial sense of an enterprise on unlawful uses (*Grokster*, 2005, pp. 937–940). It noted that the latter two indicators would not suffice on their own to establish liability based on inducement (*Grokster*, 2005, pp. 939–940).

Extent to Which Automated Filtering Helps Platforms to Escape Liability

To what extent does automated filtering help platforms to escape liability under US law? A platform does not need to filter upload attempts to receive safe harbour

[30] Contributory liability is rooted in general tort law.

[31] The US Supreme Court developed this principle based on the patent law doctrine of staple articles of commerce in 35 U.S.C. § 271(c).

protection. However, to comply with the requirements for safe harbour protection, it must establish a notice-and-takedown procedure. To review the potentially high number of notifications, it may practically need to use content recognition technology.

If a platform does not qualify for safe harbour protection, filtering mitigates the risk of liability by reducing the amount of infringing content on the platform. Moreover, automated filtering is conducive to escaping liability under each of the described doctrines of secondary liability. For vicarious liability, it is conceivable that courts would subsume detection by automated filtering under a platform's ability to supervise the infringing activity. Likewise, when transferred to platforms, the proportionality test proposed in *Aimster* (2003, p. 653) for contributory liability could result in a necessity to employ automated filtering. Finally, under the inducement rule, platforms can decrease the likelihood of being held liable by adopting automated filtering. Yet, failing to do so does not necessarily lead to liability.

2.3.1.2 EU Law

Having examined the extent to which automated filtering helps platforms to escape liability under US law, this section addresses the same question for EU law. The key provision for the liability of platforms for copyright-infringing uploads is Article 17 of the Copyright in the DSM Directive (2019).[32] This provision creates a special liability regime for online content-sharing service providers (OCSSPs), that is, services 'of which the main or one of the main purposes is to store and give the public access to a large amount of copyright-protected works or other protected subject matter uploaded by its users, which it organises and promotes for profit-making purposes' (Article 2, first sentence, no. 6 of the Copyright in the DSM Directive, 2019).[33] By and large, this definition encompasses the services considered

[32] Immediately after the adoption of the Copyright in the DSM Directive (2019), Poland brought an action to annul Article 17(4)(b) and, *in fine*, Article 17(4)(c), that is, the part requiring a staydown of notified content. The claim was based on an alleged infringement of the right to freedom of expression and information under Article 11(1) of the Charter of Fundamental Rights of the European Union (2012) resulting from the necessity to employ automated filters. The CJEU found that Article 17 of the Copyright in the DSM Directive (2019) contains sufficient safeguards for the protection of the right to freedom of expression and information (*Poland v. Parliament and Council*, 2022, para. 98). It therefore dismissed the action. Note that the CJEU considered the action for partial annulment of only Article 17(4)(b) and, *in fine*, Article 17(4)(c) of the Copyright in the DSM Directive (2019) to be inadmissible but the alternative request to annul Article 17 of the Copyright in the DSM Directive (2019) in its entirety to be admissible (*Poland v. Parliament and Council*, 2022, paras. 21–22).

[33] Recital 62 of the Copyright in the DSM Directive (2019) clarifies that the definition should 'target only online services that play an important role on the online content market by competing with other online content services, such as online audio and video streaming services, for the same audiences'. In addition, Article 2, second sentence of the Copyright in the DSM Directive (2019) provides a non-exhaustive list of services that are not covered by the definition.

in this book as user-uploaded content platforms. This section first outlines Article 17 of the Copyright in the DSM Directive (2019) and then reflects on the extent to which automated filtering helps platforms to escape liability under this provision.

Note that the Digital Services Act (2022) requires very large online platforms (VLOPs)[34] to assess (Article 34(1), first subparagraph, second subparagraph, second sentence, (a) of the Digital Services Act, 2022) and mitigate (Article 35(1), first sentence of the Digital Services Act, 2022) systemic risks associated with their services, including 'the dissemination of illegal content'. The broad definition of illegal content includes copyright infringements.[35] Mitigation measures encompass 'content moderation processes' (Article 35(1), second sentence, (c) of the Digital Services Act, 2022) such as automated filtering (see Article 3(t) of the Digital Services Act, 2022). However, the Copyright in the DSM Directive (2019) prevails as *lex specialis* (Article 2(4)(b) of the Digital Services Act, 2022).[36] The Digital Services Act (2022) thus does not influence the extent to which OCSSPs are required to use automated copyright filters.

Article 17 of the Copyright in the DSM Directive (2019)

To understand Article 17 of the Copyright in the DSM Directive (2019), it is useful to briefly outline the pre-Copyright in the DSM Directive (2019) legal framework. This framework did not contain an explicit provision that required Member States to introduce liability for platforms. Instead, it set out conditions under which Member States were not allowed to hold platforms liable for monetary relief based on (not harmonised) national rules.[37] In the absence of such a provision, the CJEU

[34] Very large online platforms are platforms that have an average of at least 45 million monthly active recipients in the EU and that are designated by the Commission (Article 33(1) of the Digital Services Act, 2022). Currently designated very large online platforms include Facebook, Instagram, TikTok, and YouTube (European Commission, 2024).

[35] Illegal content is defined in Article 3(h) of the Digital Services Act (2022). Recital 12, fourth sentence of the Digital Services Act (2022) clarifies that the definition encompasses 'the non-authorised use of copyright protected material'.

[36] The view that the Copyright in the DSM Directive (2019) 'in no way addresses' the issue of risk mitigation and thus does not preclude an application of Article 35 of the Digital Services Act (2022) (Quintais & Schwemer, 2022, p. 215) is too broad as the purpose of Article 17 of the Copyright in the DSM Directive (2019) is to mitigate the risk stemming from the dissemination of copyright-infringing content (see recitals 61 and 66, first paragraph of the Copyright in the DSM Directive, 2019).

[37] To qualify for the safe harbour provided by Article 14(1) of the E-Commerce Directive (2000) (now: Article 6(1) of the Digital Services Act, 2022), a platform had to play a neutral role, that is, its conduct had to be 'merely technical, automatic and passive, which means that it has no knowledge of or control over the content it stores' (*YouTube/Cyando*, 2021, para. 106). Whether a platform was eligible for safe harbour protection had to be decided on a case-by-case basis. For YouTube, national courts answered this question inconsistently (see Englisch & Priora, 2019, pp. 14–15). According to the AG Opinion in *YouTube/Cyando* (2020, paras. 153–168), YouTube in principle plays a passive role. The CJEU left the question for the referring court to decide. A platform forfeited immunity with respect to specific unlawful uploads of which it had actual or constructive knowledge, and which it failed to remove expeditiously (Article 14(1) of the E-Commerce Directive, 2000; now: Article 6(1) of the Digital Services Act, 2022). It gained specific knowledge

constructed a regime of primary liability of intermediaries based on right holders' right of communication to the public (Article 3(1) of the InfoSoc Directive, 2001), which is the right an uploader may infringe by uploading a right holder's work. Under certain conditions, intermediaries were considered to also perform acts of communication to the public and thus to also directly infringe this right if unauthorised uploads were made.[38] Whether this was the case had to be determined on a case-by-case basis. For YouTube, the CJEU advanced several arguments suggesting that the platform did not itself perform acts of communication to the public when uploaders uploaded copyright-protected content (*YouTube/Cyando*, 2021, paras. 92–96).[39]

Article 17(1), first subparagraph of the Copyright in the DSM Directive (2019) now stipulates that by giving the public access to copyright-protected content, OCSSPs perform acts of communication to the public or making available to the public. OCSSPs must thus obtain authorisation from right holders (Article 17(1), second subparagraph of the Copyright in the DSM Directive, 2019). Article 6(1) of the Digital Services Act (2022) does not shield platforms from liability when performing acts of communication to the public or making available to the public (Article 17(3), first subparagraph of the Copyright in the DSM Directive, 2019).[40] However, if an unauthorised upload is made, the OCSSP is not liable if it can show that it

- 'made best efforts to obtain an authorisation' from the right holder (Article 17(4)(a) of the Copyright in the DSM Directive, 2019),

---

by being notified or by detecting infringements on its own initiative (*YouTube/Cyando*, 2021, para. 115).

[38] A platform did not directly infringe a right holder's right of communication to the public unless its contribution to giving access to infringing content went beyond the mere provision of the platform (*YouTube/Cyando*, 2021, para. 102). The CJEU non-exhaustively mentioned three circumstances that amounted to a contribution beyond the mere provision of a platform: refraining from 'putting in place the appropriate technological measures that can be expected from a reasonably diligent operator [...] to counter credibly and effectively copyright infringements' despite having general actual or constructive knowledge of infringing uploads; supporting unlawful uploads by participating in selecting infringing content, providing tools intended to share unlawful content, or knowingly promoting infringements, for example, by adopting a financial model that encourages infringements; specific knowledge of an infringing upload combined with a failure to expeditiously remove it (*YouTube/Cyando*, 2021, para. 84). General knowledge of infringing activity alone did not suffice for direct liability (*YouTube/Cyando*, 2021, para. 85). Direct liability was more likely to be affirmed if a platform was mainly or predominantly used for the dissemination of unlawful content (*YouTube/Cyando*, 2021, para. 100).

[39] The CJEU emphasised that YouTube did not select or review uploads, that it informed uploaders that unlawful uploads are not tolerated, that it operated technical measures to prevent infringements (including automated filtering), that its search and recommendation functions were not targeted towards infringing uploads, and that its financial model was not based on infringements.

[40] Note that the provision refers to Article 14(1) of the E-Commerce Directive (2000). However, according to Article 89(2) of the Digital Services Act (2022), this reference shall now be construed as a reference to Article 6(1) of the Digital Services Act (2022).

- 'made, in accordance with high industry standards of professional diligence, best efforts to ensure the unavailability of specific works and other subject matter for which the rightholders have provided [it] with the relevant and necessary information' (Article 17(4)(b) of the Copyright in the DSM Directive, 2019), and
- acted expeditiously to take infringing content down upon receiving a 'sufficiently substantiated notice' and made 'best efforts' to ensure a staydown of the content (Article 17(4)(c) of the Copyright in the DSM Directive, 2019).

When applying these conditions, factors related to the OCSSP (e.g. its type, its audience, its size, and the types of works uploaded; Article 17(5)(a) of the Copyright in the DSM Directive, 2019) and the availability and suitability of effective means and their costs (Article 17(5)(b) of the Copyright in the DSM Directive, 2019) must be considered. A shortcut to escape liability exists for new and small OCSSPs.[41]

Extent to Which Automated Filtering Helps Platforms to Escape Liability
To what extent does automated filtering help platforms to escape liability under EU law? Already under the pre-Copyright in the DSM Directive (2019) legal framework automated filtering helped platforms to escape liability.[42] Article 17 of the Copyright in the DSM Directive (2019) still does not explicitly mandate automated filtering. However, if a platform is liable for infringing uploads, for example,

[41] If a platform has offered its service for less than 3 years in the EU, has an annual turnover below €10 million, and has an average number of monthly unique viewers not exceeding 5 million, it can escape liability by complying with the obligation contained in the first bullet point and the takedown element of the obligation in the third bullet point (Article 17(6), first subparagraph of the Copyright in the DSM Directive, 2019). The requirement that the number of monthly unique viewers may not exceed 5 million follows *e contrario* from the second subparagraph. If a platform falls below the thresholds in terms of age and annual turnover but exceeds the threshold of monthly unique viewers, it must comply with the obligation contained in the first bullet point and the (full) obligation contained in the third bullet point, that is, also ensure the staydown of content (Article 17(6), second subparagraph of the Copyright in the DSM Directive, 2019).

[42] While presumably not a necessary condition, automated filtering helped platforms to escape direct liability. If a platform was directly liable for infringing uploads, it effectively had to employ automated filtering to avoid paying damages. If a platform was not directly liable, automated filtering was not detrimental to playing a neutral role and thus to benefitting from the immunity of Article 14(1) of the E-Commerce Directive (2000) (now: Article 6(1) of the Digital Services Act, 2022; *YouTube/Cyando*, 2021, para. 109). If, contrary to the AG Opinion in *YouTube/Cyando* (2020, para. 194), this provision had been construed as containing a staydown obligation, a platform would have practically needed to employ automated filtering to comply with this obligation. If a platform was not covered by the safe harbour, automated filtering may have been conducive to escaping, and in any case helped to limit exposure to, secondary liability based on the national laws of Member States. Finally, even if a platform was not liable, it may have sought to mitigate its exposure to injunctive relief, which remained possible according to Article 14(3) of the E-Commerce Directive (2000) (now: Article 6(4) of the Digital Services Act, 2022) and which may have been combined with a reimbursement of associated costs of giving formal notice and court costs (cf. *McFadden*, 2016, paras. 76–78). Based on the AG Opinion in *YouTube/Cyando* (2020, paras. 221–222), injunctions may have further been associated with a staydown obligation, the compliance with which may again have practically required the employment of automated filtering.

because it has not complied with the obligation contained in the first bullet point, it effectively has to employ automated filtering to avoid paying damages.

Moreover, Article 17(4) of the Copyright in the DSM Directive (2019) makes escaping liability effectively conditional upon employing automated filtering. To fulfil their obligation contained in the second bullet point and the staydown element in the third bullet point, platforms must filter out upload attempts that copy from works for which right holders have provided the relevant and necessary information or that have been notified by right holders (*Poland v. Parliament and Council*, 2022, para. 53).[43] There appears to be no alternative to automated filtering to perform this task (*Poland v. Parliament and Council*, 2022, para. 54).

If Article 17(4) of the Copyright in the DSM Directive (2019) is interpreted in this way, the question arises how it can be reconciled with the prohibition of a general monitoring obligation, which is contained in Article 8 of the Digital Services Act (2022) (previously: Article 15(1) of the E-Commerce Directive, 2000), repeated in Article 17(8), first subparagraph of the Copyright in the DSM Directive (2019), and has additionally been based on platforms' and users' fundamental rights by the CJEU (*Netlog*, 2012, paras. 45–52). A possible line of reasoning to resolve the seeming contradiction is that the resulting monitoring obligation would not be general because the obligation contained in the second bullet point and the staydown element in the third bullet point require the prior provision of the 'relevant and necessary information' and a 'substantiated notice' of the works to be monitored, respectively (Leistner, 2020, pp. 139–141).

The CJEU goes one step further. It argues that the prohibition of a general monitoring obligation implies that platforms cannot be required to block unlawful upload attempts if determining the unlawfulness presupposes an 'independent assessment of the content [...] in the light of the information provided by the rightholders and of any exceptions and limitations to copyright' (*Poland v. Parliament and Council*, 2022, para. 90). The CJEU thus interprets the prohibition of a general monitoring obligation as substantiating the 'best efforts' requirements in the second and third bullet point.

2.3.2 Responsibilities of Right Holders and Platforms Regarding Lawful Upload Attempts

Having examined the extent to which automated filtering helps platforms to escape liability, this section reviews right holders' and platforms' responsibilities to avoid

[43] Senftleben and Angelopoulos (2020, p. 28) argue that 'other preventive measures that would comply with the wording of those paragraphs can also be envisaged' and mention measures such as account suspension, community moderation, and warning notices as examples. However, such a reading requires a rather generous interpretation of 'best efforts'.

blockings of lawful upload attempts based on US law (Sect. 2.3.2.1) and EU law (Sect. 2.3.2.2).

2.3.2.1 US Law

US law only creates responsibilities for right holders and platforms for lawful uploads with respect to notice-and-takedown. In this regard, right holders are liable for knowingly materially misrepresenting content as infringing, 17 U.S.C. § 512(f)(1).[44] Platforms are shielded from liability for good faith takedowns of lawful content pursuant to a notification by a right holder if they take reasonable steps to promptly notify uploaders, comply with procedural obligations for counter notifications, and reinstate content in due time after receipt of the counter notification (unless the right holder filed an action seeking court order), 17 U.S.C. § 512(g).

For automated filtering, no comparable responsibilities exist. Several lines of reasoning why platforms could nevertheless be liable for removing lawful content ('must-carry claims') are conceivable. To support must-carry claims,[45] plaintiffs have inter alia employed the First Amendment guarantee of free speech (e.g. *PragerU*, 2020, pp. 996–999),[46] alleged an unfair competitive practice (e.g. *PragerU*, 2020, pp. 999–1000),[47] and asserted a breach of contract (e.g. *Song fi*, 2015, pp. 884–885).[48] Platforms, on the other hand, inter alia rely on their private

---

[44] The provision enables uploaders and platforms to obtain damages, including court costs and attorneys' fees.

[45] Most existing cases concern takedowns for other reasons than alleged copyright infringement, but plaintiffs' claims and platforms' defences are nevertheless relevant. A defence based on 47 U.S.C. § 230(c)(2)(A), which shields platforms against liability for good faith takedowns of content they consider objectionable, is an exception. This provision does not apply to takedowns for alleged copyright infringement; see 47 U.S.C. § 230(e)(2).

[46] In this case, YouTube had restricted access to and demonetised videos uploaded by the controversial media organisation PragerU. PragerU sought to surmount the hurdle that the First Amendment only prohibits governmental (and not private) abridgement of speech by arguing that YouTube operates a public forum and thus must be deemed a state actor. The 9th Circuit rejected this argument, holding based on previous case law that private entities can only be deemed state actors in the rare case in which they perform a '"[...] traditionally and exclusively governmental"' function. The Court went on to argue that YouTube's function of hosting speech is hardly an activity exclusively performed by the government.

[47] PragerU claimed that public statements by YouTube in which it presented itself as being committed to free speech constituted false advertising, leading to liability under 15 U.S.C. § 1125(a)(1). The Court rejected this claim, holding that such statements were not 'commercial advertising or promotion' as required for such liability but 'classic, non-actionable opinions or puffery'.

[48] In this case, YouTube relocated a video into a non-publicly accessible location on YouTube due to alleged view count inflation. The plaintiffs argued that YouTube breached its terms of service as well as the implied covenant of good faith and fair dealing. The Court rejected these arguments because of a clause in YouTube's terms of service which allowed it to take content down at its discretion.

nature to counter claims based on free speech (e.g. *PragerU*, 2020, pp. 996–999), invoke their protection under the First Amendment (e.g. *E-Ventures*, 2016, pp. 8–9),[49] and point to their terms of service (e.g. *Song fi*, 2015, pp. 884–885), to which uploaders agree. Platforms have prevailed in all cases so far (Keller, 2019, p. 11). For the time being, uploaders therefore have little hope of succeeding in holding platforms liable for blocking lawful upload attempts through automated filtering.

2.3.2.2 EU Law

Having considered the (lack of) responsibilities of right holders and platforms to prevent blockings of lawful content under US law, this section reflects on the same issue for EU law.

The pre-Copyright in the DSM Directive (2019) legal framework did not state responsibilities of right holders or platforms to prevent blockings of lawful content.[50] Article 17(7), first subparagraph of the Copyright in the DSM Directive (2019) now provides that the cooperation between right holders and platforms shall not entail a prevention of the availability of lawful uploads.[51] The CJEU emphasised that this provision stipulates a specific result to be achieved rather than just a best efforts requirement (*Poland v. Parliament and Council*, 2022, para. 78).

Still, it remains unclear what requirements this entails for right holders. In its non-binding guidance on Article 17 of the Copyright in the DSM Directive (2019), the European Commission (2021, p. 14) states that the information provided 'should, as a minimum, be accurate about the rights ownership'. However, there is no recommendation in terms of consequences for inaccurate indications. Interestingly,

---

[49] In this case, the search engine optimisation provider e-ventures had allegedly violated Google's guidelines on search engine manipulation, resulting in a removal of its websites from the search engine. According to the Court, the First Amendment protects Google's decisions on which websites are contrary to its guidelines and thereby subject to removal, regardless of 'whether they are fair or unfair, or motivated by profit or altruism'.

[50] For right holders, the CJEU noted that the notifications they submit 'must contain sufficient information to enable the […] platform to satisfy itself, without a detailed legal examination, that that communication is illegal and that removing that content is compatible with freedom of expression' (*YouTube/Cyando*, 2021, para. 116). However, the CJEU has not formulated requirements for the information right holders enter into reference databases. For platforms, the CJEU emphasised that when platforms remove content to comply with Article 14(1) of the E-Commerce Directive (2000) (now: Article 6(1) of the Digital Services Act, 2022), they 'must do so with due regard to the principle of freedom of expression' (*YouTube/Cyando*, 2021, para. 113). Yet, it is unclear what responsibilities this entailed.

[51] The provision emphasises that non-infringing uses encompass uploads covered by copyright exceptions. Article 17(7), second subparagraph of the Copyright in the DSM Directive (2019) requires Member States to ensure that uploaders can rely on the quotation and the parody exception. These exceptions were previously optional under EU law.

in a document outlining initial ideas for the guidance, the European Commission (2020, p. 9) noted that 'Member States should be free to define sanctions for abuse of the cooperation mechanism laid down in Article 17, such as the provision of false information.' The final guidance does not contain a comparable statement. While this does not affect Member States' freedom to introduce liability for right holders who enter wrongful information (see Leistner, 2020, p. 180), as far as apparent, this option has not yet been used.[52]

For platforms, the CJEU noted that the obligations contained in Article 17(4) of the Copyright in the DSM Directive (2019) cannot lead them to take measures that would affect the essence of their users' right to freedom of expression and information (*Poland v. Parliament and Council*, 2022, para. 80). It takes the view that an automated filter that cannot distinguish adequately between unlawful and lawful content is incompatible with users' right to freedom of expression and information (*Poland v. Parliament and Council*, 2022, para. 86). However, it does not further specify the requirements for an adequately precise filter.

In its guidance, the European Commission (2021, p. 20) notes that the need to 'respect legitimate uses should be taken into account when assessing whether a service provider has made its "best efforts"'. It emphasises that the possibility of legitimate uses must be considered during the filtering process and that it is not sufficient to restore legitimate content ex post. Moreover, it states that platforms should in principle only block 'manifestly infringing uploads.' To detect manifest infringements, the European Commission (2021, p. 21) suggests to inter alia look at the 'length/size of the identified content used in the upload, the proportion of the matching/identified content in relation to the entire upload [...] and the level of modification of the work'. Exact matches of entire works and uploads that are only modified to avoid detection should generally be considered to be manifest infringements. A manifest infringement should be negated if the uploader 'has significantly modified the work in a creative manner' or the match only represents a 'small proportion of the entire work'.

The German and Austrian implementations are more specific in this regard. The German implementation introduces a rebuttable presumption that an upload is lawful if it contains less than half of a work or of several works, combines the parts taken from third-party works with other content, and uses parts of third-party works to a minor extent or is flagged as lawful (section 9(2) of the Act on the Copyright Liability of Online Content Sharing Service Providers, 2021). A minor use is defined as up to 15 s of a movie or up to 15 s of an audio track (section 10 of the Act on the

[52]The German implementation of Article 17 of the Copyright in the DSM Directive (2019) does introduce negligence-based liability of alleged right holders who request blockings of works they do not own. Compensation can be claimed by platforms or concerned users (section 18(2) of the Act on the Copyright Liability of Online Content Sharing Service Providers, 2021). Moreover, alleged right holders who repeatedly request blockings of works they do not own must be temporarily banned from the blocking procedures (section 18(1) of the Act on the Copyright Liability of Online Content Sharing Service Providers, 2021). Yet, there is neither comparable liability nor a comparable sanction for wrongful indications in the reference database.

Copyright Liability of Online Content Sharing Service Providers, 2021). The Austrian implementation stipulates that small parts of works must not be blocked unless right holders show that using them considerably compromises their ability to economically exploit their works. Small parts are defined in the same way as minor uses in the German implementation (§ 89b(3) of the Copyright Law of 1936).

The European Commission (2021, p. 21) further proposes in its guidance to take 'the type of content, the business model, as well as the risk of significant economic harm to rightholders' into account. To identify works for which copying would cause particularly high harm to right holders, the European Commission (2021, p. 22) suggests to enable right holders to earmark such works (e.g. 'pre-released music or films or highlights of recent broadcasts of sports events') and applying 'a rapid *ex ante* human review [...] of the uploads containing such earmarked content identified'.

Furthermore, Article 17(9), first subparagraph of the Copyright in the DSM Directive (2019) obliges Member States to require platforms to set up 'effective and expeditious complaint and redress mechanism[s]'. Member States must further ensure the availability of 'out-of-court redress mechanisms' and guarantee uploaders access to a court to assert copyright exceptions (Article 17(9), second subparagraph of the Copyright in the DSM Directive, 2019).

The Copyright in the DSM Directive (2019) neither requires Member States to introduce compensation for damages from wrongful blockings nor precludes them from doing so. As far as apparent, Member States have not yet used this option. However, the German implementation of Article 17 of the Copyright in the DSM Directive (2019) enables user rights organisations to claim injunctive relief if a platform repeatedly wrongfully blocks lawful uses (section 18(6) of the Act on the Copyright Liability of Online Content Sharing Service Providers, 2021).

In principle, platforms can keep non-infringing content down for other reasons than alleged copyright infringements (Leistner, 2020, p. 169). The Digital Services Act (2022) reduces VLOPs' leeway in this regard. VLOPs are required to assess (Article 34(1), first subparagraph, second subparagraph, second sentence, (b) of the Digital Services Act, 2022) and mitigate (Article 35(1), first sentence of the Digital Services Act, 2022) systemic risks associated with their services, including 'negative effects for the exercise of fundamental rights'. In doing so, VLOPs should consider how 'the applicable terms and conditions and their enforcement' affect such risks (Article 34(2), first subparagraph, (c) of the Digital Services Act, 2022). Apart from these obligations for VLOPs, EU law does not provide guidance on whether limits to the ability to keep non-infringing content down for other reasons than alleged copyright infringements exist. On the Member State level, notably German courts have affirmed must-carry obligations in individual cases (e.g. *McMahon v. Facebook*, 2020).[53] However, the exact shape of must-carry obligations under German law, and even more so in other Member States, is unsettled.

[53] The case concerns takedowns for alleged hate speech. The legal reasoning is nevertheless relevant beyond this specific field. The basis for the must-carry obligation is the contract concluded between

As with platforms' responsibilities to use automated filters (Sect. 2.3.1.2), there is an overlap between Article 17 of the Copyright in the DSM Directive (2019) and the Digital Services Act (2022) concerning responsibilities to prevent the blocking of lawful upload attempts. When assessing and mitigating systemic risks, namely, 'negative effects for the exercise of fundamental rights', platforms should consider how content moderation, such as automated filtering (see Article 3(t) of the Digital Services Act, 2022), affects such risks (Article 34(2), first subparagraph, (b) of the Digital Services Act, 2022). However, since Article 17 of the Copyright in the DSM Directive (2019) contains the above-described responsibilities of OCSSPs to prevent blockings of lawful upload attempts due to alleged copyright infringements, it prevails to this extent as *lex specialis* (Article 2(4)(b) of the Digital Services Act, 2022).[54] Besides the above-described limitations in terms of keeping non-infringing content down for other reasons than alleged copyright infringements, the Digital Services Act (2022) therefore does not influence OCSSPs' responsibilities to prevent wrongful blockings.

2.4 Main Takeaways for Analysis

This chapter served to familiarise the reader with the relevant economic, technical, and legal background for the following analysis. Five takeaways deserve to be highlighted.

First, from an economic perspective, the goal of copyright law is to efficiently navigate the trade-off between incentivising content creation by increasing right holders' profits and ensuring access to creative content. To evaluate the desirability of automated filtering, it is thus crucial to understand how filtering affects right

a platform and an uploader when the uploader creates an account. This contract has been held to contain an obligation owed by the platform to carry the uploaded content unless it is illegal or precluded by a permissible reservation in the platform's terms of service. Platforms may preclude uploads of otherwise legal content through their terms of service provided that the provisions comply with controls on unfair contract terms. Of particular relevance in this regard is the doctrine of indirect third-party effects of fundamental rights ('*mittelbare Drittwirkung der Grundrechte*'), which has been developed by the German Federal Constitutional Court in *Lüth* (1958), and according to which fundamental rights indirectly affect the relationship between private parties by guiding the interpretation of legal standards. In reconciling a platform's fundamental rights, which establish its 'virtual householder's rights' ('*virtuelles Hausrecht*'), with an uploader's right to freedom of expression, a provision that allowed a platform discretion on which content it removes has been declared ineffective (*McMahon v. Facebook*, 2020, paras. 93–118).

[54] As for OCSSPs' obligations to use automated copyright filters, the view expressed by Quintais and Schwemer (2022, p. 215) that the Copyright in the DSM Directive (2019) 'in no way addresses' the issue of risk mitigation and thus does not preclude an application of Article 35 of the Digital Services Act (2022) is too broad. Quite to the contrary, the above-described responsibilities to prevent wrongful blockings seek to reduce risks for uploaders' freedom of expression (see recital 70 of the Copyright in the DSM Directive, 2019).

holders' profits and the availability of works on a platform. Chapter 3 therefore examines these effects.

The second takeaway relates to the circumvention of fingerprinting technology. Circumvention is possible but comes at a cost as unlawful uploaders must invest in disguising content and may need several attempts to upload. The additional costs unlawful uploaders incur can be adjusted by moving the critical similarity threshold for a blocking. These insights fundamentally shape the design of the model in Chap. 3. Specifically, it is assumed that unlawful uploaders can upload when the platform filters, but that they incur higher uploading costs than right holders. Moreover, the model is designed in a way that allows the impact of different levels of filtering strictness (and thus of additional costs for unlawful uploaders) to be observed.

Third, throughout this book, it is presumed that substantive copyright law is efficient. Under this presumption, the social benefits resulting from a lawful upload exceed social costs. For unlawful uploads, the opposite is true. Automated filtering then contributes to separating the copyright-infringing and thus socially costly 'chaff' from the lawful and thus socially valuable 'wheat'. At the same time, false negatives and false positives generate net social costs. The assumption that substantive copyright law is efficient is therefore crucial for applying the error cost framework in Chap. 4.

Fourth, fingerprinting technology evaluates the similarity between a work in the reference database and an upload attempt. This observation is relevant for explaining why automated filtering cannot emulate a legal analysis. Moreover, it reveals two important sources of information to make blocking decisions, namely, indications in the reference database and observations on the overlap between a work in the reference database and an upload attempt. These insights are key when discussing the second-best efficient design of automated filtering in Chap. 4.

Finally, the current legal situations in the US and the EU do shape platforms' incentives in terms of automated filtering. It follows that observations on platforms' actual behaviour are not informative of their behaviour in the absence of regulation. It is important to keep this consideration in mind during the discussion of platforms' incentives in a *laissez-faire* regime in Sect. 5.4.1. Moreover, as the current legal situations influence platforms' incentives, there is added value in comparing the suggested measures to best approach efficient error avoidance with the current legal situations. Section 5.5.2 performs this task.

References

15 U.S.C. § 1125 (US). https://www.law.cornell.edu/uscode/text/15/1125
17 U.S.C. § 101 et seq. (US). https://www.law.cornell.edu/uscode/text/17
35 U.S.C. § 271 (US). https://www.law.cornell.edu/uscode/text/35/271
47 U.S.C. § 230 (US). https://www.law.cornell.edu/uscode/text/47/230
ACRCloud. (2024). *Copyright compliance & data deduplication: Protecting music copyright & refining media database*. https://www.acrcloud.com/copyright-compliance-data-deduplication/

Act on the Copyright Liability of Online Content Sharing Service Providers (Germany), 31 May 2021, Federal Law Gazette I, p. 1204, 1215 (2021). https://www.gesetze-im-internet.de/englisch_urhdag/index.html

AG Opinion in YouTube/Cyando (EU). AG Opinion in Frank Peterson v. Google LLC and others and Elsevier Inc. v. Cyando AG, Joined Cases C-682/18 and C-683/18, ECLI:EU:C:2020:586 (CJEU 2020). https://curia.europa.eu/juris/document/document.jsf;jsessionid=F225D083B049B019F7E3C12A692DB276?text=&docid=228712&pageIndex=0&doclang=EN&mode=lst&dir=&occ=first&part=1&cid=13288016

Aimster (US). In re Aimster copyright litigation, 334 F.3d 643 (7th Cir. 2003). https://scholar.google.com/scholar_case?case=17668008213909640659&q=334+F.3d+643+&hl=en&as_sdt=4,112,127,268,269,270,271,272,314,315,331,332,333,334,335,377,378

Audible Magic. (n.d.). *Which platforms do you work with for Identification?* Help Desk. Retrieved August 27, 2024, from https://support.audiblemagic.com/which-platforms-do-you-work-with-for-identification-1

Austin, G. W. (2000). Social policy choices and choice of law for copyright infringement in cyberspace. *Oregon Law Review, 79*(3), 575–618.

Beijing Treaty on Audiovisual Performances (adopted 24 June 2012, entered into force 28 April 2020) 51 ILM 1214 (2012). https://www.wipo.int/wipolex/en/text/295838

Betamax (US). Sony Corp. of America v. Universal City Studios, Inc., 464 U.S. 417 (1984). https://supreme.justia.com/cases/federal/us/464/417/

Bonetto, G. (2018). Internet memes as derivative works: Copyright issues under EU law. *Journal of Intellectual Property Law & Practice, 13*(12), 989–997.

Brøvig-Hanssen, R., & Jones, E. (2021). Remix's retreat? Content moderation, copyright law and mashup music. *New Media & Society*, 1–19.

Capitol Records, LLC v. Vimeo, LLC (US), 972 F. Supp. 2d 500 (S.D. New York 2013). https://scholar.google.com/scholar_case?case=7182265287680094203&q=Capitol+Records,+LLC+v+VIMEO,+LLC&hl=en&as_sdt=4,351

Charter of Fundamental Rights of the European Union (EU), OJ C 326/391 (2012). https://eur-lex.europa.eu/legal-content/EN/TXT/PDF/?uri=CELEX:12012P/TXT

Copyright in the DSM Directive (EU). Directive (EU) 2019/790 of the European Parliament and of the European Council of 17 April 2019 on copyright and related rights in the Digital Single Market and amending Directives 96/9/EC and 2001/29/EC, OJ L 130/92 (2019). https://eur-lex.europa.eu/legal-content/EN/TXT/PDF/?uri=CELEX:32019L0790

Copyright Law of 1936 (Austria). Federal Law on Copyright in Literary and Artistic Works and Related Rights. https://www.ris.bka.gv.at/GeltendeFassung.wxe?Gesetzesnummer=10001848&Abfrage=Bundesnormen

Dailymotion. (2024). *How to protect your copyrighted work?* https://faq.dailymotion.com/hc/en-us/articles/203921173-How-to-protect-your-copyrighted-work-

Digital Services Act (EU). Regulation (EU) 2022/2065 of the European Parliament and of the Council of 19 October 2022 on a Single Market For Digital Services and amending Directive 2000/31/EC, OJ L 277/1 (2022). https://eur-lex.europa.eu/legal-content/EN/TXT/PDF/?uri=CELEX:32022R2065

Dinwoodie, G. B. (2000). A new copyright order: Why national courts should create global norms. *University of Pennsylvania Law Review, 149*(2), 469–580.

Dinwoodie, G. B. (2004). Private ordering and the creation of international copyright norms: The role of public structuring. *Journal of Institutional and Theoretical Economics, 160*(1), 161–180.

E-Commerce Directive (EU). Directive 2000/31/EC of the European Parliament and of the Council of 8 June 2000 on certain legal aspects of information society services, in particular electronic commerce, in the Internal Market (Directive on electronic commerce), OJ L 178/1 (2000). https://eur-lex.europa.eu/legal-content/EN/TXT/PDF/?uri=CELEX:32000L0031

Eger, T. (2015). Copyright under fire: Some comments from a law and economics perspective on the heated debate on copyright law. *Hamburg Law Review, 2*, 25–40.

Elkin-Koren, N. (1997). Copyrights in cyberspace: Rights without laws. *Chicago-Kent Law Review, 73*(4), 1155–1202.

Elkin-Koren, N., & Salzberger, E. M. (2013). *The law and economics of intellectual property in the digital age: The limits of analysis*. Routledge.

Englisch, O., & Priora, G. (2019). Safe harbour protection for online video platforms: A time to say goodbye? Analysis of judgements by Italian and German courts on the liability of YouTube for copyright infringements. *Rivista Di Diritto Dei Media, 2*, 1–16.

Esmaeili, M. M., Fatourechi, M., & Ward, R. K. (2011). A robust and fast video copy detection system using content-based fingerprinting. *IEEE Transactions on Information Forensics and Security, 6*(1), 213–226.

European Commission. (2020, July 27). *Targeted consultation addressed to the participants to the stakeholder dialogue on Article 17 of the Directive on Copyright in the Digital Single Market*. https://www.ipi.si/wp-content/uploads/2020/07/FinalconsultationpaperonArt17pdf.pdf

European Commission. (2021, June 4). *Communication from the Commission to the European Parliament and the Council: Guidance on Article 17 of Directive 2019/790 on Copyright in the Digital Single Market*. COM(2021) 288 Final. https://eur-lex.europa.eu/legal-content/EN/TXT/?uri=CELEX:52021DC0288

European Commission. (2024, July 12). *Supervision of the designated very large online platforms and search engines under DSA*. https://digital-strategy.ec.europa.eu/en/policies/list-designated-vlops-and-vloses

European Union Intellectual Property Office. (2020, November 25). *Automated Content Recognition: Discussion Paper—Phase 1 "Existing technologies and their impact on IP"*. https://data.europa.eu/doi/10.2814/52085

Evans, D. S., & Schmalensee, R. (2007). The industrial organization of markets with two-sided platforms. *Competition Policy International, 3*(1), 151–179.

E-Ventures (US). E-Ventures Worldwide, LLC v. Google, Inc., Case No. 2:14-cv-646-FtM-PAM-CM (M.D. Florida 2016). https://digitalcommons.law.scu.edu/cgi/viewcontent.cgi?article=2410&context=historical

Fonovisa, Inc. v. Cherry Auction, Inc. (US), 76 F.3d 259 (9th Cir. 1996). https://scholar.google.com/scholar_case?case=5950768713691772923&q=76+F.3d+259+&hl=en&as_sdt=4,114,129

Frosio, G. (2020). Reforming the C-DSM reform: A user-based copyright theory for commonplace creativity. *International Review of Intellectual Property and Competition Law, 51*, 709–750.

Fullerton, D. (1991). On justifications for public support of the arts. *Journal of Cultural Economics, 15*(2), 67–82.

Gallo, L. G. (2010). The (im)possibility of "Standard Technical Measures" for UGC websites. *Columbia Journal of Law & the Arts, 34*(2), 283–315.

Gershwin Publishing Corp. v. Columbia Artists Man., Inc. (US), 443 F.2d 1159 (2d Cir. 1971). https://scholar.google.com/scholar_case?case=13919786496570065695&q=443+F.2d+1159+&hl=en&as_sdt=4,107,122

Giblin-Chen, R., & Davison, M. (2006). Kazaa goes the way of Grokster? Authorisation of copyright infringement via peer-to-peer networks in Australia. *Australian Intellectual Property Journal, 17*, 53–76.

Gilbert, R. J., & Katz, M. L. (2001). When good value chains go bad: The economics of indirect liability for copyright infringement. *Hastings Law Journal, 52*(4), 961–990.

Ginsburg, J. C. (2000). International copyright: From a "bundle" of national copyright laws to a supranational code? *Journal of the Copyright Society of the U.S.A., 47*, 265–289.

Gomes, L. d. C. T., Cano, P., Gómez, E., Bonnet, M., & Batlle, E. (2003). Audio watermarking and fingerprinting: For which applications? *Journal of New Music Research, 32*(1), 65–81.

Google. (2024). *YouTube copyright transparency report*. https://transparencyreport.google.com/youtube-copyright/intro?hl=en_GB

Google. (n.d.). *Copyright and rights management*. YouTube Help. Retrieved July 17, 2024, from https://support.google.com/youtube/topic/2676339?hl=en-GB&ref_topic=6151248&sjid=7784574668489471573-EU

Gorwa, R., Binns, R., & Katzenbach, C. (2020). Algorithmic content moderation: Technical and political challenges in the automation of platform governance. *Big Data & Society, 7*(1), 1–15.

Grokster (US). Metro-Goldwyn-Mayer Studios Inc. v. Grokster, Ltd., 545 U.S. 913 (2005). https://supreme.justia.com/cases/federal/us/545/913/

Haitsma, J., & Kalker, T. (2003). A highly robust audio fingerprinting system with an efficient search strategy. *Journal of New Music Research, 32*(2), 211–221.

Husovec, M. (2016, May 2). *Accountable, not liable: Injunctions against intermediaries* (2016–012). TILEC Discussion Paper No. 2016-012. http://www.ssrn.com/abstract=2773768

InfoSoc Directive (EU). Directive 2001/29/EC of the European Parliament and of the Council of 22 May 2001 on the harmonisation of certain aspects of copyright and related rights in the information society, OJ L 167/10 (2001). https://eur-lex.europa.eu/legal-content/EN/TXT/PDF/?uri=CELEX:32001L0029

Kaesling, K., & Knapp, J. (2020). "Massenkreativität" in sozialen Netzwerken: Überlegungen zur Plattformverantwortlichkeit nach der DSM-RL. *Multimedia Und Recht, 23*(12), 816–821.

Keller, D. (2019). *Who do you sue? State and platform hybrid power over online speech*. Hoover Institution, Aegis Series Paper No. 1902. https://www.hoover.org/sites/default/files/research/docs/who-do-you-sue-state-and-platform-hybrid-power-over-online-speech_0.pdf

Kulk, S. (2018). *Internet intermediaries and copyright law: Towards a future-proof EU legal framework*. Ridderprint.

Landes, W. M., & Posner, R. A. (1989). An economic analysis of copyright law. *The Journal of Legal Studies, 18*(2), 325–363.

Leistner, M. (2020). European copyright licensing and infringement liability under Art. 17 DSM-Directive: Can we make the new European system a global opportunity instead of a local challenge? *Zeitschrift Für Geistiges Eigentum, 12*(2), 123–214.

Lemley, M. A., & Reese, R. A. (2004). Reducing digital copyright infringement without restricting innovation. *Stanford Law Review, 56*(6), 1345–1434.

Lenz (US). Lenz v. Universal Music Corp., 801 F.3d 1126 (9th Cir. 2015). https://scholar.google.com/scholar_case?case=12567649168680108221&q=801+F.3d+1126+&hl=en&as_sdt=4,114,129

Lessig, L. (2008). *Remix: Making art and commerce thrive in the hybrid economy*. Bloomsbury Academic.

Lev-Aretz, Y. (2013). Copyright lawmaking and public choice: From legislative battles to private ordering. *Harvard Journal of Law & Technology, 27*(1), 203–256.

Liebowitz, S. J. (2014). The impacts of internet piracy. In R. Watt (Ed.), *Handbook on the economics of copyright: A guide for students and teachers* (pp. 225–240). Edward Elgar.

Litman, J. (2002). War stories. *Cardozo Arts & Entertainment Law Journal, 20*(2), 337–366.

Litman, J. (2017). *Digital copyright*. Michigan Publishing.

Lu, J. (2009). Video fingerprinting for copy identification: From research to industry applications. *Proceedings of SPIE: Media Forensics and Security, 7254*, 1–15.

Lüth (Germany), 1 BvR 400/51 (Federal Constitutional Court 1958). https://www.bundesverfassungsgericht.de/SharedDocs/Entscheidungen/DE/1958/01/rs19580115_1bvr040051.html

Matalon, L. J. (2019). Modern problems require modern solutions: Internet memes and copyright. *Texas Law Review, 98*(2), 405–437.

McFadden (EU). Tobias McFadden v. Sony Music Entertainment Germany GmbH, C-484/14, ECLI:EU:C:2016:689 (CJEU 2016). https://curia.europa.eu/juris/document/document.jsf?docid=183363&doclang=EN

McMahon v. Facebook (Germany), 18 U 1491/19 Pre (Higher Regional Court of Munich 2020). https://www.juris.de/r3/document/NJRE001414100

Meta. (2024). *Rights manager*. https://rightsmanager.fb.com/

Napster (US). A&M Records, Inc. v. Napster, Inc., 239 F.3d 1004 (9th Cir. 2001). https://scholar.google.com/scholar_case?case=14102696336550697309&q=239+F.3d+1004+&hl=en&as_sdt=4,114,129

Netlog (EU). Belgische Vereniging van Auteurs, Componisten en Uitgevers CVBA (SABAM) v. Netlog NV, C-360/10, ECLI:EU:C:2012:85 (CJEU 2012). https://curia.europa.eu/juris/document/document.jsf?text=&docid=119512&pageIndex=0&doclang=EN&mode=lst&dir=&occ=first&part=1&cid=13295281

OECD. (2010, April). *The economic and social role of internet intermediaries*. https://www.oecd.org/internet/ieconomy/44949023.pdf

Patel, R. (2013). First world problems: A fair use analysis of internet memes. *UCLA Entertainment Law Review, 20*(2), 235–256.

Patry, W. F. (1996). Copyright and the legislative process: A personal perspective. *Cardozo Arts & Entertainment Law Journal, 14*(1), 139–152.

Poland v. Parliament and Council (EU). Republic of Poland v. European Parliament and Council of the European Union, C-401/19, ECLI:EU:C:2022:297 (CJEU 2022). https://curia.europa.eu/juris/document/document.jsf?text=&docid=258261&pageIndex=0&doclang=EN&mode=req&dir=&occ=first&part=1&cid=13289381

PragerU (US). Prager University v. Google LLC, 951 F.3d 991 (9th Cir. 2020). https://scholar.google.com/scholar_case?case=16871614384391817723&q=951+F.3d+991+&hl=en&as_sdt=866000000000f81e0cc000000001f03c000000000000000000000010a0e0c2800500002141c300000000000000000004

Quintais, J. P. (2020). The new copyright in the digital single market directive: A critical look. *European Intellectual Property Review, 42*(1), 28–41.

Quintais, J. P., & Schwemer, S. F. (2022). The interplay between the digital services act and sector regulation: How special is copyright? *European Journal of Risk Regulation, 13*(2), 191–217.

Raue, B., & Steinebach, M. (2020). Uploadfilter: Funktionsweisen, Einsatzmöglichkeiten und Parametrisierung. *Zeitschrift Für Urheber- Und Medienrecht, 64*(5), 355–364.

Religious Tech. Center v. Netcom On-Line Comm. (US), 907 F. Supp. 1361 (N.D. California 1995). https://scholar.google.com/scholar_case?case=2398297825525410597&q=Religious+Tech.+Center+v+Netcom+On-Line+Comm&hl=en&as_sdt=4,323

Rossi (US). Rossi v. Motion Picture Ass'n of America, 391 F.3d 1000 (9th Cir. 2004). https://scholar.google.com/scholar_case?case=15201841502915519327&q=Rossi+v.+Motion+Picture+Ass%27n+of+America&hl=en&as_sdt=4,114,129

Samuelson, P. (2006). Regulating technical design: Should software developers be required to include infringement-inhibiting components such as filters in their technologies? *Communications of the ACM, 49*(2), 25–30.

Samuelson, P. (2021). Pushing back on stricter copyright ISP liability rules. *Michigan Technology Law Review, 27*(2), 299–343.

Sartor, G., & Loreggia, A. (2020, September 15). *The impact of algorithms for online content filtering or moderation: "Upload filters."* https://www.europarl.europa.eu/thinktank/en/document.html?reference=IPOL_STU(2020)657101

Schiavenza, M. (2015, February 14). *How YouTube changed journalism*. The Atlantic. https://www.theatlantic.com/technology/archive/2015/02/how-youtube-changed-journalism/385523/

Seidel, C. (2009). Content fingerprinting from an industry perspective. In *Proceedings of the 2009 IEEE International Conference on Multimedia and Expo* (pp. 1524–1527).

Senftleben, M. (2020). Institutionalized algorithmic enforcement: The pros and cons of the EU approach to UGC platform liability. *FIU Law Review, 14*(2), 299–328.

Senftleben, M., & Angelopoulos, C. (2020). *The Odyssey of the prohibition on general monitoring obligations on the way to the digital services act: Between Article 15 of the E-Commerce Directive and Article 17 of the Directive on Copyright in the Digital Single Market*. https://papers.ssrn.com/sol3/papers.cfm?abstract_id=3717022

Shapiro, Bernstein & Co. v. HL Green Company (US), 316 F.2d 304 (2d Cir. 1963). https://scholar.google.com/scholar_case?case=11617630515138458269&q=Shapiro,+Bernstein+%26+Co.+v.+HL+Green+Company&hl=en&as_sdt=4,107,122,323

Shapiro, C., & Varian, H. R. (1999). *Information rules: A strategic guide to the network economy.* Harvard Business School Press.

Song fi (US). Song fi Inc. v. Google, Inc., 108 F. Supp. 3d 876 (N.D. California 2015). https://scholar.google.com/scholar_case?case=12473745511769351864&q=F.+Supp.+3d+876+&hl=en&as_sdt=866000000000f81e0cc000000001f03c00000000000000000000010a0e0c2800500002141c300000000000000000004

Tillis, T. (2020, December 22). *Discussion Draft for a Digital Copyright Act of 2021.* https://www.tillis.senate.gov/2020/12/tillis-releases-landmark-discussion-draft-to-reform-the-digital-millennium-copyright-act

US Copyright Office. (2016, February 22). *The making available right in the United States: A report of the Register of Copyrights.* http://www.copyright.gov/docs/making_available/making-available-right.pdf

Viacom v. YouTube (US). Viacom International, Inc. v. YouTube, Inc., 676 F.3d 19 (2d Cir. 2012). https://scholar.google.com/scholar_case?case=13644579048975596329&q=676+F.3d+19+&hl=en&as_sdt=4,107,122

Viacom v. YouTube (US). Viacom International, Inc. v. YouTube, Inc., 940 F. Supp. 2d 110 (S.D. New York 2013). https://scholar.google.com/scholar_case?case=9781681406417936292&q=F.+Supp.+2d+110+&hl=en&as_sdt=4,351

Watt, R. (2009). *An empirical analysis of the economics of copyright: How valid are the results of studies in developed countries for developing countries?* The Economics of Intellectual Property: Suggestions for Further Research in Developing Countries and Countries with Economies in Transition. https://www.wipo.int/publications/en/details.jsp?id=289&plang=EN

WIPO Copyright Treaty (adopted 20 December 1996, entered into force 6 March 2002) 2186 UNTS 121 (1996). https://www.wipo.int/wipolex/en/text/295157

WIPO Performances and Phonograms Treaty (adopted 20 December 1996, entered into force 20 May 2002) 2186 UNTS 203 (1996). https://www.wipo.int/wipolex/en/text/295477

YouTube/Cyando (EU). Frank Peterson v. Google LLC and others and Elsevier Inc. v. Cyando AG, Joined Cases C-682/18 and C-683/18, ECLI:EU:C:2020:586 (CJEU 2021). https://curia.europa.eu/juris/document/document.jsf?text=&docid=243241&pageIndex=0&doclang=EN&mode=lst&dir=&occ=first&part=1&cid=13288846

Chapter 3
Impact of Automated Filtering on Right Holders' Profits and Availability of Works on Platform

Abstract Little research has been conducted on how automated filtering affects the key goals of copyright protection from an economic perspective, namely, to incentivise creation by increasing right holders' profits and to promote access to works. To examine this influence, this chapter develops an economic model that focuses on the competition between right holders and copyright-infringing uploaders. Unlike previous discussions, the model shows that even filters that are not intended to block all copyright-infringing upload attempts—and are therefore less likely to block lawful upload attempts—increase right holders' profits. It further finds that filtering leads right holders to upload fewer existing works, which is relevant for the social desirability and platforms' costs of filtering. Moreover, it reveals that unless a certain filtering strictness is surpassed, right holders' profits are positively correlated with the concentration of the market for supplying copyright-infringing uploads. It thereby highlights the value of combining filtering with other measures to disincentivise copyright-infringing uploading. Further results concern the impact of differentiating the filtering strictness based on the popularity of potentially copied-from works and the impact of right holders' pre-emptive activities. They carry relevance for the design of liability regimes and the design and interpretation of empirical studies, respectively.

Keywords User-uploaded content platforms · User-generated content platforms · Economic analysis of platform regulation · Economic analysis of intermediary liability · Economic analysis of copyright law · Automated filtering · Upload filters · Automated copyright enforcement · Online copyright piracy · Online copyright enforcement

The European Commission expected automated filtering to have 'a positive impact on the production and availability of content' (Proposal for the Copyright in the DSM Directive, 2016, p. 3). By contrast, YouTube's Global Head of Music claimed that what automated filtering 'could really mean: less money for artists and

O. Englisch, *Automated Copyright Filters*, International Law and Economics,
https://doi.org/10.1007/978-3-031-83161-4_3

songwriters, less music for fans' (Cohen, 2018).[1] These statements illustrate what the previous chapter concluded based on the economic rationale for copyright protection: The impact of automated filtering on right holders' profits and the availability of works on a platform is crucial for evaluating its desirability.

Nevertheless, a review of the related literature reveals that this impact has not yet been analysed when considering the competition between right holders and unlawful copiers (Sect. 3.1). Section 3.2 explains the analytical approach adopted in this chapter to address this research gap. Sections 3.3–3.7 then perform the analysis. Finally, Sect. 3.8 summarises and discusses the main findings.

For the reader's convenience, Table 3.5 in Appendix 2 provides an overview of all variables used in this chapter. To present calculations and results in a reasonably clear and accessible manner, this chapter introduces endogenous variables that function as placeholders for recurring critical thresholds. Table 3.5 also shows breakdowns of these endogenous variables to facilitate replications of calculations.

3.1 Literature Review and Research Question

The rationale for holding platforms liable for unlawful uploads, and thus for inducing them to filter, is to counteract an assumed negative effect of unlawful uploads on right holders' profits (see recital 61 of the Copyright in the DSM Directive, 2019; Gabison & Buiten, 2020, p. 249).

The assumption that unlawful uploads reduce right holders' profits is often based on the alleged observation that user-uploaded content platforms pay uploaders less per view than streaming services that are not open to user uploads (e.g. IFPI, 2016, p. 23; Liebowitz, 2018, paras. 134–158).[2] Even if empirically correct,[3] this so-called value gap[4] is not necessarily caused by unlawful uploads. The different business models pursued (see Elkin-Koren et al., 2020, pp. 20–22; Lennon, 2016) and the different types of viewers attracted (Wimmers & Barudi, 2017, p. 329) are plausible alternative explanations. Moreover, it is unclear whether streaming services that are

[1] Note that these statements refer to Article 13 of the Proposal for the Copyright in the DSM Directive (2016), which is the initial version of Article 17 of the Copyright in the DSM Directive (2019) and would have also created strong incentives for platforms to use automated filters.

[2] Liebowitz even argues that the observed difference understates the harm to right holders as without liability, user-uploaded content platforms exert higher competitive pressure on other streaming sites.

[3] Many commentators view the value gap as empirically unfounded (e.g. Frosio, 2018, p. 356; Spoerri, 2019, para. 9). One of the difficulties in assessing the differences in revenues is that licensing agreements often include non-disclosure clauses for negotiated fees (see Mazziotti, 2021, p. 214).

[4] Note that the term is sometimes also used to describe the alleged observations that revenues user-uploaded content platforms generate based on copyright-protected content are out of sync with revenues right holders receive or that revenues right holders receive have decreased over time (Elkin-Koren et al., 2020, p. 16).

not open to user uploads pay right holders the desirable amount and thus whether they are suitable benchmarks (Elkin-Koren et al., 2020, pp. 22–23).

From a theoretical perspective, a link between the possibility to upload unlawfully and payments per view has been explained based on right holders' bargaining position. A right holder is in a better bargaining position if a platform's outside option is the non-availability of his[5] work than if its outside option is the availability of his work (uploaded by an unlawful copier) (European Commission, 2016, pt. 1/3, p. 140; Liebowitz, 2018, paras. 97–98).

If this were the only mechanism at play, right holders' profits could only be increased by a strict filter (Liebowitz, 2018, paras. 12, 77): As long as some unlawful uploads pass the filter, a platform's outside option in negotiations with right holders is to display the unlawfully uploaded content to viewers. Only reducing, but not excluding, unlawful uploads would therefore not appreciably improve right holders' bargaining position. A strict filter, however, is associated with a high risk of false positives. If one relies on this rationale, there is little room for designing filters in ways that balance the interests of all concerned parties.

However, there is another mechanism through which unlawful uploads influence right holders' profits. If a right holder and unlawful uploaders can upload a work, they compete for views and the associated revenues. Right holders need to invest time and effort into winning this competition or accept that unlawful uploaders collect some of the revenues generated by their works. Either way, the presence of unlawful uploaders decreases their profits. Automated filters provide right holders with a competitive advantage: While right holders can simply upload their works, unlawful copiers face the risk of blockings and therefore need to invest time and effort into modifying the content in such a way that it passes the filter but still is attractive to viewers. This effect of automated filtering on right holders' profits has not yet been examined.[6]

The impact of automated filtering on the availability of works on a platform has received even less attention than its impact on right holders' profits. The obvious consideration that blocking reduces the number of successful unlawful uploads is not informative in this regard because a work that an unlawful uploader unsuccessfully attempted to upload can still be uploaded by that unlawful uploader in a second attempt, by another unlawful uploader, or by the right holder.

Three channels through which automated filtering affects the availability of works on a platform have been considered.[7] First, if a platform passes the filtering costs to uploaders, all else being equal, filtering makes uploading to the platform less

---

[5] In the interest of clarity, when considering the competition between right holders and unlawful copiers, male pronouns are used to refer to right holders and female pronouns to refer to unlawful copiers.

[6] Previous research has considered the competition between right holders and unlawful suppliers of their works in related contexts (e.g. Banerjee, 2003; Kiema, 2008; Lefort, 2013; Martínez-Sánchez, 2010). However, the impact on right holders' aggregate profits has not yet been examined.

[7] In addition, Zimmerman (2014, p. 273) claims that filtering is likely to increase right holders' willingness to use a platform. However, she does not substantiate this claim.

attractive (Beard et al., 2018, pp. 321–322, 325–326). Second, if filtering reduces the risk that a platform is shut down, all else being equal, filtering makes uploading to the platform more attractive (Beard et al., 2018, pp. 321–322, 325–326). Third, a negative effect of unlawful uploads on right holders' profits in a first period reduces the amount of works created and therefore uploaded in a second period (Gabison & Buiten, 2020, p. 265). Filtering counteracts this effect.

Besides these channels, automated filtering affects the availability of works on a platform through the competition for views between right holders and unlawful uploaders. This channel has not yet been explored.[8]

Based on these considerations, this chapter addresses the following research question:

Research Question 1
How does automated filtering affect right holders' profits and the number of works uploaded to a user-uploaded content platform when right holders compete with unlawful copiers for views?

3.2 Analytical Approach

To address research question 1, this chapter develops an economic model of a market for creative works. The supply side comprises right holders and unlawful copiers, who can both upload works to a platform. A game theoretical model of their competitive behaviour is developed and embedded into the market model. On the demand side, viewers can access the uploaded works.

Section 3.2.1 explains why the method of economic modelling is used. To ensure that the model does not become too convoluted, the analysis is divided into different scenarios and specifications, which are presented in Sect. 3.2.2. Next, the variables and assumptions relevant for the supply side (Sect. 3.2.3) and the demand side (Sect. 3.2.4) are introduced.

[8] Again, previous research has considered the competition between right holders and unlawful suppliers of their works in related contexts (e.g. Banerjee, 2003; Kiema, 2008; Lefort, 2013; Martínez-Sánchez, 2010). However, the impact on the availability of works on a platform has not yet been analysed. Beard et al. (2018, p. 326) briefly touch upon this issue, noting that 'one can imagine that the amount of infringing material on the Internet negatively affects the potential value obtained from uploading non-infringing material' and that the effect of 'a reduction in the value of legal property is to reduce uploading on Vetted [sic!] platforms'. However, it is unclear whether they refer to the effect of unlawful uploads on the value of lawful uploads of the same work or in general. In any case, their considerations do not go beyond these cursory remarks.

3.2.1 Choice of Method

The market model provides a framework for examining the impact of changes in right holders' and unlawful uploaders' competitive behaviour on right holders' profits and the number of works uploaded to a platform. The method of economic modelling is chosen to handle the complexity of the preceding step, namely, the impact of automated filtering on right holders' and unlawful uploaders' competitive behaviour. This competitive behaviour is characterised by the interdependency of decisions: Right holders and unlawful uploaders predict or observe the behaviour of the other actors and make decisions accordingly.

Game theoretical modelling is a method developed to examine strategic decision-making in such interdependent circumstances. It enables predictions of the relevant actors' behaviour with mathematical precision. To achieve this high degree of internal validity, the reality must be simplified and assumptions on relevant but uncertain factors must be made. As a consequence, particular caution is needed when drawing conclusions from the modelled to the real world.

While different methods than game theoretical modelling are conceivable, it is important to note that if we want to understand the competitive behaviour of right holders and unlawful uploaders, there is no way around simplifications and assumptions. The diversity of actors, behavioural options, interests, and influencing factors must be reduced to conduct a thorough analysis. Moreover, there are several relevant factors on which no conclusive empirical evidence exists. Any attempt to examine right holders' and unlawful uploaders' competitive behaviour must—at least implicitly—make assumptions in these regards.

As simplifications and assumptions are not a result of the method chosen but are inevitably connected to the research interest, the advantages of game theoretical modelling prevail. To keep negative effects in terms of external validity at check, simplifications and assumptions are carefully chosen and—whenever possible—based on empirical research. All simplifications and assumptions are disclosed and explained to make it easier for the reader to reflect on the generalisability of conclusions and for future researchers to modify the analysis. Moreover, the robustness of the results is tested by varying the most important assumptions.

3.2.2 Scenarios and Specifications

The following analysis compares right holders' profits and the number of works uploaded to a platform in three scenarios:

- Unlawful copiers are absent (scenario 1).
- Unlawful copiers are present and the platform does not filter (scenario 2.1).
- Unlawful copiers are present and the platform filters (scenario 2.2).

Throughout the analysis, the subscripts '1', '2.1', and '2.2' are used on variables that change in the three scenarios to indicate the scenario referred to.

The absence of unlawful copiers is included as a benchmark scenario. It helps to understand how the presence of unlawful copiers affects right holders' profits and the number of works uploaded. This understanding is the basis for examining the effects of automated filtering in these regards. Moreover, the results obtained enable a determination of the filtering intensities required to ensure that right holders earn the same profits as if unlawful copiers were absent.[9]

In scenarios 2.1 and 2.2, right holders compete with unlawful copiers for the revenues generated by works. The competitive pressure right holders are exposed to differs depending on how the market for supplying unlawful copies of works is structured. It is unclear which market structure is most realistic.[10] On the one hand, it can be argued that as long as it is profitable to upload copies of a work, unlawful copiers will enter the market, resulting in fierce competition among them (see Belleflamme & Peitz, 2012, pp. 512–513). On the other hand, creating copies of copyright-protected works and making them available to the public are illegal acts under copyright law that can result in claims for damages and even criminal sanctions. The number of people willing to enter such a market may be limited, resulting in a more concentrated market structure. For the analysis, it is essential to make an assumption in this regard. Given the uncertainty about the most realistic market structure, two versions of the model are considered. These versions reflect the two extreme cases: perfect competition among unlawful copiers and a per-work monopoly on supplying unlawful copies. Specifications of the model that assume perfect competition among unlawful copiers are indicated by the Roman numeral 'I' and specifications that assume a per-work monopoly on supplying unlawful copies by 'II'.

In scenario 2.2, it is assumed that a platform filters, but filtering is imperfect. For a given filtering technology, a platform can modify the filtering intensity by shifting the critical similarity score for a blocking. In the main text, it is assumed that platforms apply the most straightforward approach, that is, filter with the same intensity regardless of how popular a work is ('uniform filtering'). Absent evidence to the contrary, it can be presumed that platforms currently employ this strategy. Alternatively, it is conceivable that a platform filters more rigorously, the more popular a work is ('popularity-based filtering').[11] Appendix 1 demonstrates that the

[9]These filtering intensities become relevant in Sect. 3.7.3. Banerjee (2003, pp. 98–99) follows a similar approach: He considers a scenario in which the pirate is absent 'to study the policy variables that may restore the monopoly outcome'.

[10]Most previous studies that model the competition between unlawful copiers and right holders consider a per-work monopoly on uploading unlawful copies (e.g. Banerjee, 2003; Lefort, 2013; Martínez-Sánchez, 2010). By contrast, Kiema (2008) considers a setting in which several unlawful copiers compete.

[11]Platforms may be induced to adopt this filtering strategy if they are liable for unlawful uploads and must pay actual damages. More popular works are then associated with higher damages than less popular works as, all else being equal, the harm to a right holder caused by unlawful uploads of

Table 3.1 Scenarios and specifications of the model

	No filtering	Uniform filtering	Popularity-based filtering
No unlawful copiers	Scenario 1 (Sect. 3.3)		
Perfect competition among unlawful copiers	Scenario 2.1, specification I (Sect. 3.4.1)	Scenario 2.2, specification A.I (Sect. 3.4.2)	Scenario 2.2, specification B.I (Sect. A.1)
Per-work monopoly on uploading unlawful copies	Scenario 2.1, specification II (Sect. 3.5.1)	Scenario 2.2, specification A.II (Sect. 3.5.2)	Scenario 2.2, specification B.II (Sect. A.2)

results in terms of right holders' profits and the number of works uploaded do not differ qualitatively when assuming popularity-based filtering. Nevertheless, it is insightful to investigate whether uniform or popularity-based filtering requires a lower total filtering intensity to achieve a conceivable policy objective, namely, ensuring that right holders earn the same profits as in the absence of unlawful copiers (see Sect. 3.7.3). The specifications of the model that assume uniform filtering are indicated by the letter 'A'; the specifications in Appendix 1, which assume popularity-based filtering, are indicated by 'B'.

To square the scenarios with the assumptions on the structure of the market for supplying unlawful copies and the assumptions on the filtering strategy, the model is considered in the scenarios and specifications shown in Table 3.1.

In the first step, it is assumed that unlawful copiers are absent (scenario 1). Under this assumption, there is no reason for platforms to filter and thus no need to distinguish further specifications. In the second step, it is assumed that unlawful copiers are present and that the market for supplying unlawful copies is perfectly competitive. Under these assumptions, the model is considered without automated filtering (scenario 2.1, specification I) and with uniform filtering (scenario 2.2, specification A.I). The third step changes the assumption on the structure of the market for supplying unlawful copies. Under the assumption of a per-work monopoly on uploading unlawful copies, again, the model is considered without automated

a more popular work exceeds the harm caused by unlawful uploads of a less popular work. Note that YouTube limits the eligibility for its Content ID program to right holders of works that are 'frequently uploaded to YouTube' (Google, n.d., pt. How Content ID works). For other right holders, it offers tools with limited functionality, including the Content Verification Program, which right holders can use to find copying uploads to then issue takedown requests (Google, n.d., pt. Content Verification Program), and the Copyright Match Tool, which right holders who have submitted a takedown request can use to scan for further matches of the content reported in the request (Google, n.d., pt. Use the Copyright Match Tool). This approach is similar to popularity-based filtering. Note further that in its guidance on Article 17 of the Copyright in the DSM Directive (2019), the European Commission (2021, p. 21) includes the 'risk of significant economic harm to rightholders' as a criterion that can be considered when deciding on whether to block content. While the guidance does not envision a popularity-based strategy as modelled in Appendix 1, this recommendation can be read as a general endorsement of filtering more rigorously with respect to upload attempts copying from more popular works.

filtering (scenario 2.1, specification II) and with uniform filtering (scenario 2.2, specification A.II). The specifications in Appendix 1 presume popularity-based filtering. Specification B.I presumes perfect competition among unlawful copiers and specification B.II a per-work monopoly on uploading unlawful copies.

3.2.3 Supply Side

Having outlined the different scenarios and specifications, this section explains the setup of the model with respect to the supply side of the market. Section 3.2.3.1 introduces important variables and explains how the number of works uploaded to a platform is counted. This is followed by explanations of how the competition between right holders and unlawful copiers (Sect. 3.2.3.2) and automated filtering (Sect. 3.2.3.3) are modelled. Finally, Sect. 3.2.3.4 introduces the assumption that the number of copies right holders and unlawful copiers upload is a continuous variable and explains how right holders and unlawful copiers are presumed to behave if they are indifferent between uploading and not uploading.

3.2.3.1 Key Variables and Normalisation of Works

Creative works differ in various dimensions. The heterogeneity of works complicates an assessment of the number of works uploaded to a platform. Simply counting the number of works would assign the same value to every work, no matter how high its quality—however defined—and popularity are. In their seminal article on the economics of copyright law, Landes and Posner (1989, p. 335) overcome this challenge by counting the number of equivalent works—without, however, specifying in which dimension equivalence is assumed. Similar to their solution, this chapter normalises works with respect to popularity: A highly popular work is assigned a higher value than a less popular work.[12] Popularity is defined by some exogenous measure. Compared to the alternative approach of considering works with different levels of popularity, this approach makes it easier to understand the model and interpret the results.

Platforms are assumed to incentivise uploading by paying a reward r to an uploader every time an upload is viewed, with $r > 0$. To simplify the analysis, r is assumed to be fixed. Since works are normalised with respect to popularity, viewers distribute their views evenly among the works on the platform. v denotes the number of views per normalised work, with $v > 0$. The revenues generated by uploading a normalised work therefore are $v \cdot r$.

[12] The focus on popularity is not a normative statement about what copyright policy should focus on. It is rather a useful way of summarising and counting works.

For right holders, it is assumed that uploading a work is associated with two types of costs: uploading costs and a reduction in off-platform profits.[13] Uploading costs reflect the time and computational power required for uploading.[14] When considering works prior to normalisation ('non-normalised works'), it is likely that each work exhibits roughly the same uploading costs. Normalised works, to the contrary, are associated with heterogeneous uploading costs. For explanation, suppose that only two types of non-normalised works exist: low-popularity and high-popularity works. Suppose further that low-popularity works attract a certain benchmark level of popularity, while high-popularity works attract four times the benchmark level of popularity. A low-popularity work is then counted as one normalised work and a high-popularity work as four normalised works. If a right holder owns a low-popularity work, he therefore incurs the full uploading costs to upload one normalised work. For the owner of a high-popularity work, incurring the uploading costs once results in the upload of four normalised works. He therefore only incurs a quarter of the uploading costs for each of the four normalised works he uploads.

More realistically, many different non-normalised works exist, each attracting different levels of popularity. This chapter assumes that every right holder owns one non-normalised work, which he can upload to the platform. The uploading costs per copy of a normalised work then differ depending on the popularity of the underlying non-normalised work. To define right holders' marginal uploading cost function, normalised works are ranked based on the popularity of the underlying non-normalised work. The first work is the normalised work with the most popular underlying non-normalised work. N denotes the number assigned to a normalised work based on this ranking, with $N \geq 0$. As the popularity of the underlying non-normalised work decreases, N increases.

c denotes the costs of uploading a copy of a normalised work. As explained above, c increases as N increases. For simplification, the relationship between c and N is assumed to be linear: As N increases by one unit, c increases by t units, with $t > 0$. A normalised work with the number 0 (i.e. a normalised work based on a hypothetical non-normalised work that is slightly more popular than the most popular non-normalised work) would be associated with uploading costs of s, with $s > 0$. Right holders' marginal uploading cost function therefore is $c = s + t \cdot N$.

[13] Costs related to the creation of copies are assumed to be zero. This is a common assumption in the economic analysis of copyright law (e.g. Banerjee, 2003, p. 100; Johnson, 1985, p. 161; Lefort, 2013, p. 33; Martínez-Sánchez, 2010, p. 400). In reality, there is a spectrum of costs for creating copies. The more skill and material required to create copies, the higher the costs (Yoo, 2004, pp. 231–232). Creating digital copies of digital originals lies at the low costs end of the spectrum, rendering the assumption plausible in this analysis.

[14] In their survey among and interviews with mash-up producers, Brøvig-Hanssen and Jones (2021, p. 8) provide some evidence that uploaders perceive uploading as costly: They report that YouTube's 'uniquely large audience meant that it was usually considered worth the effort to try and upload mashups there'. This suggests that uploading costs are a factor that uploaders consider when deciding on whether to attempt to upload.

For now, it is assumed that the number of existing works is independent of the profits right holders earn through the platform. Section 3.7.2 discusses the implications of assuming that an increase in right holders' profits leads to an increase in the number of works produced.

The second type of costs a right holder incurs when his work is uploaded to a platform is a reduction in off-platform profits. Works can be consumed not only through the platform but also through off-platform channels. Three main types of relationships between the on-platform availability of a work and off-platform profits are conceivable.[15] First, viewers may substitute on-platform for off-platform consumption. Second, the on-platform availability of a work may introduce viewers to this work, generating new demand for off-platform versions of the work or complementary products. Finally, the on-platform availability of a work may not affect off-platform profits. Viewers may only find out about the work through the platform or find off-platform channels too costly or too inconvenient. They may then only consume the work because it is available on the platform. Alternatively, viewers may continue to buy off-platform versions, while in addition accessing the work through the platform. For now, the most likely and relevant case that the on-platform availability of a work has an overall negative effect on a right holder's off-platform profits is assumed.[16] Section 3.7.1 discusses the implications of an overall positive effect. For simplicity, it is further assumed that the on-platform availability of a work does not affect the off-platform profits of right holders of other works.[17]

---

[15] The described effects are adopted by analogy from the literature discussing the impact of unlawful copying on legal sales. For an overview, see Quintais and Poort (2019, pp. 816–818).

[16] Considering the empirical literature on the impact of unlawful copying on legal sales by analogy provides support for this assumption. Tyrowicz et al. (2020) review 45 empirical studies that examine the film or music industry, which contain '81 general findings about the effects of unauthorized acquisition on sales' (pp. 4–6). They report that the majority of findings (48) show a negative effect. However, since a non-negligible number of findings are inconclusive (19) or evince a positive effect (14), they conclude that 'there is no clear conclusion so far in the literature' (p. 11).

[17] For one thing, it is unclear whether and to what extent such an effect is realistic. For another, considering it in the model would provide no added value in terms of the research interest of this chapter and therefore unnecessarily convolute the analysis. Assuming that the on-platform availability of a work decreases the off-platform profits of right holders of other works would mean that o would increase as the number of works uploaded increases. As Sect. 3.4.3 explains, introducing automated filtering leads to a decrease in the number of works uploaded. It would thus decrease o and thereby shift right holders' per-work profit function upwards and increase their aggregate profits. However, this effect is a mere additional consequence of the effect of automated filtering on the number of works uploaded. It would operate in the same direction as the effect on right holders' aggregate profits described below. Moreover, assuming that the on-platform availability of a work leads to a decrease in off-platform profits of right holders of other works would not influence the mechanism of the effect of automated filtering on right holders' profits and the number of works uploaded that is explored in the model, namely, the competition between right holders and unlawful copiers for views, because right holders ignore off-platform profits when deciding how many copies they upload; see Sect. 3.4.1.4.

A right holder's off-platform profits are presumed to be determined by the popularity of his non-normalised work. Since normalised works are equally popular, every normalised work is associated with the same off-platform profits. Moreover, it is assumed that for every non-normalised work (regardless of how popular it is), the right holder loses the same proportion of off-platform profits if he uploads the work to the platform. In absolute terms, a right holder who owns a highly popular work therefore loses more by uploading than a right holder who owns a less popular work. Again, since normalised works are equally popular, the upload of every normalised work leads to the same off-platform losses. The off-platform losses resulting from the upload of the first copy of a normalised work are denoted by o, with $o > 0$.

3.2.3.2 Competition Between Right Holders and Unlawful Copiers

In scenarios 2.1 and 2.2, works can be uploaded to a platform by right holders and unlawful copiers. Right holders and unlawful copiers are assumed to compete for the revenues generated by the on-platform availability of works by uploading copies of the works, pursuing to maximise their profits.

Suppose that a right holder has uploaded his work. In the absence of unlawful copiers, he would then earn revenues of $v \cdot r$. If an unlawful copier uploads a copy of the right holder's work, a fraction of v is diverted from the right holder's upload to the unlawful copier's upload. If the same or another unlawful copier uploads the same work again, the likelihood increases that a viewer clicks on an unlawful upload instead of the right holder's upload. The right holder's per-work revenues therefore decrease further. The right holder can, however, employ the same strategy as unlawful copiers and use different accounts to upload multiple copies of his work to increase the likelihood that a viewer clicks on one of his uploads.[18]

It is difficult for viewers to find out whether a right holder or an unlawful copier has uploaded (Beard et al., 2018, p. 319). An unlawful copier can make her account appear official, for example, by using the name of the artist as an account name. Moreover, viewers may lack the relevant knowledge of copyright law or be unaware of licensing arrangements. They may therefore not be able to evaluate whether an upload infringes a right holder's rights. Even if—with some effort—viewers were able to distinguish between infringing and non-infringing uploads, most viewers presumably would not care about the source of the content—at least not enough to make the necessary effort (see Beard et al., 2018, p. 318). It is reasonable to presume that most viewers click on one of the first uploads displayed when they search for a work, but it is unclear whether it is more likely that a right holder's or an unlawful copier's upload is displayed first. Even if viewers cared enough about the source of

[18] The assumption that right holders do so is inspired by one of the rare insights into a right holder's strategy with respect to YouTube: In *Viacom v. YouTube* (2013), YouTube noted that Viacom and its marketing agents posted extensively to the platform, using various obscured accounts (YouTube Inc. et al., 2013, pp. 23–25).

the content to make the necessary investment, their decision which upload to click on could go either way. They could decide to support the right holder by viewing his upload. Alternatively, they could prefer to view an unlawful copier's upload, for example, to support the free sharing of creative works (cf. Office for Harmonization in the Internal Market (Trade Marks and Designs), 2013, p. 51). Taken together, it is impossible to predict the probabilities with which viewers click on different uploads. For simplicity, v is thus assumed to be distributed evenly among the uploads of a work.

The strategic interaction between a right holder and unlawful copiers is modelled as a Stackelberg game.[19] The right holder and unlawful copiers sequentially choose the number of copies they upload. For every normalised work, the right holder is assumed to be the Stackelberg leader, that is, to decide first on the number of uploads. Unlawful copiers are assumed to be Stackelberg followers, that is, to react to the right holder's choice.

This assumption on the sequence of choices is justified because unlawful copiers can generally only upload a work once the work has been published (see Banerjee, 2003, pp. 102–103; Lefort, 2013, p. 35). When publishing a work, a right holder can choose whether to upload the work to the platform. While it is conceivable that an unlawful copier gains access to a work prior to its first publication, such cases are arguably sufficiently rare to be excluded from the analysis. Note in this regard that right holders can take measures to prevent unlawful copiers from accessing their works before the first publication (see Martínez-Sánchez, 2010, pp. 398–399). For instance, right holders can keep their works secret prior to first publication or shorten the time during creation and publication. For works that have already been published prior to a platform's existence, right holders are assumed to have a time advantage when deciding on whether to upload to the platform.

If a right holder has decided not to upload his work, unlawful copiers can nevertheless upload it. If at least one unlawful copier uploads a right holder's work, the right holder still bears the off-platform losses o.

3.2.3.3 Automated Filtering

If a platform does not filter, right holders' and unlawful uploaders' costs of uploading a copy of a work are identical. In scenario 2.2, it is assumed that a platform filters but the filter works imperfectly. That is, unlawful copiers can still upload copies but not every unlawful upload attempt is successful. Several attempts to upload a work require unlawful copiers to invest more in uploading than a single attempt would. In addition (or alternatively), unlawful copiers may invest in disguising content so that the filter cannot detect it (Sect. 2.2). It is therefore assumed

[19] The name goes back to Heinrich von Stackelberg, who was the first to systematically analyse the strategic interaction between a firm that moves first (Stackelberg leader) and a firm that follows (Stackelberg follower) (see von Stackelberg, 2011, pp. 15–16).

that filtering increases unlawful copiers' uploading costs. Unlawful copiers' uploading costs if a platform filters are denoted by c^{co}, with $c^{co} > c$.

Right holders' uploading costs are presumed to be unaffected by automated filtering. In other words, it is assumed that right holders' upload attempts are not blocked erroneously. This assumption may strike the reader as odd since the risk of false positives is one of the main objections against automated filtering. However, note that erroneous blockings of right holders' upload attempts only represent a minor part of the problem of false positives. The hurdles to error-free blocking that are unsurmountable by state-of-the-art filters (Sect. 4.4.1) relate to upload attempts by lawful copiers, which are not considered in this chapter. A right holder's upload attempts can only be blocked erroneously if the work is entered into the reference database. By indicating the correct metadata, these errors can be avoided.

The consideration that some upload attempts by right holders may nevertheless be blocked could be reflected in the model by assuming that automated filtering also increases right holders' uploading costs. However, it is plausible to presume that unlawful copiers' uploading costs would be affected more strongly. Erroneous blockings of right holders' upload attempts would then not influence the effects explored in this chapter, but an additional effect of automated filtering on right holders' profits and the availability of works on a platform would emerge. In the interest of a focused analysis, such errors are excluded from the analysis.

3.2.3.4 Continuity Assumption and Behaviour in Case of Indifference

The number of uploads of a work by a right holder is denoted by u^{rh} and the number of uploads per work by unlawful copiers by u^{co}, with $u \geq 0$.[20] To simplify the analysis, u is treated as a continuous variable ('continuity assumption'). The calculated numbers of uploads per work are thus approximations of the actual, that is, discrete, numbers of uploads. Likewise, the calculated profits are approximations of the profits right holders and unlawful copiers would obtain if they could only upload a discrete number of copies.

For values $0 < u^{rh} < 1$, the continuity assumption allows right holders to obtain the full per-work revenues without incurring the full per-copy uploading costs. This implication of the continuity assumption is accepted unless it would allow a right holder to earn larger profits than if he uploaded the only copy of his work. Allowing a right holder to earn larger profits than if he uploaded the only copy of his work would not only be unrealistic but also inconsistent with scenario 1. The continuity assumption is therefore applied with the following qualification: The maximal profits a right holder can obtain by uploading a work must not exceed the profits he would

[20] In scenarios 2.1 and 2.2, certain variables take different values depending on whether they refer to the right holder or to unlawful copiers. This difference is indicated by using the superscript 'rh' to refer to the right holder and the superscript 'co' to refer to unlawful copiers. In the absence of unlawful copiers (scenario 1), a distinction is not necessary. For consistency, the superscript 'rh' is nevertheless used on variables that change in later scenarios.

earn if he uploaded the only copy of his work ('qualification of the continuity assumption'). If the qualification of the continuity assumption kicks in, the right holder is presumed to obtain the profits he would earn if he uploaded the only copy of his work. The corresponding qualification of the continuity assumption is applied with respect to unlawful copiers: The maximal profits an unlawful copier can obtain by uploading a work must not exceed the profits she would obtain if she uploaded the only copy of a right holder's work.

A right holder is assumed to upload a copy of his work if by uploading he earns profits that are at least as large as the profits he would obtain by not uploading. The assumption that the right holder opts for uploading if he is indifferent becomes relevant when the presence of unlawful copiers incentivises a right holder to upload copies of his work until the point at which the upload of an additional copy would cause his total uploading costs (i.e. the product of the number of copies uploaded and the per-copy uploading costs) to exceed the available per-work revenues. Due to the continuity assumption, all available revenues are then consumed by uploading costs. If instead of treating u as a continuous variable, only discrete values of u were considered, positive on-platform profits would be possible. For explanation, suppose that a right holder has uploaded $\frac{v \cdot r}{c} - \alpha$ copies of his work, with $0 \leq \alpha < 1$. Uploading an additional copy would then cause the right holder's total uploading costs to exceed the available per-work revenues.[21] When uploading $\frac{v \cdot r}{c} - \alpha$ copies, the right holder's per-work profits, which are denoted by π^{rh}, are

$$\pi^{rh} = v \cdot r - \left(\frac{v \cdot r}{c} - \alpha\right) \cdot c - o = \alpha \cdot c - o \tag{3.1}$$

Given $0 \leq \alpha < 1$, the right holder's on-platform profits ($\alpha \cdot c$) take a value above or equal to 0 and below c.[22] The calculation in the continuous case, which results in on-platform profits of 0, therefore underestimates the per-work profits a right holder obtains in all cases except for $\alpha = 0$. It never overestimates the right holder's on-platform profits. It follows that in almost all cases in which a right holder is indifferent in the continuous case, he would upload in the discrete case. At most, the right holder would also be indifferent in the discrete case. The assumption that a right holder uploads if he is indifferent therefore ensures that the continuity assumption does not alter the results. Based on the same rationale, unlawful copiers are assumed to upload if they are indifferent.

---

[21] The right holder's total uploading costs $\left(\frac{v \cdot r}{c} - \alpha + 1\right) \cdot c$ would exceed the per-work revenues $v \cdot r$ because $\left(\frac{v \cdot r}{c} - \alpha + 1\right) \cdot c > v \cdot r \Leftrightarrow \alpha < 1$.

[22] Incorporating an approximation for these additional profits would make the analysis more complicated but add no insights with respect to the research interest of this chapter.

3.2.4 Demand Side

Having introduced the key variables and assumptions with respect to the supply side of the market, the demand side is next in line. To simplify the analysis, the number of people who view works on a platform is assumed to be fixed. Presuming viewers' marginal benefits of viewing works on the platform to be decreasing, the number of views per work then decreases as the number of works uploaded to the platform increases. N^* denotes the number of normalised works uploaded to a platform in the market equilibrium and v^* the number of views per work if N^* works are uploaded. For simplicity, the relationship between N^* and v^* is assumed to be linear: If a work is uploaded to the platform, v^* decreases by d, with $d > 0$.

While most platforms do not charge viewers for accessing content, viewers 'pay' in other ways, for example, by having to view advertisements before the actual content. For simplicity, the price per view is assumed to be fixed. For a given price per view, v_{max} denotes the hypothetical number of views per work if $N^* = 0$.

Based on these considerations, v^* can be expressed as a function of N^*: $v^* = v_{max} - d \cdot N^*$.

3.3 Absence of Unlawful Copiers (Scenario 1)

Based on the variables and assumptions introduced in the previous section, this section considers the benchmark scenario in which unlawful copiers are absent. Right holders then either upload no copy or one copy of their works. They never upload more than one copy per work as uploading is costly and doing so would not increase their revenues. This section first determines the number of normalised works right holders upload to the platform (Sect. 3.3.1) and then calculates the aggregate profits right holders obtain (Sect. 3.3.2).

3.3.1 Number of Works Uploaded

To obtain the revenues of $v_1^* \cdot r$, a right holder incurs the uploading costs $s + t \cdot N$ and the off-platform losses o. By uploading a normalised work to the platform, he thus earns profits of $v_1^* \cdot r - s - t \cdot N - o$.

N_1^* is the total number of normalised works that are uploaded to a platform in the market equilibrium. It follows that every right holder who owns a normalised work which is assigned a number $N \leq N_1^*$ uploads his work to the platform, while a right holder who owns a normalised work with a number $N > N_1^*$ does not. The number N_1^* is thus assigned to the normalised work that is based on the least popular non-normalised work that a right holder is willing to upload.

If a right holder does not upload his work, he earns profits of 0. Right holders thus upload if uploading leads to profits of $\pi^{rh} \geq 0$. For the right holder who owns the normalised work with the number N_1^*, the profits from uploading must therefore be 0. It follows that $v_1^* \cdot r - s - t \cdot N_1^* - o = 0$. Inserting $v_{max} - d \cdot N_1^*$ for v_1^* and solving for N_1^* yields

$$v_1^* \cdot r - s - t \cdot N_1^* - o = 0 \Leftrightarrow N_1^* = \frac{v_{max} \cdot r - s - o}{d \cdot r + t} \tag{3.2}$$

Note that this leads to a negative value of N_1^* if

$$\frac{v_{max} \cdot r - s - o}{d \cdot r + t} < 0 \Leftrightarrow o > v_{max} \cdot r - s \tag{3.3}$$

Since the number of works on the platform is non-negative, the minimal value of N_1^* is 0. If $o > v_{max} \cdot r - s$, therefore no works are uploaded. The threshold can be explained as follows: The hypothetical right holder who owns the work with the number $N = 0$ (i.e. a normalised work based on a hypothetical non-normalised work that is slightly more popular than the most popular non-normalised work) would incur uploading costs of s. If only he uploaded his work, he would earn revenues of $v_{max} \cdot r$. He would not upload if the reduction in off-platform profits o exceeded his on-platform profits $v_{max} \cdot r - s$. The same is true for right holders who own less popular works because these right holders would incur higher uploading costs. As a result, no right holder uploads a work.

To increase the clarity of the following explanations and calculations, from now on $N = \frac{v_{max} \cdot r - s - o}{d \cdot r + t}$ is referred to by $\tilde{N}$ and the number of views if $N^* = \tilde{N}$ by $\tilde{v}$. The calculated values of $\tilde{N}$ and $\tilde{v}$ are only used if doing so generates additional insights.

To sum up, in scenario 1, right holders upload the following number of works to the platform:

$$N_1^* = \begin{cases} \tilde{N}, & \text{if } o \leq v_{max} \cdot r - s \\ 0, & \text{if } o > v_{max} \cdot r - s \end{cases} \tag{3.4}$$

3.3.2 Right Holders' Aggregate Profits

This section turns the attention from the number of works uploaded to right holders' aggregate profits, which are denoted by Π.

If $o \leq v_{max} \cdot r - s$, right holders who upload their works obtain profits of $\tilde{v} \cdot r - s - t \cdot N - o$. Right holders' per-work profit function is displayed in Fig. 3.1. The right holder who owns the work with the number $\tilde{N}$ (vertical gridline) earns profits of 0. Every right holder who owns a work with a number $N > \tilde{N}$ would earn negative profits and hence does not upload.

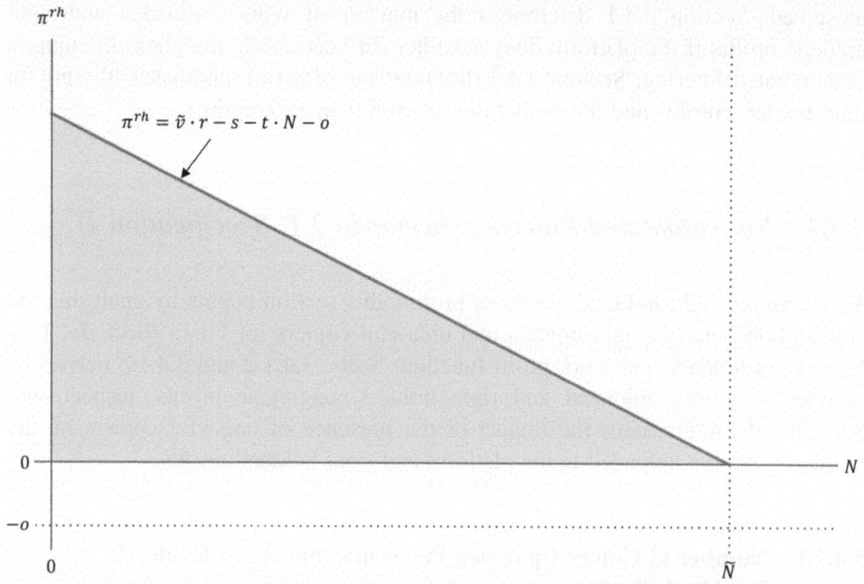

Fig. 3.1 Right holders' profits in scenario 1, presuming if $o \leq v_{max} \cdot r - s$

Π is the sum of the per-work profits of all right holders who upload their works. Right holders' aggregate profits in the market equilibrium, which are denoted by Π^*, therefore are

$$\Pi_1^* = \int_0^{\tilde{N}} (\tilde{v} \cdot r - s - t \cdot N - o) \mathrm{d}N = \frac{1}{2} \cdot \tilde{N} \cdot (\tilde{v} \cdot r - s - o) \tag{3.5}$$

In Fig. 3.1, these profits are illustrated by the grey triangle. The altitude of the vertical leg of the triangle represents the per-work profits if $N = 0$: $\tilde{v} \cdot r - s - o$. The length of the horizontal leg is determined by the number of works right holders upload: $\tilde{N}$.

If $o > v_{max} \cdot r - s$, the number of works uploaded is 0, implying $\Pi_1^* = 0$.

To sum up, right holders earn aggregate profits of

$$\Pi_1^* = \begin{cases} \frac{1}{2} \cdot \tilde{N} \cdot (\tilde{v} \cdot r - s - o), & \text{if } o \leq v_{max} \cdot r - s \\ 0, & \text{if } o > v_{max} \cdot r - s \end{cases} \tag{3.6}$$

3.4 Perfect Competition Among Unlawful Copiers

The previous section determined the number of works uploaded to the platform and right holders' aggregate profits presuming that unlawful copiers are absent. In this section, unlawful copiers enter the scene and perfect competition among them is presumed. Section 3.4.1 determines the number of works uploaded and right holders' profits if the platform does not filter. In Sect. 3.4.2, the platform engages in automated filtering. Section 3.4.3 discusses the effect of automated filtering on right holders' profits and the availability of works on a platform.

3.4.1 No Automated Filtering (Scenario 2.1, Specification I)

To determine right holders' per-work profits, this section begins by analysing the competition between right holders and unlawful copiers for views (Sect. 3.4.1.1). From right holders' per-work profit function, Sects. 3.4.1.2 and 3.4.1.3 derive the number of works uploaded and right holders' aggregate profits, respectively. Section 3.4.1.4 discusses the impact of the presence of unlawful copiers on the number of works uploaded to the platform and right holders' profits.

3.4.1.1 Number of Copies Uploaded Per Work and Right Holders' Per-Work Profits

This section determines the number of copies uploaded per work and right holders' per-work profits for a given level of $N_{2.1}^*$ and thus also a given level of $v_{2.1}^*$. Recall that as in this scenario the platform does not filter, unlawful copiers and the right holder incur the same per-copy uploading costs (c).

Due to the qualification of the continuity assumption (Sect. 3.2.3.4), the maximal profits unlawful copiers can obtain by uploading a copy of a work are $v_{2.1}^* \cdot r - c$. Note that because c is a function of N, these profits differ depending on the normalised work the unlawful copier uploads. If an unlawful copier does not upload a copy of a work, she obtains profits of 0. It follows that no unlawful copier uploads a copy of a work that fulfils the following condition:

$$v_{2.1}^* \cdot r - c < 0 \Leftrightarrow c > v_{2.1}^* \cdot r \tag{3.7}$$

The maximal profits a right holder can obtain by uploading his work are $v_{2.1}^* \cdot r - c - o$. If his work is associated with uploading costs of $c > v_{2.1}^* \cdot r$, not uploading leads to profits of 0 as unlawful copiers do not upload either. The right holder then does not upload if his work fulfils the following condition:

$$v_{2.1}^* \cdot r - c - o < 0 \Leftrightarrow c > v_{2.1}^* \cdot r - o \tag{3.8}$$

Since $c > v_{2.1}^* \cdot r$ implies $c > v_{2.1}^* \cdot r - o$, neither an unlawful copier nor the right holder uploads a copy of a work associated with uploading costs of $c > v_{2.1}^* \cdot r$. The work is then not uploaded and the right holder earns profits of 0.

By contrast, if the uploading costs of a work are $c \leq v_{2.1}^{*} \cdot r$, uploading one copy generates revenues above or equal to uploading costs. The maximal number of copies that can be uploaded of a work without the total uploading costs exceeding the per-work revenues is

$$u \cdot c = v_{2.1}^{*} \cdot r \Leftrightarrow u = \frac{v_{2.1}^{*} \cdot r}{c} \tag{3.9}$$

Neither the right holder nor unlawful copiers upload copies beyond $\frac{v_{2.1}^{*} \cdot r}{c}$. Let u^{*} denote the number of copies uploaded per work in the Stackelberg equilibrium. Since this specification assumes perfect competition among unlawful copiers, once the right holder has uploaded, unlawful copiers upload until $\frac{v_{2.1}^{*} \cdot r}{c}$ copies are uploaded, that is, $u_{2.1}^{co\,*} = \frac{v_{2.1}^{*} \cdot r}{c} - u^{rh}$. For explanation, suppose that taken together, unlawful copiers and the right holder have already uploaded $\check{u} - 1$ copies, with $\check{u} \leq \frac{v_{2.1}^{*} \cdot r}{c}$. With perfect competition, there exists another unlawful copier who can upload her first copy. She will do so if by uploading she earns non-negative profits. Her profits from uploading are $\frac{v_{2.1}^{*} \cdot r}{\check{u}} - c$. She uploads as $\frac{v_{2.1}^{*} \cdot r}{\check{u}} - c \geq 0 \Leftrightarrow \check{u} \leq \frac{v_{2.1}^{*} \cdot r}{c}$. Since u is treated as a continuous variable (Sect. 3.2.3.4), unlawful copiers continue to upload copies until $\frac{v_{2.1}^{*} \cdot r}{c}$ copies are uploaded.

The right holder's per-work revenues are the per-copy share $\frac{1}{u^{rh}+u^{co}}$ of the revenues $v_{2.1}^{*} \cdot r$ multiplied by the number of copies he uploads. By uploading his work, the right holder therefore earns profits of $\left(\frac{v_{2.1}^{*} \cdot r}{u^{rh}+u^{co}} - c\right) \cdot u^{rh} - o$. Inserting $u_{2.1}^{co\,*} = \frac{v_{2.1}^{*} \cdot r}{c} - u^{rh}$ yields the right holder's profit maximisation problem:

$$\max_{u^{rh}} \pi^{rh} = \left(\frac{v_{2.1}^{*} \cdot r}{u^{rh} + \frac{v_{2.1}^{*} \cdot r}{c} - u^{rh}} - c\right) \cdot u^{rh} - o = -o, \text{ s.t. } u^{rh} \leq \frac{v_{2.1}^{*} \cdot r}{c} \tag{3.10}$$

Due to the assumption that unlawful copiers can upload a publicly available work even if the right holder does not upload it (Sect. 3.2.3.2), the right holder also earns profits of $-o$ if he uploads 0 copies. It follows that the right holder earns profits of $-o$ regardless of whether he uploads 0 copies, $\frac{v_{2.1}^{*} \cdot r}{c}$ copies, or any number of copies in between. Since the right holder opts for uploading if he is indifferent (Sect. 3.2.3.4), he solves the maximisation problem by uploading $\frac{v_{2.1}^{*} \cdot r}{c}$ copies. Unlawful copiers then upload $\frac{v_{2.1}^{*} \cdot r}{c} - \frac{v_{2.1}^{*} \cdot r}{c} = 0$ copies.

Intuitively, this result can be explained as follows: Suppose that the right holder has uploaded a number of copies below $\frac{v_{2.1}^{*} \cdot r}{c}$. Confronted with many unlawful copiers, he anticipates that unlawful copiers will upload the remaining copies until $\frac{v_{2.1}^{*} \cdot r}{c}$ copies are uploaded. He therefore faces the following trade-off: If he uploads more copies, he can claim more (eventually all) of the work's revenues for himself but must spend more on uploading. If he does not upload more copies, he can save on uploading costs but anticipates that unlawful copiers' uploads will decrease his share of the per-work revenues. The homogenous uploading costs of the right holder and of unlawful copiers imply that whenever an unlawful copier is willing to upload (i.e. whenever the part of the revenues an unlawful copier could obtain from uploading is equal to or above c), the right holder is also willing to incur c to keep the part of the revenues. The right holder therefore uploads all copies that unlawful copiers would otherwise upload.

Note that the per-work profits of $-o$ are independent of the N assigned to a right holder's work. This is the case since a right holder who uploads a work with a small N not only incurs lower uploading costs but also needs to upload more copies to prevent unlawful copiers from uploading than a right holder who uploads a work with a large N.

To sum up, in the Stackelberg equilibrium, a right holder uploads the following number of copies of his work and earns the following per-work profits, which are denoted by π^*:

$$u_{2.1}^{rh\,*} = \begin{cases} \frac{v_{2.1}^* \cdot r}{c}, & \text{if } c \leq v_{2.1}^* \cdot r \\ 0, & \text{if } c > v_{2.1}^* \cdot r \end{cases}; \quad \pi_{2.1}^{rh\,*} = \begin{cases} -o, & \text{if } c \leq v_{2.1}^* \cdot r \\ 0, & \text{if } c > v_{2.1}^* \cdot r \end{cases} \tag{3.11}$$

By inserting $c = s + t \cdot N$, the conditions can be transformed as follows:

$$u_{2.1}^{rh\,*} = \begin{cases} \frac{v_{2.1}^* \cdot r}{c}, & \text{if } N \leq \frac{v_{2.1}^* \cdot r - s}{t} \\ 0, & \text{if } N > \frac{v_{2.1}^* \cdot r - s}{t} \end{cases}; \quad \pi_{2.1}^{rh\,*} = \begin{cases} -o, & \text{if } N \leq \frac{v_{2.1}^* \cdot r - s}{t} \\ 0, & \text{if } N > \frac{v_{2.1}^* \cdot r - s}{t} \end{cases} \tag{3.12}$$

3.4.1.2 Number of Works Uploaded

With these results in mind, this section examines the number of works uploaded to the platform. A work is counted as uploaded if $u^{rh} + u^{co} > 0$. From the previous section we know that every right holder who owns a normalised work with a number $N \leq \frac{v_{2.1}^* \cdot r - s}{t}$ uploads some copies of his work. Neither right holders nor unlawful copiers upload copies of works that are associated with a number $N > \frac{v_{2.1}^* \cdot r - s}{t}$. As normalised works are ranked according to the popularity of the underlying non-normalised works (beginning with the most popular work; Sect. 3.2.3.1), the last work uploaded is the work with the number $\frac{v_{2.1}^* \cdot r - s}{t}$.

Recall that $v_{2.1}^*$ is a function of $N_{2.1}^*$: $v_{2.1}^* = v_{max} - d \cdot N_{2.1}^*$. Therefore, when determining $N_{2.1}^*$, $v_{2.1}^*$ can no longer be treated as given. Since $N_{2.1}^*$ represents the total number of works uploaded to a platform, the last work uploaded to the platform is assigned the number $N_{2.1}^*$. Inserting $v_{2.1}^* = v_{max} - d \cdot N_{2.1}^*$ into $N_{2.1}^* = \frac{v_{2.1}^* \cdot r - s}{t}$ yields

$$N_{2.1}^{*} = \frac{\left(v_{max} - d \cdot N_{2.1}^{*}\right) \cdot r - s}{t} \Leftrightarrow N_{2.1}^{*} = \frac{v_{max} \cdot r - s}{d \cdot r + t} \tag{3.13}$$

Note that this leads to a negative value of $N_{2.1}^{*}$ if

$$\frac{v_{max} \cdot r - s}{d \cdot r + t} < 0 \Leftrightarrow s > v_{max} \cdot r \tag{3.14}$$

Because the number of works uploaded to the platform is non-negative, no works are uploaded if $s > v_{max} \cdot r$. This threshold can be explained as follows: The hypothetical right holder who owns the work with the number $N = 0$ would incur uploading costs of s. If only he uploaded his work, he would earn revenues of $v_{max} \cdot r$. He would also incur the reduction in off-platform profits of o. However, unlike in scenario 1, this reduction in off-platform profits would not affect his decision as it materialises independently of whether he or an unlawful copier uploads his work. Still, he would not upload if the on-platform profits are negative, that is, if the costs of uploading of s exceed the revenues $v_{max} \cdot r$. The same is true for right holders who own less popular works since they would incur higher uploading costs. As a result, no right holder uploads his work if $s > v_{max} \cdot r$.

By contrast, if $s \leq v_{max} \cdot r$, right holders upload $\frac{v_{max} \cdot r - s}{d \cdot r + t}$ works. As above, to increase the clarity of the following explanations and calculations, from now on $N = \frac{v_{max} \cdot r - s}{d \cdot r + t}$ is referred to by $\hat{N}$, and the number of views if $N^* = \hat{N}$ is denoted by $\hat{v}$. Right holders' per-work profits as a function of N are displayed in Fig. 3.2.

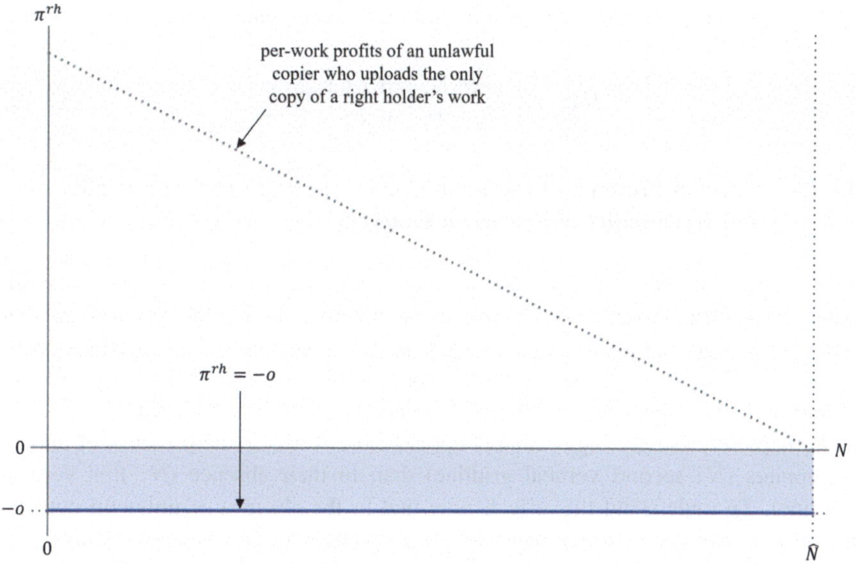

Fig. 3.2 Right holders' profits in scenario 2.1 (specification I), presuming $s \leq v_{max} \cdot r$

The dotted, downward sloping function indicates the per-work profits an unlawful copier would earn if she uploaded the only copy of a work: $\pi^{co} = \hat{v} \cdot r - s - t \cdot N$. This situation does not occur in equilibrium but helps to show why right holders upload all (and only) works associated with a number $N \leq \hat{N}$: These works would otherwise be uploaded by unlawful copiers. Unlawful copiers would earn negative profits when uploading works with a number $N > \hat{N}$. They would therefore not upload these works. As a result, there is no reason for right holders to upload works with a number $N > \hat{N}$.

To summarise, right holders upload the following number of works:

$$N_{2.1}^* = \begin{cases} \hat{N}, & \text{if } s \leq v_{max} \cdot r \\ 0, & \text{if } s > v_{max} \cdot r \end{cases} \tag{3.15}$$

3.4.1.3 Right Holders' Aggregate Profits

Having considered the number of works uploaded, right holders' aggregate profits are next in line. If $s > v_{max} \cdot r$, no works are uploaded and right holders' aggregate profits are 0. If $s \leq v_{max} \cdot r$, right holders earn per-work profits of $-o$, as indicated by the light blue function in Fig. 3.2. Right holders' aggregate profits are the sum of the individual profits of all right holders who upload their works. Since every right holder earns the same per-work profits of $-o$, aggregate profits are the per-work profits multiplied by the number of works uploaded: $\Pi_{2.1}^* = -o \cdot \hat{N}$.

In Fig. 3.2, right holders' aggregate profits are illustrated by the light blue rectangle. The height of the rectangle ($-o$) indicates right holders' per-work profits; the width ($\hat{N}$) the number of works right holders upload.

To summarise, right holders earn the following aggregate profits:

$$\Pi_{2.1}^* = \begin{cases} -o \cdot \hat{N}, & \text{if } s \leq v_{max} \cdot r \\ 0, & \text{if } s > v_{max} \cdot r \end{cases} \tag{3.16}$$

3.4.1.4 Effect of Presence of Unlawful Copiers on Right Holders' Profits and Availability of Works on Platform

This section compares the results obtained under the assumption that unlawful copiers are absent (scenario 1) with those obtained under the assumption that unlawful copiers are present and compete perfectly (scenario 2.1, specification I). Figure 3.3 displays right holders' per-work profit functions depending on N in scenarios 1 (grey function) and 2.1, specification I (light blue function).

Perhaps surprisingly, right holders upload more works in the presence of unlawful copiers ($\hat{N}$; second vertical gridline) than in their absence ($\tilde{N}$; first vertical gridline). To understand this effect, note that in the absence of unlawful copiers, the off-platform losses o only materialise if a right holder uploads a copy of his work. A right holder thus chooses to upload a copy of his work if the on-platform profits resulting from the upload at least recoup the off-platform losses.

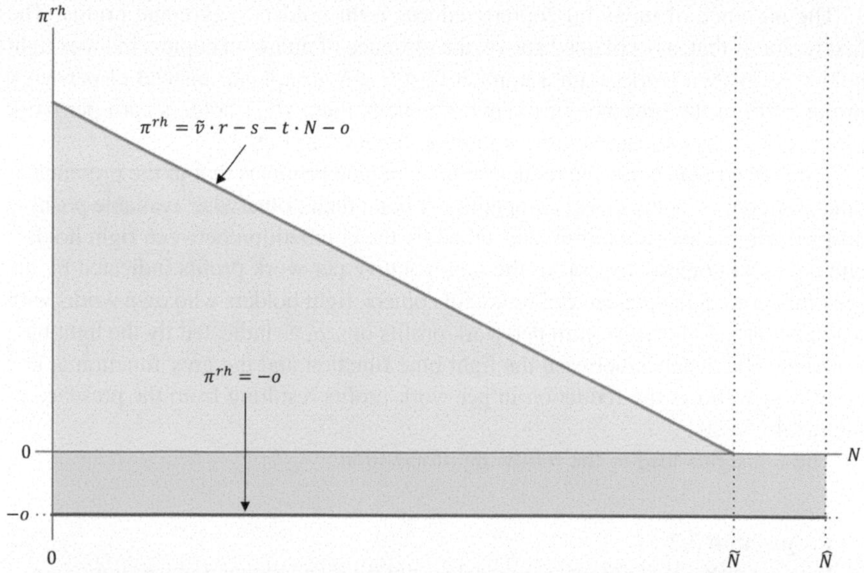

Fig. 3.3 Comparison of right holders' profits in scenario 1 and scenario 2.1 (specification I), presuming $o \leq v_{max} \cdot r - s$

In the presence of unlawful copiers, uploading the only copy of a work is associated with the same revenues and—without automated filtering—the same uploading costs for unlawful copiers as for the right holder. Unlawful copiers are willing to upload the first copy of a work if uploading produces revenues that are at least as high as the costs of uploading, that is, if the on-platform profits from uploading the first copy are non-negative. Right holders incur the off-platform losses regardless of whether they or unlawful copiers upload a copy of their works. They therefore ignore the off-platform losses when deciding on whether to upload the first copy of their works. Like unlawful copiers, they are thus willing to upload if the on-platform profits of uploading the first copy of their works are non-negative.

More works are associated with merely non-negative on-platform profits than with on-platform profits that recoup the off-platform losses. Therefore, more works are uploaded in scenario 2.1 than in scenario 1.

These insights lead to the following proposition:

Proposition 3.1
If a user-uploaded content platform does not filter, the presence of unlawful copiers induces right holders to upload works that they would not upload in the absence of unlawful copiers, namely, works for which the upload of the first copy is associated with non-negative on-platform profits that fall below the off-platform losses.

The presence of unlawful copiers reduces right holders' aggregate profits. The first reason is that, as explained above, the presence of unlawful copiers induces right holders who own works with a number $\tilde{N} < N \leq \hat{N}$ to upload. Instead of per-work profits of 0, in the presence of unlawful copiers, these right holders earn per-work profits of $-o$, as indicated by the light blue function in Fig. 3.3.

The second reason for the reduction in aggregate profits is that in the presence of unlawful copiers with perfect competition among them, otherwise available positive on-platform profits are entirely consumed by the competition between right holders and unlawful copiers. Instead of the non-negative per-work profits indicated by the grey function, in the presence of unlawful copiers, right holders who own works with a number $N \leq \tilde{N}$ therefore earn per-work profits of $-o$, as indicated by the light blue function. The distance between the light blue function and the grey function at any point $N \leq \tilde{N}$ shows the reduction in per-work profits resulting from the presence of unlawful copiers.

These insights lead to the following proposition:

Proposition 3.2
If a user-uploaded content platform does not filter and the market for supplying unlawful copies is perfectly competitive, right holders fully prevent unlawful copiers from uploading. To this end, they spend so much on uploading that all available per-work revenues are consumed by uploading costs.

Note that the reduction in profits is larger for right holders who own more popular non-normalised works (smaller N) than for right holders who own less popular non-normalised works (larger N). The reason is that the presence of unlawful copiers induces all right holders to upload until all available revenues are consumed by uploading costs. Since more popular non-normalised works are associated with higher revenues, the negative impact on profits is larger for right holders who own more popular non-normalised works.

3.4.2 *With Automated Filtering (Scenario 2.2, Specification A.I)*

The previous section considered the competition between right holders and unlawful copiers if a platform does not filter. This section presumes that the platform filters. The filtering intensity is assumed to be the same for every upload of a non-normalised work regardless of how popular the non-normalised work is. The factor by which unlawful copiers' uploading costs of a copy of a normalised work increase due to automated filtering is denoted by m, with $m > 1$. Unlawful copiers' per-copy uploading costs therefore are $c^{co} = m \cdot (s + t \cdot N)$.

Note that this leads to a larger difference between a right holder's uploading costs ($s + t \cdot N$) and unlawful copiers' uploading costs, the larger N. This is a result of the consideration that unlawful copiers who copy a work with a small N incur the uploading costs per copy of a non-normalised work fewer times than unlawful copiers who copy a work with a larger N (Sect. 3.2.3.1). Since the platform is assumed to filter uniformly, automated filtering increases the uploading costs of unlawful copiers for every non-normalised work by the same amount. Automated filtering therefore has a stronger effect if more non-normalised works need to be uploaded to obtain the revenues of one normalised work.

The analysis follows the same structure as in scenario 2.1. It begins by calculating the number of copies right holders upload per work (Sect. 3.4.2.1). Next, it determines the number of works uploaded (Sect. 3.4.2.2) and right holders' aggregate profits (Sect. 3.4.2.3).

3.4.2.1 Number of Copies Uploaded Per Work and Right Holders' Per-Work Profits

This section determines the number of copies uploaded and right holders' per-work profits for a given level of $N^*_{2.2}$ and thus also a given level of $v^*_{2.2}$. As opposed to scenario 2.1, the per-copy uploading costs differ between right holders (c) and unlawful copiers (c^{co}). Recall that c and c^{co} are functions of N.

As explained in scenario 2.1, regardless of what the right holder does, unlawful copiers do not upload works associated with uploading costs that exceed the per-work revenues ($c^{co} > v^*_{2.2} \cdot r$). If in addition the right holder's profits from uploading are negative ($c > v^*_{2.2} \cdot r - o$), the right holder does not upload and therefore earns profits of 0. If, on the other hand, the right holder's profits from uploading are non-negative ($c \leq v^*_{2.2} \cdot r - o$), he uploads the only copy of his work and earns profits of $v^*_{2.2} \cdot r - c - o$. As in scenario 1, the right holder does not upload more than one copy as doing so would not increase his revenues.

If a work is associated with uploading costs for unlawful copiers that are below or equal to the per-work revenues ($c^{co} \leq v^*_{2.2} \cdot r$), once the right holder has uploaded, unlawful copiers upload until $\frac{v^*_{2.2} \cdot r}{c^{co}}$ copies are uploaded; hence $u^{co\,*}_{2.2} = \frac{v^*_{2.2} \cdot r}{c^{co}} - u^{rh}$. As explained in scenario 2.1, right holders earn per-work profits of $\left(\frac{v^*_{2.2} \cdot r}{u^{rh} + u^{co}} - c\right) \cdot u^{rh} - o$. Inserting $u^{co\,*}_{2.2} = \frac{v^*_{2.2} \cdot r}{c^{co}} - u^{rh}$ yields

$$\pi^{rh} = \left(\frac{v^*_{2.2} \cdot r}{u^{rh} + \frac{v^*_{2.2} \cdot r}{c^{co}} - u^{rh}} - c \right) \cdot u^{rh} - o = (c^{co} - c) \cdot u^{rh} - o \tag{3.17}$$

The right holder would never upload more copies of his work than he needs to upload to prevent unlawful copiers from uploading (i.e. $\frac{v^*_{2.2} \cdot r}{c^{co}}$ copies) because doing so would not increase his revenues. He therefore faces the following profit maximisation problem:

$$\max_{u^{rh}} \pi^{rh} = (c^{co} - c) \cdot u^{rh} - o, \ \ \text{s.t.}\ u^{rh} \leq \frac{v_{2.2}^{*} \cdot r}{c^{co}} \tag{3.18}$$

Since $c^{co} > c$, this maximisation problem is solved by choosing the maximal value of u^{rh}: $\frac{v_{2.2}^{*} \cdot r}{c^{co}}$. Unlawful copiers then upload $\frac{v_{2.2}^{*} \cdot r}{c^{co}} - \frac{v_{2.2}^{*} \cdot r}{c^{co}} = 0$ copies.

This result is unsurprising as even without filtering, the right holder did not let unlawful copiers upload (Sect. 3.4.1.1). The difference is that the right holder does not need to sacrifice the full available per-work revenues to prevent unlawful copiers from uploading. By uploading $\frac{v_{2.2}^{*} \cdot r}{c^{co}}$ copies, the right holder obtains profits of $(c^{co} - c) \cdot \frac{v_{2.2}^{*} \cdot r}{c^{co}} - o$.

To summarise, in the Stackelberg equilibrium, a right holder uploads the following number of copies of his work:

$$u_{2.2}^{rh\,*} = \begin{cases} \frac{v_{2.2}^{*} \cdot r}{c^{co}}, & \text{if } c^{co} \leq v_{2.2}^{*} \cdot r \\ 1, & \text{if } c^{co} > v_{2.2}^{*} \cdot r \text{ and } c \leq v_{2.2}^{*} \cdot r - o \\ 0, & \text{if } c^{co} > v_{2.2}^{*} \cdot r \text{ and } c > v_{2.2}^{*} \cdot r - o \end{cases} \tag{3.19}$$

By doing so, he earns the following per-work profits:

$$\pi_{2.2}^{rh\,*} = \begin{cases} (c^{co} - c) \cdot \frac{v_{2.2}^{*} \cdot r}{c^{co}} - o, & \text{if } c^{co} \leq v_{2.2}^{*} \cdot r \\ v_{2.2}^{*} \cdot r - c - o, & \text{if } c^{co} > v_{2.2}^{*} \cdot r \text{ and } c \leq v_{2.2}^{*} \cdot r - o \\ 0, & \text{if } c^{co} > v_{2.2}^{*} \cdot r \text{ and } c > v_{2.2}^{*} \cdot r - o \end{cases} \tag{3.20}$$

By inserting $c^{co} = m \cdot (s + t \cdot N)$ and $c = s + t \cdot N$, the number of copies uploaded can be transformed as follows:

$$u_{2.2}^{rh\,*} = \begin{cases} \frac{v_{2.2}^{*} \cdot r}{m \cdot (s + t \cdot N)}, & \text{if } N \leq \frac{v_{2.2}^{*} \cdot r}{t \cdot m} - \frac{s}{t} \\ 1, & \text{if } \frac{v_{2.2}^{*} \cdot r}{t \cdot m} - \frac{s}{t} < N \leq \frac{v_{2.2}^{*} \cdot r - s - o}{t} \\ 0, & \text{if } N > \frac{v_{2.2}^{*} \cdot r}{t \cdot m} - \frac{s}{t} \text{ and } N > \frac{v_{2.2}^{*} \cdot r - s - o}{t} \end{cases} \tag{3.21}$$

Likewise, the right holder's per-work profits can be transformed as follows:

$$\pi_{2.2}^{rh\,*} = \begin{cases} v_{2.2}^{*} \cdot r - \frac{v_{2.2}^{*} \cdot r}{m} - o, \text{ if } N \leq \frac{v_{2.2}^{*} \cdot r}{t \cdot m} - \frac{s}{t} \\ v_{2.2}^{*} \cdot r - s - t \cdot N - o, \text{ if } \frac{v_{2.2}^{*} \cdot r}{t \cdot m} - \frac{s}{t} < N \leq \frac{v_{2.2}^{*} \cdot r - s - o}{t} \\ 0, \text{ if } N > \frac{v_{2.2}^{*} \cdot r}{t \cdot m} - \frac{s}{t} \text{ and } N > \frac{v_{2.2}^{*} \cdot r - s - o}{t} \end{cases} \tag{3.22}$$

3.4.2.2 Number of Works Uploaded

With the results of the previous section in mind, this section considers the number of works right holders upload to the platform. The last work a right holder can upload profitably is the work with the number $\frac{v_{2.2}^{*} \cdot r - s - o}{t}$. Right holders therefore upload at least the works with numbers $N \leq \frac{v_{2.2}^{*} \cdot r - s - o}{t}$. The last work unlawful copiers can upload profitably is the work with the number $\frac{v_{2.2}^{*} \cdot r}{t \cdot m} - \frac{s}{t}$. If $\frac{v_{2.2}^{*} \cdot r - s - o}{t} \geq \frac{v_{2.2}^{*} \cdot r}{t \cdot m} - \frac{s}{t}$, the last right holder who uploads his work is the right holder who owns the work with the number $\frac{v_{2.2}^{*} \cdot r - s - o}{t}$. Inserting $v_{2.2}^{*} = v_{max} - d \cdot N_{2.2}^{*}$ into $N_{2.2}^{*} = \frac{v_{2.2}^{*} \cdot r - s - o}{t}$ yields

$$N_{2.2}^{*} = \frac{\left(v_{max} - d \cdot N_{2.2}^{*}\right) \cdot r - s - o}{t} \Leftrightarrow N_{2.2}^{*} = \tilde{N} \tag{3.23}$$

Recall from Sect. 3.3.1 that uploading $\tilde{N}$ works leads to a negative value of $N_{2.2}^{*}$ if $o > v_{max} \cdot r - s$. Right holders therefore upload $\tilde{N}$ works if $o \leq v_{max} \cdot r - s$ and

$$\tilde{N} \geq \frac{\tilde{v} \cdot r}{t \cdot m} - \frac{s}{t} \Leftrightarrow m \geq \frac{(v_{max} \cdot t + d \cdot s) \cdot r + d \cdot r \cdot o}{(v_{max} \cdot t + d \cdot s) \cdot r - t \cdot o} \tag{3.24}$$

To increase the clarity of the following explanations and calculations, $m = \frac{(v_{max} \cdot t + d \cdot s) \cdot r + d \cdot r \cdot o}{(v_{max} \cdot t + d \cdot s) \cdot r - t \cdot o}$ is referred to by $\tilde{m}$.[23] For an explanation of this threshold, recall that a right holder's and unlawful copiers' per-work profits in scenario 2.2 differ in two respects. First, for every work uploaded to the platform, the right holder incurs the off-platform losses o, while unlawful copiers do not. The work with the number $\tilde{N}$ is the work for which the right holder's on-platform profits of uploading the only copy exactly compensate the off-platform losses, leading to overall profits of 0 for the right holder. Second, due to automated filtering, uploading is m times more costly for unlawful copiers than for the right holder. Without automated filtering ($m = 1$), an unlawful copier would make positive profits from uploading the only copy of the

[23] The tilde illustrates that $\tilde{m}$ is the threshold that m must reach for right holders to upload $\tilde{N}$ works.

work $\tilde{N}$ since she does not incur the off-platform losses. As m increases, unlawful copiers' profits from uploading decrease. If $m = \tilde{m}$, unlawful copiers' costs of uploading are increased to such an extent that by uploading the only copy of the work $\tilde{N}$, an unlawful copier also earns profits of 0. Hence, $\tilde{v} \cdot r = \tilde{m} \cdot (s + t \cdot \tilde{N})$. In other words, $\tilde{m}$ is the smallest value of m for which unlawful copiers cannot upload more works profitably than right holders can, and right holders therefore do not need to upload works for which the on-platform profits fall below the off-platform losses.

If $m < \tilde{m}$, unlawful copiers can upload more works profitably than right holders. The last right holder who uploads his work then is the right holder who owns the work with the number $\frac{v_{2.2}^* \cdot r}{t \cdot m} - \frac{s}{t}$, that is, the last work unlawful copiers can upload profitably. This work is then assigned the number $N_{2.2}^*$. Inserting $v_{2.2}^* = v_{max} - d \cdot N_{2.2}^*$ yields

$$N_{2.2}^* = \frac{\left(v_{max} - d \cdot N_{2.2}^*\right) \cdot r}{t \cdot m} - \frac{s}{t} \Leftrightarrow N_{2.2}^* = \frac{v_{max} \cdot r - m \cdot s}{d \cdot r + m \cdot t} \tag{3.25}$$

To increase the clarity of the following explanations, $N = \frac{v_{max} \cdot r - m \cdot s}{d \cdot r + m \cdot t}$ is referred to by $\overline{N}$, and the number of views per work if $N^* = \overline{N}$ is denoted by $\overline{v}$. Uploading $N_{2.2}^* = \overline{N}$ works would lead to a negative value of $N_{2.2}^*$ if

$$\frac{v_{max} \cdot r - m \cdot s}{d \cdot r + m \cdot t} < 0 \Leftrightarrow m > \frac{v_{max} \cdot r}{s} \tag{3.26}$$

It follows that right holders upload $\overline{N}$ works if $m < \tilde{m}$ and $m \leq \frac{v_{max} \cdot r}{s}$.[24] If $m > \frac{v_{max} \cdot r}{s}$ and $o > v_{max} \cdot r - s$, even uploading the most popular work is unprofitable for the right holder and for unlawful copiers. As a result, no works are uploaded.

The number of works uploaded to the platform for the different combinations of m and o is shown in Fig. 3.4.

At or above the dotted function $m = \tilde{m}$, the filtering intensity is so high that right holders can upload at least as many works profitably as unlawful copiers can upload profitably. If there were no off-platform losses ($o = 0$), unlawful copiers could not upload more works profitably than right holders even if the platform did not filter ($m = 1$). Therefore, the vertical intercept of $m = \tilde{m}$ is 1. As o increases, a higher filtering intensity is required to ensure that unlawful copiers cannot upload more works profitably than right holders. For all combinations of m and o at or above $m = \tilde{m}$ and at or left of the vertical gridline indicating $o = v_{max} \cdot r - s$, right holders upload $\tilde{N}$ works, that is, only (and all) works that they can upload profitably.

At $o = v_{max} \cdot r - s$, the dotted function $m = \tilde{m}$ intersects with the horizontal gridline $m = \frac{v_{max} \cdot r}{s}$, which indicates the lowest value of m for which unlawful copiers cannot upload any works profitably. For explanation, note that $o = v_{max} \cdot r - s$ implies $\tilde{N} = 0$. Recall that if $m = \tilde{m}$, unlawful copiers' profits from uploading the

[24]For a graphical explanation of the threshold $\overline{N}$, see Sect. 3.4.2.3.

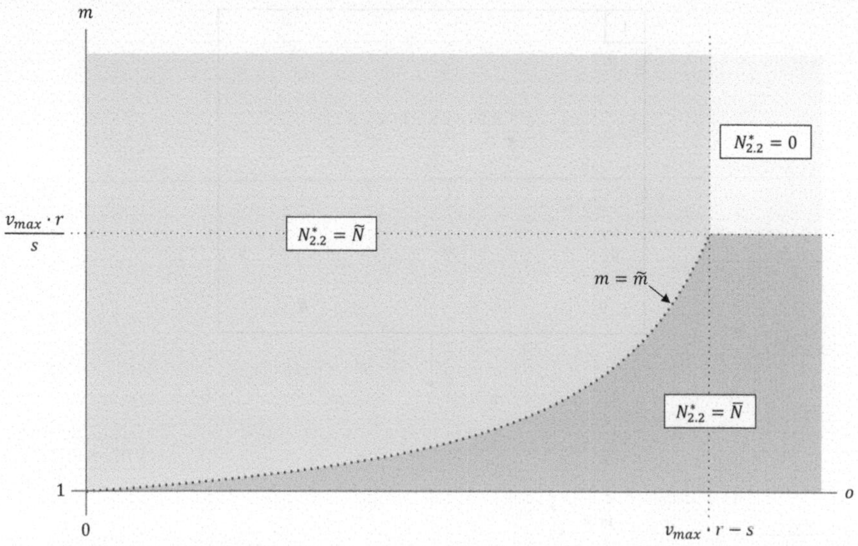

Fig. 3.4 Number of works uploaded for the different combinations of m and o in scenario 2.2 (specification A.I), presuming $s \leq v_{max} \cdot r$

work with the number $\tilde{N}$ are 0. It follows that if $o = v_{max} \cdot r - s$, $\tilde{m}$ is the smallest value of m for which unlawful copiers cannot upload any works profitably. It is thus equivalent to the threshold $m = \frac{v_{max} \cdot r}{s}$.

Right of the vertical gridline, the decisive question for determining the number of works uploaded is whether unlawful copiers can upload works profitably. If not ($m > \frac{v_{max} \cdot r}{s}$), no works are uploaded. If yes ($m \leq \frac{v_{max} \cdot r}{s}$), right holders upload as many works as unlawful copiers can upload profitably: $\overline{N}$. The same result materialises in the area at or left of the vertical gridline and below the dotted function $m = \tilde{m}$, that is, when right holders can upload some works profitably, but the filtering intensity is so low that unlawful copiers can upload more works profitably than right holders.

To summarise, right holders upload the following number of works to the platform:

$$N^*_{2.2} = \begin{cases} \tilde{N}, \text{ if } o \leq v_{max} \cdot r - s \text{ and } m \geq \tilde{m} \\ \overline{N}, \text{ if } \left(\begin{array}{c} (o \leq v_{max} \cdot r - s \text{ and } m < \tilde{m}) \text{ or} \\ \left(o > v_{max} \cdot r - s \text{ and } m \leq \frac{v_{max} \cdot r}{s} \right) \end{array} \right) \\ 0, \text{ if } o > v_{max} \cdot r - s \text{ and } m > \frac{v_{max} \cdot r}{s} \end{cases} \tag{3.27}$$

3.4.2.3 Right Holders' Aggregate Profits

Based on right holders' per-work profits and the number of works uploaded to the platform, this section calculates right holders' aggregate profits. Right holders'

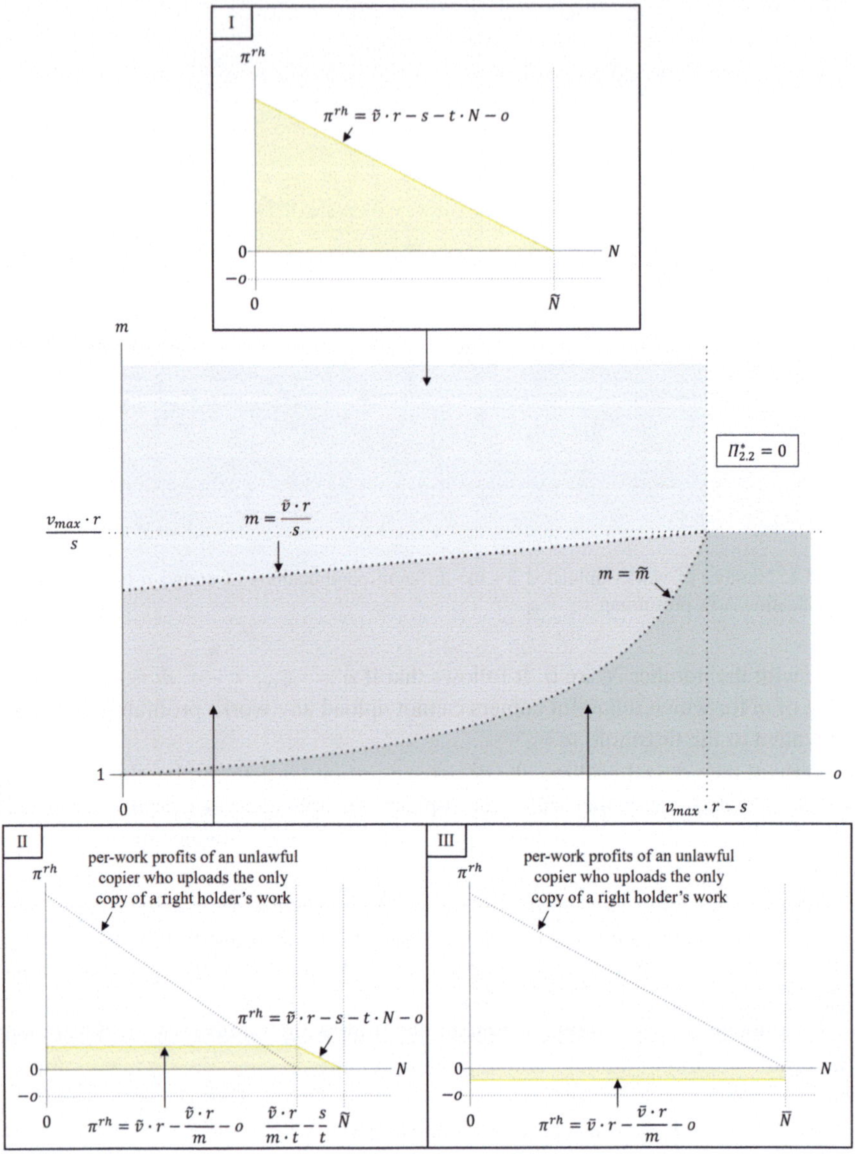

Fig. 3.5 Right holders' profits for the different combinations of m and o in scenario 2.2 (specification A.I), presuming $s \leq v_{max} \cdot r$

per-work profit functions for the different combinations of m and o are displayed in Fig. 3.5.

The coordinate system in the centre corresponds to the coordinate system in Fig. 3.4 but contains one addition. Recall that for all combinations of m and o located at or to the left of the vertical gridline and at or above the dotted function $m = \tilde{m}$, right holders upload $\tilde{N}$ works. When considering profits, the area must be further divided as right holders' per-work profits differ depending on whether unlawful copiers would upload their works. From above, we know that the last right holder who is exposed to competition from unlawful copiers is the right holder who owns the work with the number $\frac{\tilde{v} \cdot r}{t \cdot m} - \frac{s}{t}$.[25] It follows that no right holder is exposed to competition from unlawful copiers if

$$\frac{\tilde{v} \cdot r}{t \cdot m} - \frac{s}{t} \leq 0 \Leftrightarrow m \geq \frac{\tilde{v} \cdot r}{s} \tag{3.28}$$

The function $m = \frac{\tilde{v} \cdot r}{s}$ increases in o because the number of works uploaded to the platform ($\tilde{N}$) decreases as o increases. A decrease in the number of works uploaded results in an increase in the number of views per uploaded work ($\tilde{v}$).

Again, if $o = v_{max} \cdot r - s$, the number of works uploaded to the platform is $\tilde{N} = 0$. Hence, $\tilde{v} = v_{max}$. This explains the intersection of $m = \frac{\tilde{v} \cdot r}{s}$ and $m = \frac{v_{max} \cdot r}{s}$ at $o = v_{max} \cdot r - s$. The intersection of $m = \frac{\tilde{v} \cdot r}{s}$ (and $m = \frac{v_{max} \cdot r}{s}$) with $m = \tilde{m}$ at the same point follows the same rationale as explained in the previous section.

The light yellow functions in coordinate systems I to III in Fig. 3.5 indicate right holders' per-work profit functions for the respective combinations of m and o. The light yellow areas between the per-work profit functions and the horizontal axes indicate right holders' aggregate profits.

Coordinate system I shows right holders' per-work profit function if the off-platform losses are low enough for some right holders to be able to upload works profitably ($o \leq v_{max} \cdot r - s$), and the filtering intensity is so high that no right holder is exposed to competition from unlawful copiers ($m \geq \frac{\tilde{v} \cdot r}{s}$). Every right holder then only needs to upload one copy of his work and earns per-work profits of $\tilde{v} \cdot r - s - t \cdot N - o$. As in scenario 1 (Sect. 3.3.2), aggregate profits then are $\frac{1}{2} \cdot \tilde{N} \cdot (\tilde{v} \cdot r - s - o)$.

Coordinate system II displays right holders' per-work profit function if right holders can upload at least as many works profitably as unlawful copiers can ($m \geq \tilde{m}$) and some right holders are exposed to competition from unlawful copiers ($m < \frac{\tilde{v} \cdot r}{s}$).[26] The number of works uploaded to the platform then is also $\tilde{N}$. Right holders who own works with a number $N \leq \frac{\tilde{v} \cdot r}{m \cdot t} - \frac{s}{t}$ are exposed to competition from unlawful copiers. They therefore earn per-work profits of $\tilde{v} \cdot r - \frac{\tilde{v} \cdot r}{m} - o$. Since $m \geq \tilde{m}$, this per-work profit function is non-negative.

---

[25] The threshold is derived at the end of Sect. 3.4.2.1.

[26] Note that if unlawful copiers can upload some works profitably ($m < \frac{\tilde{v} \cdot r}{s}$) and right holders can upload at least as many works profitably as unlawful copiers can ($m \geq \tilde{m}$), it is implied that right holders can upload some works profitably ($o \leq v_{max} \cdot r - s$). Formally, $\tilde{m} \leq m < \frac{\tilde{v} \cdot r}{s}$ can only be fulfilled if $\tilde{m} < \frac{\tilde{v} \cdot r}{s} \Leftrightarrow o < v_{max} \cdot r - s$.

The threshold $N = \frac{\tilde{v} \cdot r}{m \cdot t} - \frac{s}{t}$ can be explained by reference to the dotted, downward sloping function, which shows the per-work profits of an unlawful copier who uploads the only copy of a work: $\tilde{v} \cdot r - m \cdot (s + t \cdot N)$. Again, this situation does not occur in equilibrium but helps to show why right holders who own works with a number $N > \frac{\tilde{v} \cdot r}{m \cdot t} - \frac{s}{t}$ are not exposed to competition from unlawful copiers: Unlawful copiers earn negative profits if they upload these works and therefore refrain from doing so. Right holders who own works with a number $\frac{\tilde{v} \cdot r}{m \cdot t} - \frac{s}{t} < N \leq \tilde{N}$ thus only upload one copy of their works and earn per-work profits of $\tilde{v} \cdot r - s - t \cdot N - o$.

Right holders earn the following aggregate profits:

$$\begin{aligned} \Pi^*_{2.2} &= \int_0^{\frac{\tilde{v} \cdot r}{m \cdot t} - \frac{s}{t}} \left(\tilde{v} \cdot r - \frac{\tilde{v} \cdot r}{m} - o \right) \mathrm{d}N + \int_{\frac{\tilde{v} \cdot r}{m \cdot t} - \frac{s}{t}}^{\tilde{N}} (\tilde{v} \cdot r - s - t \cdot N - o) \mathrm{d}N \\ &= \frac{1}{2} \cdot \left(\tilde{N} + \frac{\tilde{v} \cdot r}{m \cdot t} - \frac{s}{t} \right) \cdot \left(\tilde{v} \cdot r - \frac{\tilde{v} \cdot r}{m} - o \right) \end{aligned} \tag{3.29}$$

These aggregate profits are illustrated by the light yellow trapezium in coordinate system II. The factor $\frac{1}{2} \cdot \left(\tilde{N} + \frac{\tilde{v} \cdot r}{m \cdot t} - \frac{s}{t} \right)$ is the unweighted average of the widths of the two bases; the factor $\tilde{v} \cdot r - \frac{\tilde{v} \cdot r}{m} - o$ the height of the trapezium.

If right holders can upload no works profitably ($o > v_{max} \cdot r - s$), but unlawful copiers can upload some works profitably ($m \leq \frac{v_{max} \cdot r}{s}$), the total number of works uploaded to the platform is $\overline{N}$. The same is true if right holders can upload some works profitably ($o \leq v_{max} \cdot r - s$), but unlawful copiers can upload more works profitably ($m < \tilde{m}$). In both cases, the per-work profits of every right holder are $\overline{v} \cdot r - \frac{\overline{v} \cdot r}{m} - o$. This per-work profit function is shown in coordinate system III. The per-work profits are negative but larger than $-o$.

The dotted, downward sloping function shows per-work profits of an unlawful copier who uploads the only copy of a work: $\overline{v} \cdot r - m \cdot (s + t \cdot N)$. The horizontal intercept of this function ($\overline{N}$) helps to explain why right holders upload only works with a number $N \leq \overline{N}$: Unlawful copiers would not upload works with a number $N > \overline{N}$. Hence, there is no reason for right holders to upload these works. Since the per-work profit function is independent of N, every right holder earns the same per-work profits. Right holders' aggregate profits therefore are $\left(\overline{v} \cdot r - \frac{\overline{v} \cdot r}{m} - o \right) \cdot \overline{N}$.

If neither right holders ($o > v_{max} \cdot r - s$) nor unlawful copiers ($m > \frac{v_{max} \cdot r}{s}$) can upload works profitably, no works are uploaded. Right holders' aggregate profits earned through the platform then are 0.

To summarise, right holders earn the following aggregate profits:

$$\Pi_{2.2}^{*}=\begin{cases}\frac{1}{2}\cdot\tilde{N}\cdot(\tilde{v}\cdot r-s-o), & \text{if } o\leq v_{max}\cdot r-s \text{ and } m\geq\frac{\tilde{v}\cdot r}{s}\\ \frac{1}{2}\cdot\left(\tilde{N}+\frac{\tilde{v}\cdot r}{m\cdot t}-\frac{s}{t}\right)\cdot\left(\tilde{v}\cdot r-\frac{\tilde{v}\cdot r}{m}-o\right), & \text{if } \tilde{m}\leq m<\frac{\tilde{v}\cdot r}{s}\\ \left(\tilde{v}\cdot r-\frac{\tilde{v}\cdot r}{m}-o\right)\cdot\overline{N}, & \text{if }\left(\begin{array}{c}(o\leq v_{max}\cdot r-s \text{ and } m<\tilde{m}) \text{ or}\\ \left(o>v_{max}\cdot r-s \text{ and } m\leq\frac{v_{max}\cdot r}{s}\right)\end{array}\right)\\ 0, & \text{if } o>v_{max}\cdot r-s \text{ and } m>\frac{v_{max}\cdot r}{s}\end{cases}\tag{3.30}$$

3.4.3 *Effect of Automated Filtering on Right Holders' Profits and Availability of Works on Platform*

Taken together, the results of the previous sections provide the basis for a discussion of the effect of automated filtering on the number of works uploaded and on right holders' profits. Right holders' per-work profit functions in scenario 1 (grey functions), scenario 2.1, specification I (light blue functions), and scenario 2.2, specification A.I (light yellow functions) are compared in Fig. 3.6. Note that not filtering is equivalent to filtering with an intensity of $m = 1$. For scenario 2.2, two situations are considered: Coordinate system I displays right holders' profits for $m < \tilde{m}$ and coordinate system II for $\tilde{m} \leq m < \frac{\tilde{v}\cdot r}{s}$.

The number of works uploaded decreases as m increases. Note that $\overline{N} = \hat{N}$ if the platform does not filter. If the platform filters with an intensity of $m < \tilde{m}$ (coordinate system I), the number of works uploaded in scenario 2.2 is $\overline{N}$. As m increases, $\overline{N}$ decreases. This is the reverse effect of the increase in the number of works uploaded that results from the presence of unlawful copiers (Sect. 3.4.1.4): As unlawful copiers' uploading costs increase, there are fewer works which can be uploaded profitably by unlawful copiers but lead to negative profits for right holders.

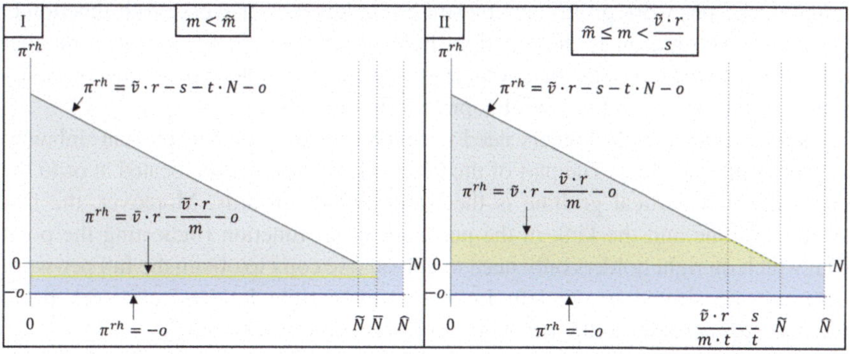

Fig. 3.6 Comparison of right holders' profits in scenario 1, scenario 2.1 (specification I), and scenario 2.2 (specification A.I), presuming $o \leq v_{max} \cdot r - s$

Once m has reached the threshold $\tilde{m}$, right holders upload the same number of works as they would upload if no unlawful copiers existed: $\tilde{N}$. A further increase in m does not affect the number of works uploaded (coordinate system II).

These insights lead to the following proposition:

Proposition 3.3
Automated filtering leads right holders to upload fewer of those works that they would not upload in the absence of unlawful copiers. Once automated filtering ensures that unlawful copiers do not upload a copy of the most popular work that a right holder cannot upload profitably, a further increase in the filtering intensity does not affect the number of existing works right holders upload.

Moreover, automated filtering increases right holders' aggregate profits. For one thing, as explained above, right holders need to upload fewer works that they cannot upload profitably. For another, per-work profits increase. In coordinate system I, automated filtering therefore decreases the light blue loss rectangle by shifting the right side of the rectangle to the left and by shifting the lower side of the rectangle upwards.

The increase in per-work profits (graphically: the upward shifting of the lower side of the rectangle) is the result of two effects. First, as m increases, right holders need to upload fewer copies of their works to prevent unlawful copiers from uploading. As a result, the available revenues are no longer fully consumed by uploading costs. Second, as the number of works uploaded decreases, the number of views per work increases from $\hat{v}$ to $\overline{v}$, leading to an increase in per-work revenues.

Nevertheless, if $m < \tilde{m}$, per-work profits continue to be negative. Once $m = \tilde{m}$, the right side of the loss rectangle is shifted so far to the left that $\overline{N} = \tilde{N}$. Moreover, the lower side of the loss rectangle is shifted so far upwards that $\pi^{rh} = 0$; that is, it is located on the horizontal axis.

For $m \geq \tilde{m}$ (coordinate system II), the number of works uploaded and thus also the number of views per work are the same as in scenario 1. However, given $m < \frac{\tilde{v} \cdot r}{s}$, right holders' per-work profit function still lies below the per-work profit function in scenario 1. The reason is that all right holders who own a work with a number located at or to the left of the first vertical gridline need to upload more than one copy of their works to prevent unlawful copiers from uploading.

As m increases, right holders need to upload fewer copies to prevent unlawful copiers from uploading. The part of the per-work profit function located at or to the left of the first vertical gridline is therefore shifted upwards. Moreover, the first vertical gridline and the kink in the per-work profit function (indicating the point from which on right holders only need to upload one copy to obtain the full per-work revenues) are shifted to the left. In other words, right holders' per-work profit function moves closer to the per-work profit function in scenario 1.

These insights lead to the following proposition:

Proposition 3.4
If the market for supplying unlawful copies is perfectly competitive, automated filtering increases right holders' profits as they need to spend less to obtain the full revenues generated by their works.

Note that unlike for $m < \tilde{m}$, for $m \geq \tilde{m}$ the increase in per-work profits is not reinforced by an increase in per-work revenues. In the region $m < \tilde{m}$, an increase in m therefore shifts right holders' per-work profit function upwards more strongly than in the region $m \geq \tilde{m}$.

Once m reaches the threshold $\frac{\tilde{v} \cdot r}{s}$, right holders earn the same profits as if no unlawful copiers existed. A further increase in m then does not affect right holders' aggregate profits.

3.5 Per-Work Monopoly on Uploading Unlawful Copies

The previous section reflected on the number of works uploaded and right holders' profits presuming perfect competition among unlawful copiers. As explained in Sect. 3.2.2, this section changes this presumption, assuming instead a per-work monopoly on uploading unlawful copies. Like Sect. 3.4, this section begins by determining the number of works uploaded and right holders' profits if unlawful copiers are present and the platform does not filter (Sect. 3.5.1). Next, Sect. 3.5.2 calculates the number of works uploaded and right holders' profits if the platform filters. Finally, Sect. 3.5.3 discusses the effects of automated filtering on the availability of works on a platform and right holders' profits.

3.5.1 No Automated Filtering (Scenario 2.1, Specification II)

Following the same structure as above, this section begins by analysing the competition between right holders and unlawful copiers for views (Sect. 3.5.1.1). Next, Sect. 3.5.1.2 considers the number of works right holders upload and determines their aggregate profits. Section 3.5.1.3 discusses the effect of the presence of unlawful copiers on the availability of works on a platform and right holders' profits. Finally, Sect. 3.5.1.4 reflects on the influence of the structure of the market for supplying unlawful copies on the discussed effects of the presence of unlawful copiers.

3.5.1.1 Number of Copies Uploaded Per Work and Right Holders' Per-Work Profits

As above, this section determines the number of copies uploaded and right holders' per-work profits for a given level of $N^*_{2.1}$ and thus a given level of $v^*_{2.1}$. Recall that as in this scenario the platform does not filter, an unlawful copier and the right holder incur the same per-copy uploading costs (c). Note that because c is a function of N, these uploading costs differ between normalised works.

When determining the level of c from which on a work is not uploaded, it does not make a difference whether one or many unlawful copiers per work exist. If a work is associated with uploading costs of $c > v^*_{2.1} \cdot r$, neither the right holder nor the unlawful copier uploads a copy, implying that the work is not uploaded. Right holders who own works associated with uploading costs of $c > v^*_{2.1} \cdot r$ thus earn per-work profits of 0.

To the contrary, if a work is associated with uploading costs of $c \leq v^*_{2.1} \cdot r$, the number of unlawful copiers who compete with a right holder influences his profits. As explained in Sect. 3.4.1.1, if many unlawful copiers upload copies of the same work, competition among them incentivises them to upload until $\frac{v^*_{2.1} \cdot r}{c}$ copies are uploaded. The right holder then earns profits of $-o$ regardless of how many copies he uploads.

If only one unlawful copier competes with the right holder, the right holder's incentives change because the marginal profits an unlawful copier earns by uploading a copy are decreasing. For explanation, suppose that a right holder has uploaded $\check{u}$ copies of his work. If the unlawful copier uploads her first copy, she obtains (marginal) profits of $\frac{v^*_{2.1} \cdot r}{\check{u}+1} - c$. If she uploads a second copy, her total profits are $2 \cdot \left(\frac{v^*_{2.1} \cdot r}{\check{u}+2} - c\right)$. The marginal profits of uploading the second copy therefore are $2 \cdot \left(\frac{v^*_{2.1} \cdot r}{\check{u}+2} - c\right) - \left(\frac{v^*_{2.1} \cdot r}{\check{u}+1} - c\right)$. They are below the marginal profits of uploading the first copy as

$$2 \cdot \left(\frac{v^*_{2.1} \cdot r}{\check{u}+2} - c\right) - \left(\frac{v^*_{2.1} \cdot r}{\check{u}+1} - c\right) = \frac{v^*_{2.1} \cdot r}{\check{u}+1} - c - \frac{2 \cdot v^*_{2.1} \cdot r}{(\check{u}+1) \cdot (\check{u}+2)} \tag{3.31}$$

Intuitively, the decreasing marginal profits of uploading copies can be explained as follows: If an unlawful copier uploads her first copy, she takes a piece of the revenues previously obtained by the right holder and claims it for herself. If the unlawful copier has already uploaded a copy and uploads a further copy, she takes some of the revenues previously earned by the right holder and some of the revenues earned by her first copy. She therefore obtains an additional piece of the work's revenues but also reduces the revenues generated by her first copy. The more copies the unlawful copier has uploaded relative to the number of copies the right holder has uploaded, the larger the proportion of the revenues generated by an additional upload that results from a reduction in revenues of her previously uploaded copies.

Due to the decreasing marginal profits of uploading copies, unlike in specification I, the unlawful copier does not necessarily upload until $\frac{v_{2.1}^* \cdot r}{c}$ copies are uploaded. The number of copies an unlawful copier uploads follows from her profit maximisation problem:

$$\max_{u^{co}} \pi^{co} = \left(\frac{v_{2.1}^* \cdot r}{u^{rh} + u^{co}} - c \right) \cdot u^{co} \tag{3.32}$$

The first-order condition yields $u_{2.1}^{co\,*} = \sqrt{\frac{v_{2.1}^* \cdot r \cdot u^{rh}}{c}} - u^{rh}$.[27]

Anticipating the unlawful copier's reaction function, the right holder chooses u^{rh} to maximise his profits. Again, the right holder will never choose $u^{rh} > \frac{v_{2.1}^* \cdot r}{c}$ since $u^{rh} = \frac{v_{2.1}^* \cdot r}{c}$ already leads the unlawful copier to upload 0 copies. The right holder's maximisation problem therefore is

$$\max_{u^{rh}} \pi^{rh} = \left(\frac{v_{2.1}^* \cdot r}{u^{rh} + \sqrt{\frac{v_{2.1}^* \cdot r \cdot u^{rh}}{c}} - u^{rh}} - c \right) \cdot u^{rh} - o, \text{ s.t. } u^{rh} \leq \frac{v_{2.1}^* \cdot r}{c} \tag{3.33}$$

The first-order condition yields $u_{2.1}^{rh\,*} = \frac{v_{2.1}^* \cdot r}{4 \cdot c}$.[28] Put differently, the right holder maximises profits by uploading a quarter of the maximal number of copies that can be uploaded of his work without the total uploading costs exceeding the per-work revenues. He accepts that the unlawful copier uploads some copies of his work. Inserting $u_{2.1}^{rh\,*} = \frac{v_{2.1}^* \cdot r}{4 \cdot c}$ into the unlawful copier's reaction function yields

$$u_{2.1}^{co\,*} = \sqrt{\frac{v_{2.1}^* \cdot r \cdot \frac{v_{2.1}^* \cdot r}{4 \cdot c}}{c}} - \frac{v_{2.1}^* \cdot r}{4 \cdot c} = \frac{v_{2.1}^* \cdot r}{4 \cdot c} \tag{3.34}$$

---

[27] Inserting $\sqrt{\frac{v_{2.1}^* \cdot r \cdot u^{rh}}{c}} - u^{rh}$ into the second derivative of π^{co} with respect to u^{co} yields $-2 \cdot \sqrt{\frac{c^3}{u^{rh} \cdot v_{2.1}^* \cdot r}}$. Given the assumptions on the variables, this result is negative. The second-order condition for a maximum is thus fulfilled. Note that $u^{co} = -\sqrt{\frac{v_{2.1}^* \cdot r \cdot u^{rh}}{c}} - u^{rh}$ also fulfils the first-order condition. Inserting $u^{co} = -\sqrt{\frac{v_{2.1}^* \cdot r \cdot u^{rh}}{c}} - u^{rh}$ into the second derivative of π^{co} with respect to u^{co} yields $2 \cdot \sqrt{\frac{c^3}{u^{rh} \cdot v_{2.1}^* \cdot r}}$. Given the assumptions on the variables, this result is positive. It follows that $u^{co} = -\sqrt{\frac{v_{2.1}^* \cdot r \cdot u^{rh}}{c}} - u^{rh}$ is a minimum.

[28] Inserting $\frac{v_{2.1}^* \cdot r}{4 \cdot c}$ into the second derivative of π^{rh} with respect to u^{rh} yields $-\frac{2 \cdot c^2}{v_{2.1}^* \cdot r}$. Given the assumptions on the variables, this result is negative. The second-order condition for a maximum is therefore fulfilled. $\frac{v_{2.1}^* \cdot r}{4 \cdot c}$ also fulfils the constraint $u^{rh} \leq \frac{v_{2.1}^* \cdot r}{c}$.

Like the right holder, the unlawful copier uploads a quarter of the maximal number of copies that can be uploaded of the right holder's work without the total uploading costs exceeding the per-work revenues. This explains why the right holder refrains from fully preventing the unlawful copier from uploading: He anticipates that the decreasing marginal profits of uploading copies induce the unlawful copier to not upload all copies until $\frac{v_{2.1}^* \cdot r}{c}$ copies are uploaded. Despite losing half of the available per-work revenues to the unlawful copier, the right holder earns positive on-platform profits of $\frac{v_{2.1}^* \cdot r}{2} - \frac{v_{2.1}^* \cdot r}{4 \cdot c} \cdot c = \frac{v_{2.1}^* \cdot r}{4}$. By contrast, if the right holder uploaded $\frac{v_{2.1}^* \cdot r}{c}$ copies, he would obtain the full per-work revenues, but the entire revenues would be consumed by uploading costs: $v_{2.1}^* \cdot r - \frac{v_{2.1}^* \cdot r}{c} \cdot c = 0$.

These insights lead to the following proposition:

Proposition 3.5
If a user-uploaded content platform does not filter, a right holder who only competes with one unlawful copier for views of his work maximises profits by tolerating that the unlawful copier uploads some copies of his work.

By uploading $\frac{v_{2.1}^* \cdot r}{4 \cdot c}$ copies, the right holder earns per-work profits of $\frac{v_{2.1}^* \cdot r}{4} - o$. Note that these per-work profits are independent of N. As above, this is a result of the fact that right holders with lower uploading costs upload more copies to obtain their share of the revenues than right holders with higher uploading costs.

Note further that due to the continuity assumption, $\pi_{2.1}^{rh\ *} = \frac{v_{2.1}^* \cdot r}{4} - o$ is an approximation. Recall that the continuity assumption is qualified by only allowing for per-work profits smaller than or equal to the profits a right holder would earn if he uploaded the only copy of his work (Sect. 3.2.3.4). It is therefore assumed that a right holder uploads the only copy of his work and earns per-work profits of $v_{2.1}^* \cdot r - c - o$ if his work fulfils the following condition:[29]

$$v_{2.1}^* \cdot r - c - o < \frac{v_{2.1}^* \cdot r}{4} - o \Leftrightarrow c > \frac{3}{4} \cdot v_{2.1}^* \cdot r \tag{3.35}$$

[29] Note that if the right holder and the unlawful copier can either upload one or no copy of a work, the unlawful copier chooses not to upload if a work is associated with uploading costs of $\frac{3}{4} \cdot v_{2.1}^* \cdot r < c \leq v_{2.1}^* \cdot r$ and the right holder has uploaded as by uploading she would obtain profits of $\pi^{co} = \left(\frac{v_{2.1}^* \cdot r}{1+1} - c\right) \cdot 1 = \frac{v_{2.1}^* \cdot r}{2} - c$. For works with uploading costs of $\frac{3}{4} \cdot v_{2.1}^* \cdot r < c \leq v_{2.1}^* \cdot r$, the unlawful copier would therefore obtain negative profits. Note further that the same argument could be made for works with uploading costs of $\frac{1}{2} \cdot v_{2.1}^* \cdot r < c \leq \frac{3}{4} \cdot v_{2.1}^* \cdot r$ as the unlawful copier would then also earn negative profits by uploading one copy once the right holder has uploaded one copy. However, as explained in Sect. 3.2.3.4, the qualification of the continuity assumption only applies in cases in which a right holder's per-work profits would otherwise exceed the profits a right holder would earn if he uploaded the only copy of his work. This is not the case for works with uploading costs of $\frac{1}{2} \cdot v_{2.1}^* \cdot r < c \leq \frac{3}{4} \cdot v_{2.1}^* \cdot r$. Further extending the qualification of the continuity assumption would entail additional discontinuities in the right holders' per-work profit function. It would thereby undermine the very purpose of the continuity assumption.

To sum up, a right holder uploads the following number of copies in the Stackelberg equilibrium:

$$u_{2.1}^{rh\,*} = \begin{cases} \frac{v_{2.1}^* \cdot r}{4 \cdot c}, & \text{if } c \leq \frac{3}{4} \cdot v_{2.1}^* \cdot r \\ 1, & \text{if } \frac{3}{4} \cdot v_{2.1}^* \cdot r < c \leq v_{2.1}^* \cdot r \\ 0, & \text{if } c > v_{2.1}^* \cdot r \end{cases} \tag{3.36}$$

By doing so, he earns the following per-work profits:

$$\pi_{2.1}^{rh\,*} = \begin{cases} \frac{v_{2.1}^* \cdot r}{4} - o, & \text{if } c \leq \frac{3}{4} \cdot v_{2.1}^* \cdot r \\ v_{2.1}^* \cdot r - c - o, & \text{if } \frac{3}{4} \cdot v_{2.1}^* \cdot r < c \leq v_{2.1}^* \cdot r \\ 0, & \text{if } c > v_{2.1}^* \cdot r \end{cases} \tag{3.37}$$

By inserting $c = s + t \cdot N$, the number of copies the right holder uploads can be transformed as follows:

$$u_{2.1}^{rh\,*} = \begin{cases} \frac{v_{2.1}^* \cdot r}{4 \cdot (s + t \cdot N)}, & \text{if } N \leq \frac{3}{4} \cdot \frac{v_{2.1}^* \cdot r}{t} - \frac{s}{t} \\ 1, & \text{if } \frac{3}{4} \cdot \frac{v_{2.1}^* \cdot r}{t} - \frac{s}{t} < N \leq \frac{v_{2.1}^* \cdot r - s}{t} \\ 0, & \text{if } N > \frac{v_{2.1}^* \cdot r - s}{t} \end{cases} \tag{3.38}$$

Likewise, the right holder's per-work profits can be transformed as follows:

$$\pi_{2.1}^{rh\,*} = \begin{cases} \frac{v_{2.1}^* \cdot r}{4} - o, & \text{if } N \leq \frac{3}{4} \cdot \frac{v_{2.1}^* \cdot r}{t} - \frac{s}{t} \\ v_{2.1}^* \cdot r - s - t \cdot N - o, & \text{if } \frac{3}{4} \cdot \frac{v_{2.1}^* \cdot r}{t} - \frac{s}{t} < N \leq \frac{v_{2.1}^* \cdot r - s}{t} \\ 0, & \text{if } N > \frac{v_{2.1}^* \cdot r - s}{t} \end{cases} \tag{3.39}$$

3.5.1.2 Number of Works Uploaded and Right Holders' Aggregate Profits

As was the case under the presumption of perfect competition among unlawful copiers (Sect. 3.4.1.2), the last work a right holder uploads is the work with the number $\frac{v_{2.1}^* \cdot r - s}{t}$. As above, right holders therefore upload the following number of works:

$$N_{2.1}^* = \begin{cases} \hat{N}, & \text{if } s \leq v_{max} \cdot r \\ 0, & \text{if } s > v_{max} \cdot r \end{cases} \tag{3.40}$$

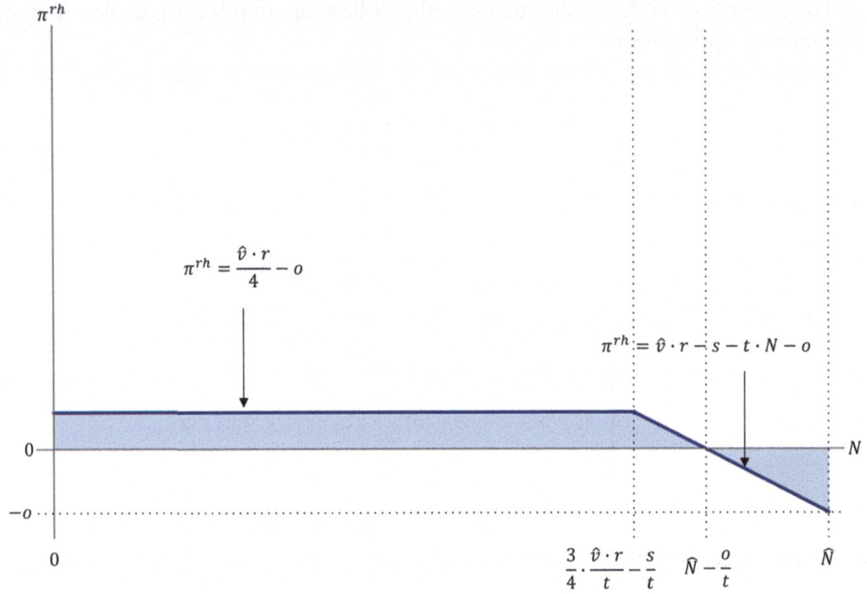

Fig. 3.7 Right holders' profits in scenario 2.1 (specification II), presuming $s \leq v_{max} \cdot r$ and $o < \frac{\hat{v} \cdot r}{4}$

Right holders' per-work profit function if $s \leq v_{max} \cdot r$ is displayed in Fig. 3.7. The part of the per-work profit function that is located at or to the left of the first vertical gridline shows right holders' per-work profits approximated based on the continuity assumption. As explained above, the approximated per-work profits are independent of N. Note that this profit function can also be located on or below the horizontal axis. This is the case if $o \geq \frac{\hat{v} \cdot r}{4}$. However, given $\hat{v} \cdot r > 0$, the function cannot be located on or below the horizontal gridline indicating per-work profits of $-o$.

The first vertical gridline marks the level of N from which on the per-work profits a right holder earns if he uploads the only copy of his work exceed the per-work profits approximated based on the continuity assumption: $\frac{3}{4} \cdot \frac{\hat{v} \cdot r}{t} - \frac{s}{t}$. As explained above, from this point on, it is assumed that right holders earn per-work profits of $\hat{v} \cdot r - s - t \cdot N - o$. Note that if $\frac{3}{4} \cdot \frac{\hat{v} \cdot r}{t} - \frac{s}{t} \leq 0$, all right holders only need to upload one copy to prevent unlawful copiers from uploading. Considering this case would add no insights and thus unnecessarily convolute the analysis. It is thus ignored in the following analysis. Note that if $o < \frac{\hat{v} \cdot r}{4}$, only those right holders earn non-positive per-work profits who own a work with a number

$$\hat{v} \cdot r - s - t \cdot N - o \leq 0 \Leftrightarrow N \geq \hat{N} - \frac{o}{t} \quad (3.41)$$

The threshold $\hat{N} - \frac{o}{t}$ is marked by the second vertical gridline in Fig. 3.7. The third vertical gridline indicates the last normalised work that is uploaded: $\hat{N}$.

The dark blue area illustrates right holders' aggregate profits, which are

$$\begin{aligned}\Pi_{2.1}^{*} &= \int_{0}^{\frac{3}{4}\cdot\frac{\hat{v}\cdot r}{t}-\frac{s}{t}} \left(\frac{\hat{v}\cdot r}{4} - o\right)\mathrm{d}N + \int_{\frac{3}{4}\cdot\frac{\hat{v}\cdot r}{t}-\frac{s}{t}}^{\hat{N}} (\hat{v}\cdot r - s - t\cdot N - o)\mathrm{d}N \\ &= \frac{1}{2}\cdot\left(\hat{N} - \frac{o}{t} + \frac{3}{4}\cdot\frac{\hat{v}\cdot r}{t} - \frac{s}{t}\right)\cdot\left(\frac{\hat{v}\cdot r}{4} - o\right) - \frac{o^2}{2\cdot t}\end{aligned} \tag{3.42}$$

This result can be interpreted as the sum of a trapezium and a triangle. The term $\frac{1}{2}\cdot\left(\hat{N} - \frac{o}{t} + \frac{3}{4}\cdot\frac{\hat{v}\cdot r}{t} - \frac{s}{t}\right)\cdot\left(\frac{\hat{v}\cdot r}{4} - o\right)$ is the dark blue trapezium between the vertical axis and the second vertical gridline. The factor $\frac{1}{2}\cdot\left(\hat{N} - \frac{o}{t} + \frac{3}{4}\cdot\frac{\hat{v}\cdot r}{t} - \frac{s}{t}\right)$ represents the unweighted average of the widths of the two bases and the factor $\frac{\hat{v}\cdot r}{4} - o$ the height of the trapezium. The trapezium illustrates the sum of the profits of all right holders who earn positive per-work profits.

The term $-\frac{o^2}{2\cdot t}$ is the dark blue triangle between the second and the third vertical gridline. The vertical leg of the triangle represents the per-work profits of the right holder who owns the work with the number $\hat{N}$, that is, $-o$. The horizontal leg is the number of right holders who earn negative per-work profits: $\hat{N} - \left(\hat{N} - \frac{o}{t}\right) = \frac{o}{t}$. The triangle illustrates the sum of the profits of all right holders who earn non-positive per-work profits.

If $o \geq \frac{\hat{v}\cdot r}{4}$, right holders' aggregate profits are the same as calculated above but have a slightly different geometrical interpretation.[30]

Finally, if $s > v_{max}\cdot r$, no works are uploaded and right holders obtain aggregate profits of 0.[31]

After further simplifications, right holders' aggregate profits can be summarised as follows:

$$\Pi_{2.1}^{*} = \begin{cases} \left(\frac{\hat{v}\cdot r}{4} - o\right)\cdot\hat{N} - \frac{(\hat{v}\cdot r)^2}{32\cdot t}, & \text{if } s \leq v_{max}\cdot r \\ 0, & \text{if } s > v_{max}\cdot r \end{cases} \tag{3.43}$$

[30] As noted above, the part of the per-work profit function that is located left of the first vertical gridline would then be located on or below the horizontal axis. Aggregate profits can be re-written as $\Pi_{2.1}^{*} = \left(\frac{\hat{v}\cdot r}{4} - o\right)\cdot\hat{N} - \frac{1}{2}\cdot\frac{\hat{v}\cdot r}{4}\cdot\frac{\hat{v}\cdot r}{4\cdot t}$. Every right holder who uploads a work makes (negative) profits of $\frac{\hat{v}\cdot r}{4} - o$. The sum of these profits is represented by the term $\left(\frac{\hat{v}\cdot r}{4} - o\right)\cdot\hat{N}$, that is, a rectangle, which is limited in height by the horizontal axis and the per-work profit function $\frac{\hat{v}\cdot r}{4} - o$, and in width by the vertical axis and $\hat{N}$. Right holders who upload works with a number $N \geq \frac{3}{4}\cdot\frac{\hat{v}\cdot r}{t} - \frac{s}{t}$ earn additional profits of $-\frac{1}{2}\cdot\frac{\hat{v}\cdot r}{4}\cdot\frac{\hat{v}\cdot r}{4\cdot t}$. This term can be interpreted as a right-angled triangle with a vertical leg of $-o - \left(\frac{\hat{v}\cdot r}{4} - o\right) = -\frac{\hat{v}\cdot r}{4}$ and a horizontal leg of $\hat{N} - \left(\frac{3}{4}\cdot\frac{\hat{v}\cdot r}{t} - \frac{s}{t}\right) = \frac{\hat{v}\cdot r}{4\cdot t}$.

[31] In Fig. 3.7, the third vertical gridline representing $\hat{N}$ would then be located left of the vertical axis.

3.5.1.3 Effect of Presence of Unlawful Copiers on Right Holders' Profits and Availability of Works on Platform

Based on the results of the previous sections, this section considers the effect of the presence of unlawful copiers on the number of works uploaded and right holders' aggregate profits, assuming that only one unlawful copier per work exists. Right holders' per-work profits in scenario 1 (grey function) and in scenario 2.1, specification II (dark blue function) are displayed in Fig. 3.8.

As explained in Sect. 3.4.1.4, right holders upload more works in the presence of unlawful copiers than in their absence.

Moreover, the presence of unlawful copiers reduces right holders' aggregate profits. As above, the presence of unlawful copiers induces right holders who own works with a number $\tilde{N} < N \leq \hat{N}$ to upload. Instead of per-work profits of 0, in the presence of unlawful copiers, these right holders earn the per-work profits indicated by the dark blue function. Note that the increase in the number of works uploaded leads to a decrease in the number of views per work (Sect. 3.2.4). As a result, even if in both scenarios right holders only upload one copy of a work, that is, if they own a work with a number of $\frac{3}{4} \cdot \frac{\hat{v} \cdot r}{t} - \frac{s}{t} < N \leq \tilde{N}$, the dark blue function is located below the grey function.

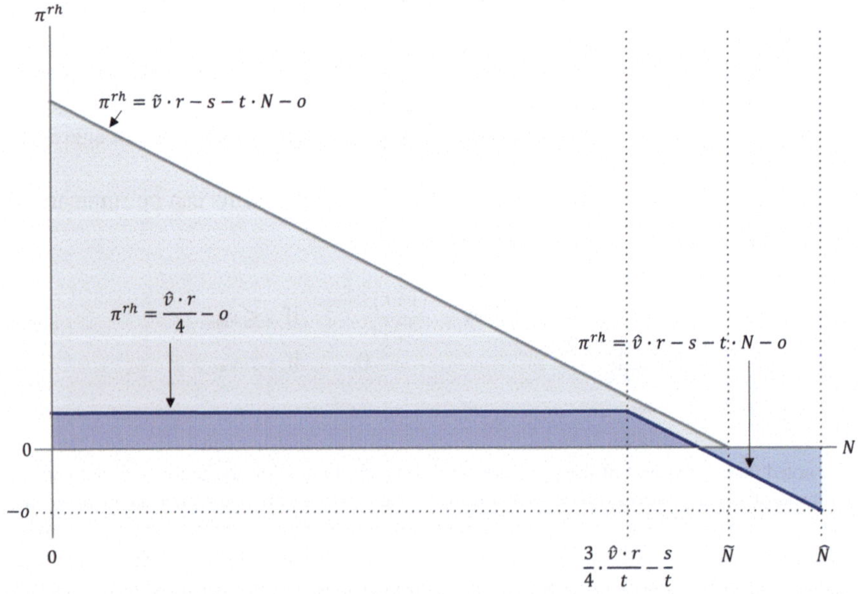

Fig. 3.8 Comparison of right holders' profits in scenario 1 and scenario 2.1 (specification II), presuming $o \leq v_{max} \cdot r - s$ and $o < \frac{\hat{v} \cdot r}{4}$

Besides this reduction in the number of views per work, the presence of unlawful copiers reduces the profits of right holders who own works with a number of $N \leq \frac{3}{4} \cdot \frac{\hat{v} \cdot r}{t} - \frac{s}{t}$ for two reasons. First, it induces them to upload more than one copy, that is, to spend more on uploading than in the absence of unlawful copiers. Second, since right holders and unlawful copiers upload copies of works with a number of $N \leq \frac{3}{4} \cdot \frac{\hat{v} \cdot r}{t} - \frac{s}{t}$, they share the per-work revenues, leaving only half of the per-work revenues for right holders.

3.5.1.4 Influence of Structure of Market for Supplying Unlawful Copies on Effect of Presence of Unlawful Copiers on Right Holders' Profits

This section examines the influence of the structure of the market for supplying unlawful copies on the effect of the presence of unlawful copiers on right holders' profits. As noted above, the number of works uploaded is not affected by the structure of the market for supplying unlawful copies. If at least one unlawful copier competes with each right holder, right holders upload all works that unlawful copiers would otherwise upload. As a result, regardless of how many unlawful copiers per work exist, all works associated with non-negative on-platform profits are uploaded.

By contrast, the market structure influences the effect of the presence of unlawful copiers on right holders' profits. The light blue function in Fig. 3.9 shows right holders' per-work profit function if the market for supplying unlawful copies is perfectly competitive and the dark blue function right holders' per-work profit function if only one unlawful copier competes with a right holder.

If the market for supplying unlawful copies is perfectly competitive, a right holder anticipates that unlawful copiers would collectively upload copies until the maximal number of copies that can be uploaded of the right holder's work without the total uploading costs exceeding the per-work revenues is uploaded. The right holder thus uploads all these copies himself. As illustrated by the light blue function, he then earns on-platform profits of 0 and incurs the off-platform losses.

If a right holder is only confronted with one unlawful copier, he knows that the unlawful copier's marginal profits from uploading copies are decreasing (Sect. 3.5.1.1). He thus anticipates that the unlawful copier does not necessarily upload until the maximal number of copies that can be uploaded of the right holder's work without the total uploading costs exceeding the per-work revenues is uploaded. The right holder chooses to upload a quarter of this maximal number of copies, knowing that the unlawful copier will upload the same number of copies. The right holder and the unlawful copier then earn positive on-platform profits. These positive on-platform profits explain why the right holder is willing to leave copies for the unlawful copier to upload: By accepting that the unlawful copier uploads copies of his work, he ensures that not all available revenues are consumed by uploading costs.

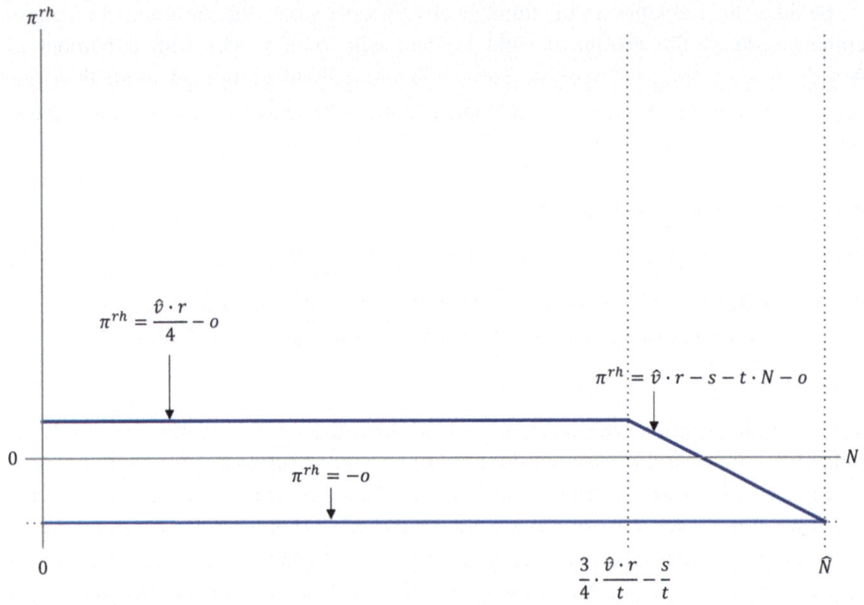

Fig. 3.9 Comparison of right holders' profits in scenario 2.1 (specification I) and scenario 2.1 (specification II), presuming $s \leq v_{max} \cdot r$ and $o < \frac{\hat{v} \cdot r}{4}$

The on-platform profits mitigate ($o \geq \frac{\hat{v} \cdot r}{4}$) or even exceed off-platform losses ($o < \frac{\hat{v} \cdot r}{4}$). The latter case is illustrated by the dark blue function.

These insights lead to the following proposition:

Proposition 3.6
If every right holder only competes with one unlawful copier and the off-platform losses from uploading works to a user-uploaded content platform are sufficiently small relative to the revenues that can be obtained through the platform, the existence of the platform is beneficial for right holders even if the platform does not filter.

3.5.2 With Automated Filtering (Scenario 2.2, Specification A.II)

This section reflects on the impact of automated filtering, presuming that every right holder only competes with one unlawful copier and that the platform filters uniformly. The analysis follows the same structure as above. After analysing the competition between right holders and unlawful copiers for views (Sect. 3.5.2.1),

Sect. 3.5.2.2 considers the number of works right holders upload. Section 3.5.2.3 determines right holders' aggregate profits.

3.5.2.1 Number of Copies Uploaded Per Work and Right Holders' Per-Work Profits

As in specification A.I, this section determines the number of copies uploaded and right holders' per-work profits for a given level of $N^*_{2.2}$ and thus a given level of $v^*_{2.2}$. As opposed to scenario 2.1, the per-copy uploading costs differ between right holders (c) and unlawful copiers (c^{co}). Recall that c and c^{co} are functions of N.

The unlawful copier does not upload a copy of a work if it is associated with uploading costs of $c^{co} > v^*_{2.2} \cdot r$. The right holder then does not upload a copy either if uploading entails negative profits, that is, if his work is associated with uploading costs of $c > v^*_{2.2} \cdot r - o$. He then earns per-work profits of 0. If, on the other hand, the right holder can upload at least one copy of his work profitably ($c \leq v^*_{2.2} \cdot r - o$), he uploads the only copy of his work and earns profits of $v^*_{2.2} \cdot r - c - o$.

If a work is associated with uploading costs of $c^{co} \leq v_{2.2} \cdot r$, the unlawful copier's reaction function is $u^{co\,*}_{2.2} = \sqrt{\frac{v^*_{2.2} \cdot r \cdot u^{rh}}{c^{co}}} - u^{rh}$.[32] The right holder's profit maximisation problem then is

$$\max_{u^{rh}} \pi^{rh} = \left(\frac{v^*_{2.2} \cdot r}{u^{rh} + \sqrt{\frac{v^*_{2.2} \cdot r \cdot u^{rh}}{c^{co}}} - u^{rh}} - c \right) \cdot u^{rh} - o, \quad \text{s.t. } u^{rh} \leq \frac{v^*_{2.2} \cdot r}{c^{co}} \tag{3.44}$$

The first-order condition yields $u^{rh\,*}_{2.2} = \frac{v^*_{2.2} \cdot r \cdot c^{co}}{4 \cdot c^2}$.[33] The number of copies uploaded by the unlawful copier is obtained by inserting $u^{rh\,*}_{2.2} = \frac{v^*_{2.2} \cdot r \cdot c^{co}}{4 \cdot c^2}$ into her reaction function:

$$u^{co\,*}_{2.2} = \sqrt{\frac{v^*_{2.2} \cdot r \cdot \frac{v^*_{2.2} \cdot r \cdot c^{co}}{4 \cdot c^2}}{c^{co}}} - \frac{v^*_{2.2} \cdot r \cdot c^{co}}{4 \cdot c^2} = \frac{v^*_{2.2} \cdot r \cdot (2 \cdot c - c^{co})}{4 \cdot c^2} \tag{3.45}$$

---

[32] For an explanation, see Sect. 3.5.1.1. The c in the reaction function obtained above is replaced by c^{co} as in this section, the platform filters and unlawful copiers thus incur uploading costs of c^{co}.

[33] Inserting $\frac{v^*_{2.2} \cdot r \cdot c^{co}}{4 \cdot c^2}$ into the second derivative of π^{rh} with respect to u^{rh} yields $-\frac{2 \cdot c^3}{v^*_{2.2} \cdot r \cdot c^{co}}$. Given the assumptions on the variables, this result is negative. The second-order condition for a maximum is thus fulfilled.

The right holder thus earns the following profits:

$$\pi_{2.2}^{rh\ *} = \left(\frac{v_{2.2}^{*} \cdot r}{\frac{v_{2.2}^{*} \cdot r \cdot c^{co}}{4 \cdot c^{2}} + \frac{v_{2.2}^{*} \cdot r \cdot (2 \cdot c - c^{co})}{4 \cdot c^{2}}} - c \right) \cdot \frac{v_{2.2}^{*} \cdot r \cdot c^{co}}{4 \cdot c^{2}} - o = \frac{v_{2.2}^{*} \cdot r \cdot c^{co}}{4 \cdot c} - o \quad (3.46)$$

Again, due to the qualification of the continuity assumption, a right holder uploads the only copy of his work and earns per-work profits of $v_{2.2}^{*} \cdot r - c - o$ if his work is associated with uploading costs for the unlawful copier of[34]

$$\frac{v_{2.2}^{*} \cdot r \cdot c^{co}}{4 \cdot c} - o > v_{2.2}^{*} \cdot r - c - o \Leftrightarrow c^{co} > 4 \cdot c - \frac{4 \cdot c^{2}}{v_{2.2}^{*} \cdot r} \quad (3.47)$$

Note that the maximal point $\frac{v_{2.2}^{*} \cdot r \cdot c^{co}}{4 \cdot c^{2}}$ is located at or outside the upper boundary of $\frac{v_{2.2}^{*} \cdot r}{c^{co}}$ if

$$\frac{v_{2.2}^{*} \cdot r \cdot c^{co}}{4 \cdot c^{2}} \geq \frac{v_{2.2}^{*} \cdot r}{c^{co}} \Leftrightarrow c^{co} \geq 2 \cdot c \quad (3.48)$$

By inserting $c^{co} = m \cdot c$, $c^{co} \geq 2 \cdot c$ can be transformed as follows:

$$m \cdot c \geq 2 \cdot c \Leftrightarrow m \geq 2 \quad (3.49)$$

From the second derivative, we know that π^{rh} is a concave function of u^{rh}.[35] π^{rh} increases in u^{rh} until the point $\frac{v_{2.2}^{*} \cdot r \cdot c^{co}}{4 \cdot c^{2}}$. Since $\frac{v_{2.2}^{*} \cdot r}{c^{co}} \leq \frac{v_{2.2}^{*} \cdot r \cdot c^{co}}{4 \cdot c^{2}}$ if $m \geq 2$, the right holder then maximises profits by choosing the maximal value allowed by the maximisation constraint: $\frac{v_{2.2}^{*} \cdot r}{c^{co}}$. In other words, the right holder then behaves in the same way and thus earns the same profits as in specification A.I (Sect. 3.4.2.1).

[34] Note that if the right holder and the unlawful copier can either upload one or no copy of a work, the unlawful copier chooses not to upload if the right holder has uploaded as by uploading she would obtain profits of $\pi^{co} = \left(\frac{v_{2.2}^{*} \cdot r}{1+1} - c^{co}\right) \cdot 1 = \frac{v_{2.2}^{*} \cdot r}{2} - c^{co}$. For works associated with uploading costs of $c^{co} > 4 \cdot c - \frac{4 \cdot c^{2}}{v_{2.2}^{*} \cdot r}$, the unlawful copier would obtain negative profits as even $c^{co} = c$ would yield $c^{co} > \frac{3}{4} \cdot v_{2.2}^{*} \cdot r$ and thus produce negative per-work profits. The qualification of the continuity assumption is not extended to works associated with uploading costs of $c^{co} \leq 4 \cdot c - \frac{4 \cdot c^{2}}{v_{2.2}^{*} \cdot r}$ as doing so would entail additional discontinuities in the right holders' per-work profit function and thereby undermine the very purpose of the continuity assumption.

[35] The second derivative of π^{rh} with respect to u^{rh} is $\frac{\Delta^{2} \pi^{rh}}{\Delta (u^{rh})^{2}} = -\frac{\sqrt{v_{2.2}^{*} \cdot r \cdot c^{co} \cdot u^{rh}}}{4 \cdot (u^{rh})^{2}}$. Given the assumptions on the variables, it is non-positive.

For $m < 2$, right holders upload the following number of copies per work:

$$u_{2.2}^{rh\,*} = \begin{cases} \dfrac{v_{2.2}^{*} \cdot r \cdot c^{co}}{4 \cdot c^{2}}, & \text{if } c^{co} \leq 4 \cdot c - \dfrac{4 \cdot c^{2}}{v_{2.2}^{*} \cdot r} \text{ and } c^{co} \leq v_{2.2}^{*} \cdot r \\ 1, & \text{if } \left(\begin{array}{c} 4 \cdot c - \dfrac{4 \cdot c^{2}}{v_{2.2}^{*} \cdot r} < c^{co} \leq v_{2.2}^{*} \cdot r \\ \text{or } \left(c^{co} > v_{2.2}^{*} \cdot r \text{ and } c \leq v_{2.2}^{*} \cdot r - o \right) \end{array} \right) \\ 0, & \text{if } c^{co} > v_{2.2}^{*} \cdot r \text{ and } c > v_{2.2}^{*} \cdot r - o \end{cases} \tag{3.50}$$

By doing so, they earn the following per-work profits:

$$\pi_{2.2}^{rh\,*} = \begin{cases} \dfrac{v_{2.2}^{*} \cdot r \cdot c^{co}}{4 \cdot c} - o, & \text{if } c^{co} \leq 4 \cdot c - \dfrac{4 \cdot c^{2}}{v_{2.2}^{*} \cdot r} \text{ and } c^{co} \leq v_{2.2}^{*} \cdot r \\ v_{2.2}^{*} \cdot r - c - o, & \text{if } \left(\begin{array}{c} 4 \cdot c - \dfrac{4 \cdot c^{2}}{v_{2.2}^{*} \cdot r} < c^{co} \leq v_{2.2}^{*} \cdot r \\ \text{or } \left(c^{co} > v_{2.2}^{*} \cdot r \text{ and } c \leq v_{2.2}^{*} \cdot r - o \right) \end{array} \right) \\ 0, & \text{if } c^{co} > v_{2.2}^{*} \cdot r \text{ and } c > v_{2.2}^{*} \cdot r - o \end{cases} \tag{3.51}$$

By inserting $c^{co} = m \cdot (s + t \cdot N)$ and $c = s + t \cdot N$, the number of copies uploaded can be transformed as follows:

$$u_{2.2}^{rh\,*} = \begin{cases} \dfrac{v_{2.2}^{*} \cdot r \cdot m}{4 \cdot (s + t \cdot N)}, & \text{if } N \leq \dfrac{4-m}{4} \cdot \dfrac{v_{2.2}^{*} \cdot r}{t} - \dfrac{s}{t} \text{ and } N \leq \dfrac{v_{2.2}^{*} \cdot r}{t \cdot m} - \dfrac{s}{t} \\ 1, & \text{if } \left(\begin{array}{c} \dfrac{4-m}{4} \cdot \dfrac{v_{2.2}^{*} \cdot r}{t} - \dfrac{s}{t} < N \leq \dfrac{v_{2.2}^{*} \cdot r}{t \cdot m} - \dfrac{s}{t} \\ \text{or } \dfrac{v_{2.2}^{*} \cdot r}{t \cdot m} - \dfrac{s}{t} < N \leq \dfrac{v_{2.2}^{*} \cdot r - s - o}{t} \end{array} \right) \\ 0, & \text{if } N > \dfrac{v_{2.2}^{*} \cdot r}{t \cdot m} - \dfrac{s}{t} \text{ and } N > \dfrac{v_{2.2}^{*} \cdot r - s - o}{t} \end{cases} \tag{3.52}$$

Likewise, right holders' per-work profits can be transformed as follows:

$$\pi_{2.2}^{rh\,*} = \begin{cases} \dfrac{v_{2.2}^{*} \cdot r}{4} \cdot m - o, & \text{if } N \leq \dfrac{4-m}{4} \cdot \dfrac{v_{2.2}^{*} \cdot r}{t} - \dfrac{s}{t} \text{ and } N \leq \dfrac{v_{2.2}^{*} \cdot r}{t \cdot m} - \dfrac{s}{t} \\ v_{2.2}^{*} \cdot r - s - t \cdot N - o, & \text{if } \left(\begin{array}{c} \dfrac{4-m}{4} \cdot \dfrac{v_{2.2}^{*} \cdot r}{t} - \dfrac{s}{t} < N \leq \dfrac{v_{2.2}^{*} \cdot r}{t \cdot m} - \dfrac{s}{t} \\ \text{or } \dfrac{v_{2.2}^{*} \cdot r}{t \cdot m} - \dfrac{s}{t} < N \leq \dfrac{v_{2.2}^{*} \cdot r - s - o}{t} \end{array} \right) \\ 0, & \text{if } N > \dfrac{v_{2.2}^{*} \cdot r}{t \cdot m} - \dfrac{s}{t} \text{ and } N > \dfrac{v_{2.2}^{*} \cdot r - s - o}{t} \end{cases} \tag{3.53}$$

3.5.2.2 Number of Works Uploaded

If right holders can upload at least as many works profitably as unlawful copiers can ($m \geq \tilde{m}$),[36] the number of works uploaded is determined by the number assigned to the last work for which uploading results in non-negative profits for the right holder. If $m < \tilde{m}$, the number of works uploaded is determined by the number assigned to the last work for which uploading results in non-negative profits for the unlawful copier. The number of works uploaded if only one unlawful copier per work exists thus is the same as in specification A.I (Sect. 3.4.2.2).

3.5.2.3 Right Holders' Aggregate Profits

This section considers right holders' aggregate profits. If the uploading costs of the unlawful copier are at least twice as large as the uploading costs of the right holder ($m \geq 2$), right holders' per-work profit functions are the same as in specification A.I.[37]

Right holders' per-work profit functions if $m < 2$ are shown in Fig. 3.10. Right holders who are exposed to competition from one unlawful copier can then earn higher profits than if the market for uploading unlawful copies were perfectly competitive.

Considering cases in which, despite $m < 2$, no right holder is exposed to competition from an unlawful copier would add no insights. In the interest of a focused analysis, it is therefore presumed that if $m < 2$, some right holders are exposed to competition from unlawful copiers. This assumption is applied even for the smallest number of views per work that occurs in equilibrium: $\hat{v}$. If $\hat{N}$ works were uploaded, no right holder would be exposed to competition from an unlawful copier if $m \geq \frac{\hat{v} \cdot r}{s}$.[38] Formally, it is thus presumed that

$$\frac{\hat{v} \cdot r}{s} > 2 \Leftrightarrow s < \frac{v_{max} \cdot r \cdot t}{d \cdot r + 2 \cdot t} \tag{3.54}$$

In the light blue area, right holders upload $\tilde{N}$ works. In the dark blue area, unlawful copiers can upload more works profitably than right holders can. Right holders then upload $\overline{N}$ works. The dark yellow functions in coordinate systems I

[36] The threshold $\tilde{m}$ is introduced in Sect. 3.4.2.2.

[37] These per-work profit functions are displayed in Fig. 3.5.

[38] Note that if the platform filters, fewer than $\hat{N}$ works are uploaded. Nevertheless, to identify the condition that ensures that even for the smallest conceivable filtering intensity some right holders are exposed to competition from unlawful uploaders, the threshold value of $\hat{v}$ is used. Note further that as $\hat{v}$ is independent of o and as $\tilde{v} = \hat{v}$ if $o = 0$, in the coordinate system in the centre of Fig. 3.10, $m = \frac{\hat{v} \cdot r}{s}$ would be a horizontal line that would intersect with $m = \frac{\tilde{v} \cdot r}{s}$ at the vertical axis.

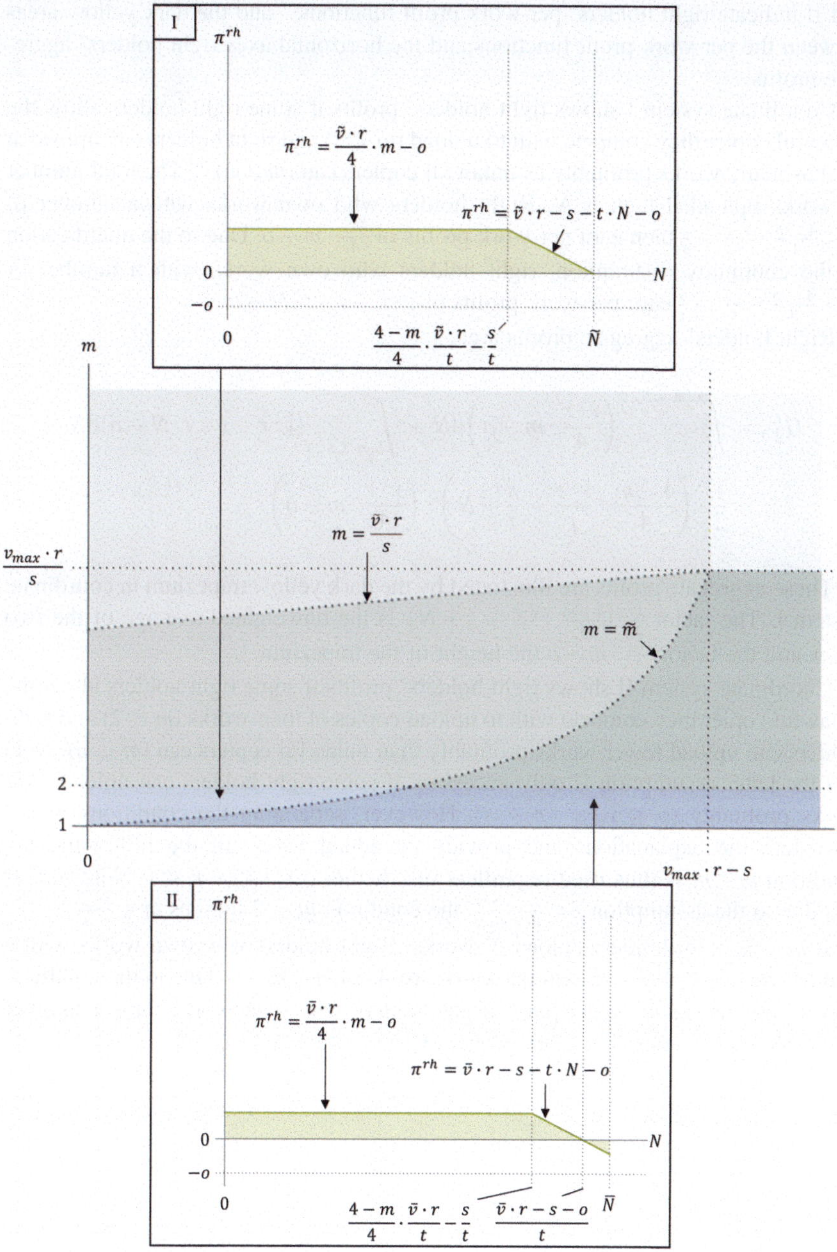

Fig. 3.10 Right holders' profits for different combinations of m and o in scenario 2.2 (specification A.II), presuming $s < \frac{v_{max} \cdot r \cdot t}{d \cdot r + 2 \cdot t}$

and II indicate right holders' per-work profit functions[39] and the dark yellow areas between the per-work profit functions and the horizontal axes right holders' aggregate profits.

Coordinate system I shows right holders' profits if some right holders allow the unlawful copier they compete with to upload ($m < 2$) and right holders can upload at least as many works profitably as unlawful copiers can ($m \geq \tilde{m}$).[40] The total number of works uploaded then is $\tilde{N}$. Right holders who own works with a number of $N \leq \frac{4-m}{4} \cdot \frac{\tilde{v} \cdot r}{t} - \frac{s}{t}$ then earn per-work profits of $\frac{\tilde{v} \cdot r}{4} \cdot m - o$. Due to the qualification of the continuity assumption, right holders who own works with a number of $N > \frac{4-m}{4} \cdot \frac{\tilde{v} \cdot r}{t} - \frac{s}{t}$ earn per-work profits of $\tilde{v} \cdot r - s - t \cdot N - o$.

Right holders' aggregate profits are:

$$\Pi^*_{2.2} = \int_0^{\frac{4-m}{4} \cdot \frac{\tilde{v} \cdot r}{t} - \frac{s}{t}} \left(\frac{\tilde{v} \cdot r}{4} \cdot m - o \right) \mathrm{d}N + \int_{\frac{4-m}{4} \cdot \frac{\tilde{v} \cdot r}{t} - \frac{s}{t}}^{\tilde{N}} (\tilde{v} \cdot r - s - t \cdot N - o) \mathrm{d}N$$
$$= \frac{1}{2} \cdot \left(\frac{4-m}{4} \cdot \frac{\tilde{v} \cdot r}{t} - \frac{s}{t} + \tilde{N} \right) \cdot \left(\frac{\tilde{v} \cdot r}{4} \cdot m - o \right)$$

These aggregate profits are illustrated by the dark yellow trapezium in coordinate system I. The factor $\frac{1}{2} \cdot \left(\frac{4-m}{4} \cdot \frac{\tilde{v} \cdot r}{t} - \frac{s}{t} + \tilde{N} \right)$ is the unweighted average of the two bases and the factor $\frac{\tilde{v} \cdot r}{4} \cdot m - o$ the height of the trapezium.

Coordinate system II shows right holders' profits if some right holders allow the unlawful copier they compete with to upload copies of their works ($m < 2$) and right holders can upload fewer works profitably than unlawful copiers can ($m < \tilde{m}$). Note that the latter assumption is only necessary if some right holders can upload their works profitably ($o \leq v_{max} \cdot r - s$). However, separating the conditions would convolute the explanations and provide no added value. In the following, the condition $m < \tilde{m}$ is thus used regardless of whether $o \leq v_{max} \cdot r - s$. Note further that due to the assumption $s < \frac{v_{max} \cdot r \cdot t}{d \cdot r + 2 \cdot t}$, the condition $m < 2$ implies $m < \frac{v_{max} \cdot r}{s}$.

If $m < \tilde{m}$, right holders upload $\overline{N}$ works. Right holders who own works with a number $N \leq \frac{4-m}{4} \cdot \frac{\overline{v} \cdot r}{t} - \frac{s}{t}$ earn per-work profits of $\frac{\overline{v} \cdot r}{4} \cdot m - o$. Due to the qualification of the continuity assumption, right holders who own works with a number $N > \frac{4-m}{4} \cdot \frac{\overline{v} \cdot r}{t} - \frac{s}{t}$ earn per-work profits of $\overline{v} \cdot r - s - t \cdot N - o$.

[39] Note that coordinate system II presumes $o < \frac{\overline{v} \cdot r}{4} \cdot m$. The implications of $o \geq \frac{\overline{v} \cdot r}{4} \cdot m$ are discussed below.

[40] Note that $o \leq v_{max} \cdot r - s$ is implied by these two conditions as they can only be fulfilled simultaneously if $2 > \tilde{m} \Leftrightarrow o < \frac{v_{max} \cdot t + d \cdot s}{d \cdot r + 2 \cdot t} \cdot r$. With $o < \frac{v_{max} \cdot t + d \cdot s}{d \cdot r + 2 \cdot t} \cdot r$, the condition $o > v_{max} \cdot r - s$ could only be fulfilled if $\frac{v_{max} \cdot t + d \cdot s}{d \cdot r + 2 \cdot t} \cdot r > v_{max} \cdot r - s \Leftrightarrow s > \frac{v_{max} \cdot r}{2}$. However, $s > \frac{v_{max} \cdot r}{2}$ is precluded by the presumption $s < \frac{v_{max} \cdot r \cdot t}{d \cdot r + 2 \cdot t}$ as given the assumptions on the variables, no solution for the following inequality exists $\frac{v_{max} \cdot r}{2} < \frac{v_{max} \cdot r \cdot t}{d \cdot r + 2 \cdot t}$.

Right holders' aggregate profits are

$$\Pi_{2.2}^* = \int_0^{\frac{4-m}{4}\cdot\frac{\overline{v}\cdot r}{t}-\frac{s}{t}} \left(\frac{\overline{v}\cdot r}{4}\cdot m - o\right)\mathrm{d}N + \int_{\frac{4-m}{4}\cdot\frac{\overline{v}\cdot r}{t}-\frac{s}{t}}^{\overline{N}} (\overline{v}\cdot r - s - t\cdot N - o)\mathrm{d}N$$
$$= \frac{1}{2}\cdot\left(\frac{4-m}{4}\cdot\frac{\overline{v}\cdot r}{t} - \frac{s}{t} + \frac{\overline{v}\cdot r - s - o}{t}\right)\cdot\left(\frac{\overline{v}\cdot r}{4}\cdot m - o\right)$$
$$+\frac{1}{2}\cdot(\overline{v}\cdot r - s - t\cdot\overline{N} - o)\cdot\left(\overline{N} - \frac{\overline{v}\cdot r - s - o}{t}\right) \tag{3.55}$$

These aggregate profits can be interpreted as the sum of a trapezium and a triangle. The trapezium is represented by the term $\frac{1}{2}\cdot\left(\frac{4-m}{4}\cdot\frac{\overline{v}\cdot r}{t} - \frac{s}{t} + \frac{\overline{v}\cdot r - s - o}{t}\right)\cdot\left(\frac{\overline{v}\cdot r}{4}\cdot m - o\right)$. It is illustrated by the dark yellow area between the horizontal axis and the per-work profit function left of the second vertical gridline.

The term $\frac{1}{2}\cdot(\overline{v}\cdot r - s - t\cdot\overline{N} - o)\cdot\left(\overline{N} - \frac{\overline{v}\cdot r - s - o}{t}\right)$ can be interpreted as the triangle located below the horizontal axis. The vertical leg ranges from the horizontal axis to the profits of the right holder who uploads the work with the number $\overline{N}$, i.e. $\overline{v}\cdot r - s - t\cdot\overline{N} - o$, and the horizontal leg from the second to the third vertical gridline. Note that the per-work profit function is fully located on or below the horizontal axis if $o \geq \frac{\overline{v}\cdot r}{4}\cdot m$. The aggregate profits then are the same as calculated above but the geometrical interpretation is slightly different.[41]

After further simplifications, right holders' aggregate profits if $m < 2$ (and presuming $s < \frac{v_{max}\cdot r\cdot t}{d\cdot r + 2\cdot t}$) can be summarised as follows:

$$\Pi_{2.2}^* = \begin{cases} \frac{1}{2}\cdot\left(\frac{4-m}{4}\cdot\frac{\overline{v}\cdot r}{t} - \frac{s}{t} + \tilde{N}\right)\cdot\left(\frac{\overline{v}\cdot r}{4}\cdot m - o\right), & \text{if } m \geq \tilde{m} \\ \left(\frac{\overline{v}\cdot r}{4}\cdot m - o\right)\cdot\overline{N} - \frac{\left(\overline{v}\cdot r\cdot(m-2)^2\right)^2}{32\cdot t\cdot m^2}, & \text{if } m < \tilde{m} \end{cases} \tag{3.56}$$

[41] The aggregate profits can be re-written as $\Pi_{2.2}^* = \left(\frac{\overline{v}\cdot r}{4}\cdot m - o\right)\cdot\overline{N} + \frac{1}{2}\cdot\left(\overline{v}\cdot r - s - t\cdot\overline{N} - \frac{\overline{v}\cdot r}{4}\cdot m\right)\cdot\left(\overline{N} - \left(\frac{4-m}{4}\cdot\frac{\overline{v}\cdot r}{t} - \frac{s}{t}\right)\right)$. Every right holder who uploads a work makes the (negative) profits of $\frac{\overline{v}\cdot r}{4}\cdot m - o$. This part of the aggregate profits is represented by a rectangle, limited in height by the horizontal axis and the per-work profit function and in width by the vertical axis and $\overline{N}$. Right holders who upload works with a number $N \geq \frac{4-m}{4}\cdot\frac{\overline{v}\cdot r}{t} - \frac{s}{t}$ earn additional negative profits, represented by a right-angled triangle with a vertical leg of the length $\overline{v}\cdot r - s - t\cdot\overline{N} - \frac{\overline{v}\cdot r}{4}\cdot m$, that is, the distance between $\overline{v}\cdot r - s - t\cdot\overline{N} - o$ and $\frac{\overline{v}\cdot r}{4}\cdot m - o$, and a horizontal leg of the length $\overline{N} - \left(\frac{4-m}{4}\cdot\frac{\overline{v}\cdot r}{t} - \frac{s}{t}\right)$, that is, the distance between $\overline{N}$ and $\frac{4-m}{4}\cdot\frac{\overline{v}\cdot r}{t} - \frac{s}{t}$.

3.5.3 *Effect of Automated Filtering on Right Holders' Profits and Availability of Works on Platform*

This section discusses the effect of automated filtering, assuming only one unlawful copier per work and uniform filtering. As explained in Sect. 3.5.2.2, the number of works uploaded does not differ between this specification and specification A.I. Likewise, as explained in Sect. 3.5.2.1, if $m \geq 2$, right holders' profits do not differ between this specification and specification A.I.

Figure 3.11 compares right holders' profits in scenario 2.2, specification A.II (dark yellow functions), for $m < 2$ with right holders' profits in scenario 1 (grey function) and scenario 2.1, specification II (dark blue functions). For scenario 2.2, two situations are considered: Coordinate system I assumes $m < \tilde{m}$ and coordinate system II $m \geq \tilde{m}$. Note that scenario 2.1 corresponds to filtering with an intensity of $m = 1$.

Right holders' profits increase as m increases. As in specification A.I, this increase in profits can in part be attributed to the fact that right holders need to upload fewer (if $m < \tilde{m}$) or no (if $m \geq \tilde{m}$) works for which uploading is overall unprofitable. In Fig. 3.11, the endpoints of the dark blue functions ($m = 1$) are therefore located to the right of the endpoints of the dark yellow functions ($m > 1$). Moreover, the endpoint of the dark yellow function in coordinate system I ($m < \tilde{m}$) is located to the right of the endpoint of the dark yellow function in coordinate system II ($m \geq \tilde{m}$). Once m has reached $\tilde{m}$, a further increase in m does not affect the number of works uploaded. The endpoint of the dark yellow function in coordinate system II therefore remains at $\tilde{N}$ if m is increased further.

In addition, right holders obtain higher per-work profits as m increases. The first reason for the increase in per-work profits is that—as in specification A.I—the views per work and thus per-work profits increase as the number of works uploaded decreases. Even if in each scenario a right holder only needs to upload one copy of his work to prevent the unlawful copier from uploading, the right holder's per-work profits in scenario 2.1 are therefore smaller than in scenario 2.2. Moreover, if $m < \tilde{m}$, the right holder's per-work profits in scenario 2.2 are smaller than in scenario 1. This explains why in coordinate system I the downward sloping part of the dark yellow function is located above the downward sloping part of the dark blue function but below the grey function. The described effect only materialises until m has reached $\tilde{m}$. From then on, a further increase in m does not affect the number of works uploaded and thus the number of views per work. In coordinate system II, the downward sloping part of the dark yellow function therefore overlaps with the grey function. Note further that since an increase in m up until $\tilde{m}$ results in an upward shift of the downward sloping part of the dark yellow function in coordinate system I, it also shifts the horizontal intercept of this function to the right. At the same time, the fourth vertical gridline in coordinate system I ($\overline{N}$) is shifted to the left. If $m = \tilde{m}$, the two thresholds converge at $\tilde{N}$. An increase in m beyond $\tilde{m}$ leaves the horizontal intercept and the number of works uploaded unaffected.

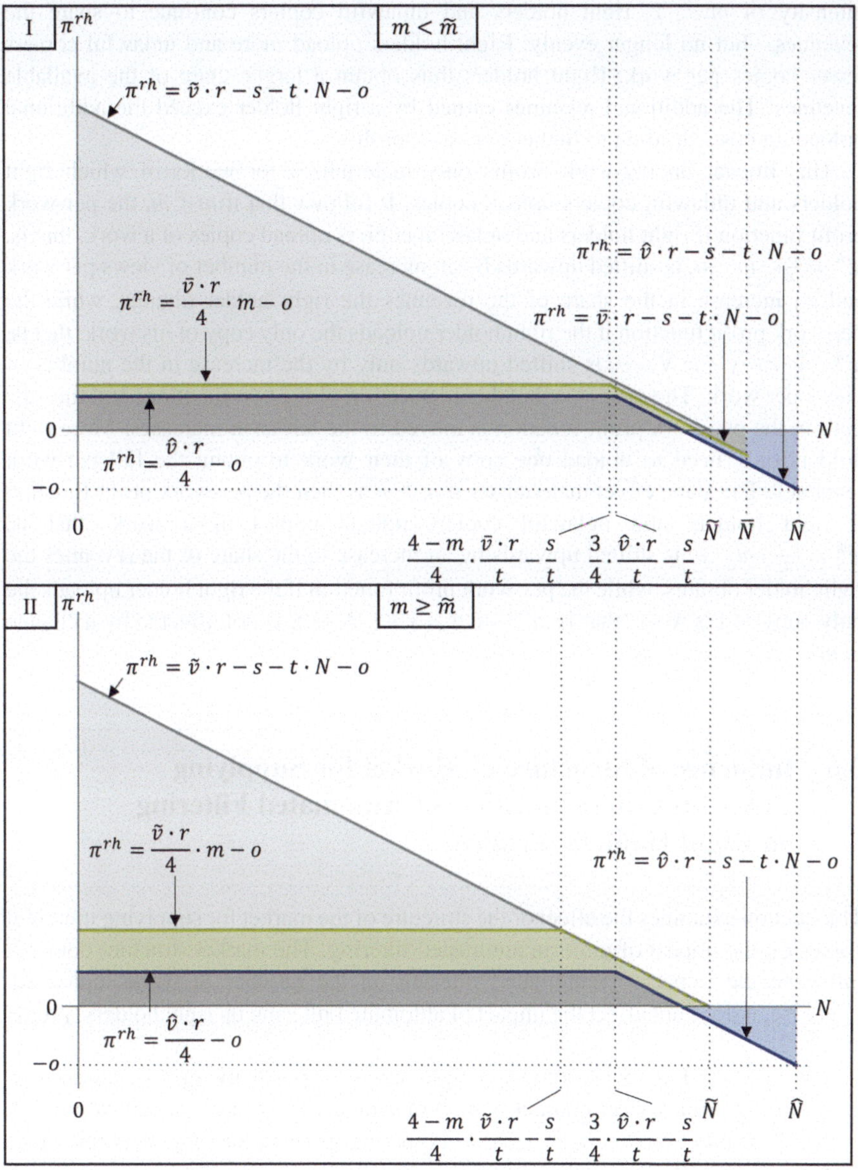

Fig. 3.11 Comparison of right holders' profits in scenario 1, scenario 2.1 (specification II) and scenario 2.2 (specification A.II), presuming $m < 2$, $s < \frac{v_{max} \cdot r \cdot I}{d \cdot r + 2 \cdot I}$, $o \leq v_{max} \cdot r - s$, and $o < \frac{\hat{v} \cdot r}{4}$

The second reason for the increase in per-work profits is that right holders earn a larger share of the per-work revenues as m increases. Recall that in scenario 2.1, right holders and unlawful copiers upload the same number of copies per work and thus evenly share the available revenues (Sect. 3.5.1.1). As the platform filters with an intensity of $m < 2$, right holders and unlawful copiers continue to share the revenues—but no longer evenly. Right holders upload more and unlawful copiers fewer copies per work. Right holders thus obtain a larger share of the available revenues. The additional revenues earned by a right holder exceed the additional uploading costs, leading to higher per-work profits.

This impact on per-work profits only materialises for works of which right holders and unlawful copiers upload copies. It follows that if $m < \tilde{m}$, the per-work profit function if right holders and unlawful copiers upload copies of a work, that is, $\pi^{rh} = \frac{\overline{v} \cdot r}{4} \cdot m - o$, is shifted upwards by an increase in the number of views per work and an increase in the share of the revenues the right holder obtains, while the per-work profit function if the right holder uploads the only copy of his work, that is, $\pi^{rh} = \overline{v} \cdot r - s - t \cdot N - o$, is shifted upwards only by the increase in the number of views per work. The upshot is that the intersection of the two functions and thus the kink in the per-work profit function is moved to the left as m increases: More right holders only need to upload one copy of their work to obtain the full per-work revenues. The same effect materialises if $m \geq \tilde{m}$ as then the per-work profit function if right holders and unlawful copiers upload copies of a work, that is, $\pi^{rh} = \frac{\tilde{v} \cdot r}{4} \cdot m - o$, is shifted upwards by an increase in the share of the revenues the right holder obtains, while the per-work profit function if the right holder uploads the only copy of his work, that is, $\pi^{rh} = \tilde{v} \cdot r - s - t \cdot N - o$, is not affected by a change in m.

3.6 Influence of Structure of Market for Supplying Unlawful Copies on Effect of Automated Filtering on Right Holders' Profits

This section examines the effect of the structure of the market for supplying unlawful copies on the impact of uniform automated filtering. The market structure does not influence the impact of automated filtering on the number of works uploaded. Likewise, it does not affect the impact of automated filtering on right holders' profits if $m \geq 2$.

For $m < 2$, Fig. 3.12 compares right holders' per-work profit functions in scenario 2.2 with perfect competition among unlawful copiers (specification A.I, light yellow function) and with a per-work monopoly on uploading unlawful copies (specification A.II, dark yellow function). It only displays right holders' per-work profit functions for $m \geq \tilde{m}$ as a comparison for $m < \tilde{m}$ would follow the same rationale and thus add no insights.

If the market for supplying unlawful copies is perfectly competitive, a right holder anticipates that unlawful copiers would collectively upload until the maximal number of copies they can upload of the right holder's work without their total uploading costs exceeding the per-work revenues is uploaded. The right holder therefore uploads all these copies himself. If a right holder is only confronted with one

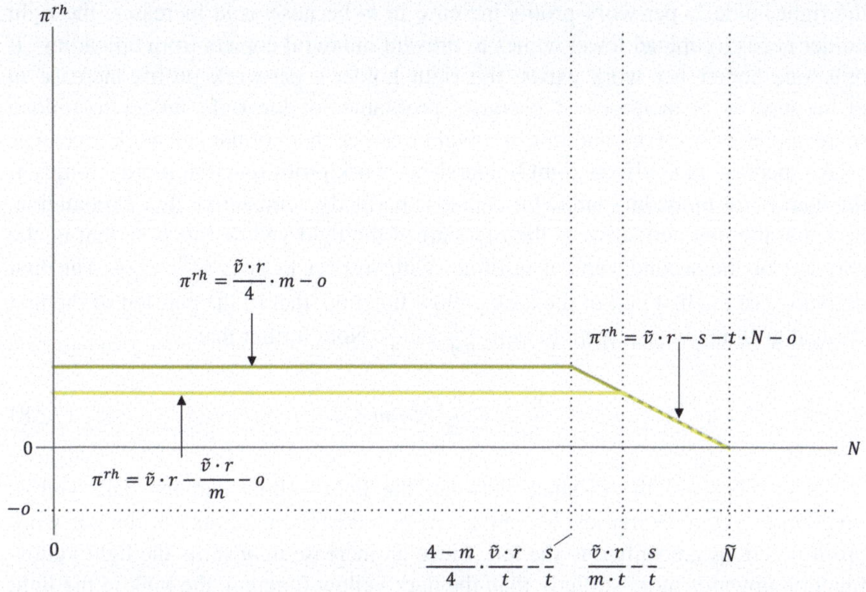

Fig. 3.12 Comparison of right holders' profits in scenario 2.2 (specification A.I) and scenario 2.2 (specification A.II), presuming $\tilde{m}\leq m<2$ and $s<\frac{v_{max}\cdot r\cdot t}{d\cdot r+2\cdot t}$

unlawful copier, the unlawful copier's marginal profits from uploading copies are decreasing (Sect. 3.5.1.1). The right holder thus anticipates that the unlawful copier does not necessarily upload until the maximal number of copies she can upload of the right holder's work without her total uploading costs exceeding the per-work revenues is uploaded. By uploading $\frac{\tilde{v}\cdot r\cdot m}{4\cdot(s+t\cdot N)}$ instead of $\frac{\tilde{v}\cdot r}{m\cdot(s+t\cdot N)}$ copies, the right holder spends $\frac{\tilde{v}\cdot r\cdot m}{4}$ instead of $\frac{\tilde{v}\cdot r}{m}$ on uploading. At the same time, he obtains revenues of $\frac{\tilde{v}\cdot r\cdot m}{2}$ instead of $\tilde{v}\cdot r$.[42] The right holder chooses to upload $\frac{\tilde{v}\cdot r\cdot m}{4\cdot(s+t\cdot N)}$ copies as

$$\frac{\tilde{v}\cdot r\cdot m}{2}-\frac{\tilde{v}\cdot r\cdot m}{4}\geq\tilde{v}\cdot r-\frac{\tilde{v}\cdot r}{m}\Leftrightarrow(m-2)^2\geq 0 \tag{3.57}$$

If the right holder is only confronted with one unlawful copier, he can thus earn larger profits than if the market for uploading unlawful copies is perfectly competitive. As m increases, both functions are shifted upwards. However, the reasons for the upward shifts differ. In the case of perfect competition among unlawful copiers,

[42] From Sect. 3.5.2.1, we know that if the right holder uploads $\frac{\tilde{v}\cdot r\cdot m}{4\cdot(s+t\cdot N)}$ copies, the unlawful copier uploads $\frac{\tilde{v}\cdot r\cdot(2\cdot(s+t\cdot N)-m\cdot(s+t\cdot N))}{4\cdot(s+t\cdot N)^2}=\frac{\tilde{v}\cdot r\cdot(2-m)}{4\cdot(s+t\cdot N)}$ copies. The right holder then earns revenues of $\frac{\tilde{v}\cdot r}{\frac{\tilde{v}\cdot r\cdot m}{4\cdot(s+t\cdot N)}+\frac{\tilde{v}\cdot r\cdot(2-m)}{4\cdot(s+t\cdot N)}}\cdot\frac{\tilde{v}\cdot r\cdot m}{4\cdot(s+t\cdot N)}=\frac{\tilde{v}\cdot r\cdot m}{2}$. If the right holder uploads $\frac{\tilde{v}\cdot r}{m\cdot(s+t\cdot N)}$ copies, the unlawful copier uploads 0 copies. The right holder then earns the full per-work revenues of $\tilde{v}\cdot r$.

the right holder's per-work profits increase in m because as m increases, the right holder needs to upload fewer copies to prevent unlawful copiers from uploading. If only one copier per work exists, the right holder's per-work profits increase in m because as m increases, it becomes profitable for the right holder to upload more copies of his work and thus to obtain a larger share of the per-work revenues.

An increase in m affects right holders' per-work profit function more strongly if the market for uploading unlawful copies is perfectly competitive. For explanation, note that the first derivative of the first part of the light yellow function, that is, the part left of the second vertical gridline, with respect to m is $\frac{\Delta\pi^{rh}}{\Delta m} = \frac{\tilde{v} \cdot r}{m^2}$. The first derivative of the first part of the dark yellow function, that is, the part left of the first vertical gridline, with respect to m is $\frac{\Delta\pi^{rh}}{\Delta m} = \frac{\tilde{v} \cdot r}{4}$. Note further that

$$\frac{\tilde{v} \cdot r}{m^2} > \frac{\tilde{v} \cdot r}{4} \Leftrightarrow m < 2 \tag{3.58}$$

As m increases, the distance between the light yellow and the dark yellow function therefore decreases. Moreover, as m increases, the kinks in the per-work profit functions are shifted to the left. Since an increase in m shifts the light yellow function upwards more strongly than the dark yellow function, the kink in the light yellow function also moves more strongly to the left. As a result, the part in which the functions overlap, which is indicated by the dashed line, becomes larger.

Once $m = 2$, the functions are identical. Perfect competition among unlawful copiers and one unlawful copier per work then leads to the same aggregate profits. These insights lead to the following proposition:

Proposition 3.7
If a right holder only competes with one unlawful copier, automated filtering increases his profits as he lets unlawful copiers upload fewer or—once the filtering intensity reaches a critical threshold (here: $m = 2$)—no copies of his work and thus obtains higher or the full per-work revenues.

3.7 Variation of Key Assumptions

This section reflects on the implications of varying three important assumptions that have been made in the above analysis: uploading a work to a platform has a negative effect on the right holder's off-platform profits (Sect. 3.7.1), the number of existing works is independent of the profits right holders obtain through the platform (Sect. 3.7.2), and the platform filters uniformly (Sect. 3.7.3).

3.7.1 *Overall Positive Effect of On-Platform Availability of Right Holder's Work on His Off-Platform Profits*

Uploading a work to a platform has an ambiguous effect on the right holder's off-platform profits (Sect. 3.2.3.1). The analysis above presumed—as appears most plausible—an overall negative effect. Assuming instead an overall positive effect has qualitatively the same impact on right holders' per-work profits as decreasing o in the analysis above: Per-work profit functions are shifted upwards; the slopes are not affected.

In terms of the number of works uploaded, two observations can be made. First, some right holders who cannot upload profitably if the effect of uploading a work to a platform on the right holder's off-platform profits is overall negative can upload profitably if the effect is overall positive. Second, an overall positive effect implies that right holders' per-work profits exceed unlawful copiers' per-work profits even if the platform does not filter. Right holders can thus upload more works profitably than unlawful copiers can. It follows that neither the presence of unlawful copiers nor automated filtering affects the number of works uploaded. Regardless of the specification and scenario, all and only those right holders upload their works who can do so profitably.

Since an overall positive effect of uploading a work to a platform on off-platform profits shifts right holders' per-work profit functions upwards, right holders earn higher aggregate profits than if the effect is overall negative. Nevertheless, the presence of unlawful copiers decreases right holders' aggregate profits. The competition among right holders and unlawful copiers for views is not affected by the assumption on the sign of the effect of uploading a work to a platform on off-platform profits. Automated filtering can thus still be employed to increase right holders' profits by providing them with an advantage over unlawful copiers when competing for views.

3.7.2 *Positive Effect of Increase in Right Holders' Aggregate Profits on Number of Works Created*

This section considers the implications of assuming a positive effect of an increase in right holders' aggregate profits on the number of works created. While it is unclear to what extent right holders' profits influence the production of creative content, some positive effect can be assumed (Sect. 2.1).

From above, we know that—regardless of the specification—the presence of unlawful copiers decreases right holders' aggregate profits and that automated filtering mitigates or even eliminates this effect. It follows that

$$\Pi_1^* \geq \Pi_{2.2}^* > \Pi_{2.1}^* \tag{3.59}$$

Table 3.2 Number of works uploaded if t decreases as Π increases, presuming uniform filtering

		N_1^*	$N_{2.1}^*$	$N_{2.2}^*$
$-o$	$m<\tilde{m}$	$\frac{v_{max}\cdot r-s-o}{d\cdot r+t_1}$	$\frac{v_{max}\cdot r-s}{d\cdot r+t_{2.1}}$	$\frac{v_{max}\cdot r-m\cdot s}{d\cdot r+m\cdot t_{2.2}}$
	$m\geq\tilde{m}$			$\frac{v_{max}\cdot r-s-o}{d\cdot r+t_{2.2}}$
$+o$		$\frac{v_{max}\cdot r-s+o}{d\cdot r+t_1}$	$\frac{v_{max}\cdot r-s+o}{d\cdot r+t_{2.1}}$	$\frac{v_{max}\cdot r-s+o}{d\cdot r+t_{2.2}}$

Recall that right holders' per-copy uploading costs increase with a slope of t as N increases because more non-normalised works need to be uploaded to reach one normalised work (Sect. 3.2.3.1). If more works exist, this effect remains, but costs increase with a slower pace, implying a smaller t. If higher aggregate profits imply that more works are produced, the relative size of t in the different scenarios can be deduced from the relative size of aggregate profits:[43]

$$t_1 \leq t_{2.2} < t_{2.1} \tag{3.60}$$

Table 3.2 displays the number of works uploaded in the three scenarios. The first two lines consider the case that uploading a work to a platform has an overall negative effect on off-platform profits ('$-o$'). The last line shows the number of works uploaded if uploading a work to a platform has an overall positive effect on off-platform profits ('$+o$').

Suppose first that uploading a work to a platform has an overall negative effect on off-platform profits ('$-o$'). From above, we know that in scenario 1, right holders only upload works they can upload profitably. In scenario 2.1, they upload all works associated with per-work profits of $\pi^{rh} \geq -o$. This effect is represented by the larger numerator of $N_{2.1}^*$ compared to N_1^*. If the number of works produced decreases as right holders' aggregate profits decrease, a second effect materialises: The number of works associated with per-work profits of $\pi^{rh} \geq -o$ is smaller in scenario 2.1 than in scenario 1. This effect is represented by the larger denominator of $N_{2.1}^*$ compared to N_1^*. The two effects run in opposite directions, leading to an ambiguous effect of the presence of unlawful copiers on the number of works uploaded.

If the platform filters, instead of uploading all works associated with per-work profits of $\pi^{rh} \geq -o$, right holders require minimal per-work profits located in the region $-o < \pi^{rh} \leq 0$ to upload their works. This effect is represented by the smaller numerators of $N_{2.2}^*$ compared to $N_{2.1}^*$. If the platform filters with an intensity of $m<\tilde{m}$, it is reinforced by the factor m in the denominator of $N_{2.2}^*$. Automated filtering increases right holders' aggregate profits. If higher aggregate profits lead to a larger number of works produced, in scenario 2.2, the number of works

[43] It is assumed that creators cannot predict the popularity of the work they are about to create and that profits thus influence the production of works of all levels of popularity in the same way. The cost function thus remains linear.

associated with per-work profits that exceed the threshold of π^{rh} that is critical for right holders to upload is larger than the number of works that would exceed the same threshold in scenario 2.1. This effect is represented by the change in the factor t from $t_{2.1}$ in the denominator of $N^*_{2.1}$ to $t_{2.2}$ in the denominator of $N^*_{2.2}$. As above, the two effects run in opposite directions, leading to an ambiguous effect of automated filtering on the number of works uploaded.

If $m \geq \tilde{m}$, right holders upload only works they can upload profitably. Unless the filtering intensity applied by the platform ensures that right holders earn the same aggregate profits as in scenario 1, the resulting higher level of t compared to scenario 1 leads to a larger denominator and thus a smaller number of works uploaded.

Suppose next that the upload of a work has an overall positive effect on the right holder's off-platform profits ('+o'). Right holders then upload all works associated with non-negative per-work profits, regardless of whether unlawful copiers are present and of whether the platform filters. As above, the presence of unlawful copiers leads to a decrease in right holders' aggregate profits, implying a larger t. The presence of unlawful copiers therefore increases the denominator and thus reduces the number of works uploaded. Automated filtering has the opposite effects.

3.7.3 Popularity-Based Filtering

Instead of filtering uniformly, a platform can filter more rigorously, the more popular a work is (Sect. 3.2.2). The assumption of popularity-based filtering requires more complex calculations but does not lead to qualitatively different results in terms of the effect of automated filtering on right holders' profits and the number of works uploaded. The analysis under this assumption is therefore placed in Appendix 1.

Nevertheless, as a policymaker can encourage—or at least refrain from discouraging—the use of a filtering strategy[44] and as a higher total filtering intensity leads to higher costs associated with erroneous blockings of lawful upload attempts,[45] it is insightful to investigate which strategy requires a lower total filtering intensity. The total filtering intensity is defined as the sum of unlawful copiers' additional per-copy uploading costs for works with a number $N \leq \hat{N}$.

The total filtering intensity required depends on the policy objective pursued. Comparing the required filtering intensities presupposes a precise definition of the policy objective. Two conceivable policy objectives that are relevant for research

[44] An example of a policy that encourages popularity-based filtering is the award of actual damages to right holders for unlawful content that a platform hosts (Sect. 3.2.2). An example of a policy that encourages uniform filtering is imposing a uniform standard of care that platforms must meet to escape liability.

[45] As explained in Sect. 3.2.3.3, the analysis above presumed that no erroneous blockings occur. When considering the relevance of the total filtering intensity, it is, however, important to acknowledge that automated filters produce false positives.

question 1 can be precisely defined: maximisation of the number of works uploaded to a platform and maximisation of right holders' aggregate profits.

The effect of filtering on the number of works uploaded depends on the sign and the size of the off-platform losses and on the extent to which increased aggregate profits translate into more content created. Given the uncertainties on these aspects, the total filtering intensities that maximise the number of works uploaded cannot be determined. The exception is a case in which the on-platform availability of a work increases the right holder's off-platform profits. The maximal number of works produced, which is achieved if right holders earn maximal aggregate profits, then leads to the maximal number of works uploaded. Based on these considerations, this section focuses on comparing the minimal filtering intensities needed to maximise right holders' aggregate profits.

The maximal aggregate profits automated filtering can achieve for right holders are the profits right holders would obtain in the absence of unlawful copiers. Right holders earn the same aggregate profits as if unlawful copiers were absent if no right holder is exposed to competition from unlawful copiers. From Sect. 3.4.2.3, we know that if the platform filters uniformly, this is the case if $m \geq \frac{\tilde{v} \cdot r}{s}$. The minimal filtering intensity needed to ensure that right holders earn the same aggregate profits as if unlawful copiers were absent therefore is $m = \frac{\tilde{v} \cdot r}{s}$. Unlawful copiers' per-copy uploading cost function then is

$$c^{co} = \frac{\tilde{v} \cdot r}{s} \cdot (s + t \cdot N) = \tilde{v} \cdot r + \frac{\tilde{v} \cdot r}{s} \cdot t \cdot N \qquad (3.61)$$

With respect to popularity-based filtering, it is assumed that the impact of automated filtering, that is, the difference between a right holder's and unlawful copiers' costs of uploading a copy of a non-normalised work, is proportional to a non-normalised work's popularity. Proportionality presupposes a linear relationship and a vertical intercept of 0. Presuming a linear relationship between the impact of automated filtering and the non-normalised work's popularity simplifies the analysis. Moreover, there does not appear to be a reason for a platform to opt for a smaller or larger influence of popularity on the impact of automated filtering for lower than for higher levels of popularity. Presuming a vertical intercept of 0 means that the platform filters purely based on popularity. Alternatively, it is conceivable that a platform filters in such a way that unlawful copiers' costs of uploading copies of non-normalised works are increased partially independent of popularity and partially as a function of popularity. To keep the analysis focused, such mixed approaches are excluded from the scope of analysis.

The upshot of presuming that the impact of automated filtering is proportional to a non-normalised work's popularity is that as works are normalised with respect to popularity, the impact of automated filtering on unlawful copiers' uploading costs is the same for every normalised work.[46] It follows that a right holder's and unlawful

[46] For the purpose of explanation, suppose that right holders' costs of uploading copies of non-normalised works are $\check{c}$. Suppose further that the platform filters in such a way that unlawful

copiers' uploading costs of a copy of a normalised work as a function of N only differ with respect to the vertical intercept. Instead of multiplying the right holder's uploading costs of a copy of a normalised work by m, for popularity-based filtering a different vertical intercept for unlawful copiers' marginal uploading cost function is introduced: s^{co}, with $s^{co} > s$. Unlawful copiers' costs of uploading a copy of a normalised work thus are $c^{co} = s^{co} + t \cdot N$.

From Sect. 3.4.2.1, we know that right holders who own works that are associated with uploading costs for unlawful copiers of $c^{co} \leq v_{2.2}^{*} \cdot r$ are exposed to competition from unlawful copiers. Inserting $c^{co} = s^{co} + t \cdot N$ and solving for N yields

$$s^{co} + t \cdot N \leq v_{2.2}^{*} \cdot r \Leftrightarrow N \leq \frac{v_{2.2}^{*} \cdot r - s^{co}}{t} \tag{3.62}$$

It follows that the last right holder who is exposed to competition from unlawful copiers is the right holder who owns the work with the number $\frac{v_{2.2}^{*} \cdot r - s^{co}}{t}$. Therefore, no right holder is exposed to competition from unlawful copiers if:

$$\frac{v_{2.2}^{*} \cdot r - s^{co}}{t} \leq 0 \Leftrightarrow s^{co} \geq v_{2.2}^{*} \cdot r \tag{3.63}$$

The last right holder who uploads his work then is the right holder who owns the work with the number $\tilde{N}$, leading to a number of views per work of $\tilde{v}$. It follows that the minimal filtering intensity needed to ensure that right holders earn the same profits as in the absence of unlawful copiers is $s^{co} = \tilde{v} \cdot r$, resulting in a per-copy uploading cost function of $c^{co} = \tilde{v} \cdot r + t \cdot N$.

Unlawful copiers' per-copy uploading cost functions under uniform filtering and under popularity-based filtering have the same vertical intercept but different slopes. The vertical intercept of $\tilde{v} \cdot r$ ensures that no unlawful copier would upload a copy of the normalised work with the most popular underlying non-normalised work.

Presuming $s < \tilde{v} \cdot r$,[47] the slope of unlawful copiers' per-copy uploading cost function for uniform filtering, namely, $\frac{\tilde{v} \cdot r}{s} \cdot t$, exceeds the slope of unlawful copiers'

copiers' costs of uploading the work with the benchmark level of popularity are $\check{c} + g$, with $g > 0$. As a platform adapts the filtering intensity in such a way that the difference between a right holder's and unlawful copiers' costs of uploading a copy of a non-normalised work is proportional to the non-normalised work's popularity, a copy of a non-normalised work that is $h > 0$ times as popular as the benchmark non-normalised work is associated with uploading costs of $\check{c} + h \cdot g$ for unlawful copiers. As works are normalised with respect to popularity, the costs of uploading a copy of a normalised work for the right holder who owns the non-normalised work that is h times as popular as the benchmark non-normalised work are $\frac{\check{c}}{h}$. For an unlawful copier, the costs of uploading a copy of this normalised work are $\frac{\check{c}+h \cdot g}{h}$. The difference between unlawful copiers' and the right holder's costs of uploading a copy of a normalised work is $\frac{\check{c}+h \cdot g}{h} - \frac{\check{c}}{h} = g$. This difference is independent of h. That is, the difference between a right holder's and unlawful copiers' costs of uploading a copy of a normalised work is independent of the underlying non-normalised work's popularity.

[47] If $s \geq \tilde{v} \cdot r$, neither unlawful copiers nor right holders upload works.

per-copy uploading cost function for popularity-based filtering, namely, t. It follows that the total filtering intensity needed to ensure that right holders earn the same profits as in the absence of unlawful copiers is smaller if the platform filters based on popularity than if it filters uniformly.

Intuitively, this can be explained as follows: If the platform filters uniformly, it must apply the filtering intensity that ensures that unlawful copiers would not upload a copy of the most popular work to all works. If the platform filters based on popularity, this filtering intensity is only applied to the most popular work, and a lower filtering intensity is applied to less popular works.

These insights lead to the following proposition:

Proposition 3.8
If the filtering intensity increases in the popularity of the copied-from work, the total filtering intensity required to maximise right holders' aggregate profits is lower than if it does not.

3.8 Summary and Discussion of Main Findings

This section summarises and discusses the main findings obtained in the above analysis, that is, findings regarding the mechanism through which automated filtering increases right holders' profits (Sect. 3.8.1), regarding the effect of automated filtering on the availability of works on a platform (Sect. 3.8.2), regarding the impact of the concentration of the market for uploading unlawful copies (Sect. 3.8.3), regarding the benefits of popularity-based filtering (Sect. 3.8.4), and regarding the plurality of reasons for the absence of unlawful uploads on a platform (Sect. 3.8.5).

3.8.1 Mechanism Through Which Automated Filtering Increases Right Holders' Profits

The model shows that without automated filtering, the presence of unlawful copiers reduces right holders' profits. The first reason is that if the on-platform availability of a work decreases the right holder's off-platform profits, the presence of unlawful copiers induces right holders to upload some works they cannot upload profitably (proposition 3.1). The second reason is that right holders incur costs to prevent unlawful copiers from uploading or lose some of the available per-work revenues to unlawful uploaders (propositions 3.2 and 3.5). By providing right holders with a competitive advantage vis-à-vis unlawful copiers, automated filtering mitigates or even eliminates both the first (proposition 3.3) and the second (propositions 3.4 and 3.7) effect. It thereby increases right holders' profits.

The result that automated filtering increases right holders' profits is in line with the existing literature, which is reviewed in Sect. 3.1. However, the channel explored in the literature so far requires the blocking of all unlawful upload attempts to improve right holders' profits. By contrast, the model demonstrates that by creating a competitive advantage for right holders, a filter that does not block all unlawful upload attempts can nevertheless increase right holders' profits or even ensure that they earn the same profits as if unlawful copiers were absent. In other words, more cautiously designed filters can still further the goal of incentivising content creation.

This finding is crucial as—unlike presumed in the analysis above—in reality automated filters produce false positives, which are associated with net social costs. A more cautiously designed filter is less likely to produce false positives. Different levels of strictness of a filter entail different balances between right holders' profits and the risk of false positives. The upshot is that the use of automated filters is not an either-or decision. This insight is an important theoretical underpinning for the analysis of how automated filters should be designed in Chap. 4.

It is hard to conceive how the social costs and benefits of false negatives and positives can be quantified. However, even if one takes the view that currently used filters produce so many false positives that the social costs they entail outweigh the benefits, this allegation does not imply that no filters should be used. It is still possible that a design of automated filtering exists that leads to net social benefits.

3.8.2 *Effect of Automated Filtering on Availability of Works*

The model demonstrates that the presence of unlawful copiers has an ambiguous effect on the availability of works on a platform if the on-platform availability of a work decreases the right holder's off-platform profits. On the one hand, as the presence of unlawful copiers reduces right holders' aggregate profits, it also leads to a lower number of works created and thus uploaded.

On the other hand, the presence of unlawful copiers induces right holders to upload works they would not upload in the absence of unlawful copiers, namely, works for which the upload of the first copy is associated with non-negative on-platform profits that fall below the off-platform losses (proposition 3.1). In such cases, right holders anticipate that if they do not upload, unlawful copiers will do so instead. Right holders thus incur off-platform losses regardless of whether they upload. They then choose to upload to at least collect on-platform profits.

Which of these opposing effects on the number of works uploaded prevails depends on the magnitude of off-platform losses and on the strength of the effect of profits on content creation.

Automated filtering mitigates or even nullifies both effects. Since right holders' aggregate profits increase, more works are created and therefore uploaded. At the same time, if automated filtering increases unlawful copiers' costs of uploading a copy of a work beyond the per-work revenues, the right holder regains the choice on whether his work becomes available on the platform. Right holders therefore need to upload fewer works they cannot upload profitably (proposition 3.3).

This effect of automated filtering on right holders' incentives to upload existing works has not yet been explored in the literature, which is reviewed in Sect. 3.1. While it remains unclear whether filtering overall leads to fewer or more works on a platform, the identified effect must be considered when discussing the social desirability of filtering. As viewers can access works on platforms at low transaction costs, the availability of works on platforms contributes to wider access. Therefore, the social costs of filtering depend on how it affects the availability of works on a platform. Likewise, the identified effect must be considered when reflecting on platforms' private costs of filtering because the attractiveness of a platform to viewers depends on the variety of works it displays.

Proposition 3.3 further highlights a limitation of the identified effect that is relevant when reflecting on the social and private costs of increasing the filtering intensity: If automated filtering ensures that unlawful copiers do not upload a copy of the most popular work that a right holder cannot upload profitably, right holders upload the same number of works as if no unlawful copiers existed. A further increase in the filtering intensity then does not affect the number of existing works right holders upload. At the same time, as an increase in the filtering intensity still increases right holders' aggregate profits, it leads to the creation and thus the upload of more works. An increase in the filtering intensity beyond the described threshold therefore unambiguously increases the number of works uploaded to the platform.

3.8.3 Impact of Concentration of Market for Uploading Unlawful Copies

The analysis shows that the structure of the market for uploading unlawful copies influences the strategy right holders pursue in the competition with unlawful copiers. The market structure thereby also affects their profits.

If the market for supplying unlawful copies is perfectly competitive, right holders fully prevent unlawful copiers from uploading. Without automated filtering, this requires them to spend so much on uploading that the per-work revenues are entirely consumed by uploading costs (proposition 3.2), leading to on-platform profits of zero. Presuming that the on-platform availability of a work decreases the right holder's off-platform profits, the existence of the platform therefore affects right holders' profits overall in a negative way. If the platform filters, right holders need to spend less to obtain the full per-work revenues (proposition 3.4). They therefore earn positive on-platform profits.

By contrast, if a right holder only competes with one unlawful copier, without automated filtering, he maximises profits by tolerating some unlawful uploads (proposition 3.5). An equilibrium emerges in which the right holder and the unlawful copier each spend a quarter of the per-work revenues on uploading and therefore evenly share the per-work revenues. As not all of the revenues right holders obtain are consumed by uploading costs, right holders make positive on-platform profits. They benefit from having a platform that does not filter compared to no platform at all if the off-platform losses from uploading works are sufficiently small relative to the revenues that can be obtained through the platform (proposition 3.6).

Automated filtering induces right holders to tolerate fewer unlawful uploads. They then earn higher profits. As long as automated filtering has not doubled unlawful copiers' uploading costs, right holders still tolerate some unlawful uploads and earn larger profits than if the market for uploading unlawful copies were perfectly competitive. If unlawful copiers' uploading costs are at least twice as high as right holders' uploading costs, right holders fully prevent unlawful copiers from uploading and thus behave—and earn the same profits—as if they competed with many unlawful copiers (proposition 3.7).

In sum, a more concentrated market enables right holders to earn higher profits if the platform does not filter or if it filters with an intensity that falls below the described threshold. This effect of the structure of the market for supplying unlawful copies on right holders' profits has not yet been considered in the literature.

It is important as—in addition to filtering—platforms may adopt other measures to disincentivise unlawful uploading, for example, sanctioning unlawful uploaders[48] and awareness campaigns.[49] While these measures can reduce incentives to upload unlawfully, they cannot ensure that no unlawful uploads of a work appear on a platform. Based on the described effect, if at most a rather cautious filter is used, merely reducing the number of people who are willing to upload a work can nevertheless benefit right holders. In other words, the observation that unlawful uploads are made despite a measure to deter them does not suffice to discard the measure as ineffective. Counterintuitively, if the platform employs a lenient filter, the absence of unlawful uploads may even indicate that other measures to deter unlawful uploading have been unsuccessful as it may show that the right holder

[48] Platforms can take legal actions against unlawful uploaders based on violations of their terms and conditions or introduce internal sanctioning mechanisms. Many platforms apply so-called three-strikes policies (e.g. Google, n.d., pt. Copyright strike basics; SoundCloud, n.d., pt. How do copyright strikes work?; Vimeo, 2022). Upon notification for takedown by a right holder, an uploader gets a strike. The first two strikes may already be associated with sanctions (e.g. an inability to monetise content). The third strike usually leads to an account termination.

[49] Informing users about copyright law may reduce unlawful uploads because not being aware of what copyright law prohibits is one reason to upload unlawful content. Article 17(9), fourth subparagraph of the Copyright in the DSM Directive (2019), stipulates that platforms 'shall inform their users in their terms and conditions that they can use works and other subject matter under exceptions or limitations to copyright and related rights provided for in Union law'. On YouTube, upon receiving the first strike, an uploader needs to attend YouTube's 'copyright school', comprising a 5-min video and a four-question multiple choice test on the basics of copyright law and the relevant processes at YouTube (Google, n.d., pt. Copyright strike basics). Most platforms also provide general information on copyright law (e.g. Google, n.d., pt. What is copyright?; Instagram, n.d.; SoundCloud, n.d., pt. How do I avoid infringing someone's copyright?; Twitch, n.d.). Moreover, stigmatising infringements may help to reduce unlawful uploads (Hill, 2007, p. 23).

competes with many unlawful copiers and therefore fully prevents them from uploading.

3.8.4 Benefits of Popularity-Based Filtering

Given the goal of copyright policy to incentivise the production of creative content, a conceivable policy objective is to maximise right holders' profits, that is, to ensure that right holders earn the same profits as if unlawful copiers were absent. Automated filtering can achieve this objective regardless of whether a platform applies the same filtering intensity to every upload or varies the intensity depending on the popularity of the copied-from work. However, as filtering produces net social costs in the form of false positives, it is desirable to maximise right holders' profits with the lowest possible total filtering intensity. It has not yet been examined in the literature which of the two filtering strategies performs better in this regard.

The analysis shows that popularity-based filtering requires a lower total filtering intensity to maximise right holders' profits than uniform filtering (proposition 3.8). The reason is that if the platform filters uniformly, it must apply the filtering intensity that ensures that unlawful copiers would not upload a copy of the most popular work to all works. By contrast, if the platform filters based on popularity, this filtering intensity is only applied to the most popular work, and a lower filtering intensity is applied to less popular works.

This result is relevant for the design of liability regimes. Stipulating exact rules on the strictness of filters that platforms must comply with to escape liability (e.g. similarity thresholds) would prevent platforms from differentiating between works. Likewise, a liability regime that requires platforms to pay statutory rather than actual damages would discourage them from differentiating based on popularity. Such policies would therefore limit platforms' leeway to design automated filtering in ways that reduce the total filtering intensity and therefore the risk of false positives.

3.8.5 Plurality of Reasons for Absence of Unlawful Uploads

To evaluate the effectiveness of platforms' efforts to protect right holders' interests, one may be tempted to look at the number of unlawful uploads available on platforms. However, the described mechanism suggests that this approach may be fallacious as an alternative explanation for the absence of unlawful uploads exists, which has not yet been explored in the literature.

Besides successful filtering, the absence of unlawful uploads can be the result of right holders' activities to pre-empt unlawful uploading (propositions 3.4 and 3.7). Right holders need to invest time and effort into pre-emptive activities. The presence of unlawful uploaders therefore reduces their profits even if no unlawful uploads are actually made.

This alternative explanation must be considered when designing empirical studies on automated filtering and when interpreting their results. It is particularly important as due to the reporting requirements in the Digital Services Act (2022) (Sect. 5.5.2.2) more empirical studies can be expected in the future.

The difficulty in terms of measuring the success of a filter further has implications for the design of legal rules on automated filtering. The analysis in Chap. 4 shows that for many important questions, conclusions on the efficient design of automated filtering cannot yet be drawn. The identified alternative explanation for the absence of unlawful uploads dampens the hope that empirical studies will be created in the future that allow for such conclusions. The upshot is that instead of seeking to prescribe performance targets or a specific design of automated filtering, a more promising approach is to rely on the distributed knowledge of the relevant actors. This consideration has implications for the specification of a standard of care for platforms. It is therefore important for the analysis in Sect. 5.3.2.2.

Appendix 1: Popularity-Based Filtering

So far we have assumed that a platform applies the same filtering intensity to every upload attempt. This appendix looks at a platform that makes the filtering intensity dependent on the popularity of the copied-from non-normalised work. As above, two assumptions on the structure of the market for uploading unlawful copies are considered: perfect competition (Sect. A.1) and a per-work monopoly (Sect. A.2). Section A.3 compares the results obtained under these two assumptions. Finally, Sect. A.4 reflects on the impact of assuming a positive effect of an increase in right holders' aggregate profits on the number of works created.

A.1 Perfect Competition Among Unlawful Copiers (Scenario 2.2, Specification B.I)

This section determines right holders' per-work profits (Sect. A.1.1), the number of works uploaded (Sect. A.1.2), and right holders' aggregate profits (Sect. A.1.3), presuming popularity-based filtering and perfect competition among unlawful copiers. Section A.1.4 discusses the effect of popularity-based filtering.

A.1.1 Right Holders' Per-Work Profits

Right holders' per-work profits as a function of c^{co} in the Stackelberg equilibrium are unaffected by the presumed filtering strategy. As explained in Sect. 3.7.3, under the assumption of popularity-based filtering, unlawful copiers' per-copy uploading cost function is $c^{co} = s^{co} + t \cdot N$. By inserting $c^{co} = s^{co} + t \cdot N$ and $c = s + t \cdot N$ into right holders' equilibrium per-work profits determined in Sect. 3.4.2.1, right holders' per-work profits can be transformed as follows:

$$\pi_{2.2}^{rh\,*} = \begin{cases} \frac{v_{2.2}^{*} \cdot r \cdot \left(s^{co} - s\right)}{s^{co} + t \cdot N} - o, & \text{if } N \leq \frac{v_{2.2}^{*} \cdot r - s^{co}}{t} \\ v_{2.2}^{*} \cdot r - s - t \cdot N - o, & \text{if } \frac{v_{2.2}^{*} \cdot r - s^{co}}{t} < N \leq \frac{v_{2.2}^{*} \cdot r - s - o}{t} \\ 0, & \text{if } N > \frac{v_{2.2}^{*} \cdot r - s^{co}}{t} \text{ and } N > \frac{v_{2.2}^{*} \cdot r - s - o}{t} \end{cases} \tag{3.64}$$

A.1.2 Number of Works Uploaded

Right holders can upload at least as many works profitably as unlawful copiers can if

$$\frac{v_{2.2}^{*} \cdot r - s - o}{t} \geq \frac{v_{2.2}^{*} \cdot r - s^{co}}{t} \Leftrightarrow s^{co} \geq s + o \tag{3.65}$$

For the purpose of explanation, recall that right holders' and unlawful copiers' per-work profits in scenario 2.2 differ in two regards. First, only right holders incur the off-platform losses. Since every normalised work entails the same off-platform losses, o only affects the vertical intercept of right holders' per-work profit function. As o increases, right holders' per-work profit function is shifted downwards, but the slope is unaffected. Second, automated filtering only increases unlawful copiers' uploading costs. Popularity-based filtering only affects the vertical intercept of unlawful copiers' per-work profit function. If $s^{co} = s + o$, the two effects have the same intensity. Right holders' and unlawful copiers' per-work profit functions are then identical. If $s^{co} > s + o$, right holders' per-work profit function is located above unlawful copiers' per-work profit function; if $s^{co} < s + o$, it is located below.

If $s^{co} \geq s + o$, the last right holder who uploads his work is the right holder who owns the work with the number $\frac{v_{2.2}^{*} \cdot r - s - o}{t}$. As explained in Sect. 3.3.1, right holders then upload $\tilde{N}$ works if $o \leq v_{max} \cdot r - s$.

If $s^{co} < s + o$, unlawful copiers can upload more works profitably than right holders. The last work a right holder uploads then is the work with the number $\frac{v_{2.2}^{*} \cdot r - s^{co}}{t}$. This work is thus assigned the number $N_{2.2}^{*}$. Inserting $v_{2.2}^{*} = v_{max} - d \cdot N_{2.2}^{*}$ into $N_{2.2}^{*} = \frac{v_{2.2}^{*} \cdot r - s^{co}}{t}$ yields

$$N_{2.2}^{*} = \frac{\left(v_{max} - d \cdot N_{2.2}^{*}\right) \cdot r - s^{co}}{t} \Leftrightarrow N_{2.2}^{*} = \frac{v_{max} \cdot r - s^{co}}{d \cdot r + t} \tag{3.66}$$

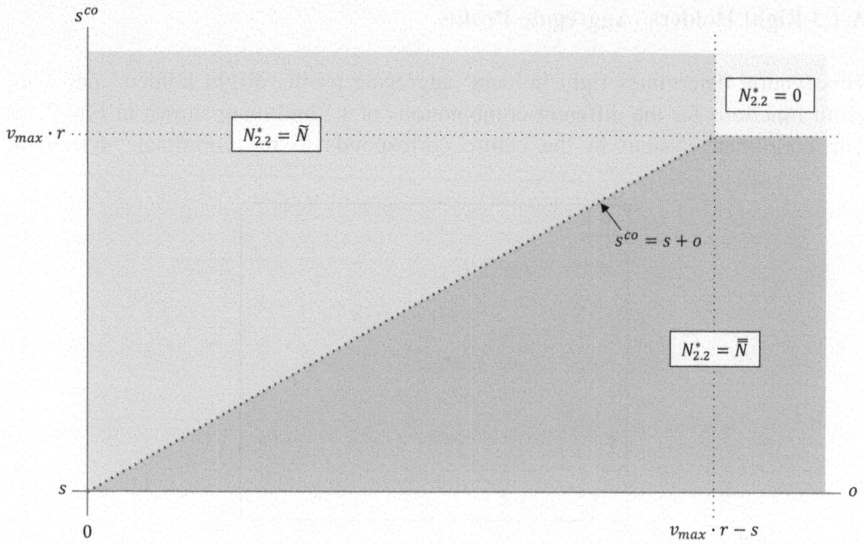

Fig. 3.13 Number of works uploaded for the different combinations of s^{co} and o in scenario 2.2 (specification B.I), presuming $s \leq v_{max} \cdot r$

Note that $N^*_{2.2} = \frac{v_{max} \cdot r - s^{co}}{d \cdot r + t}$ leads to a negative value of $N^*_{2.2}$ if

$$\frac{v_{max} \cdot r - s^{co}}{d \cdot r + t} < 0 \Leftrightarrow s^{co} > v_{max} \cdot r \tag{3.67}$$

To increase the clarity of the following explanations, from now on $\frac{v_{max} \cdot r - s^{co}}{d \cdot r + t}$ is referred to by $\overline{\overline{N}}$ and the number of views per work if $N^* = \overline{\overline{N}}$ by $\overline{\overline{v}}$.

Right holders upload $\overline{\overline{N}}$ works if $s^{co} \leq v_{max} \cdot r$ and $s^{co} < s + o$. If $s^{co} > v_{max} \cdot r$ and $o > v_{max} \cdot r - s$, even uploading the most popular work is unprofitable for the right holder and for unlawful copiers. Therefore, no works are uploaded.

The number of works uploaded for the different combinations of s^{co} and o is shown in Fig. 3.13. Note that $s + o = v_{max} \cdot r$ if $o = v_{max} \cdot r - s$. The reason is that if $o = v_{max} \cdot r - s$, only a hypothetical right holder whose normalised work is based on a hypothetical non-normalised work that is slightly more popular than the most popular non-normalised work could upload profitably and therefore $\tilde{N} = 0$. The upshot is that the threshold determining whether unlawful copiers can upload some works profitably ($s^{co} = v_{max} \cdot r$) must be equivalent to the threshold determining whether unlawful copiers can upload more works profitably than right holders can ($s^{co} = s + o$).

To summarise, right holders upload the following number of works:

$$N^*_{2.2} = \begin{cases} \tilde{N}, & \text{if } o \leq v_{max} \cdot r - s \text{ and } s^{co} \geq s + o \\ \overline{\overline{N}}, & \text{if } \left(\begin{matrix} (o \leq v_{max} \cdot r - s \text{ and } s^{co} < s + o) \text{ or} \\ (o > v_{max} \cdot r - s \text{ and } s^{co} \leq v_{max} \cdot r) \end{matrix} \right) \\ 0, & \text{if } o > v_{max} \cdot r - s \text{ and } s^{co} > v_{max} \cdot r \end{cases} \tag{3.68}$$

A.1.3 Right Holders' Aggregate Profits

This section determines right holders' aggregate profits. Right holders' per-work profit functions for the different combinations of s^{co} and o are shown in Fig. 3.14. The coordinate system in the centre corresponds to the coordinate system in

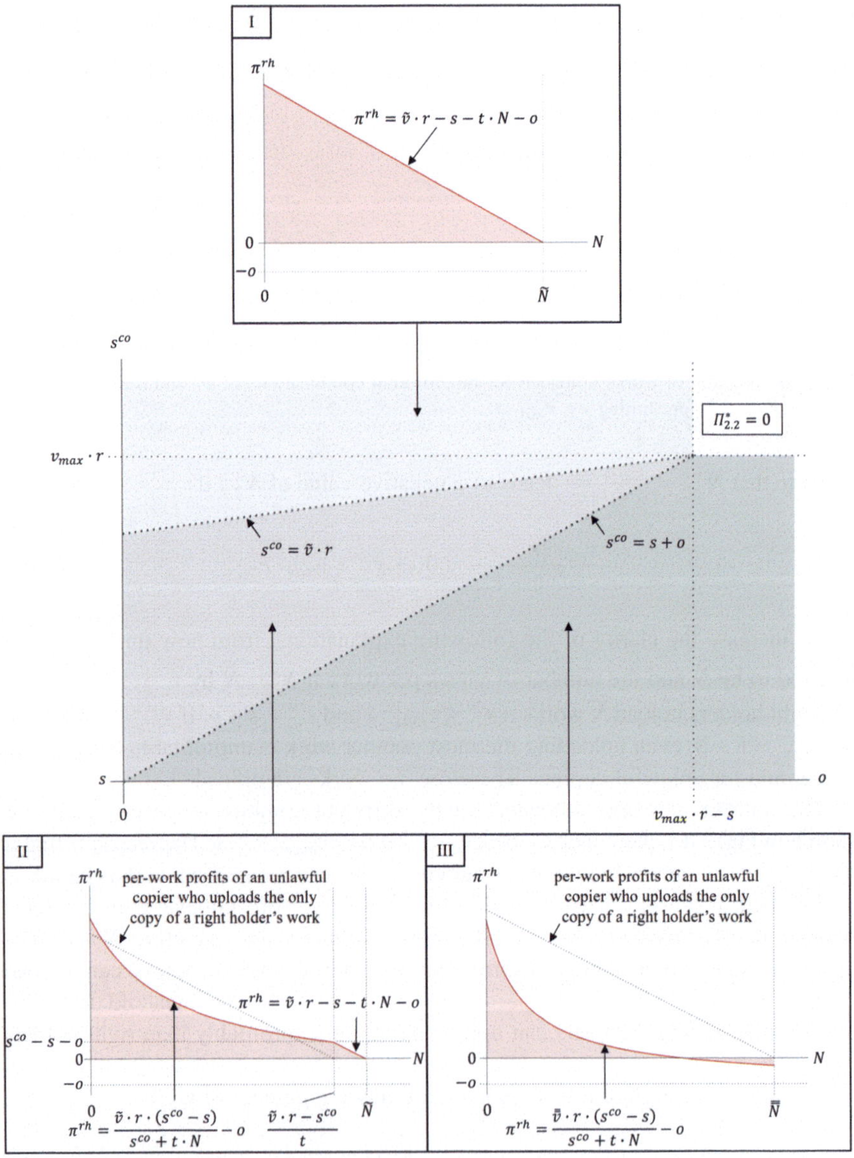

Fig. 3.14 Right holders' profits for the different combinations of s^{co} and o in scenario 2.2 (specification B.I), presuming $s \leq v_{max} \cdot r$

Fig. 3.13 but contains an additional threshold. When considering profits, the area in which right holders upload $\tilde{N}$ works must be further divided as right holders' per-work profits differ depending on whether they are exposed to competition from unlawful copiers. As explained in Sect. 3.7.3, no right holder is exposed to competition from unlawful copiers if $s^{co} \geq \tilde{v} \cdot r$.

For all combinations of s^{co} and o below the dotted function representing $s^{co} = \tilde{v} \cdot r$, some right holders are exposed to competition from unlawful copiers. The light red functions in coordinate systems I–III indicate right holders' per-work profit functions for the respective range of combinations of s^{co} and o. The light red areas between the per-work profit functions and the horizontal axes illustrate right holders' aggregate profits.

Coordinate system I shows right holders' per-work profit function if some right holders can upload works profitably ($o \leq v_{max} \cdot r - s$) and no right holder is exposed to competition from unlawful copiers ($s^{co} \geq \tilde{v} \cdot r$). As explained in Sect. 3.3.2, right holders then earn per-work profits of $\tilde{v} \cdot r - s - t \cdot N - o$, leading to aggregate profits of $\frac{1}{2} \cdot \tilde{N} \cdot (\tilde{v} \cdot r - s - o)$.

If some right holders are exposed to competition from unlawful copiers ($s^{co} < \tilde{v} \cdot r$) and right holders can upload at least as many works profitably as unlawful copiers can ($s^{co} \geq s + o$), the number of works uploaded is also $\tilde{N}$.[50] As shown in coordinate system II, right holders' per-work profit function then differs depending on whether right holders are exposed to competition from unlawful copiers. Right holders who own works with a number $N \leq \frac{\tilde{v} \cdot r - s^{co}}{t}$ are exposed to competition from unlawful copiers and therefore earn per-work profits of $\frac{\tilde{v} \cdot r \cdot (s^{co} - s)}{s^{co} + t \cdot N} - o$.

The threshold $\frac{\tilde{v} \cdot r - s^{co}}{t}$ can be explained by reference to the dotted, downward sloping function, which shows the per-work profits an unlawful copier would earn if she uploaded the only copy of a work ($\tilde{v} \cdot r - s^{co} - t \cdot N$). Again, this situation does not occur in equilibrium, but it helps to show why right holders who own works with a number $N > \frac{\tilde{v} \cdot r - s^{co}}{t}$ are not exposed to competition from unlawful copiers: Unlawful copiers would earn negative profits by uploading these works and thus refrain from doing so. Right holders who own works with a number $\frac{\tilde{v} \cdot r - s^{co}}{t} < N \leq \tilde{N}$ thus only need to upload one copy of their works. Hence, they earn per-work profits of $\tilde{v} \cdot r - s - t \cdot N - o$.

[50] Note that if unlawful copiers can upload some works profitably ($s^{co} < \tilde{v} \cdot r$) and right holders can upload at least as many works profitably as unlawful copiers can ($s^{co} \geq s + o$), it is implied that right holders can upload some works profitably ($o \leq v_{max} \cdot r - s$). Formally, $s + o \leq s^{co} < \tilde{v} \cdot r$ can only be fulfilled if $s + o < \tilde{v} \cdot r \Leftrightarrow o < v_{max} \cdot r - s$.

The aggregate profits are

$$\Pi_{2.2}^{*} = \int_0^{\frac{\tilde{v}\cdot r - s^{co}}{t}} \left(\frac{\tilde{v}\cdot r\cdot (s^{co}-s)}{s^{co}+t\cdot N} - o \right) \mathrm{d}N + \int_{\frac{\tilde{v}\cdot r - s^{co}}{t}}^{\tilde{N}} (\tilde{v}\cdot r - s - t\cdot N - o)\mathrm{d}N$$
$$= \frac{1}{2}\cdot\left(\tilde{N} + \frac{\tilde{v}\cdot r - s^{co}}{t}\right)\cdot(s^{co}-s-o) + (s^{co}-s)\cdot\left(\frac{\tilde{v}\cdot r}{t}\cdot \ln\left(\frac{\tilde{v}\cdot r}{s^{co}}\right) - \frac{\tilde{v}\cdot r - s^{co}}{t}\right) \tag{3.69}$$

This result can be interpreted by considering the two addends separately. The first addend is a trapezium with a height of $s^{co} - s - o$, that is, the distance between the horizontal axis and the upper horizontal gridline. The bases have the widths $\tilde{N}$, that is, the distance between the vertical axis and the second vertical gridline, and $\frac{\tilde{v}\cdot r - s^{co}}{t}$, that is, the distance between the vertical axis and the first vertical gridline. The second addend is the light red area on top of the trapezium.

If right holders can upload no works profitably ($o > v_{max}\cdot r - s$) but unlawful copiers can upload some works profitably ($s^{co} \leq v_{max}\cdot r$), right holders upload $\overline{\overline{N}}$ works. The same is true if some right holders can upload their works profitably ($o \leq v_{max}\cdot r - s$) but unlawful copiers can upload more works profitably ($s^{co} < s + o$). In both cases, every right holder who uploads is exposed to competition from unlawful copiers and thus earns per-work profits of $\frac{\overline{\overline{v}}\cdot r\cdot(s^{co}-s)}{s^{co}+t\cdot N} - o$. The per-work profit function is displayed in coordinate system III.

The dotted, downward sloping function in coordinate system III shows the per-work profits of an unlawful copier who uploads the only copy of a work ($\overline{\overline{v}}\cdot r - s^{co} - t\cdot N$). The horizontal intercept of this function ($\overline{\overline{N}}$) helps to explain why right holders upload only works with a number $N \leq \overline{\overline{N}}$: Unlawful copiers would not upload works with a number $N > \overline{\overline{N}}$. Hence, there is no reason for right holders to upload these works.

Right holders' aggregate profits are

$$\Pi_{2.2}^{*} = \int_0^{\overline{\overline{N}}} \left(\frac{\overline{\overline{v}}\cdot r\cdot (s^{co}-s)}{s^{co}+t\cdot N} - o \right) dN = \frac{\overline{\overline{v}}\cdot r}{t}\cdot(s^{co}-s)\cdot \ln\left(\frac{\overline{\overline{v}}\cdot r}{s^{co}}\right) - o\cdot\overline{\overline{N}} \tag{3.70}$$

For the purpose of explanation, note that the per-work profit function $\pi^{rh} = \frac{\overline{\overline{v}}\cdot r\cdot(s^{co}-s)}{s^{co}+t\cdot N} - o$ can be separated into two terms. The term $\frac{\overline{\overline{v}}\cdot r\cdot(s^{co}-s)}{s^{co}+t\cdot N}$ represents right holders' on-platform profits, which differ depending on the level of N. Since a change in N only affects the denominator, the antiderivative of this part of the per-work profit function is a logarithmic function. Aggregate on-platform profits are $\frac{\overline{\overline{v}}\cdot r}{t}\cdot(s^{co}-s)\cdot\ln\left(\frac{\overline{\overline{v}}\cdot r}{s^{co}}\right)$. Since $\frac{\overline{\overline{v}}\cdot r}{s^{co}} \geq 1$,[51] on-platform profits are non-negative.

The second term of the per-work profit function reflects the off-platform losses, which are the same for every right holder who uploads his work. In sum, aggregate

[51] Since $\frac{\overline{\overline{v}}\cdot r}{s^{co}} \geq 1 \Leftrightarrow s^{co} \leq v_{max}\cdot r$, this inequality is fulfilled.

profits can be positive or negative, depending on whether aggregate on-platform profits or aggregate off-platform losses have a larger value.

If neither right holders ($o > v_{max} \cdot r - s$) nor unlawful copiers ($s^{co} > v_{max} \cdot r$) can upload works profitably, no works are uploaded. Right holders' aggregate profits then are 0.

To summarise, right holders earn the following aggregate profits:

$$\Pi_{2.2}^{*}=\begin{cases} \frac{1}{2}\cdot(\tilde{v}\cdot r-s-o)\cdot\tilde{N}, & \text{if } o\leq v_{max}\cdot r-s \text{ and } s^{co}\geq\tilde{v}\cdot r \\ \left(\begin{array}{c} \frac{1}{2}\cdot\left(\tilde{N}+\frac{\tilde{v}\cdot r-s^{co}}{t}\right)\cdot(s^{co}-s-o)+ \\ (s^{co}-s)\cdot\left(\frac{\tilde{v}\cdot r}{t}\cdot\ln\left(\frac{\tilde{v}\cdot r}{s^{co}}\right)-\frac{\tilde{v}\cdot r-s^{co}}{t}\right)\end{array}\right), & \text{if } s+o\leq s^{co}<\tilde{v}\cdot r \\ \frac{\bar{\bar{v}}\cdot r}{t}\cdot(s^{co}-s)\cdot\ln\left(\frac{\bar{\bar{v}}\cdot r}{s^{co}}\right)-o\cdot\bar{\bar{N}}, & \text{if } \left(\left(\begin{array}{c} o\leq v_{max}\cdot r-s \\ \text{and } s^{co}<s+o \end{array}\right) \text{or} \left(\begin{array}{c} o>v_{max}\cdot r-s \\ \text{and } s^{co}\leq v_{max}\cdot r \end{array}\right)\right) \\ 0, & \text{if } o>v_{max}\cdot r-s \text{ and } s^{co}>v_{max}\cdot r \end{cases} \tag{3.71}$$

A.1.4 Effect of Automated Filtering on Right Holders' Profits and Availability of Works on Platform

This section discusses the effect of automated filtering on the number of works uploaded and on right holders' profits, presuming popularity-based filtering and perfect competition among unlawful copiers. Figure 3.15 compares right holders' per-work profits in scenario 1 (grey functions), scenario 2.1, specification I (light

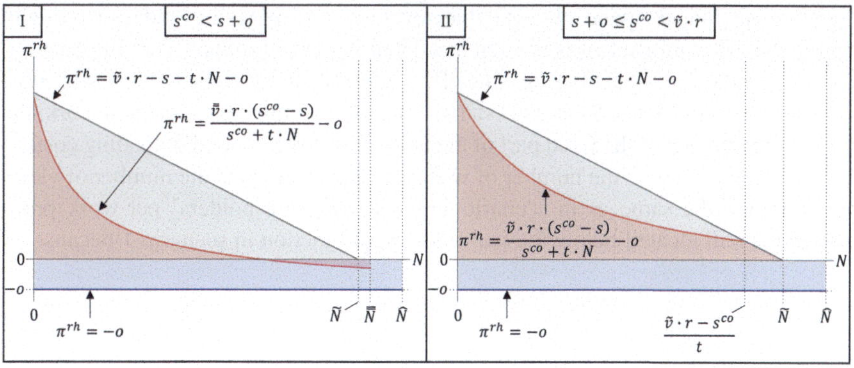

Fig. 3.15 Comparison of right holders' profits in scenario 1, scenario 2.1 (specification I), and scenario 2.2 (specification B.I), presuming $o \leq v_{max} \cdot r - s$

blue functions), and scenario 2.2, specification B.I (light red functions). Note that not filtering is equivalent to filtering with an intensity $s^{co} = s$. For scenario 2.2 (light red functions), two situations are considered: Coordinate system I displays right holders' profits for $s^{co} < s + o$ and coordinate system II for $s + o \leq s^{co} < \tilde{v} \cdot r$.

The effect of automated filtering on the number of works uploaded follows the same rationale as in specification A.I. As unlawful copiers' uploading costs increase, they would upload fewer works. Right holders therefore need to upload fewer works to prevent unlawful copiers from uploading. If $s^{co} < s + o$ (coordinate system I), unlawful copiers can upload more works profitably than right holders can. Right holders therefore upload all works that unlawful copiers can upload profitably: $\overline{\overline{N}}$. Note that $\overline{\overline{N}} = \hat{N}$ if the platform does not filter ($s^{co} = s$).

As s^{co} increases, $\overline{\overline{N}}$ decreases. The effect continues until the threshold $s^{co} = s + o$ is reached. Once the difference between s^{co} and s compensates for the off-platform losses, which only right holders incur, the number of works uploaded is the same as in the absence of unlawful copiers: $\tilde{N}$. A further increase in s^{co} does not affect the number of works uploaded (see coordinate system II).

Like uniform filtering, popularity-based filtering increases right holders' aggregate profits. If $s^{co} < s + o$, right holders' profits increase as s^{co} increases because right holders need to upload fewer works and because per-work profits increase.

As above, the increase in per-work profits follows from two effects. First, as the number of works uploaded decreases from $\hat{N}$ to $\overline{\overline{N}}$, the number of views per work increases from $\hat{v}$ to $\overline{\overline{v}}$, leading to an increase in per-work revenues. Second, as s^{co} increases, right holders need to upload fewer copies of their works to prevent unlawful copiers from uploading. Right holders upload copies until unlawful copiers are no longer willing to upload. In scenario 2.1, specification I, this leads right holders to upload so many copies that all available revenues are consumed by uploading costs, leaving per-work profits of $-o$ for them (light blue function in Fig. 3.15; Sect. 3.4.1.1). Since due to automated filtering, unlawful copiers' uploading costs are higher than right holders' uploading costs, right holders need to upload fewer copies to prevent unlawful copiers from uploading. Right holders therefore no longer spend all available revenues on uploading and can partially recoup the off-platform losses or even make non-negative profits. Given the assumption of popularity-based filtering, this effect is stronger for right holders who own more popular non-normalised works: The lower the number assigned to a work, the stronger the impact of the fixed part of the uploading costs on total uploading costs.[52]

If $s + o \leq s^{co} < \tilde{v} \cdot r$, the number of works uploaded and thus the number of views per work are the same as in scenario 1. However, right holders' per-work profit function is still located below the per-work profit function in scenario 1 because all

[52] For low levels of N, an increase in N by one unit has a larger impact on the importance of the fixed part of the per-copy uploading costs relative to the total per-copy uploading costs than for larger levels of N. This explains the convexity of the light red function.

right holders who own a work with a number located to the left of the first vertical gridline are exposed to competition from unlawful copiers. Unlike for $s^{co} < s + o$, for $s^{co} \geq s + o$, the increase in per-work profits is not reinforced by the fact that an increase in s^{co} results in larger per-work revenues. In the region $s^{co} < s + o$, an increase in s^{co} therefore shifts right holders' per-work profit function upwards more strongly than in the region $s^{co} \geq s + o$.

Nevertheless, as s^{co} increases, right holders' per-work profit function moves closer to the per-work profit function in scenario 1. Consequently, the first vertical gridline (indicating the point from which on right holders only need to upload one copy to obtain the full per-work revenues) and thus the kink in the per-work profit function are shifted to the left. Once s^{co} has reached $\tilde{v} \cdot r$, right holders earn the same profits as if unlawful copiers were absent. A further increase in s^{co} does not affect right holders' profits.

A.2 Per-Work Monopoly on Uploading Unlawful Copies (Scenario 2.2, Specification B.II)

Having examined the impact of popularity-based filtering with perfect competition among unlawful copiers, this section considers the same issue for a per-work monopoly on uploading unlawful copies. It determines right holders' per-work profits (Sect. A.2.1), the number of works uploaded (Sect. A.2.2), and right holders' aggregate profits (Sect. A.2.3). Section A.2.4 analyses the effect of automated filtering in this specification.

A.2.1 Right Holders' Per-Work Profits

Right holders' per-work profits as a function of c^{co} in the Stackelberg equilibrium are unaffected by the presumed filtering strategy. As explained in Sect. 3.5.2.1, when determining right holders' per-work profits, it is necessary to distinguish between works that fulfil the condition $c^{co} < 2 \cdot c$ and works that do not. By inserting $c^{co} = s^{co} + t \cdot N$ and $c = s + t \cdot N$, this condition can be transformed as follows:

$$s^{co} + t \cdot N < 2 \cdot (s + t \cdot N) \Leftrightarrow N > \frac{s^{co} - 2 \cdot s}{t} \tag{3.72}$$

Right holders who own a work with a number $N \leq \frac{s^{co} - 2 \cdot s}{t}$ fully prevent unlawful copiers from uploading. They thus earn the same per-work profits as in specification B.I.

Right holders who own works with a number $N > \frac{s^{co} - 2 \cdot s}{t}$ allow unlawful copiers to upload some copies of their works. However, if by doing so a right holder would earn higher per-work profits than if he uploaded the only copy of his work, that is, if his work fulfils the condition $c^{co} > 4 \cdot c - \frac{4 \cdot c^2}{v_{2.2}^* \cdot r}$ (Sect. 3.5.2.1), the qualification of the continuity assumption kicks in. The right holder is then presumed to upload the only copy of his work. By inserting $c^{co} = s^{co} + t \cdot N$ and $c = s + t \cdot N$, the condition $c^{co} > 4 \cdot c - \frac{4 \cdot c^2}{v_{2.2}^* \cdot r}$ can be transformed as follows:[53]

$$s^{co} + t \cdot N > 4 \cdot (s + t \cdot N) - \frac{4 \cdot (s + t \cdot N)^2}{v_{2.2}^* \cdot r} \Leftrightarrow$$

$$N > \frac{3 \cdot v_{2.2}^* \cdot r}{8 \cdot t} - \frac{s}{t} + \frac{\sqrt{v_{2.2}^* \cdot r \cdot \left(9 \cdot v_{2.2}^* \cdot r - 16 \cdot (s^{co} - s)\right)}}{8 \cdot t} \tag{3.73}$$

This threshold does not play a role if

$$\frac{s^{co} - 2 \cdot s}{t} \geq \frac{3 \cdot v_{2.2}^* \cdot r}{8 \cdot t} - \frac{s}{t} + \frac{\sqrt{v_{2.2}^* \cdot r \cdot \left(9 \cdot v_{2.2}^* \cdot r - 16 \cdot (s^{co} - s)\right)}}{8 \cdot t} \Leftrightarrow s^{co} \geq \frac{v_{2.2}^* \cdot r}{2} + s \tag{3.74}$$

If $s^{co} \geq \frac{v_{2.2}^* \cdot r}{2} + s$, all right holders fully prevent unlawful copiers from uploading, and per-work profits are the same as in specification B.I (Sect. A.1.1).

[53] Note that solving this inequality for N also yields $N < \frac{3 \cdot v_{2.2}^* \cdot r}{8 \cdot t} - \frac{s}{t} - \frac{\sqrt{v_{2.2}^* \cdot r \cdot \left(9 \cdot v_{2.2}^* \cdot r - 16 \cdot (s^{co} - s)\right)}}{8 \cdot t}$. However, this result is excluded by $N > \frac{s^{co} - 2 \cdot s}{t}$ because no solution for the following inequality exists $\frac{s^{co} - 2 \cdot s}{t} < \frac{3 \cdot v_{2.2}^* \cdot r}{8 \cdot t} - \frac{s}{t} - \frac{\sqrt{v_{2.2}^* \cdot r \cdot \left(9 \cdot v_{2.2}^* \cdot r - 16 \cdot (s^{co} - s)\right)}}{8 \cdot t}$. Note further that $\frac{3 \cdot v_{2.2}^* \cdot r}{8 \cdot t} - \frac{s}{t} + \frac{\sqrt{v_{2.2}^* \cdot r \cdot \left(9 \cdot v_{2.2}^* \cdot r - 16 \cdot (s^{co} - s)\right)}}{8 \cdot t}$ is only defined for $9 \cdot v_{2.2}^* \cdot r - 16 \cdot (s^{co} - s) \geq 0 \Leftrightarrow s^{co} \leq \frac{9}{16} \cdot v_{2.2}^* \cdot r + s$. However, as explained below, the threshold $N = \frac{3 \cdot v_{2.2}^* \cdot r}{8 \cdot t} - \frac{s}{t} + \frac{\sqrt{v_{2.2}^* \cdot r \cdot \left(9 \cdot v_{2.2}^* \cdot r - 16 \cdot (s^{co} - s)\right)}}{8 \cdot t}$ is only relevant if $s^{co} < \frac{v_{2.2}^* \cdot r}{2} + s$, which implies $s^{co} \leq \frac{9}{16} \cdot v_{2.2}^* \cdot r + s$.

If $s^{co} < \frac{v^*_{2.2} \cdot r}{2} + s$, right holders earn the following per-work profits:[54]

$$\pi^{rh\ *}_{2.2} = \begin{cases} \frac{v^*_{2.2} \cdot r \cdot (s^{co} - s)}{s^{co} + t \cdot N} - o, & \text{if } N \leq \frac{s^{co} - 2 \cdot s}{t} \\ \frac{v^*_{2.2} \cdot r}{4} \cdot \frac{s^{co} + t \cdot N}{s + t \cdot N} - o, & \text{if } \left(\frac{s^{co} - 2 \cdot s}{t} < N \leq \frac{3 \cdot v^*_{2.2} \cdot r}{8 \cdot t} - \frac{s}{t} + \frac{\sqrt{v^*_{2.2} \cdot r \cdot (9 \cdot v^*_{2.2} \cdot r - 16 \cdot (s^{co} - s))}}{8 \cdot t} \right) \\ v^*_{2.2} \cdot r - s - t \cdot N - o, & \text{if } \left(\left(\frac{3 \cdot v^*_{2.2} \cdot r}{8 \cdot t} - \frac{s}{t} + \frac{\sqrt{v^*_{2.2} \cdot r \cdot (9 \cdot v^*_{2.2} \cdot r - 16 \cdot (s^{co} - s))}}{8 \cdot t} < N \leq \frac{v^*_{2.2} \cdot r - s^{co}}{t} \right) \text{ or } \frac{v^*_{2.2} \cdot r - s^{co}}{t} < N \leq \frac{v^*_{2.2} \cdot r - s - o}{t} \right) \\ 0, & \text{if } N > \frac{v^*_{2.2} \cdot r - s^{co}}{t} \text{ and } N > \frac{v^*_{2.2} \cdot r - s - o}{t} \end{cases} \tag{3.75}$$

A.2.2 Number of Works Uploaded

The number of works uploaded is determined by the number assigned to the last work for which uploading results in non-negative profits for an unlawful copier (if $s^{co} < s + o$) or the right holder (if $s^{co} \geq s + o$). The number of works uploaded if only one unlawful copier per work exists thus is the same as in specification B.I (Sect. A.1.2).

A.2.3 Right Holders' Aggregate Profits

This section determines right holders' aggregate profits. It first considers the cases in which right holders' aggregate profits are the same as in specification B.I. These cases are indicated by the grey area in the coordinate system in the centre of Fig. 3.16.

The first case is that all right holders fully prevent unlawful copiers from uploading. If some right holders can upload works profitably ($o \leq v_{max} \cdot r - s$) and more right holders than unlawful copiers can upload works profitably ($s^{co} \geq s + o$),

[54] Note that in the first and second line, the condition $N \leq \frac{v^*_{2.2} \cdot r - s^{co}}{t}$ has been omitted as given $s^{co} < \frac{v^*_{2.2} \cdot r}{2} + s$, the condition $N \leq \frac{s^{co} - 2 \cdot s}{t}$ and the condition $N \leq \frac{3 \cdot v^*_{2.2} \cdot r}{8 \cdot t} - \frac{s}{t} + \frac{\sqrt{v^*_{2.2} \cdot r \cdot (9 \cdot v^*_{2.2} \cdot r - 16 \cdot (s^{co} - s))}}{8 \cdot t}$ imply $N \leq \frac{v^*_{2.2} \cdot r - s^{co}}{t}$.

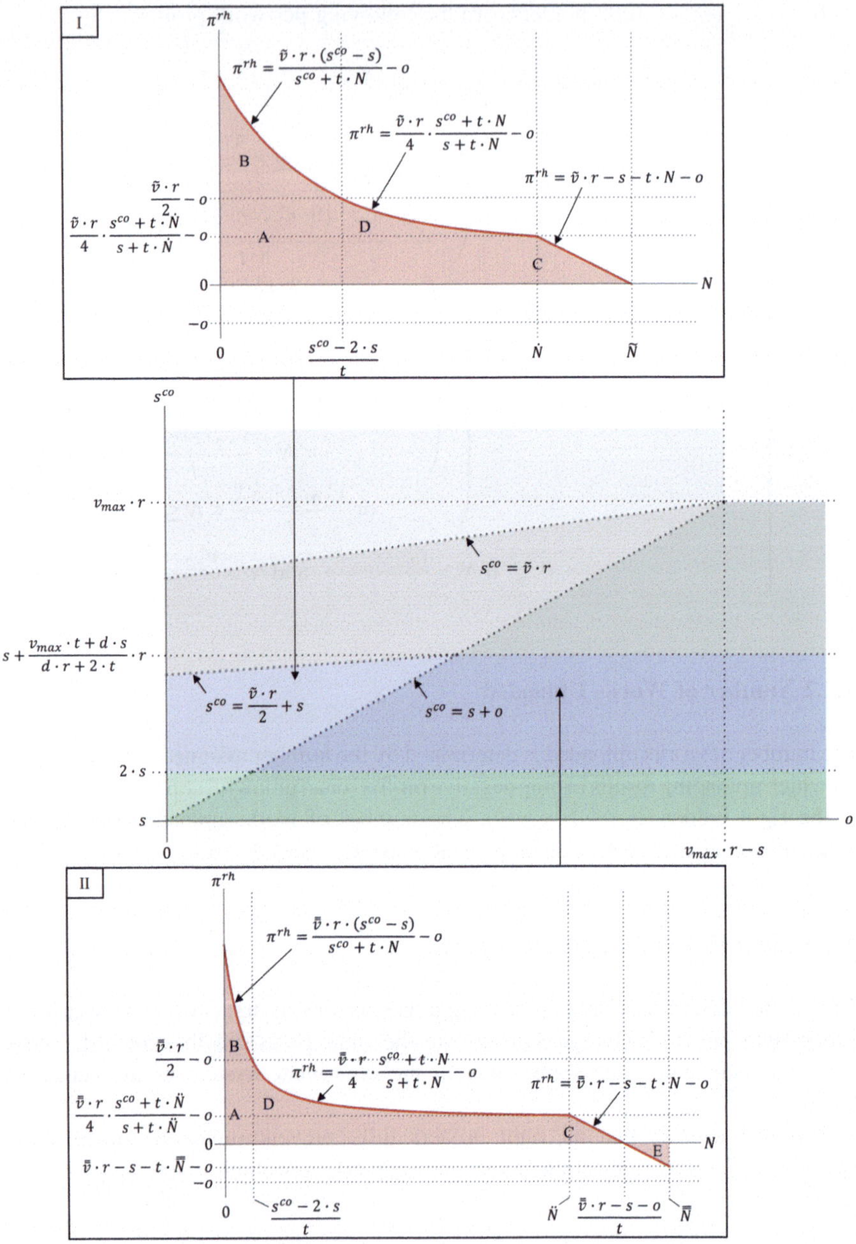

Fig. 3.16 Right holders' profits for different combinations of s^{co} and o in scenario 2.2 (specification B.II), presuming $s < \frac{v_{max} \cdot r \cdot t}{d \cdot r + 2 \cdot t}$

right holders upload $\tilde{N}$ works. As explained in Sect. A.2.1, all right holders then fully prevent unlawful copiers from uploading if $s^{co} \geq \frac{\tilde{v} \cdot r}{2} + s$. For explanation, note that this condition can be transformed as follows:

$$s^{co} \geq \frac{\tilde{v} \cdot r}{2} + s \Leftrightarrow s^{co} + t \cdot \frac{\tilde{v} \cdot r - s^{co}}{t} \geq 2 \cdot \left(s + t \cdot \frac{\tilde{v} \cdot r - s^{co}}{t} \right) \tag{3.76}$$

Given $s^{co} \geq s + o$, the last work an unlawful copier would upload is the work with the number $\frac{\tilde{v} \cdot r - s^{co}}{t}$. If this work is associated with at least two times higher uploading costs for the unlawful copier ($s^{co} + t \cdot \frac{\tilde{v} \cdot r - s^{co}}{t}$) than for the right holder ($s + t \cdot \frac{\tilde{v} \cdot r - s^{co}}{t}$), all right holders fully prevent unlawful copiers from uploading.

If some right holders can upload their works profitably ($o \leq v_{max} \cdot r - s$) but unlawful copiers can upload more works profitably ($s^{co} < s + o$), right holders upload $\overline{\overline{N}}$ works. The same is true if no right holder can upload his work profitably ($o > v_{max} \cdot r - s$), but unlawful copiers can upload some works profitably ($s^{co} \leq v_{max} \cdot r$). If one of these pairs of conditions is fulfilled, right holders fully prevent unlawful copiers from uploading if

$$s^{co} \geq \frac{\overline{\overline{v}} \cdot r}{2} + s \Leftrightarrow s^{co} \geq s + \frac{v_{max} \cdot t + d \cdot s}{d \cdot r + 2 \cdot t} \cdot r \tag{3.77}$$

The intuition behind this condition follows the same rationale as above.[55]

The second case in which right holders' profits are the same as in specification B.I is that no right holder is exposed to competition from an unlawful copier. If $\tilde{N}$ works are uploaded, no right holder is exposed to competition from an unlawful copier if $s^{co} \geq \tilde{v} \cdot r$. The same is true if neither right holders ($o > v_{max} \cdot r - s$) nor unlawful copiers ($s^{co} > v_{max} \cdot r$) can upload works profitably.

Considering cases in which $o \leq v_{max} \cdot r - s$ and $s^{co} \geq s + o$ but, despite $s^{co} < \frac{\tilde{v} \cdot r}{2} + s$, no right holder is exposed to competition from an unlawful copier ($s^{co} \geq \tilde{v} \cdot r$) would add no insights. In the interest of a focused analysis, it is therefore presumed that if $s^{co} < \frac{\tilde{v} \cdot r}{2} + s$, some right holders are exposed to competition from unlawful copiers. As in specification A.II (Sect. 3.5.2.3), the assumption is applied even for the smallest number of views per work that occurs in equilibrium, namely, $\hat{v}$, which occurs if $o = 0$ and thus $\tilde{v} = \hat{v}$. Formally, as above, it is therefore presumed that

$$\hat{v} \cdot r > \frac{\hat{v} \cdot r}{2} + s \Leftrightarrow s < \frac{v_{max} \cdot r \cdot t}{d \cdot r + 2 \cdot t} \tag{3.78}$$

---

[55] The condition can be transformed as follows: $s^{co} \geq s + \frac{v_{max} \cdot t + d \cdot s}{d \cdot r + 2 \cdot t} \cdot r \Leftrightarrow s^{co} + t \cdot \overline{\overline{N}} \geq 2 \cdot \left(s + t \cdot \overline{\overline{N}} \right)$. $\overline{\overline{N}}$ is the last work an unlawful copier would upload. As above, if this work is associated with at least two times higher uploading costs for the unlawful copier ($s^{co} + t \cdot \overline{\overline{N}}$) than for the right holder ($s + t \cdot \overline{\overline{N}}$), all right holders fully prevent unlawful copiers from uploading.

Note that under this presumption, the threshold $s^{co} = s + \frac{v_{max} \cdot t + d \cdot s}{d \cdot r + 2 \cdot t} \cdot r$ is located below the threshold $s^{co} = v_{max} \cdot r$. It follows that this presumption also precludes cases in which $o > v_{max} \cdot r - s$, but despite $s^{co} < s + \frac{v_{max} \cdot t + d \cdot s}{d \cdot r + 2 \cdot t} \cdot r$, no right holder is exposed to competition from an unlawful copier ($s^{co} > v_{max} \cdot r$).

Having considered the cases in which right holders' aggregate profits are the same as in specification B.I, the cases in which aggregate profits differ are next in line. These cases are indicated by the blue and the green areas in the coordinate system in the centre of Fig. 3.16. Right holders' aggregate profits differ from the profits in specification B.I if some right holders do not fully prevent unlawful copiers from uploading.

If $o \leq v_{max} \cdot r - s$ and $s^{co} \geq s + o$, this is the case if $s^{co} < \frac{\bar{v} \cdot r}{2} + s$. Note that $s + o \leq s^{co} < \frac{\bar{v} \cdot r}{2} + s$ implies $o \leq v_{max} \cdot r - s$.[56] In such cases, as explained in Sect. A.2.1, the qualification of the continuity assumption applies to works with a number $N > \frac{3 \cdot \bar{v} \cdot r}{8 \cdot t} - \frac{s}{t} + \frac{\sqrt{\bar{v} \cdot r \cdot (9 \cdot \bar{v} \cdot r - 16 \cdot (s^{co} - s))}}{8 \cdot t}$. To increase the clarity of the following explanations, $\dot{N}$ is used to refer to the work with the number $\frac{3 \cdot \bar{v} \cdot r}{8 \cdot t} - \frac{s}{t} + \frac{\sqrt{\bar{v} \cdot r \cdot (9 \cdot \bar{v} \cdot r - 16 \cdot (s^{co} - s))}}{8 \cdot t}$.

If $o \leq v_{max} \cdot r - s$ and $s^{co} < s + o$, some right holders do not fully prevent unlawful copiers from uploading if $s^{co} < s + \frac{v_{max} \cdot t + d \cdot s}{d \cdot r + 2 \cdot t} \cdot r$.[57] The same is true if $o > v_{max} \cdot r - s$. In such cases, the qualification of the continuity assumption applies to works with a number $N > \frac{3 \cdot \bar{\bar{v}} \cdot r}{8 \cdot t} - \frac{s}{t} + \frac{\sqrt{\bar{\bar{v}} \cdot r \cdot \left(9 \cdot \bar{\bar{v}} \cdot r - 16 \cdot (s^{co} - s)\right)}}{8 \cdot t}$. Again, in the interest of clarity, $\ddot{N}$ is used to refer to the work with the number $\frac{3 \cdot \bar{\bar{v}} \cdot r}{8 \cdot t} - \frac{s}{t} + \frac{\sqrt{\bar{\bar{v}} \cdot r \cdot \left(9 \cdot \bar{\bar{v}} \cdot r - 16 \cdot (s^{co} - s)\right)}}{8 \cdot t}$.

Note that—except for right holders who own a work with a number $N > \dot{N}$ or $N > \ddot{N}$—no right holder fully prevents an unlawful copier from uploading if

$$\frac{s^{co} - 2 \cdot s}{t} < 0 \Leftrightarrow s^{co} < 2 \cdot s \tag{3.79}$$

Note further that the presumption $s < \frac{v_{max} \cdot r \cdot t}{d \cdot r + 2 \cdot t}$ implies that the threshold $s^{co} = 2 \cdot s$ is located below the threshold $s^{co} = \frac{\bar{v} \cdot r}{2} + s$ and below the threshold $s^{co} = s + \frac{v_{max} \cdot t + d \cdot s}{d \cdot r + 2 \cdot t} \cdot r$.

The dark red function in coordinate system I in Fig. 3.16 shows right holders' per-work profit function if $s^{co} \geq s + o$ and $2 \cdot s \leq s^{co} < \frac{\bar{v} \cdot r}{2} + s$. The dark red function in coordinate system II shows right holders' per-work profit function if $s^{co} < s + o$

---

[56] The conditions can only be simultaneously fulfilled if $s + o < \frac{\bar{v} \cdot r}{2} + s \Leftrightarrow o < \frac{v_{max} \cdot t + d \cdot s}{d \cdot r + 2 \cdot t} \cdot r$. With $o < \frac{v_{max} \cdot t + d \cdot s}{d \cdot r + 2 \cdot t} \cdot r$, $o > v_{max} \cdot r - s$ could only be fulfilled if $\frac{v_{max} \cdot t + d \cdot s}{d \cdot r + 2 \cdot t} \cdot r > v_{max} \cdot r - s \Leftrightarrow s > \frac{v_{max} \cdot r}{2}$. However, $s > \frac{v_{max} \cdot r}{2}$ is precluded by the presumption $s < \frac{v_{max} \cdot r \cdot t}{d \cdot r + 2 \cdot t}$ since given the assumptions on the variables, no solution for the following inequality exists $\frac{v_{max} \cdot r}{2} < \frac{v_{max} \cdot r \cdot t}{d \cdot r + 2 \cdot t}$.

[57] Note that $s^{co} < s + o$ implies $s^{co} < s + \frac{v_{max} \cdot t + d \cdot s}{d \cdot r + 2 \cdot t} \cdot r$ if $s + o < s + \frac{v_{max} \cdot t + d \cdot s}{d \cdot r + 2 \cdot t} \cdot r \Leftrightarrow o < \frac{v_{max} \cdot t + d \cdot s}{d \cdot r + 2 \cdot t} \cdot r$. From then on, $s^{co} < s + \frac{v_{max} \cdot t + d \cdot s}{d \cdot r + 2 \cdot t} \cdot r$ implies $s^{co} < s + o$. However, separating the conditions in this way would convolute the following explanations and provide no added value. The following explanations therefore use the conditions $s^{co} < s + o$ and $s^{co} < s + \frac{v_{max} \cdot t + d \cdot s}{d \cdot r + 2 \cdot t} \cdot r$.

and $2 \cdot s \leq s^{co} < s + \frac{v_{max} \cdot t + d \cdot s}{d \cdot r + 2 \cdot t} \cdot r$.[58] The dark red areas between the per-work profit functions and the horizontal axes indicate right holders' aggregate profits.

Right holders' profits if $s^{co} < 2 \cdot s$ (green area in the coordinate system in the centre) are described in the text following Fig. 3.16. Note that if despite a filtering intensity of $s^{co} < 2 \cdot s$, $\dot{N} \leq 0$ (if $s^{co} \geq s + o$) or $\ddot{N} \leq 0$ (if $s^{co} < s + o$), all right holders only need to upload one copy of their works to fully prevent unlawful copiers from uploading. As above, these cases are not considered in the following as doing so would add no insights and thus unnecessarily convolute the analysis. Right holders' profits for the combinations of s^{co} and o in the grey area in the coordinate system in the centre are not considered because in such cases right holders earn the same profits as in specification B.I.

In coordinate system I, more right holders than unlawful copiers can upload works profitably ($s^{co} \geq s + o$) and some ($s^{co} < \frac{\tilde{v} \cdot r}{2} + s$)—but not all ($s^{co} \geq 2 \cdot s$)—right holders do not fully prevent unlawful copiers from uploading. Since in this specification, automated filtering only affects the fixed part of unlawful copiers' uploading costs, the impact of automated filtering decreases as N increases.

The first vertical gridline shows the threshold at which the impact of automated filtering has decreased to such an extent that it is no longer profitable for a right holder to prevent an unlawful copier from uploading: $N = \frac{s^{co} - 2 \cdot s}{t}$. From this threshold on, right holders and unlawful copiers (unevenly) share the revenues per uploaded work. The second vertical gridline marks the point from which on the continuity assumption would allow right holders to earn higher per-work profits than they would earn if they uploaded the only copy of their works.

Right holders' aggregate profits in the case displayed in coordinate system I are

$$\begin{aligned}
\Pi^*_{2.2} = & \int_0^{\frac{s^{co} - 2 \cdot s}{t}} \left(\frac{\tilde{v} \cdot r \cdot (s^{co} - s)}{s^{co} + t \cdot N} - o \right) \mathrm{d}N + \int_{\frac{s^{co} - 2 \cdot s}{t}}^{\dot{N}} \left(\frac{\tilde{v} \cdot r}{4} \cdot \frac{s^{co} + t \cdot N}{s + t \cdot N} - o \right) \mathrm{d}N \\
& + \int_{\dot{N}}^{\tilde{N}} (\tilde{v} \cdot r - s - t \cdot N - o) \mathrm{d}N \\
= & \left(\frac{\tilde{v} \cdot r}{2} - o \right) \cdot \frac{s^{co} - 2 \cdot s}{t} + \frac{\tilde{v} \cdot r}{t} \cdot \left(s - \frac{s^{co}}{2} + (s^{co} - s) \cdot \ln \left(2 \cdot \frac{s^{co} - s}{s^{co}} \right) \right) \\
& + \frac{1}{2} \cdot \left(\dot{N} + \tilde{N} - 2 \cdot \frac{s^{co} - 2 \cdot s}{t} \right) \cdot \left(\frac{\tilde{v} \cdot r}{4} \cdot \frac{s^{co} + t \cdot \dot{N}}{s + t \cdot \dot{N}} - o \right) \\
& + \frac{\tilde{v} \cdot r}{4 \cdot t} \cdot (s^{co} - s) \cdot \left(\frac{s^{co} - 2 \cdot s - t \cdot \dot{N}}{s + t \cdot \dot{N}} + \ln \left(\frac{s + t \cdot \dot{N}}{s^{co} - s} \right) \right)
\end{aligned} \tag{3.80}$$

[58] Note that coordinate system II presumes $o < \frac{\bar{\bar{v}} \cdot r}{4} \cdot \frac{s^{co} + t \cdot \ddot{N}}{s + t \cdot \ddot{N}}$. If $o \geq \frac{\bar{\bar{v}} \cdot r}{4} \cdot \frac{s^{co} + t \cdot \ddot{N}}{s + t \cdot \ddot{N}}$, the horizontal intercept of the dark red function would be located at or to the left of the second vertical gridline. Aggregate profits would nevertheless be the same as calculated below.

Table 3.3 Graphical interpretation of right holders' aggregate profits in scenario 2.2 (specification B.II) for $s < \frac{v_{max} \cdot r \cdot t}{d \cdot r + 2 \cdot t}$, $s^{co} \geq s + o$, and $2 \cdot s \leq s^{co} < \frac{\tilde{v} \cdot r}{2} + s$

Term	Graphical interpretation (coordinate system I)
$\left(\frac{\tilde{v} \cdot r}{2} - o\right) \cdot \frac{s^{co} - 2 \cdot s}{t}$	Rectangle A, limited in height by the horizontal axis and the upper horizontal gridline and in width by the vertical axis and the first vertical gridline
$\frac{\tilde{v} \cdot r}{t} \cdot \left(s - \frac{s^{co}}{2} + (s^{co} - s) \cdot \ln\left(2 \cdot \frac{s^{co} - s}{s^{co}}\right)\right)$	Area B, located on top of rectangle A
$\frac{1}{2} \cdot \left(\dot{N} + \tilde{N} - 2 \cdot \frac{s^{co} - 2 \cdot s}{t}\right) \cdot \left(\frac{\tilde{v} \cdot r}{4} \cdot \frac{s^{co} + t \cdot \dot{N}}{s + t \cdot \dot{N}} - o\right)$	Trapezium C, limited in height by the horizontal axis and the middle horizontal gridline, with a long base running from the first to the third vertical gridline and a short base running from the first to the second vertical gridline
$\frac{\tilde{v} \cdot r}{4 \cdot t} \cdot (s^{co} - s) \cdot \left(\frac{s^{co} - 2 \cdot s - t \cdot \dot{N}}{s + t \cdot \dot{N}} + \ln\left(\frac{s + t \cdot \dot{N}}{s^{co} - s}\right)\right)$	Area D, located on top of the short base of trapezium C

Table 3.3 explains these aggregate profits by dividing the dark red area in coordinate system I into four parts.

If $s^{co} < 2 \cdot s$ (light green area in the coordinate system in the centre of Fig. 3.16), the threshold $N = \frac{s^{co} - 2 \cdot s}{t}$ no longer plays a role. Right holders then earn aggregate profits of

$$\Pi^*_{2.2} = \int_0^{\dot{N}} \left(\frac{\tilde{v} \cdot r}{4} \cdot \frac{s^{co} + t \cdot N}{s + t \cdot N} - o\right) \mathrm{d}N + \int_{\dot{N}}^{\tilde{N}} (\tilde{v} \cdot r - s - t \cdot N - o) \mathrm{d}N$$
$$= \frac{1}{2} \cdot (\tilde{N} + \dot{N}) \cdot \left(\frac{\tilde{v} \cdot r}{4} \cdot \frac{s^{co} + t \cdot \dot{N}}{s + t \cdot \dot{N}} - o\right) + \frac{\tilde{v} \cdot r}{4 \cdot t} \cdot (s^{co} - s) \cdot \left(\ln\left(\frac{s + t \cdot \dot{N}}{s}\right) - \frac{t \cdot \dot{N}}{s + t \cdot \dot{N}}\right) \tag{3.81}$$

Graphically, this result can be interpreted by presuming that the first vertical gridline in coordinate system I is located to the left of the vertical axis. The first summand can then be interpreted as a trapezium that is comparable to the trapezium C in coordinate system I. Its bases begin at the vertical axis and end at $\tilde{N}$ (long base) and $\dot{N}$ (short base). As above, its height is $\frac{\tilde{v} \cdot r}{4} \cdot \frac{s^{co} + t \cdot \dot{N}}{s + t \cdot \dot{N}} - o$. The second summand is the area located on top of the trapezium. It is comparable to the area D in coordinate system I.

To summarise, if $s + o \leq s^{co} < \frac{\tilde{v}\cdot r}{2} + s$ (and presuming $s < \frac{v_{max}\cdot r\cdot t}{d\cdot r+2\cdot t}$), right holders' aggregate profits are

$$\Pi^*_{2.2} = \begin{cases} \begin{pmatrix} \left(\frac{\tilde{v}\cdot r}{2} - o\right)\cdot\frac{s^{co}-2\cdot s}{t} \\ +\frac{\tilde{v}\cdot r}{t}\cdot\left(s - \frac{s^{co}}{2} + (s^{co}-s)\cdot\ln\left(2\cdot\frac{s^{co}-s}{s^{co}}\right)\right) \\ +\frac{1}{2}\cdot\left(\dot{N}+\tilde{N}-2\cdot\frac{s^{co}-2\cdot s}{t}\right)\cdot\left(\frac{\tilde{v}\cdot r}{4}\cdot\frac{s^{co}+t\cdot\dot{N}}{s+t\cdot\dot{N}} - o\right) \\ +\frac{\tilde{v}\cdot r}{4\cdot t}\cdot(s^{co}-s)\cdot\left(\frac{s^{co}-2\cdot s-t\cdot\dot{N}}{s+t\cdot\dot{N}} + \ln\left(\frac{s+t\cdot\dot{N}}{s^{co}-s}\right)\right) \end{pmatrix}, & \text{if } s^{co} \geq 2\cdot s \\ \begin{pmatrix} \frac{1}{2}\cdot(\tilde{N}+\dot{N})\cdot\left(\frac{\tilde{v}\cdot r}{4}\cdot\frac{s^{co}+t\cdot\dot{N}}{s+t\cdot\dot{N}} - o\right) \\ +\frac{\tilde{v}\cdot r}{4\cdot t}\cdot(s^{co}-s)\cdot\left(\ln\left(\frac{s+t\cdot\dot{N}}{s}\right) - \frac{t\cdot\dot{N}}{s+t\cdot\dot{N}}\right) \end{pmatrix}, & \text{if } s^{co} < 2\cdot s \end{cases} \tag{3.82}$$

In coordinate system II, more unlawful copiers than right holders can upload works profitably ($s^{co} < s + o$) and some ($s^{co} < s + \frac{v_{max}\cdot t+d\cdot s}{d\cdot r+2\cdot t}\cdot r$)—but not all ($s^{co} \geq 2\cdot s$)—right holders do not fully prevent unlawful copiers from uploading. Right holders earn aggregate profits of

$$\begin{aligned} \Pi^*_{2.2} &= \int_0^{\frac{s^{co}-2\cdot s}{t}}\left(\frac{\bar{\bar{v}}\cdot r\cdot(s^{co}-s)}{s^{co}+t\cdot N} - o\right)\mathrm{d}N + \int_{\frac{s^{co}-2\cdot s}{t}}^{\ddot{N}}\left(\frac{\bar{\bar{v}}\cdot r}{4}\cdot\frac{s^{co}+t\cdot N}{s+t\cdot N} - o\right)\mathrm{d}N \\ &\quad + \int_{\ddot{N}}^{\bar{\bar{N}}}\left(\bar{\bar{v}}\cdot r - s - t\cdot N - o\right)\mathrm{d}N \\ &= \left(\frac{\bar{\bar{v}}\cdot r}{2} - o\right)\cdot\frac{s^{co}-2\cdot s}{t} + \frac{\bar{\bar{v}}\cdot r}{t}\cdot\left(s - \frac{s^{co}}{2} + (s^{co}-s)\cdot\ln\left(2\cdot\frac{s^{co}-s}{s^{co}}\right)\right) \\ &\quad + \frac{1}{2}\cdot\left(\ddot{N} + \frac{\bar{\bar{v}}\cdot r - s - o}{t} - 2\cdot\frac{s^{co}-2\cdot s}{t}\right)\cdot\left(\frac{\bar{\bar{v}}\cdot r}{4}\cdot\frac{s^{co}+t\cdot\ddot{N}}{s+t\cdot\ddot{N}} - o\right) \\ &\quad + \frac{\bar{\bar{v}}\cdot r}{4\cdot t}\cdot(s^{co}-s)\cdot\left(\frac{s^{co}-2\cdot s-t\cdot\ddot{N}}{s+t\cdot\ddot{N}} + \ln\left(\frac{s+t\cdot\ddot{N}}{s^{co}-s}\right)\right) \\ &\quad + \frac{1}{2}\cdot\left(\bar{\bar{v}}\cdot r - s - t\cdot\bar{\bar{N}} - o\right)\cdot\left(\bar{\bar{N}} - \frac{\bar{\bar{v}}\cdot r - s - o}{t}\right) \end{aligned} \tag{3.83}$$

The interpretation of the first four summands corresponds to the interpretation in Table 3.3. The fifth summand is the triangle E, which is located below the horizontal axis.

Finally, if $s^{co} < 2\cdot s$ (dark green area in the coordinate system in the centre of Fig. 3.16), right holders earn aggregate profits of

$$
\begin{aligned}
\Pi_{2.2}^{*} &= \int_{0}^{\ddot{N}} \left(\frac{\overline{\overline{v}} \cdot r}{4} \cdot \frac{s^{co} + t \cdot N}{s + t \cdot N} - o \right) \mathrm{d}N + \int_{\ddot{N}}^{\overline{\overline{N}}} \left(\overline{\overline{v}} \cdot r - s - t \cdot N - o \right) \mathrm{d}N \\
&= \frac{1}{2} \cdot \left(\ddot{N} + \frac{\overline{\overline{v}} \cdot r - s - o}{t} \right) \cdot \left(\frac{\overline{\overline{v}} \cdot r}{4} \cdot \frac{s^{co} + t \cdot \ddot{N}}{s + t \cdot \ddot{N}} - o \right) \\
&\quad + \frac{\overline{\overline{v}} \cdot r}{4 \cdot t} \cdot (s^{co} - s) \cdot \left(\ln\left(\frac{s + t \cdot \ddot{N}}{s} \right) - \frac{t \cdot \ddot{N}}{s + t \cdot \ddot{N}} \right) \\
&\quad + \frac{1}{2} \cdot \left(\overline{\overline{v}} \cdot r - s - t \cdot \overline{\overline{N}} - o \right) \cdot \left(\overline{\overline{N}} - \frac{\overline{\overline{v}} \cdot r - s - o}{t} \right)
\end{aligned} \tag{3.84}
$$

Graphically, this result can be interpreted by presuming that the first vertical gridline in coordinate system II is located to the left of the vertical axis. The first summand can be interpreted as a trapezium that is comparable to the trapezium C in coordinate system II. Its bases begin at the vertical axis and end at $\frac{\overline{\overline{v}} \cdot r - s - o}{t}$ (long base) and $\ddot{N}$ (short base). As in coordinate system II, its height is $\frac{\overline{\overline{v}} \cdot r}{4} \cdot \frac{s^{co} + t \cdot \ddot{N}}{s + t \cdot \ddot{N}} - o$. The second summand is the area located on top of the trapezium. It is comparable to the area D in coordinate system II. Finally, the third summand represents a right-angled triangle which is comparable to triangle E in coordinate system II.

To summarise, if $s^{co} < s + o$ and $s^{co} < s + \frac{v_{max} \cdot t + d \cdot s}{d \cdot r + 2 \cdot t} \cdot r$ (and presuming $s < \frac{v_{max} \cdot r \cdot t}{d \cdot r + 2 \cdot t}$), right holders' aggregate profits are

$$
\Pi_{2.2}^{*} = \begin{cases}
\left(\begin{array}{c}
\left(\frac{\overline{\overline{v}} \cdot r}{2} - o \right) \cdot \frac{s^{co} - 2 \cdot s}{t} \\
+ \frac{\overline{\overline{v}} \cdot r}{t} \cdot \left(s - \frac{s^{co}}{2} + (s^{co} - s) \cdot \ln\left(2 \cdot \frac{s^{co} - s}{s^{co}} \right) \right) \\
+ \frac{1}{2} \cdot \left(\ddot{N} + \frac{\overline{\overline{v}} \cdot r - s - o}{t} - 2 \cdot \frac{s^{co} - 2 \cdot s}{t} \right) \cdot \left(\frac{\overline{\overline{v}} \cdot r}{4} \cdot \frac{s^{co} + t \cdot \ddot{N}}{s + t \cdot \ddot{N}} - o \right) \\
+ \frac{\overline{\overline{v}} \cdot r}{4 \cdot t} \cdot (s^{co} - s) \cdot \left(\frac{s^{co} - 2 \cdot s - t \cdot \ddot{N}}{s + t \cdot \ddot{N}} + \ln\left(\frac{s + t \cdot \ddot{N}}{s^{co} - s} \right) \right) \\
+ \frac{1}{2} \cdot \left(\overline{\overline{v}} \cdot r - s - t \cdot \overline{\overline{N}} - o \right) \cdot \left(\overline{\overline{N}} - \frac{\overline{\overline{v}} \cdot r - s - o}{t} \right)
\end{array} \right), & \text{if } s^{co} \geq 2 \cdot s \\
\left(\begin{array}{c}
\frac{1}{2} \cdot \left(\ddot{N} + \frac{\overline{\overline{v}} \cdot r - s - o}{t} \right) \cdot \left(\frac{\overline{\overline{v}} \cdot r}{4} \cdot \frac{s^{co} + t \cdot \ddot{N}}{s + t \cdot \ddot{N}} - o \right) \\
+ \frac{\overline{\overline{v}} \cdot r}{4 \cdot t} \cdot (s^{co} - s) \cdot \left(\ln\left(\frac{s + t \cdot \ddot{N}}{s} \right) - \frac{t \cdot \ddot{N}}{s + t \cdot \ddot{N}} \right) \\
+ \frac{1}{2} \cdot \left(\overline{\overline{v}} \cdot r - s - t \cdot \overline{\overline{N}} - o \right) \cdot \left(\overline{\overline{N}} - \frac{\overline{\overline{v}} \cdot r - s - o}{t} \right)
\end{array} \right), & \text{if } s^{co} < 2 \cdot s
\end{cases} \tag{3.85}
$$

A.2.4 Effect of Automated Filtering on Right Holders' Profits and Availability of Works on Platform

This section discusses the effect of automated filtering on the number of works uploaded and on right holders' profits, presuming popularity-based filtering and a per-work monopoly on uploading unlawful copies. As explained in Sect. A.2.2, the number of works uploaded does not differ between this specification and specification B.I. Likewise, as explained in Sect. A.2.3, if either $s^{co} \geq s + o$ and $s^{co} \geq \frac{\tilde{v} \cdot r}{2} + s$, or if $s^{co} < s + o$ and $s^{co} \geq s + \frac{v_{max} \cdot t + d \cdot s}{d \cdot r + 2 \cdot t} \cdot r$, right holders' profits do not differ between this specification and specification B.I.

The cases in which right holders' profits differ between this specification and specification B.I are shown in Fig. 3.17. It displays right holders' per-work profit functions in scenario 1 (grey functions), scenario 2.1, specification II (dark blue functions), and scenario 2.2, specification B.II (dark red functions). For scenario 2.2, two situations are considered. Coordinate system I presumes $s^{co} < s + o$ and $s^{co} < s + \frac{v_{max} \cdot t + d \cdot s}{d \cdot r + 2 \cdot t} \cdot r$. Coordinate system II presumes $s + o \leq s^{co} < \frac{\tilde{v} \cdot r}{2} + s$. Note that, as above, not filtering is equivalent to filtering with an intensity of $s^{co} = s$.

Like uniform filtering, popularity-based filtering increases right holders' aggregate profits because right holders need to upload fewer (coordinate system I) or no (coordinate system II) works for which uploading is overall unprofitable and because right holders obtain higher per-work profits.

The first reason for the increase in per-work profits is that the number of views per work increases as the number of works uploaded decreases. This explains why in coordinate system I, the part of the dark red function located to the right of the second vertical gridline is located above the downward sloping part of the dark blue function but below the grey function. This effect only materialises until $s^{co} = s + o$ because further increases in s^{co} do not affect the number of works uploaded. In coordinate system II, the part of the dark red function located to the right of the second vertical gridline is thus identical to the grey function. Note that because an increase in s^{co} until $s + o$ results in an upward shift of the part of the dark red function located to the right of the second vertical gridline, it also shifts the horizontal intercept of the dark red function in coordinate system I to the right. At the same time, an increase in s^{co} shifts the fifth vertical gridline in coordinate system I ($\overline{\overline{N}}$, i.e. the number of works uploaded) to the left. Once $s^{co} = s + o$, the two thresholds converge at $\tilde{N}$. An increase in s^{co} beyond $s + o$ leaves the horizontal intercept and the number of works uploaded unaffected.

The second reason for the increase in per-work profits is that right holders who prevent unlawful copiers from uploading need to upload fewer copies of their works as s^{co} increases. In scenario 2.2, these are the right holders who own works with a number located to the left of the first vertical gridlines in coordinate systems I and II.

The third reason for the increase in per-work profits is that as s^{co} increases, right holders who (unevenly) share revenues with unlawful copiers upload more copies of

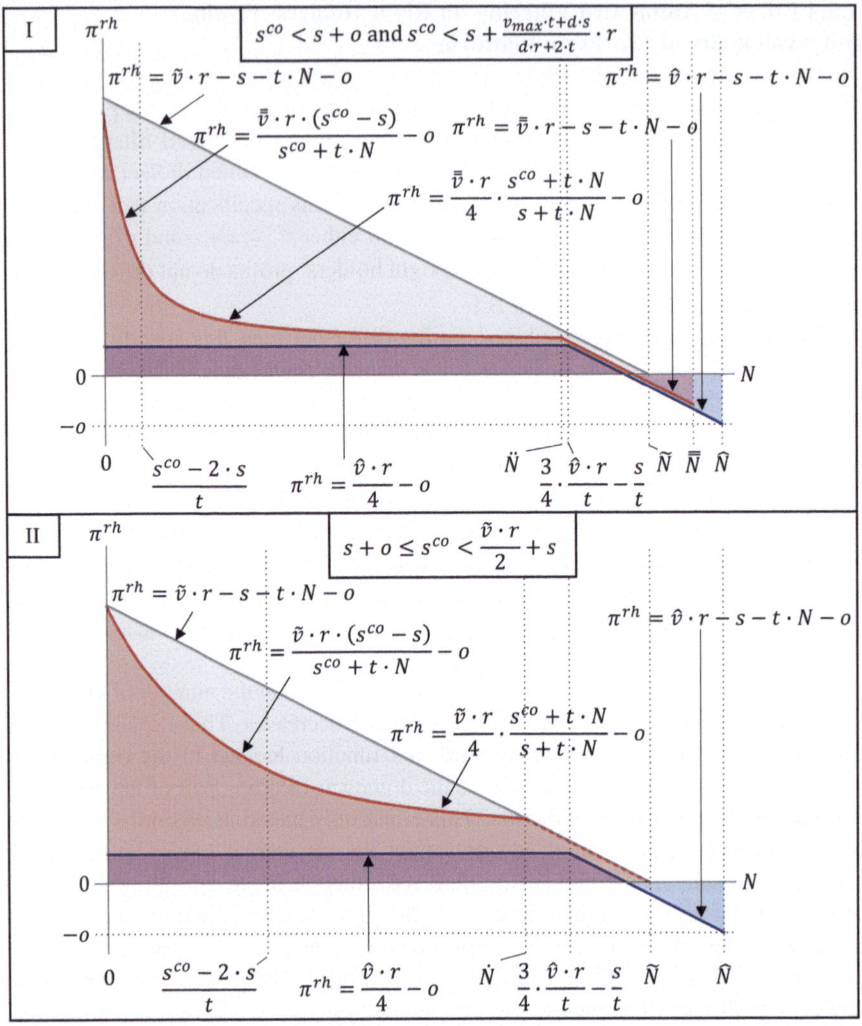

Fig. 3.17 Comparison of right holders' profits in scenario 1, scenario 2.1 (specification II), and scenario 2.2 (specification B.II), presuming $s < \frac{v_{max} \cdot r \cdot t}{d \cdot r + 2 \cdot t}$, $s^{co} \geq 2 \cdot s$, $o \leq v_{max} \cdot r - s$, and $o < \frac{\hat{v} \cdot r}{4}$

their works and therefore earn a larger share of the revenues. In scenario 2.2, these are the right holders who own works with a number located between the first and the second vertical gridlines in coordinate systems I and II. Since the increase in revenues obtained outweighs the increase in costs from uploading more copies, right holders earn higher per-work profits. Note that the first vertical gridlines are shifted to the right as s^{co} increases because more right holders fully prevent unlawful copiers from uploading. Moreover, note that the part of the dark red function located between the first and the second vertical gridline in coordinate system I is shifted upwards by an increase in the number of views per work and by an increase in the share of the revenues the right holder obtains. At the same time, the part of the per-work profit function located to the right of the second vertical gridline is shifted upwards only by the increase in the number of views per work. As a result, the intersection of the two functions and hence the kink in the dark red function (second vertical gridline) are moved to the left as s^{co} increases. In other words, more right holders only need to upload one copy of their works to obtain the full per-work revenues. In coordinate system II, the same effect materialises as then the part of the dark red function located between the first and the second vertical gridline is shifted upwards by an increase in the share of the revenues the right holder obtains, while the part of the dark red function located to the right of the second vertical gridline is not affected by a change in s^{co}.

A.3 Influence of Structure of Market for Supplying Unlawful Copies on Effect of Automated Filtering on Right Holders' Profits

This section discusses how the structure of the market for supplying unlawful copies influences the effect of popularity-based automated filtering. As explained in Sect. A.2.2, the market structure does not influence the impact of automated filtering on the number of works uploaded. Moreover, as explained in Sect. A.2.3, it does not affect right holders' aggregate profits if either $s^{co} \geq s + o$ and $s^{co} \geq \frac{\tilde{v} \cdot r}{2} + s$ or $s^{co} < s + o$ and $s^{co} \geq s + \frac{v_{max} \cdot t + d \cdot s}{d \cdot r + 2 \cdot t} \cdot r$.

Figure 3.18 shows right holders' per-work profit functions in scenario 2.2 presuming popularity-based filtering with perfect competition among unlawful copiers (light red function) and with a per-work monopoly on uploading unlawful copies (dark red function). It only shows right holders' per-work profit functions for $s + o \leq s^{co} < \frac{\tilde{v} \cdot r}{2} + s$. It does not compare right holders' per-work profit functions for $s^{co} < s + o$ and $s^{co} < s + \frac{v_{max} \cdot t + d \cdot s}{d \cdot r + 2 \cdot t} \cdot r$. Such a comparison would follow the same rationale and therefore add no insights.

Right holders who upload works with a number $N \leq \frac{s^{co} - 2 \cdot s}{t}$ fully prevent unlawful copiers from uploading, regardless of how the market is structured. Right holders who own works with a number $\frac{s^{co} - 2 \cdot s}{t} < N \leq \frac{\tilde{v} \cdot r - s^{co}}{t}$ pursue different strategies depending on how the market for supplying unlawful copies is structured.

The reasons for the different strategies are the same as proffered in Sect. 3.6 for uniform filtering. To repeat, when competing with many unlawful copiers, a right holder anticipates that unlawful copiers would collectively upload until the maximal number of copies they can upload of the right holder's work without their total uploading costs exceeding the per-work revenues is uploaded. The right holder then

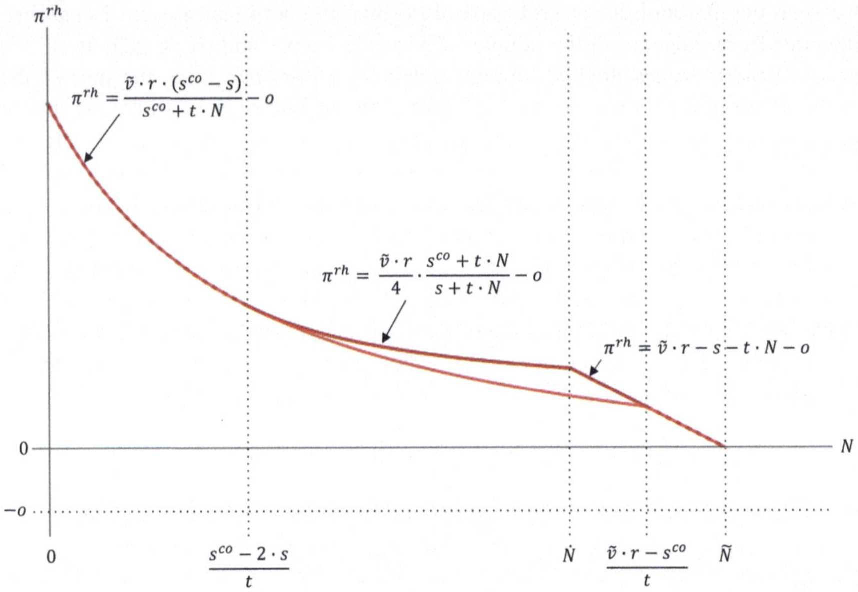

Fig. 3.18 Comparison of right holders' profits in scenario 2.2 (specification B.I) and scenario 2.2 (specification B.II), presuming $s < \frac{v_{max} \cdot r \cdot t}{d \cdot r + 2 \cdot t}$, $s + o \leq s^{co} < \frac{\tilde{v} \cdot r}{2} + s$, and $s^{co} \geq 2 \cdot s$

chooses to upload all these copies himself. When only competing with one unlawful copier, the right holder anticipates that the unlawful copier does not necessarily upload until the maximal number of copies she can upload of the right holder's work without her total uploading costs exceeding the per-work revenues is uploaded because the unlawful copier's marginal profits from uploading copies are decreasing. By uploading $\frac{\tilde{v} \cdot r}{4} \cdot \frac{s^{co} + t \cdot N}{(s + t \cdot N)^2}$ copies instead of the $\frac{\tilde{v} \cdot r}{s^{co} + t \cdot N}$ copies he would upload if the market for uploading unlawful copies were perfectly competitive, a right holder who owns a work with a number $N > \frac{s^{co} - 2 \cdot s}{t}$ earns profits of $\frac{\tilde{v} \cdot r}{4} \cdot \frac{s^{co} + t \cdot N}{s + t \cdot N} - o$ instead of profits of $\frac{\tilde{v} \cdot r \cdot (s^{co} - s)}{s^{co} + t \cdot N} - o$. The former profits are larger than the latter since[59]

$$\frac{\tilde{v} \cdot r}{4} \cdot \frac{s^{co} + t \cdot N}{s + t \cdot N} - o > \frac{\tilde{v} \cdot r \cdot (s^{co} - s)}{s^{co} + t \cdot N} - o \Leftrightarrow (2 \cdot s + t \cdot N - s^{co})^2 > 0 \qquad (3.86)$$

As s^{co} increases, the part of the dark red function located to the left of the second vertical gridline and the part of the light red function located to the left of the third vertical gridline move upwards. At the same time, the gap between the two functions decreases. The first reason why the gap decreases is that the first vertical gridline is shifted to the right. Put differently, more right holders who are confronted with only

[59]Note that this inequality would not be fulfilled if $2 \cdot s + t \cdot N = s^{co}$, which is, however, excluded as the right holder owns a work with a number $N > \frac{s^{co} - 2 \cdot s}{t} \Leftrightarrow 2 \cdot s + t \cdot N > s^{co}$.

one unlawful copier fully prevent the unlawful copier from uploading and thus behave as if they competed with many unlawful copiers.

The second reason why the gap between the two functions diminishes is that an increase in s^{co} shifts the part of the light red function located between the first and the third vertical gridline upwards more strongly than the part of the dark red function located between the first and the second vertical gridline. For explanation, note that the first derivative of the described part of the light red function with respect to s^{co} is $\frac{\Delta\pi^{rh}}{\Delta s^{co}} = \tilde{v} \cdot r \cdot \frac{s+t \cdot N}{(s^{co}+t \cdot N)^2}$. The first derivative of the described part of the dark red function with respect to s^{co} is $\frac{\Delta\pi^{rh}}{\Delta s^{co}} = \frac{\tilde{v} \cdot r}{4 \cdot (s+t \cdot N)}$. An increase in s^{co} affects the described part of the light red function more strongly than the described part of the dark red function because $\tilde{v} \cdot r \cdot \frac{s+t \cdot N}{(s^{co}+t \cdot N)^2} > \frac{\tilde{v} \cdot r}{4 \cdot (s+t \cdot N)} \Leftrightarrow N > \frac{s^{co} - 2 \cdot s}{t}$.

The third reason why the gap between the two functions diminishes as s^{co} increases follows from the second. As the parts of the light red function and of the dark red function located to the right of the first vertical gridline move closer together, the points at which they intersect with the profit function of right holders who upload the only copy of their works also move closer together.

Note that the described effects of an increase in s^{co} are in accordance with proposition 3.7, which states that as the filtering intensity applied by a platform increases, a right holder who only competes with one unlawful copier for views of his work tolerates fewer unlawful uploads of his work, and that, once the filtering intensity has reached a critical threshold (here: $s^{co} = 2 \cdot s + t \cdot N$), the right holder fully prevents the unlawful copier from uploading and thus behaves as if he competed with many unlawful copiers (Sect. 3.6). However, unlike above, with popularity-based filtering, the critical threshold from which on a right holder fully prevents the unlawful copier from uploading is dependent on the work's popularity rank.

A.4 Positive Effect of Increase in Right Holders' Aggregate Profits on Number of Works Created

This section considers the implications of assuming a positive effect of an increase in right holders' aggregate profits on the number of works created for popularity-based filtering. The presence of unlawful copiers decreases right holders' aggregate profits. Regardless of whether a platform filters uniformly or based on popularity, automated filtering mitigates or even eliminates this effect. As explained in Sect. 3.7.2, if higher aggregate profits imply that more works are produced, it can therefore be concluded that:

$$t_1 \leq t_{2.2} < t_{2.1} \tag{3.87}$$

Table 3.4 shows the number of works uploaded in the three scenarios.

Table 3.4 Number of works uploaded if t decreases as Π increases, presuming popularity-based filtering

	N_1^*	$N_{2.1}^*$	$N_{2.2}^*$
$s^{co} < s + o$	$\frac{v_{max} \cdot r - s - o}{d \cdot r + t_1}$	$\frac{v_{max} \cdot r - s}{d \cdot r + t_{2.1}}$	$\frac{v_{max} \cdot r - s^{co}}{d \cdot r + t_{2.2}}$
$s^{co} \geq s + o$			$\frac{v_{max} \cdot r - s - o}{d \cdot r + t_{2.2}}$

In scenario 2.1, right holders upload all works associated with per-work profits of $\pi^{rh} \geq -o$. As is the case with uniform filtering, if the platform filters based on popularity, right holders require minimal per-work profits of $-o < \pi^{rh} \leq 0$ to upload their works. This reduced willingness to upload is represented by the smaller numerators of $N_{2.2}^*$ compared to $N_{2.1}^*$. Like uniform filtering, popularity-based filtering increases right holders' aggregate profits and thereby leads to a larger number of works produced. The upshot is that in scenario 2.2, the number of works associated with per-work profits that exceed the threshold of π^{rh} that is critical for right holders to upload is larger than the number of works that would exceed the same threshold in scenario 2.1. The decrease in the factor t from $t_{2.1}$ in the denominator of $N_{2.1}^*$ to $t_{2.2}$ in the denominator of $N_{2.2}^*$ represents this effect. The two effects run in opposite directions, leading to an overall ambiguous effect of automated filtering on the number of works uploaded.

If $s^{co} \geq s + o$, right holders upload only works they can upload profitably. Unless the filtering intensity applied by the platform ensures that right holders earn the same aggregate profits as in scenario 1, the resulting higher level of t compared to scenario 1 implies that right holders upload fewer works than in scenario 1.

Appendix 2: Explanation of Variables

Table 3.5 Explanation of variables

Variable	Explanation	Introduced in Section
α	Some value larger than or equal to 0 and smaller than 1; used to explain the assumption that right holders and unlawful copiers upload if they are indifferent	3.2.3.4
c	Right holders' costs of uploading a copy of a normalised work; also: unlawful copiers' costs of uploading a copy of a normalised work if the platform does not filter	3.2.3.1
c^{co}	Unlawful copiers' costs of uploading a copy of a normalised work if the platform filters	3.2.3.3
$\check{c}$	Right holders' costs of uploading a copy of a non-normalised work; used to explain the assumed filtering strategy for popularity-based filtering	3.7.3
d	Decrease in v^* resulting from a one-unit increase in N^*	3.2.4
g	Some value larger than 0; used to explain the assumed filtering strategy for popularity-based filtering	3.7.3
h	Factor with which the platform adapts the filtering intensity to a non-normalised work's popularity; used to explain the assumed filtering strategy for popularity-based filtering	3.7.3
m	Factor by which automated filtering increases unlawful copiers' per-copy uploading costs if the platform filters uniformly	3.4.2 (introduction)
$\tilde{m}$	Smallest value of m for which unlawful copiers cannot upload more works profitably than right holders can; $\tilde{m}=\frac{(v_{max}\cdot t+d\cdot s)\cdot r+d\cdot r\cdot o}{(v_{max}\cdot t+d\cdot s)\cdot r-t\cdot o}$	3.4.2.2
N	Number assigned to a normalised work	3.2.3.1
N^*	Number of normalised works uploaded to the platform in the market equilibrium; the subscripts '1', '2.1', and '2.2' indicate the scenario to which this variable refers	3.3.1

(continued)

Table 3.5 (continued)

Variable	Explanation	Introduced in Section
$\tilde{N}$	Number of the last normalised work a right holder uploads if unlawful copiers are absent; also: number of the last normalised work a right holder uploads if unlawful copiers are present and the platform filters in such a way that $m \geq \tilde{m}$ (uniform filtering) or $s^{co} \geq s + o$ (popularity-based filtering); $\tilde{N} = \frac{v_{max} \cdot r - s - o}{d \cdot r + t}$	3.3.1
$\hat{N}$	Number of the last normalised work a right holder uploads if unlawful copiers are present and the platform does not filter; $\hat{N} = \frac{v_{max} \cdot r - s}{d \cdot r + t}$	3.4.1.2
$\overline{N}$	Number of the last normalised work a right holder uploads if unlawful copiers are present and the platform filters uniformly in such a way that $m < \tilde{m}$; $\overline{N} = \frac{v_{max} \cdot r - m \cdot s}{d \cdot r + m \cdot t}$	3.4.2.2
$\overline{\overline{N}}$	Number of the last normalised work a right holder uploads if unlawful copiers are present and the platform filters based on popularity in such a way that $s^{co} < s + o$; $\overline{\overline{N}} = \frac{v_{max} \cdot r - s^{co}}{d \cdot r + t}$	A.1.2
$\dot{N}$	Number of the last normalised work to which the continuity assumption applies if only one copier per normalised work exists and the platform filters based on popularity in such a way that $s^{co} \geq s + o$; $\dot{N} = \frac{3 \cdot \tilde{v} \cdot r}{8 \cdot t} - \frac{s}{t} + \frac{\sqrt{\tilde{v} \cdot r \cdot (9 \cdot \tilde{v} \cdot r - 16 \cdot (s^{co} - s))}}{8 \cdot t} = \frac{3 \cdot \left(v_{max} - d \cdot \frac{v_{max} \cdot r - s - o}{d \cdot r + t}\right) \cdot r}{8 \cdot t}$ $- \frac{s}{t} + \frac{\sqrt{\left(v_{max} - d \cdot \frac{v_{max} \cdot r - s - o}{d \cdot r + t}\right) \cdot r \cdot \left(9 \cdot \left(v_{max} - d \cdot \frac{v_{max} \cdot r - s - o}{d \cdot r + t}\right) \cdot r - 16 \cdot (s^{co} - s)\right)}}{8 \cdot t}$	A.2.3

$\ddot{N}$	Number of the last normalised work to which the continuity assumption applies if only one copier per normalised work exists and the platform filters based on popularity in such a way that $s^{co} < s + o$; $\ddot{N} = \frac{3 \cdot \bar{\bar{v}} \cdot r}{8 \cdot t} - \frac{s}{t} + \frac{\sqrt{\bar{\bar{v}} \cdot r \cdot \left(9 \cdot \bar{\bar{v}} \cdot r - 16 \cdot (s^{co} - s)\right)}}{8 \cdot t} = \frac{3 \cdot \left(v_{max} - d \cdot \frac{v_{max} \cdot r - s^{co}}{d \cdot r + t}\right) \cdot r}{8 \cdot t} - \frac{s}{t} + \frac{\sqrt{\left(v_{max} - d \cdot \frac{v_{max} \cdot r - s^{co}}{d \cdot r + t}\right) \cdot r \cdot \left(9 \cdot \left(v_{max} - d \cdot \frac{v_{max} \cdot r - s^{co}}{d \cdot r + t}\right) \cdot r - 16 \cdot (s^{co} - s)\right)}}{8 \cdot t}$	A.2.3
o	A right holder's off-platform losses resulting from the upload of the first copy of his normalised work to a platform	3.2.3.1
π	Profits per normalised work a right holder or an unlawful copier obtains through the platform; for right holders—besides on-platform profits—profits obtained through the platform include off-platform losses resulting from an upload of a work to a platform (o); for the subscripts, see explanation to N^*; the superscripts indicate whether this variable refers to right holders ('rh') or to unlawful copiers ('co')	3.2.3.4
π^*	Profits per normalised work a right holder or an unlawful copier obtains through the platform in the Stackelberg equilibrium; for more details on the notion 'obtains through the platform', see explanation to π; for the subscripts, see explanation to N^*; for the superscripts, see explanation to π	3.4.1.1
Π	Right holders' aggregate profits obtained through the platform; for more details on the notion 'obtained through the platform', see explanation to π	3.3.2
Π^*	Right holders' aggregate profits obtained through the platform in the market equilibrium; for more details on the notion 'obtained through the platform', see explanation to π; for the subscripts, see explanation to N^*	3.3.2
r	Reward paid by the platform to a right holder or to an unlawful copier for a view of the copy of a normalised work that he or she has uploaded	3.2.3.1
s	Fixed part of right holders' per-copy uploading costs as a function of N; also: fixed part of unlawful copiers' per-copy uploading costs as a function of N if the platform does not filter	3.2.3.1

(continued)

Table 3.5 (continued)

Variable	Explanation	Introduced in Section
s^{co}	Fixed part of unlawful copiers' per-copy uploading costs as a function of N if the platform filters based on popularity	3.7.3
t	Increase in c resulting from a one-unit increase in N; also: increase in c^{co} resulting from a one-unit increase in N if the platform filters based on popularity; for the subscripts, see explanation to N^*	3.2.3.1
u	Number of copies of a normalised work uploaded to the platform; for the subscripts, see explanation to N^*; for the superscripts, see explanation to π	3.2.3.4
$\breve{u}$	Some number of copies uploaded of a normalised work; used to explain why unlawful copiers would collectively upload until the maximal number of copies that can be uploaded of a right holder's work without total uploading costs exceeding the per-work revenues is uploaded if the market for uploading unlawful copies of a work is perfectly competitive (Sect. 3.4.1.1); also: used to explain why an unlawful copier's marginal profits of uploading copies of a work are decreasing if only one unlawful copier per work exists (Sect. 3.5.1.1)	3.4.1.1; 3.5.1.1
u^*	Number of copies of a normalised work uploaded to the platform in the Stackelberg equilibrium; for the subscripts, see explanation to N^*; for the superscripts, see explanation to π	3.4.1.1
v	Number of views per normalised work	3.2.3.1
v_{max}	Hypothetical number of views per normalised work if $N^* = 0$ for a given price per view	3.2.4
v^*	Number of views per normalised work in the market equilibrium; for the subscripts, see explanation to N^*; $v^* = v_{max} - d \cdot N^*$	3.2.4
$\tilde{v}$	Number of views per normalised work if unlawful copiers are absent; also: number of views per normalised work if unlawful copiers are present and the platform filters in such a way that $m \geq \tilde{m}$ (uniform filtering) or $s^{co} \geq s + o$ (popularity-based filtering); $\tilde{v} = v_{max} - d \cdot \tilde{N} = v_{max} - d \cdot \frac{v_{max} \cdot r - s - o}{d \cdot r + t}$	3.3.1

$\hat{v}$	Number of views per normalised work if unlawful copiers are present and the platform does not filter; $\hat{v} = v_{max} - d \cdot \hat{N} = v_{max} - d \cdot \frac{v_{max} \cdot r - s}{d \cdot r + t}$	3.4.1.2
$\overline{v}$	Number of views per normalised work if unlawful copiers are present and the platform filters uniformly in such a way that $m < \tilde{m}$; $\overline{v} = v_{max} - d \cdot \overline{N} = v_{max} - d \cdot \frac{v_{max} \cdot r - m \cdot s}{d \cdot r + m \cdot t}$	3.4.2.2
$\overline{\overline{v}}$	Number of views per normalised work if unlawful copiers are present and the platform filters based on popularity in such a way that $s^{co} < s + o$; $\overline{\overline{v}} = v_{max} - d \cdot \overline{\overline{N}} = v_{max} - d \cdot \frac{v_{max} \cdot r - s^{co}}{d \cdot r + t}$	A.1.2

References

Banerjee, D. S. (2003). Software piracy: A strategic analysis and policy instruments. *International Journal of Industrial Organization, 21*(1), 97–127.

Beard, T. R., Ford, G. S., & Stern, M. (2018). Safe harbors and the evolution of online platform markets: An economic analysis. *Cardozo Arts & Entertainment Law Journal, 36*(2), 309–330.

Belleflamme, P., & Peitz, M. (2012). Digital piracy: Theory. In M. Peitz & J. Waldfogel (Eds.), *The Oxford handbook of the digital economy* (pp. 489–530). Oxford University Press.

Brøvig-Hanssen, R., & Jones, E. (2021). Remix's retreat? Content moderation, copyright law and mashup music. *New Media & Society*, 1–19.

Cohen, L. (2018, November 20). *Lyor Cohen: Article 13 could mean "less money for artists and songwriters on YouTube"*. Music Business Worldwide. https://www.musicbusinessworldwide.com/lyor-cohen-article-13-could-mean-less-money-for-artists-and-songwriters/

Copyright in the DSM Directive (EU). Directive (EU) 2019/790 of the European Parliament and of the European Council of 17 April 2019 on copyright and related rights in the Digital Single Market and amending Directives 96/9/EC and 2001/29/EC, OJ L 130/92 (2019). https://eur-lex.europa.eu/legal-content/EN/TXT/PDF/?uri=CELEX:32019L0790

Digital Services Act (EU). Regulation (EU) 2022/2065 of the European Parliament and of the Council of 19 October 2022 on a Single Market For Digital Services and amending Directive 2000/31/EC, OJ L 277/1 (2022). https://eur-lex.europa.eu/legal-content/EN/TXT/PDF/?uri=CELEX:32022R2065

Elkin-Koren, N., Nahmias, Y., & Perel, M. (2020). Is it time to abolish safe harbor? When rhetoric clouds policy goals. *Stanford Law & Policy Review, 31*(1), 1–50.

European Commission. (2016, September 14). *Commission staff working document: Impact assessment on the modernisation of EU copyright rules*. SWD(2016) 301 Final. https://digital-strategy.ec.europa.eu/en/library/impact-assessment-modernisation-eu-copyright-rules

European Commission. (2021, June 4). *Communication from the Commission to the European Parliament and the Council: Guidance on Article 17 of Directive 2019/790 on Copyright in the Digital Single Market*. COM(2021) 288 Final. https://eur-lex.europa.eu/legal-content/EN/TXT/?uri=CELEX:52021DC0288

Frosio, G. (2018). To filter, or not to filter? That is the question in EU copyright reform. *Cardozo Arts & Entertainment Law Journal, 36*(2), 331–368.

Gabison, G. A., & Buiten, M. C. (2020). Platform liability in copyright enforcement. *Science & Technology Law Review, 21*(2), 237–281.

Google. (n.d.). *Copyright and rights management*. YouTube Help. Retrieved July 17, 2024, from https://support.google.com/youtube/topic/2676339?hl=en-GB&ref_topic=6151248&sjid=7784574668489471573-EU

Hill, C. W. L. (2007). Digital piracy: Causes, consequences, and strategic responses. *Asia Pacific Journal of Management, 24*(1), 9–25.

IFPI. (2016). *Global music report: Music consumption exploding worldwide*. https://www.musikindustrie.de/fileadmin/bvmi/upload/06_Publikationen/GMR/Global-Music-Report-2016.pdf

Instagram. (n.d.). *Copyright*. Help Centre. Retrieved August 27, 2024, from https://help.instagram.com/126382350847838?helpref=faq_content

Johnson, W. R. (1985). The economics of copying. *Journal of Political Economy, 93*(1), 158–174.

Kiema, I. (2008). Commercial piracy and intellectual property policy. *Journal of Economic Behavior & Organization, 68*(1), 304–318.

Landes, W. M., & Posner, R. A. (1989). An economic analysis of copyright law. *The Journal of Legal Studies, 18*(2), 325–363.

Lefort, M. (2013). Copyright enforcement and quality differentiation on the internet. *Review of Economic Research on Copyright Issues, 10*(2), 27–54.

Lennon, J. (2016, May 3). *The real value gap in the music business*. https://medium.com/@joelennon/the-real-value-gap-in-the-music-business-5361d03b8f7a

Liebowitz, S. J. (2018, February 27). *Economic analysis of safe harbor provisions*. https://papers.ssrn.com/sol3/papers.cfm?abstract_id=3143811

Martínez-Sánchez, F. (2010). Avoiding commercial piracy. *Information Economics and Policy, 22*(4), 398–408.

Mazziotti, G. (2021). A data-driven approach to copyright in the age of online platforms. In D. J. Gervais (Ed.), *The future of intellectual property* (pp. 207–228). Edward Elgar.

Office for Harmonization in the Internal Market (Trade Marks and Designs). (2013, November). *European Citizens and Intellectual Property: Perception, Awareness and Behaviour*. https://euipo.europa.eu/tunnel-web/secure/webdav/guest/document_library/observatory/documents/IPContributionStudy/25-11-2013/european_public_opinion_study_web.pdf

Proposal for the Copyright in the DSM Directive (EU). Proposal for a Directive of the European Parliament and of the Council on copyright in the Digital Single Market, COM(2016) 593 Final (2016). https://eur-lex.europa.eu/legal-content/EN/TXT/?uri=CELEX%3A52016PC0593

Quintais, J. P., & Poort, J. (2019). The decline of online piracy: How markets—not enforcement—drive down copyright infringement. *American University International Law Review, 34*(4), 807–876.

SoundCloud. (n.d.). *Copyright information & policies*. SoundCloud Help Center. Retrieved July 17, 2024, from https://help.soundcloud.com/hc/en-us/sections/4402635879707-Copyright-Information-Policies

Spoerri, T. (2019). On upload-filters and other competitive advantages for big tech companies under Article 17 of the Directive on Copyright in the Digital Single Market. *Journal of Intellectual Property, Information Technology and Electronic Commerce Law, 10*(2), 173–186.

Twitch. (n.d.). *Music guidelines*. Retrieved July 2, 2024, from https://www.twitch.tv/p/en-gb/legal/community-guidelines/music/

Tyrowicz, J., Krawczyk, M., & Hardy, W. (2020). Friends or foes? A meta-analysis of the relationship between "online piracy" and the sales of cultural goods. *Information Economics and Policy, 53*.

Viacom v. YouTube (US). Viacom International, Inc. v. YouTube, Inc., 940 F. Supp. 2d 110 (S.D. New York 2013). https://scholar.google.com/scholar_case?case=9781681406417936292&q=F.+Supp.+2d+110+&hl=en&as_sdt=4,351

Vimeo. (2022, September 1). *Vimeo copyright policy*. https://vimeo.com/dmca

von Stackelberg, H. (2011). *Market structure and equilibrium* (D. Bazin (Scientific Director), L. Urch, & R. Hill, Trans.). Springer.

Wimmers, J., & Barudi, M. (2017). Der Mythos vom Value Gap: Kritik zur behaupteten Wertschöpfungslücke bei der Nutzung urheberrechtlich geschützter Inhalte auf Hosting-Diensten. *Gewerblicher Rechtsschutz Und Urheberrecht, 119*(4), 327–338.

Yoo, C. S. (2004). Copyright and product differentiation. *New York University Law Review, 79*(1), 212–280.

YouTube Inc., YouTube LLC, & Google Inc. (2013, March 29). *Memorandum of law in support of defendants' renewed motion for summary judgment*. https://casetext.com/brief/viacom-international-inc-et-al-v-youtube-inc-et-al_memorandum-of-law-in-support-re-440-motion-for-summary-judgment-document

Zimmerman, D. L. (2014). Copyright and social media: A tale of legislative abdication. *Pace Law Review, 35*(1), 260–284.

Chapter 4
Design of Automated Filtering to Approach Efficient Error Avoidance

Abstract State-of-the-art automated filters cannot perfectly emulate the analysis necessary to evaluate whether an upload attempt infringes copyright law. Existing discussions on how to design filtering mostly neglect some facets and rarely apply an efficiency perspective. This chapter conducts the first comprehensive analysis of why filters produce errors and what design choices best approach optimal error avoidance. For this, it applies the error cost framework, which states that decisions under uncertainty should strive to minimise the sum of direct costs of decision-making and expected net costs of errors. The analysis finds that a central reference database should be established, right holders should be responsible for preventing deficiencies of the database, and the database should comprise features to reduce right holders' costs of providing information. For other key questions, conclusive answers cannot yet be given. Platforms should thus experiment with different approaches, track and disclose probabilities of errors, and disclose filtering designs. The resulting insights would also reduce uncertainties that cause inefficient levels of divergence between national approaches to filtering. Furthermore, the analysis points to possible uses of the information collected by filters that go beyond blocking, namely, notifying right holders of potentially infringing uploads and improving selection into the manual review.

Keywords User-uploaded content platforms · User-generated content platforms · Economic analysis of platform regulation · Economic analysis of intermediary liability · Automated filtering · Upload filters · Automated decision-making · Automated copyright enforcement · Content moderation · Ubiquitous copyright infringement

The previous chapter demonstrated that automated filtering promotes right holders' interests even if it does not block all unlawful uploads of a work, that is, produces errors in the form of false negatives. As the avoidance of false negatives requires investments in filtering or leads to a higher probability of false positives, this finding begs the question how automated filtering should be designed to efficiently avoid errors. A review of the related literature shows that despite some relevant contributions, this question has not been answered comprehensively (Sect. 4.1). Section 4.2

O. Englisch, *Automated Copyright Filters*, International Law and Economics,
https://doi.org/10.1007/978-3-031-83161-4_4

explains the analytical approach adopted to address this research gap. The analysis is performed in Sects. 4.3–4.5. Finally, Sect. 4.6 summarises and discusses the main findings.

4.1 Literature Review and Research Question

The design of the reference database has received little attention so far. Suggestions include a central reference database (e.g., Arsham, 2013, p. 793; Bechtel, 2020, p. 267; Helman & Parchomovsky, 2011, pp. 1221–1223; Leistner, 2020, p. 183) and a reference database that is open to all right holders (e.g., Bechtel, 2020, p. 267; Grosse Ruse-Khan, 2021, pp. 163–164).

By contrast, numerous ideas on how to design the analysis of upload attempts to address the risk of errors have been advanced. They include:

- a privileged treatment of upload attempts flagged as lawful (e.g., Leistner, 2020, pp. 201–203; Raue & Steinebach, 2020, p. 363; Spindler, 2019, para. 107),
- a privileged treatment of upload attempts by trusted uploaders (e.g., Peukert et al., 2022, pp. 372–373; Schwartmann & Hentsch, 2020, p. 212; Spindler, 2019, para. 108),
- a specification of automatable rules (e.g., Elkin-Koren, 2017, pp. 1095–1096; M. Lambrecht, 2020, paras. 52–57; Yu, 2020, pp. 206–210),
- usage of machine learning to estimate probabilities of lawfulness (e.g., Burk, 2019, pp. 292–294; Elkin-Koren, 2017, pp. 1096–1099; M. Lambrecht, 2020, paras. 58–65; McJohn & McJohn, 2020, pp. 131–151; Senftleben, 2020, p. 324; Yu, 2020, pp. 210–212), and
- a manual review of certain upload attempts (e.g., Boroughf, 2015, pp. 116–117; Buiten et al., 2020, pp. 163–164; Elkin-Koren, 2017, p. 1098; Helman & Parchomovsky, 2011, pp. 1230–1233).

The question how automated filtering should be designed to reflect differences in national copyright laws has received almost no attention.

The above-mentioned design suggestions have mostly been considered regarding their implications for users' fundamental rights or the balance struck by copyright law. Efficiency considerations are rare. The main exception is the division of labour between right holders and platforms. In this regard, the 'cheapest cost avoider' principle has been applied (e.g., Helman & Parchomovsky, 2011, pp. 1212–1215; Husovec, 2016, pp. 35–37). The design of automated filtering has not yet been examined comprehensively from an efficiency perspective.

Note that the first-best efficient design of automated filtering would minimise the sum of aggregate expected net social costs of errors and aggregate direct costs.[1]

[1] Alternatively, a hypothetical filtering design that produces no errors and is associated with no direct costs may be defined as first-best efficient (see Kaesling & Knapp, 2020, pp. 817–818). This

Solving this minimisation problem presupposes information that is not available, notably on net social costs of errors and probabilities of errors associated with different designs of automated filtering. This chapter therefore focusses on the design that best approaches efficient error avoidance ('second-best efficient' design). It addresses the following research question:

Research Question 2
What design of automated filtering best approaches efficient error avoidance?

4.2 Analytical Approach

To address research question 2, this chapter verbally applies the error cost framework to automated filtering. By means of this framework, it analyses the efficiency of design choices that influence probabilities of errors. The design options to be analysed are identified based on a comprehensive examination of the reasons why automated filters produce errors.

The error cost framework is a tool to analyse efficient decision-making under uncertainty. It is usually stated as a cost minimisation problem (Posner, 1973, pp. 399–400; Rubinfeld & Sappington, 1987, p. 309): When deciding under uncertainty, the goal is to minimise the sum of expected net costs of errors and direct costs associated with decision-making. The framework is frequently used in the economic analysis of criminal procedure (e.g., *In re Winship*, 1970, US, Harlan, J., concurring, pp. 369–372; Kaplan, 1968; Posner, 1973), plays an important role in antitrust law (e.g., Beckner & Salop, 1999; Joskow & Klevorick, 1979; Lambert, 2011), and has been applied to other areas of law, including intellectual property law (e.g., Miller, 2014).

The error cost framework is useful for the research interest of this chapter. For one thing, it evaluates decision-making based on efficiency and thus applies the same evaluation standard as research question 2. For another, it focusses on decision-making under uncertainty, which is the key challenge in designing automated filtering. The uncertainty arises because—as the analysis in this chapter will show—filters cannot emulate the standard-based and context-dependent analysis required to determine whether an upload attempt infringes copyright law.

The error cost framework could be presented in a formalised manner. This approach would be useful if the goal were to better understand decision-making under uncertainty in general. However, existing analyses have already developed a profound understanding in this regard. This chapter therefore relies on the existing literature and focusses on applying the error cost framework to automated filtering.

---

difference in the definition is irrelevant for the analysis. A hypothetical filter that produces no errors and no direct costs is not considered in the following discussion because doing so would provide no added value.

For this application, modelling would not provide added value. This chapter therefore conducts a verbal economic analysis.

To ensure that the analysis does not become too convoluted, it is conducted separately for three sources of errors. An automated analysis using fingerprinting technology compares the similarity between a work in the reference database and an upload attempt. Errors may be caused by deficiencies of the reference database or by failures of the analysis of upload attempts to take relevant legal considerations into account. Errors may further be caused by technical shortcomings. For instance, the filtering software may have bugs or get hacked (Westcott-Baker et al., 2012, p. 195). For a focussed discussion, this chapter leaves possible technical shortcomings aside, presuming that content recognition technology does not err in measuring the similarity between works and upload attempts. Sections 4.3 and 4.4 focus on design choices to avoid errors resulting from deficiencies of the reference database and errors resulting from the analysis of upload attempts, respectively.

Both sections presume that a platform only operates in one jurisdiction, that is, that it only makes uploaded content available to viewers from one jurisdiction and prevents viewers from other jurisdictions from accessing it. This assumption helps to disentangle challenges related to automation from challenges related to multi-jurisdictional platform operation. However, it is an unrealistic assumption. Section 4.5 thus considers the implications of multi-jurisdictional platform operation for approaching the efficient design of automated filtering.

4.3 Reference Database

The reference database is crucial for the accuracy of automated filtering. It is a gateway to incorporate manual assessments of questions regarding copied-from content that are relevant for whether upload attempts are lawful, namely, subsistence of copyright protection, copyright ownership, and licensing arrangements. This section analyses how deficiencies of the reference database can be prevented to contribute to efficient error avoidance. Before answering this question in Sect. 4.3.2, it is useful to explain why deficiencies arise (Sect. 4.3.1).

4.3.1 Reasons for Deficiencies of Reference Database

Incompleteness is a first type of deficiency of the reference database. Public[2] and private[3] databases exist, but they are far from complete. Since creative content does

[2]Some countries incentivise right holders to register and deposit their works by attaching procedural benefits to registration and deposition. For a survey of voluntary registration systems, see WIPO - Standing Committee on Copyright and Related Rights (2005).

[3]Several private database operators claim to run databases that contain large numbers of works, for example, 'over 100 million tracks' (ACRCloud, n.d.), songs by '[m]ore than 140,000 music labels'

not need to be registered or deposited to be protected,[4] compiling a complete reference database is practically impossible (Helman & Parchomovsky, 2011, pp. 1219–1221). Besides by being incomplete, the reference database may cause errors if it contains unprotected content (Sect. 4.3.1.1) or incorrect metadata on who may upload (Sect. 4.3.1.2).

4.3.1.1 Unprotected Content in Reference Database

To explain why the reference database may contain unprotected content, it is useful to briefly outline the requirements for copyright protection. For protection to subsist, content must be original and the term of protection must not have lapsed.[5]

The definition of originality differs among jurisdictions. US law requires independent creation and a modicum of creativity: Independent creation establishes the boundary to copies from other works; the degree of creativity needed is 'extremely low' (*Feist,* 1991, p. 345). In the EU, the CJEU has developed a harmonised standard of originality, requiring a work to be 'its author's own intellectual creation' (*Infopaq*, 2009, para. 37) in the sense that it reflects 'the author's personality' (*Painer*, 2011, para. 88). Note, however, that this requirement does not apply to neighbouring rights.

If a work fulfils the requirements for protection, it enjoys copyright protection unless the term of protection has lapsed. US and EU law generally grant economic rights for 70 years *post mortem auctoris* (17 U.S.C. § 302(a); Article 1(1) of the Copyright Term Directive, 2006), but exceptions exist.[6]

Why may the reference database contain unoriginal or no longer protected content? One possibility is that the content is wrongfully entered as a protected work (Google, 2024, pt. Creating a balanced ecosystem). Given the low originality thresholds, the likelihood that the entered content in its entirety does not meet the applicable threshold is rather small. Content generated by artificial intelligence is an

---

and 'hundreds of thousands of titles of TV and film content' (Audible Magic Corporation, n.d.), 'millions of copyrighted videos and sound recordings' (Pex, n.d.), or 'more than 80 million files of audio and visual content' (Google, 2018, p. 25).

[4] Article 5(2) of the Berne Convention (1886) prohibits signatory states from making the enjoyment and exercise of copyrights in countries other than a work's country of origin subject to formalities. The notion formalities encompasses registration and deposition requirements (Ficsor, 2003, para. BC-5.7).

[5] In some countries, copyright protection only subsists in works that are fixed in some material form. Yet, this condition is irrelevant for the present discussion because all content entered into the reference database is fixed.

[6] Different rules apply, for instance, to works made for hire, anonymous or pseudonymous works, and neighbouring rights. Moreover, protection terms differ depending on the date of creation as they have been extended over time.

example of content that may be entered despite being unoriginal.[7] Content in which copyright protection has lapsed may be contained as a still protected work if it is entered despite the expiration of protection, if it is not removed from the reference database when the term of protection ends, or if the wrong end date of protection is indicated.

Alternatively, unprotected content may be incorporated in works entered into the reference database (Google, 2024, pt. Creating a balanced ecosystem). If unprotected elements are not marked, a filter may block upload attempts that contain the same or similar elements. For instance, suppose that the reference database contains a video that features no longer protected background music. A filter may then block an attempt to upload an otherwise distinct video that features the same background music.

4.3.1.2 Incorrect Metadata on Who May Upload

This section turns to reasons for inaccuracies of the metadata on who may upload a work. Before exploring these reasons, it is useful to briefly explain which person is entitled to upload a work.

Evidently, right holders may upload their works. Generally, the author of a work is the initial right holder.[8] The author may no longer be the right holder if copyright ownership has been transferred or the author has granted an exclusive licence. One reason for the transfer of copyrights is the death of an author. Copyright ownership is then transferred to the author's heirs based on rules of succession and—if applicable—the author's will. Another possibility is a contractual transfer. Contractual transfers of copyright ownership are not allowed in all countries.[9] Note, however, that even if contractual transfers are not permitted, the relevant rights may still be granted through exclusive licences.

[7] The protectability of content generated by artificial intelligence is an open question. Under EU law, the decisive question in terms of authors' rights is likely to be whether the production process involved sufficient creative choices by a human (Hartmann et al., 2020, p. 79). In addition, protection under neighbouring rights is conceivable (Hartmann et al., 2020, pp. 88–94). Under US law, a similar question is likely to be decisive (see Hristov, 2017, pp. 435–437).

[8] Some countries apply exceptions to works created within employment relationships and commissioned works. For example, the US 'works made for hire'-doctrine provides that works created by employees within the scope of employment relationships are owned by the employers, 17 U.S.C. § 201(b) in conjunction with § 101. It also applies to certain commissioned works.

[9] Under US law, copyright ownership and the individual exclusive rights can be transferred, 17 U.S.C. § 201(d). In the EU, rules on transfers are not harmonised. German copyright law is an example of a copyright regime that does not allow contractual transfers, section 29(1) of the Act on Copyright and Related Rights (1965).

Besides the right holder, a person who has obtained a non-exclusive licence encompassing the relevant use of a work for the relevant country may upload the work. Moreover, right holders can attach creative commons (or comparable) licences to their works, allowing anyone to use the works in ways otherwise restricted.[10]

Why may the metadata on copyright ownership or licensing arrangements be inaccurate? One possibility is that the metadata is wrongfully entered, either inadvertently or deliberately.[11] Moreover, if a work is incorporated in a work entered into the reference database, the incorporated work may be treated as belonging to the same right holder and as being associated with the same licensing arrangements as the work it is contained in (Google, 2024, pt. Creating a balanced ecosystem). For example, suppose that the reference database contains a documentary that features excerpts of movies that are covered by the quotation exception but are not marked as belonging to a different work. An automated analysis would then treat the excerpts as belonging to the same right holder and as being subject to the same licensing arrangements as the documentary.

4.3.2 Approaching an Efficient Prevention of Deficiencies of Reference Database

The previous section explained why the reference database is necessarily incomplete, may contain unprotected content, and may contain incorrect metadata on who may upload. These deficiencies may cause erroneous filtering decisions. The probabilities of errors can be reduced by adding works to the reference database, excluding unprotected content from it, and indicating correct metadata on who may upload.

This section examines how efficient prevention of deficiencies of the reference database can best be approached. Efficiency requires deficiencies to be prevented as cheaply as possible (Sect. 4.3.2.1) and only those deficiencies to be prevented that are worthy of being prevented (Sect. 4.3.2.2).

[10] For more information on the different types of licenses, see Creative Commons (n.d.).

[11] YouTube reports that between July 2023 and December 2023 more than 6% of removal requests through its public webform 'were the subject of abusive copyright removal requests, meaning these requests were assessed and rejected by our review team as a likely false assertion of copyright ownership' and that this 'attempted abuse rate […] was more than 10 times higher […] than the attempted abuse rate across all other copyright removal tools' (Google, 2024, pt. Creating a balanced ecosystem). For Content ID, no abuse rate is reported. However, it is stated that 'the limited availability of Content ID also helps to limit abuse of that tool' (Google, 2024, pt. Creating a balanced ecosystem).

4.3.2.1 Reducing Direct Costs of Preventing Deficiencies

This section examines how deficiencies of the reference database can be prevented most cheaply. One cost component relates to the collection of the required information. To add protected works, one must learn about their existence, gain access to copies, and assess the subsistence of protection, which inter alia requires information on creation processes and end dates of protection. To mark elements that are unprotected or owned by other right holders ('external elements'), one must identify these elements. Correctly indicating metadata on who may upload requires information on copyright ownership and licensing arrangements.

Actors' costs diverge with respect to gathering this information. It is socially desirable that the actor who can gather information most cheaply ('cheapest cost avoider')[12] prevents deficiencies.

Right holders can be presumed to be cheapest cost avoiders in this regard. Unlike other actors, they do not incur costs to find protected content and obtain copies. They may be uncertain about whether content is (still) protected but presumably have more information than other actors on the relevant facts. Right holders are further likely to be best placed to evaluate whether elements of their works are external. They may not be in the best position to assess whether external elements are protected and—if yes—to collect the relevant metadata. However, it suffices that they indicate that the elements are external. External elements that are protected can then still be entered by their owners along with the relevant metadata. Moreover, right holders generally incur negligible costs to find out that they are right holders and which licensing arrangements apply to their works (see Husovec, 2018, p. 66). Exceptions are conceivable, for instance, if copyright ownership is transferred upon the death of an author or sublicenses are granted. However, even then, right holders appear best placed to collect the needed information.

It is further desirable to reduce right holders' costs of gathering information, provided that the measures taken entail a reduction in right holders' aggregate direct costs that exceeds the associated costs. A database operator can reduce right holders' costs by setting up an automated calculation of end dates of protection.[13] Instead of determining end dates, right holders would then only have to indicate the information needed for the calculation, for example, the date of the death of the author. Translating rules on the duration of protection into an algorithm is laborious but for many countries such algorithms already exist.[14] Moreover, reductions in costs materialise for every work in the reference database. For a substantial number of

[12]The concept has been developed by Calabresi (1970, p. 135) as a rule for allocating costs of accidents.

[13]Calculators of end dates of protection have already been created (e.g., IP Squared, n.d.).

[14]For flowcharts for all EU Members States except Croatia (plus Iceland, Norway, Switzerland, and UK), see IP Squared (n.d.).

works in the database, it is thus likely that the associated costs fall below the reduction in right holders' aggregate direct costs.

Another measure that the database operator can take to reduce right holders' informational costs is to employ content recognition technology to screen for overlapping entries.[15] In this way, external elements can be identified that belong to other right holders' works, that originate from no longer protected works which are contained in the reference database and labelled as unprotected, or that have been marked by other right holders as unprotected. The aggregate reduction in right holders' costs of identifying external elements is likely to exceed the social costs of employing (existing) content recognition technology.

Furthermore, database operators and platforms can reduce right holders' costs of identifying external elements by making it easy for uploaders whose upload attempts have been blocked to notify right holders of unmarked potentially external elements. Database operators and platforms can facilitate such notifications by setting up a time-saving communication channel for uploaders and right holders. This measure is cost-justified as the costs of establishing a communication channel are not overly high. Moreover, platforms can facilitate notifications by informing uploaders about the parts of their upload attempts that triggered the blockings and about the allegedly infringed works.[16] The costs associated with notifications can further be reduced by informing right holders who have been notified by uploaders about the parts of their entries that matched with the upload attempts. Providing this information is cost-justified as it is collected during the filtering process anyway.

Besides informational costs, the opportunity costs of the time spent on adding protected works to the reference database, marking external elements, and entering correct metadata on who may upload arise (see Meyers, 2009, p. 948). As right holders are best placed to collect the needed information, it is sensible that right holders also take these actions. To reduce right holders' costs, the database operator

[15]For example, YouTube screens entries into the reference database for overlaps with existing entries (Google, 2022, pt. Fix reference overlaps): The right holder who made the second entry is informed about overlaps and can either exclude the critical part or assert ownership. Asserting ownership triggers a notification to the right holder who made the first entry. He can then either exclude the critical part or counter-assert ownership. Until the issue is resolved, ownership is assigned to the right holder who made the first entry. A counter-assertion prevents the right holder who made the second entry from asserting ownership. In addition, an option to message the other right holder is provided. Pex (n.d.) also provides 'an ownership conflict resolution system that works to resolve ownership disputes and inconsistencies in the data' but does not provide information on the functioning of the process. Likewise, it has been reported that Audible Magic, Facebook, and INA-Signature take measures to resolve overlaps between entries in the reference database (French Ministry of Culture, 2020, p. 42).

[16]For example, YouTube e-mails uploaders the name of the right holder of the allegedly infringed work and a link to YouTube Studio, where uploaders can see the concerned segment of their upload attempt and find further information on the allegedly infringed work (see TunePocket, 2021).

can set up time-saving ways for entering works, marking external elements,[17] and indicating metadata. Moreover, expiration of protection can trigger automated labelling as unprotected. The costs of establishing the infrastructure needed for these measures are not overly high. They are likely to be dwarfed by the reduction in right holders' aggregate direct costs.

Finally, a duplication of costs can be prevented by using the same reference database for automated filtering on all platforms[18] (Arsham, 2013, p. 793; Bechtel, 2020, p. 267; Helman & Parchomovsky, 2011, pp. 1221–1223; Leistner, 2020, p. 183) and potentially for additional purposes.[19] Keeping the completeness and accuracy of reference databases constant, this avoids a duplication of the costs associated with entering works, marking external elements, and indicating metadata.[20] Intermediaries who collect right holders' information and then distribute it to different reference databases may somewhat decrease the duplication of costs, but a central reference database still promises efficiency gains. As the needed information does not diverge between platforms, a central reference database is as useful for platforms as an individual reference database would be. In addition, a central reference database prevents a duplication of the costs of establishing the relevant infrastructure, which includes the above-discussed automated calculation of end dates of protection, automated screening for overlaps, and time-saving ways to enter works, mark external elements as well as indicate metadata.

4.3.2.2 Selecting Deficiencies Worthy of Being Prevented

Besides reducing the direct costs of preventing deficiencies of the reference database, efficiency requires right holders to only prevent deficiencies if the associated costs fall below the resulting reduction in aggregate expected net social costs of errors.

Adding a work to the reference database increases the probability that a filter blocks upload attempts that unlawfully copy from it. At the same time, it also

[17] For example, YouTube enables right holders to exclude segments by specifying the start and end time of elements that are not part of the creation (Google, 2022, pt. Exclude parts of your references).

[18] A central reference database must contain a copy of each work so that platforms can create their own fingerprints.

[19] Of note, the reference database may be used to facilitate rights clearing (see Landes & Posner, 2003, p. 477; Samuelson et al., 2010, p. 1186).

[20] A constant level of completeness and accuracy is assumed to simplify the argument. Alternatively, one could keep the total investment in the reference databases constant. Establishing several less accurate reference databases instead of one more accurate reference database would then entail higher aggregate expected net social costs of errors. Of course, one could also vary the investment and the completeness and accuracy. In any case, the sum of aggregate direct costs and aggregate expected net social error costs increases if more than one reference database is created.

increases the probability that the filter blocks upload attempts that lawfully copy from the work. Entering a work further carries the risk of including unmarked external elements into the reference database. Due to these costs, not all works are worthy of being entered.

One may entertain the idea that an eligibility check by the database operator would help to exclude works that are not worthy of being entered.[21] However, it is hard to conceive how a database operator can assess the relevant costs. Right holders are in a better position to make assessments in this regard, at least when it comes to estimating the direct costs of entering works and the costs of unlawful uploads that copy from their works.

In any case, even if suitable variables were found, platforms could use such variables in a more fine-tuned way to differentiate the 'strictness' of filtering upload attempts copying from different works. Overall, a reference database that is open to all right holders therefore appears preferable (cf. Bechtel, 2020, p. 267; Grosse Ruse-Khan, 2021, pp. 163–164).

The consideration that not all deficiencies of the reference database deserve to be prevented further implies that external elements are only worthy of being marked if they have been automatically flagged, if they have been notified by concerned uploaders, or if the costs of identifying them fall below the resulting reduction in aggregate expected net social costs of errors.

The same consideration may also render separate entries of unprotected content acceptable. Yet, this implication is of little relevance. For one thing, as explained in Sect. 4.3.1.1, cases in which entered content does not qualify for copyright protection are rare. For another, at least if an automated calculation of the term of protection is implemented, correctly indicating the end date of protection is likely to be cost-justified.

A final implication of the consideration that right holders should only prevent deficiencies for which the resulting reduction in aggregate expected net social costs of errors exceeds the associated direct costs is that some inaccuracies in terms of the metadata on who may upload are acceptable. However, in most cases identifying the right holder or licensees is rather straightforward. A high level of accuracy therefore appears justified in these regards.

---

[21] For example, YouTube limits the eligibility for its Content ID program to right holders who 'own exclusive rights to a substantial body of original material that is frequently uploaded to YouTube' (Google, n.d., pt. How Content ID works). Note, however, that right holders who are not eligible for using Content ID can commission service providers to manage their rights for them (Google, 2024, pt. Introduction). Alternatively, such right holders have access to tools with limited functionality, including the Content Verification Program, which right holders can use to find copying uploads to then issue takedown requests (Google, n.d., pt. Content Verification Program), and the Copyright Match Tool, which right holders who have submitted a takedown request can use to scan for further matches of the content they have reported in the request (Google, n.d., pt. Use the Copyright Match Tool).

4.4 Analysis of Upload Attempts

Having reflected on design options that contribute to an efficient prevention of deficiencies of the reference database, this section turns to errors caused by the analysis of upload attempts. It considers an analysis of upload attempts that consists of up to two steps. First, all upload attempts go through an automated analysis performed by state-of-the-art fingerprinting technology. In a second step, selected automated decisions are manually reviewed. Sections 4.4.2 and 4.4.3 examine how the automated analysis and the manual review can be designed to contribute to efficient error avoidance, respectively. To do so, it is useful to first explain why an automated analysis cannot observe the aspects that a legal analysis would consider (Sect. 4.4.1).

4.4.1 Reasons for Unobservability of Relevant Legal Aspects by Automated Analysis

To assess the lawfulness of upload attempts, essentially two questions must be addressed:

- Is the potentially infringed content copyright-protected?
- Does the upload attempt infringe the right holder's rights?

An upload attempt infringes copyright if both questions are answered in the affirmative. The second question must be answered in the negative if the uploader is the right holder or a licensee, the uploader has created the uploaded content independently, the uploader only copies a fragment of a work and copying the fragment does not amount to an infringement, the upload is sufficiently distinct from the allegedly infringed work, or the use of the copied content is covered by a copyright exception.

Right holders can assess the subsistence of copyright protection, copyright ownership, and licensing arrangements when entering content into the reference database. This section explains why assessing the remaining aspects, namely, parallel independent creation (Sect. 4.4.1.1), fragmented copying (Sect. 4.4.1.2), non-literal copying (Sect. 4.4.1.3), and relevant copyright exceptions (Sect. 4.4.1.4), requires considerations that a state-of-the-art automated analysis cannot carry out.

4.4.1.1 Parallel Independent Creation

If a creator creates a work independently, it is irrelevant whether the work bears resemblance to another work (Goldstein & Hugenholtz, 2013, p. 193). However, independent creation may already be denied if the other work subconsciously inspired the creator (see e.g. *Bright Tunes Music Corp. v. Harrisongs Music, Ltd.*,

1976, US, pp. 180–181; *Magdalenenarie*, 1970, Germany, para. 22). An automated analysis cannot figure out whether the creation has been independent because such an assessment requires evidence on the creation process and the knowledge (and subconscious inspiration) of the creator.

The risk of errors resulting from a failure to consider the possibility of parallel independent creation should not be overstated as parallel independent creation is unlikely for sophisticated works. The likelihood is higher if low creativity content, such as a sufficiently original fragment of a work, is concerned. Moreover, two authors are more likely to create closely related works if both base their creation on public domain content.

4.4.1.2 Fragmented Copying

The lawfulness of an upload attempt that exhibits similarities to a fragment of a copyright-protected work further depends on characteristics of the fragment. User-generated, but also professionally generated content (e.g., sampled music), often incorporates fragments of other works. To understand why a filter cannot observe considerations relevant for an evaluation of whether an upload attempt that copies a fragment of a work is lawful, an outline of the legal standards is useful.

Under US law, copying a fragment of a work only falls within the scope of the right holder's rights if the fragment is original (*Feist*, 1991, p. 348). *De minimis* copying, namely, copying that is so 'meager and fragmentary that the average audience would not recognize the appropriation', does not infringe right holders' rights (*Fisher v. Dees*, 1986, p. 434, n. 2). Courts are divided on whether the *de minimis* standard also applies to sound recordings.[22]

In the EU, fragments of works must be treated like whole works (*Infopaq*, 2009, para. 38). Hence, protection of fragments presupposes originality (*Infopaq*, 2009, para. 39). For sound recordings, the copying of a fragment in principle falls within the producer's exclusive rights 'even if very short' (*Pelham*, 2019, para. 29).

Why can an automated filter not observe considerations relevant for upload attempts that copy fragments of works? US and EU copyright law require an assessment of whether a fragment is sufficiently original. Since existing standards of originality cannot be condensed into bright-line rules, an automated analysis cannot reflect them. Likewise, the standard developed under US law for *de minimis* copying cannot be translated into a clear-cut threshold. The CJEU's approach to sound recordings could be translated into the—albeit extremely strict—bright-line rule that any upload of a fragment of a sound recording may interfere with a producer's rights. An automated analysis could enforce this rule.

[22] The 6th Circuit ruled that the *de minimis* doctrine is not applicable to sound recordings (*Bridgeport Music, Inc. v. Dimension Films*, 2005, pp. 800–802). The 9th Circuit considered the reasoning of the 6th Circuit to be unpersuasive and held that the *de minimis* doctrine also applies to sound recordings (*Vmg Salsoul, LLC v. Ciccone*, 2016, pp. 880–885).

4.4.1.3 Non-literal Copying

Having reasoned why—possibly except for the CJEU's approach to sound recordings—an automated analysis cannot reflect legal considerations relevant to assess whether upload attempts that copy fragments of works are lawful, this section argues that the same is true for non-literally copying upload attempts. An upload attempt may copy content non-literally to circumvent detection. Unless covered by a copyright exception, such upload attempts are almost certainly unlawful.

Alternatively, new creative content may partially rely on a modified pre-existing work. If no copyright exception applies, the lawfulness of such upload attempts depends on whether the similarity relates to the underlying idea or to the expression and on the degree of similarity.

Idea-Expression Dichotomy

An upload attempt that exhibits non-literal similarity to a copyright-protected work is not infringing if the similarity arises at the level of the underlying idea. To explain why an automated analysis cannot carry out the relevant considerations, an outline of the legal standards is useful.

In terms of copyright protection, an author's expression is not limited to the concrete fixation of a work but extends more abstractly to the creative structures developed. For instance, copyright protection is not limited to the exact way in which a story is told but extends to the patterns of the story (Chafee, 1945, pp. 513–514)[23] or even to individual characters.[24] Once the threshold to some level of abstraction is crossed, the creative structures become so general that they constitute an idea, which is not protected.

US courts have developed two doctrines to provide guidance on when the threshold is reached (Goldstein & Hugenholtz, 2013, pp. 220–221): The *scènes à faire*-doctrine provides that elements of a work that are customary for a given genre constitute ideas (*Reyher v. Children's Television Workshop*, 1976, p. 91); the merger-doctrine that, as the degrees of freedom in articulating a thought decrease, ideas and expressions merge, thereby shifting the articulation into the category of ideas (*Morrisey v. Procter & Gamble Company*, 1967, pp. 678–679). In the EU, no harmonised approach to demarcating the boundary exists.

Why can a filter not reflect these considerations? An automated analysis that checks not only for infringements of the concrete articulation of a work but also for infringements of its more abstract expression would need to compare the creative structures of a work in the reference database with the creative structures of an upload attempt. A state-of-the-art automated analysis cannot perform this task.

[23] For examples in the case law, see *Nichols* (1930, US, pp. 121–123); *Laras Tochter* (1999, Germany, paras. 25–52).

[24] For examples in the case law, see *Anderson v. Stallone* (1989, US, pp. 20–23); *Pippi-Langstrumpf-Kostüm I* (2013, Germany, paras. 24–31).

Required Level of Similarity

Another reason why an upload attempt that exhibits non-literal similarity to a copyright-protected work may not be deemed an infringement is if the level of similarity is insufficient. Again, to explain why the required analysis cannot be automated, it is useful to first outline the relevant considerations.

US copyright law defines the level of similarity needed for an infringement as substantial similarity (see *Nichols*, 1930, p. 121). However, consensus ends with the label of the concept. Courts have developed different tests to assess whether the threshold is surpassed.[25] An important test is the ordinary observer test.[26] The decisive question has been specified as whether, when comparing two pieces of content, an 'ordinary observer, unless he set out to detect the disparities, would be disposed to overlook them, and regard their aesthetic appeal as the same' (*Peter Pan Fabrics, Inc. v. Martin Weiner Corp.*, 1960, p. 489). This version of the test neglects that an ordinary observer would not distinguish between copyright-protected and not protected elements of a work (Rogers, 2013, pp. 904–905). In a later version, the characteristics of the observer have thus been refined: The more discerning ordinary observer disregards non-protected elements when forming his opinion (*Folio Impressions, Inc. v. Byer California*, 1991, pp. 765–766). Another important test is the extrinsic/intrinsic test:[27] The extrinsic part analyses similarities using objective criteria; The intrinsic part compares the '"total concept and feel"' from the perspective of an ordinary reasonable person (*Krofft*, 1977, pp. 1164, 1167). The test affirms substantial similarity if it finds similarity in both parts.

EU copyright law does not define the degree of similarity required for a use to fall within the exclusive rights of a right holder. To determine the scope of exclusive rights, a balance between right holders' interests in the protection of their intellectual property, uploaders' interests in the protection of the freedom of their artistic expression, and the public interest must be struck (*Pelham*, 2019, para. 32). It follows that the scope of right holders' exclusive rights is limited by uploaders' fundamental rights. For sound recordings, the CJEU provides further guidance. A producer's rights are interfered with unless the similarity between the pre-existing sound recording and the non-literal copy is 'unrecognisable to the ear' (*Pelham*, 2019, para. 31). This criterion suggests that the required degree of similarity for a use to fall within the scope of a producer's rights is low, but the CJEU did not elaborate on the subtleties of the standard.[28]

Why can a filter not reflect these considerations? A state-of-the-art automated analysis cannot observe decisive parts of the tests under US law (e.g., aesthetic

---

[25] For an overview of the different tests, see Rogers (2013, pp. 903–911).

[26] For an overview of the case law and the subtleties in applying the test, see Rogers (2013, pp. 904–907).

[27] For an overview of the case law and the subtleties in applying the test, see Rogers (2013, pp. 907–909).

[28] For example, it remains unclear to the ear of whom similarity should be recognisable: An average listener? An attentive listener? A casual listener?

appeal; total concept and feel). Moreover, it cannot separate protected and non-protected elements. Likewise, an automated analysis cannot perform the balancing of rights required under EU law. It can also not decide whether the standard of 'recognisability to the ear' for sound recordings is fulfilled.

4.4.1.4 Copyright Exceptions

Finally, the lawfulness of an upload attempt that exhibits similarity to a copyright-protected work depends on whether a copyright exception applies. Copyright exceptions render some upload attempts permissible that would otherwise be infringing. This may, for instance, include movie reviews, sampled music, parodies, and uploads that incidentally include protected content.

This section explains why an automated analysis can neither consider the aspects that are decisive for the applicability of the US fair use doctrine nor those decisive for the applicability of the relevant exceptions under EU law. Both sections first outline the exceptions.

Fair Use

The most important copyright exception in US law is fair use. This doctrine has been developed in the case law (see e.g. *Folsom v. Marsh*, 1841, p. 348). The Copyright Act of 1976 codified it in 17 U.S.C. § 107.[29] It requires the four factors listed in § 107 to be explored and weighed together in light of the purposes of copyright (*Campbell*, 1994, p. 578).

The first factor is the 'purpose and character of the use', § 107(1). It includes an assessment of whether a use is commercial, § 107(1), and of whether it is transformative, that is, 'adds something new, with a further purpose or different character, altering the first with new expression, meaning, or message' (*Campbell*, 1994, p. 579).[30] Parodies are among the uses that may be transformative (*Campbell*, 1994, p. 579).

The 'nature of the copyrighted work' is the second factor, § 107(2). This factor puts the spotlight on the copied-from work. It inter alia renders the scope of fair use narrower for works possessing a higher degree of creative expression (see *Campbell*, 1994, p. 586).[31]

Third, the 'amount and substantiality of the portion used' must be considered, § 107(3). This factor focusses on the overlap between the use and the copied-from work. The overlap is considered on a quantitative and on a qualitative basis (see *Harper & Row*, 1985, pp. 564–566).

---

[29] All further references to statutory provisions in this section refer to title 17 U.S.C.

[30] In the same decision, the US Supreme Court also held that the more transformative a use is, the less weight is assigned to other subfactors, such as the commercial nature of a use.

[31] In the same decision, the US Supreme Court also noted that this consideration is of little use for parodies as parodies almost always copy from 'publicly known, expressive works.'

Finally, the fourth factor 'effect [...] upon the potential market for or value of the copyrighted work', § 107(4), considers the economic impact of the use. In addition to potential harm to the market of the copied-from work, harm to the market for derivative works must be taken into account (*Harper & Row*, 1985, p. 568). Market harm stemming from negative criticism or ridicule must not be considered (*Campbell*, 1994, pp. 591–592).

Why can an automated analysis not reflect the considerations relevant for the fair use doctrine? An automated analysis cannot observe some of the relevant aspects, including the transformative purpose, the qualitative overlap between the copied-from work and the use, the market harm (in particular for transformative uses), and the weighing together of the four factors in light of the purposes of copyright. While an automated analysis can reflect other relevant aspects, such as the commercial nature of a use and its quantitative overlap with the copied-from work, solely considering these aspects would alter the fair use doctrine beyond recognition.

EU Copyright Exceptions

In contrast to the US approach of applying an open-ended standard, EU copyright law provides a list of 'stencils' that Member States can (and sometimes must) use to carve out specific uses from the scope of exclusive rights.[32] For platforms, the exceptions for quotations, parodies, incidental inclusions, news reporting, and the use of political speeches as well as extracts of public lectures or similar works are of relevance.[33]

---

[32] Apart from certain 'cases of minor importance', Article 5(3)(o) of the InfoSoc Directive (2001), Member States must not apply further exceptions (*Pelham*, 2019, para. 58). If a Member State implements an exception, it must do so in accordance with EU law (*ACI Adam and others*, 2014, para. 34).

[33] M. Lambrecht (2020, para. 124) notes that besides the quotation and parody exception, which he considers in detail, the incidental inclusion and the freedom of panorama exception are potentially relevant. This section neglects the freedom of panorama exception, which is contained in Article 5(3)(h) of the InfoSoc Directive (2001), as this book focusses on copyright in music and videos (Sect. 1.2). One may further argue that the teaching exception in Article 5(3)(a) of the InfoSoc Directive (2001) is relevant for educational content. While the exception encompasses distance learning, recital 42 of the InfoSoc Directive (2001), it arguably only applies to educational institutions (Triaille et al., 2013, pp. 359–360). Moreover, it requires an identifiable group of students (Triaille et al., 2013, p. 354). Uses typically relevant for platforms (e.g., use of protected content during video tutorials or recorded lectures) are therefore excluded. Likewise, in cases of distance learning, the mandatory education exception introduced by Article 5(1) of the Copyright in the DSM Directive (2019) only applies if the use is 'accessible only by the educational establishment's pupils or students and teaching staff'. Finally, one may entertain the idea that the exception for uses in connection with the demonstration or repair of equipment in Article 5(3)(l) of the InfoSoc Directive (2001) is relevant. However, this exception has not yet played a role in the online context.

The quotation exception in Article 5(3)(d) of the InfoSoc Directive (2001)[34] may, for instance, render uploads of movie reviews or sampled music permissible.[35] To be covered by the quotation exception, a functional purpose (e.g., a criticism or review of the quoted work) must justify the quotation, Article 5(3)(d). A sound sample incorporated into a new work may also amount to a quotation if it is intended to enter into dialogue with the copied-from work (*Pelham*, 2019, para. 72). The upper limit of the amount that may be quoted is defined as the extent required by the specific purpose of the quotation, Article 5(3)(d). Moreover, the portion taken must be secondary to the uploader's own assertions and may not 'be so extensive as to conflict with a normal exploitation of the work' (*Spiegel Online*, 2019, para. 79).

A second potentially relevant exception is the parody exception in Article 5(3)(k).[36] A parody has two essential characteristics: First, it evokes an existing work while being noticeably different from it; Second, it is an expression of humour or mockery (*Deckmyn*, 2014, para. 20). To assess whether a parody infringes a right holder's rights, a fair balance between the right holder's and the uploader's rights and interests must be struck (*Deckmyn*, 2014, para. 27).

A third potentially relevant exception concerns incidental inclusions, Article 5(3)(i). EU copyright law does not provide guidance on how to distinguish incidental from relevant inclusions. On the Member State level, German courts inter alia address the question whether the included part can be deleted or replaced without attracting the average observer's attention or influencing the overall impression (e.g., *Möbelkatalog*, 2014, para. 27).

Finally, exceptions for news reporting, Article 5(3)(c), and the use of political speeches as well as extracts of public lectures or similar works, Article 5(3)(f), may be relevant. According to Article 5(3)(c) and (f), these exceptions require an informatory purpose to justify the use of protected content.

Why can an automated analysis not reflect the considerations relevant for these copyright exceptions? An automated analysis cannot observe the functional purpose of a quotation and answer the question whether the specific purpose of a quotation justifies the amount copied. Regarding parodies, the same is true for an assessment whether an upload contains an expression of humour or mockery and for the required balancing of interests. Likewise, an automated filter cannot observe the role copyright-protected content plays in an upload, as relevant under German law to determine whether an inclusion is incidental. The same is true for the question whether an informatory purpose justifies the copying for news reporting and political speeches as well as public lectures or similar works.

---

[34] Unless indicated otherwise, all further references to statutory provisions in this section refer to the InfoSoc Directive (2001).

[35] Article 17(7), second subparagraph, (a) of the Copyright in the DSM Directive (2019) renders the quotation exception mandatory for user-generated content uploaded to a platform.

[36] Article 17(7), second subparagraph, (b) of the Copyright in the DSM Directive (2019) renders the parody exception mandatory for user-generated content uploaded to a platform.

As with the fair use doctrine, the similarity between a work and an upload attempt is not irrelevant for addressing these copyright exceptions. However, evaluating the compliance of an upload attempt with these exceptions solely on a quantitative basis would omit crucial considerations (see French Ministry of Culture, 2021, pp. 49–51).

4.4.2 Approaching an Efficient Automated Analysis

The previous section explained why an automated analysis cannot reflect the considerations that determine whether an upload attempt that bears resemblance to another work (and is not uploaded by a licensee or the right holder) is lawful. An automated analysis must therefore rely on observable variables that are alien to or at least not decisive for a legal analysis. Section 4.4.2.1 outlines approaches to make blocking decisions based on observable variables. Due to a lack of experience with these approaches, it is not yet possible to answer the question how an automated analysis can best be designed to contribute to efficient error avoidance (Sect. 4.4.2.2). Given this somewhat disappointing conclusion, for now experimentation with different approaches is desirable (Sect. 4.4.2.3).

4.4.2.1 Approaches to Make Blocking Decisions Based on Observable Variables

Table 4.1 displays examples of observable variables presumably correlated with the probability of lawfulness of upload attempts.

In addition, the idea of considering observable variables correlated with net social costs of false negatives or false positives could come to mind.[37] However, conceivable variables, for example, recency (Raue & Steinebach, 2020, p. 363) or popularity of copied-from work, are likely to be strongly correlated with net social costs of false negatives and false positives. For blocking decisions, these variables would thus only be informative if it were known which correlation is stronger.

Two main approaches to make blocking decisions based on observable variables are conceivable. The first is to specify automatable rules.[38] An automatable rule can rely on a single variable. For instance, it can mandate a blocking if the similarity between an upload attempt and a work exceeds a certain threshold.[39] Alternatively,

[37] In terms of false negatives, see Raue and Steinebach (2020, pp. 363–364).

[38] This approach has mostly been discussed in terms of automating fair use analyses (e.g., Elkin-Koren, 2017, pp. 1095–1096; Helman & Parchomovsky, 2011, pp. 1231–1232; Yu, 2020, pp. 206–210). It has further been considered in the context of assessing EU copyright exceptions (e.g., M. Lambrecht, 2020, paras. 52–57).

[39] For example, Boroughf (2015, pp. 115–116) proposes to only block 'egregious uses', that is, uses exhibiting 'a 95 percent proportion of a single reference file to other content in an uploaded video'.

Table 4.1 Examples of observable variables presumably correlated with the probability of lawfulness of upload attempts

Variables related to	Examples
Overlap between upload attempt and work in reference database	Duration, similarity, proportion overlap accounts for in upload attempt or copied-from work
Upload attempt	Trigger words in title or description,[a] choice to display advertisements along with upload,[b] self-assessment of whether copyright exception applies (e.g., Elkin-Koren, 2017, p. 1096; Leistner, 2020, p. 202; Raue & Steinebach, 2020, p. 363)
Uploader	Previously blocked and unchallenged upload attempts (Raue & Steinebach, 2020, p. 363),[c] profile information,[d] number of followers, viewer ratings[e]
Copied-from work	Subject matter, genre[f]

[a]Mentions of trigger words can increase (e.g., 'parody of' or 'review of') or decrease (e.g., 'full movie') the probability of lawfulness. Moreover, a mention of the copied-from work indicates the dependency of creation and suggests that the uploader seeks to attract viewers by referring to the work. However, it may also point to some potentially lawful uses, for example, parodies or movie reviews

[b]If an uploader opts for advertisements, this choice indicates commerciality (Elkin-Koren, 2017, p. 1096). This information is relevant for fair use analyses, 17 U.S.C. § 107(1)

[c]The same consideration underlies the privileged treatment of 'trusted uploaders', which has, for instance, been suggested by Peukert et al. (2022, pp. 372–373), Schwartmann and Hentsch (2020, p. 212), Spindler (2019, para. 108)

[d]Personal information in a profile may be informative of the probability of lawfulness as disclosing personal information increases the risk of being held directly liable for unlawful uploads

[e]Uploaders with more followers or more favourable ratings have more to lose if their accounts are blocked (see Brøvig-Hanssen & Jones, 2021, p. 7; Elkin-Koren et al., 2022, p. 998). Note in this regard that—presumably encouraged by the requirement under US law to introduce repeat infringer policies, 17 U.S.C. § 512(i)(1)(A)—many platforms apply 'three-strikes' policies, that is, upon notification for takedown by a right holder, an uploader gets a strike, and the third strike results in an account termination (e.g., Google, n.d., pt. Copyright strike basics; SoundCloud, n.d., pt. How do copyright strikes work?; Vimeo, 2022)

[f]For example, Danaher et al. (2014, p. 550) provide empirical evidence indicating that some genres are more prone to piracy than others

values for several observable variables can be factored into a blocking score (see French Ministry of Culture, 2021, p. 26). Another possibility is to build a decision tree in which several observable variables function as split nodes. For instance, a first split can be made based on whether an uploader has a history of blocked and unchallenged upload attempts, a second based on whether the uploader has indicated full personal information, and so forth. The leaf nodes can then specify the degree of similarity needed for a blocking.

The second approach is to estimate the probability of lawfulness of upload attempts based on observable variables. A machine learning algorithm can be employed to train a prediction model.[40] For this, a data set of upload attempts containing information on relevant observable variables and on the lawfulness of upload attempts is needed. The prediction model can then be used to estimate the probability of lawfulness of upload attempts. A blocking decision is triggered if the probability of lawfulness exceeds a pre-specified threshold. The threshold can account for assumptions on the relative magnitude of net social costs of false negatives and false positives.

4.4.2.2 Uncertainty About Approaches

Efficiency requires an adoption of the approach that achieves the lowest sum of aggregate direct costs and aggregate expected net social costs of errors. Note that technically, probabilities of errors with respect to automatable rules can be reduced to zero. However, in terms of net social costs or foregone net social benefits, deviations in the outcome of a legal analysis based on existing copyright law and an analysis using automatable rules are tantamount to errors. This section thus continues to speak of error costs.

How do the two outlined approaches compare in terms of efficiency? Existing copyright law offers little guidance on suitable automatable rules. Given a lack of justifications, proposed[41] and adopted[42] automatable rules appear to be largely guesswork. Stakeholders can be consulted to identify suitable rules. However, even extensive stakeholder involvement would not deliver a clear answer to the question what the best rules are. Moreover, stakeholder consultations produce costs.

---

[40] Again, this approach has mostly been discussed in terms of automating fair use analyses (e.g., Burk, 2019, pp. 292–294; Elkin-Koren, 2017, pp. 1096–1099; McJohn & McJohn, 2020, pp. 131–151; Yu, 2020, pp. 210–212). It has further been considered in the context of assessing EU copyright exceptions (e.g., M. Lambrecht, 2020, paras. 58–65; Senftleben, 2020, p. 324). An alternative is to estimate net social costs of upload attempts (see Yu, 2020, pp. 213–214). However, it is hard to imagine how social costs and benefits of upload attempts can be measured.

[41] For example, Parchomovsky and Goldman (2007, pp. 1510–1518) propose clear-cut thresholds of how much uploaders should be allowed to copy without permission, but they do not substantiate the chosen thresholds, stating instead that '[v]irtually all rules display a certain level of arbitrariness.' Boroughf (2015, pp. 115–116) bases his proposal to only block uses exhibiting 'a 95 percent proportion of a single reference file to other content in an uploaded video' on the claim that it is 'a good proxy for verbatim copying and an initial determination of no fair use.' However, no clear method used to define this threshold is discernible.

[42] The 15 s *de minimis* thresholds in section 10 of the Act on the Copyright Liability of Online Content Sharing Service Providers (2021, Germany), see Sect. 2.3.2.2, are justified in the grounds of the Law by reference to the proportion they would account for in a 3½-min song and a 90-min movie (German Federal Government, 2021, p. 140). However, no justification is given as to why about 7% of a song and about 0.3% of a movie are deemed *de minimis*. Interestingly, the discussion draft stipulated thresholds of 20 s (German Federal Ministry of Justice and Consumer Protection, 2020, Article 3 § 6(1) no 1, 2). The grounds of the Law of § 89b(3) of the Copyright Law of 1936 (Austria), which also uses the 15 s thresholds, see Sect. 2.3.2.2, do not provide justifications for the thresholds.

For the second approach, rather accurate predictions and thus low aggregate expected net social costs of errors are conceivable if a prediction model is trained on a randomly selected, sufficiently accurate, and sufficiently large data set. Establishing such a data set is associated with enormous costs. Cheaper approaches to compile a data set are conceivable. For instance, one may compile a data set of decisions that have already been manually reviewed (see McJohn & McJohn, 2020, p. 122). However, unless the selection into the manual review is random, this strategy produces a biased prediction model.

The upshot is that a prediction of lawfulness has greater potential for reducing aggregate expected net social costs of errors than automatable rules, at least if the latter approach is performed without information collected through an analysis of a data set of upload attempts.[43] However, once aggregate direct costs are considered, it becomes unclear which approach is more efficient: To what extent can the two approaches reduce aggregate expected net social costs of errors? How costly are these approaches? These questions cannot yet be answered on a substantiated basis.

Even if the superiority of one approach could be established, the concrete design of the approach poses myriad further questions that cannot yet be answered. For automatable rules, inter alia the following open questions arise: Which variables should be part of the rules? How should they be weighted? Which thresholds should be applied? Open questions in terms of the creation of a prediction model include: How large should the data set be? Which machine learning algorithm should be used? How should the critical probability of lawfulness for a blocking be specified?

Insights into current practices of platforms and resulting probabilities of errors would provide starting points for addressing open questions. However, such insights are not available. Absent evidence to the contrary, it appears reasonable to presume that platforms use automatable rules to decide when to trigger a blocking decision. Yet, little is known on what these rules are and how they have developed over time (Elkin-Koren & Perel, 2018, pp. 8–9; Gallo, 2010, p. 297; Gray & Suzor, 2020, p. 3).[44]

The level of information on probabilities of errors is also unsatisfactory. Relevant empirical research is lacking and, in any case, could not be linked to platforms'

[43] This conclusion would have to be reconsidered if—unlike in this book, see Sect. 2.1—existing copyright law were presumed to be inefficient. By predicting lawfulness, one would then strive for an inefficient target. Automatable rules could correct inefficiencies.

[44] One may try to get a sense of platforms' internal design choices by consulting reports by uploaders or instructions on how to avoid blockings. However, unless a platform applies a simple rule (e.g., blocks all upload attempts that include a copying fragment of a certain length), such reports can hardly be expected to reflect actually applied decision-making rules. With respect to YouTube, Leistner (2020, p. 184) states that 'for blocking or monetization purposes, protected subject matter will be identified and monetization will be typically assigned to the registering rightholder if 90% of an uploaded video are at least 90% similar with an existing ID file (so-called 90:90-rule)' and that 'for takedown, the algorithm will check whether at least a sequence of ten seconds of the video is identical with an uploaded ID file.' However, there is no indication of the source of this information.

design choices.[45] Creating meaningful empirical studies is cumbersome because to determine whether a filter produced an error, the lawfulness of the upload attempt that the filter evaluated must be manually assessed. Moreover, unless a platform publishes information on blocked upload attempts, only successful uploads can be observed. However, filtering designs cannot reliably be evaluated solely based on the availability of unlawful uploads. For one thing, this would neglect false positives. For another, the availability of unlawful uploads may be a misleading indicator because it is also influenced by right holders' pre-emptive activities (Sect. 3.8.5).

4.4.2.3 Case for Experimentation

The somewhat disappointing conclusion drawn in the previous section is a result of the lack of experience with different approaches. It highlights the importance of trying out different approaches and of gathering data on probabilities of errors.

The results of experimentation are most informative if one platform tries out different approaches. A platform can randomly assign upload attempts to one of the approaches.

Alternatively or additionally, different approaches on different platforms can be compared ('between-platform distinction'). However, the selection of upload attempts into the approaches is then biased: For instance, some platforms may be popular for uploading unlawfully, while other platforms may be popular for uploading parodies or movie reviews. Moreover, the generalisability of the impact of the approaches is limited due to differences between platforms: For instance, discrimination based on user ratings may have different effects on different platforms as the meaning of user ratings differs between platforms. Still, because of the current lack of understanding of the effects of different approaches, between-platform distinction can generate valuable learnings. Unlike a uniform approach by all platforms, it further allows platforms' approaches to better reflect platform specificities.

[45] Existing empirical evidence centres around notice-and-takedown. For an overview, see Erickson and Kretschmer (2020, pp. 107–119). Studies on automated filtering (e.g., Erickson & Kretschmer, 2018; Jacques et al., 2018) show that—as expectable, see Sect. 4.4.1.4—YouTube's Content ID blocks parodies. Yet, they do not allow conclusions on probabilities of errors. Gray and Suzor (2020) conducted a large-scale study of Content ID removals. Their data set of 76.7 million YouTube videos contained information on whether and why videos were removed. They further categorised videos as full movies, gameplay, sports, or tutorials for copyright circumvention. They conclude that filtering worked 'relatively well to remove apparently infringing content' but also voice concerns regarding 'potential misidentification and over blocking' (p. 11). However, their analysis does not provide insights on probabilities of errors because they do not observe blockings during the uploading process and their data set does not include information on whether content is lawful.

At the same time, experimentation produces costs. Keeping the accuracy of the automated analysis constant,[46] applying different approaches entails a duplication of the costs of designing the automated analysis. Still, given the high potential of experimentation for achieving more efficient automated analyses in the future and the additional benefit of better reflecting platform specificities, at least between-platform distinction appears desirable.

To make experimentation useful for policymakers, researchers, and other platforms, platforms should disclose the designs of their automated analyses (Access Now et al., 2021, Foundational Principle 2; Grosse Ruse-Khan, 2021, pp. 171–172; Montagnani, 2020, pp. 34–35, 39–41), including information on how they have developed the designs. The latter information is important because uncertainty not only relates to the designs as such but also to the best approach to determine them.

One may argue that disclosing filtering designs generates costs by providing guidance to unlawful uploaders on how to trick filters. The relevance of this concern is limited to automatable rules and, within this approach, to rules that relate to variables that uploaders can observe and control. If automatable rules—at least also—rely on variables like the similarity between an overlapping part in the copied-from work and the upload attempt or characteristics of the copied-from work, unlawful uploaders derive little benefit from being aware of the filtering designs in place. In addition, even if filtering designs are secret, unlawful uploaders can deduce automatable rules through trial and error and publish their observations. While a disclosure obligation makes circumvention less costly, the same argument applies to lawful uploads: To the extent that lawful uploaders can assess and control relevant variables, disclosed filtering designs make it less costly for them to find ways to upload successfully. Taken together, the net costs of revealing filtering designs to unlawful uploaders can be presumed to be negligible. In any case, even if the net costs were substantial, they could be averted by only sharing filtering designs with policymakers, researchers, and other platforms.

Moreover, platforms should track and disclose metrics informative of the performance of the automated analysis (Access Now et al., 2021, Operational Principle 1; Lefouili & Madio, 2022, pp. 344, 349; Lester & Pachamanova, 2017, pp. 70–71). While other metrics are conceivable, this section and the analysis below focus on probabilities of errors, which is the metric most directly relevant for the present discussion.

Platforms can estimate probabilities of errors by manually analysing randomly selected upload attempts that underwent the analysis or by uploading test data. Determining probabilities of errors produces the costs of manually reviewing selected upload attempts[47] or of compiling a suitable test data set. However, given

[46] For a justification that applies *mutatis mutandis* to keeping the accuracy of the automated analysis constant, see Sect. 4.3.2.1.

[47] One could come up with the idea that a cheaper way to collect information on probabilities of errors is to analyse the percentage of decisions overturned in the manual review. However, inter alia because one goal pursued in selecting decisions for manual review is to find decisions for which

the great uncertainty about the best possible design of the automated analysis, a determination of probabilities of errors can contribute considerably to reducing aggregate expected net social costs of errors going forward. At least until greater clarity on probabilities of errors associated with different approaches emerges, it is thus plausible that keeping track of probabilities of errors is cost-justified.

4.4.3 Approaching an Efficient Manual Review

There is not yet a substantiated basis for designing an automated analysis in a way that approaches efficiency. And even if there were, the automated analysis would not be error-free: An efficient automated analysis only prevents errors that it can cost-justifiably avoid.

To shorten the time during which errors persist and thus to decrease the resulting net social costs, platforms can manually review automated decisions. This section examines how the manual review can be designed in a way that contributes to efficient error avoidance.

For this, it is useful to first outline the costs and benefits of a manual review (Sect. 4.4.3.1). As a next step, Sect. 4.4.3.2 discusses how automated decisions that deserve to be manually reviewed can be selected. Section 4.4.3.3 reflects on additional ways to discriminate between automated decisions. Finally, Sect. 4.4.3.4 argues that—like for the automated analysis—experimentation with different approaches is needed.

4.4.3.1 Costs and Benefits of Manual Review

If a platform reviews an erroneous automated decision, the net social costs of the error arise until the platform corrects the decision. However, the review may also mistakenly confirm the automated decision (see Helman & Parchomovsky, 2011, p. 1230). The product of the probability of correcting an erroneous automated decision and the reduction in net social costs of the erroneous automated decision that results from the manual correction is referred to as the expected reduction in net social costs of an erroneous automated decision.

A manual review may also mistakenly overturn a correct automated decision. Like errors caused by the automated analysis, errors caused by the manual review create net social costs. The product of the probability of overturning a correct automated decision and the net social costs that arise due to the incorrect manual decision is referred to as the expected net social costs of an error produced by the manual review.

---

errors are particularly likely, the selection of decisions for manual review is not random. This strategy would thus produce biased results.

Table 4.2 Costs and benefits of manual review

Costs	Benefits
Sum of • direct costs of the review and • product of – probability of a correct automated decision and – expected net social costs of an error produced by the manual review	Product of • probability of an erroneous automated decision and • expected reduction in net social costs of an erroneous automated decision

An automated decision deserves to be manually reviewed if the costs associated with the review fall below the benefits it brings about. Table 4.2 lists the costs and benefits.

4.4.3.2 Selection of Automated Decisions for Manual Review

It is widely acknowledged that some automated decisions should be reviewed (e.g., Boroughf, 2015, pp. 116–117; Buiten et al., 2020, pp. 163–164; Elkin-Koren, 2017, p. 1098; Helman & Parchomovsky, 2011, pp. 1230–1233). At the same time, reviewing all automated decisions is unfeasible.[48] This section examines how platforms can select automated decisions for the manual review in a way that contributes to efficient error avoidance. It considers the probability of erroneous automated decisions and net social costs of errors as selection criteria.

Selection Based on Probability of Erroneous Automated Decision

All else equal, a higher probability that an automated decision is erroneous makes it more likely that the costs of the manual review fall below the benefits (see Table 4.2) and thus that the decision deserves to be manually reviewed (Buiten et al., 2020, pp. 163–164). But how can the probability of an erroneous automated decision be estimated?

A first source of information is whether the automated decision has been challenged. Uploaders and right holders may not be sure whether an automated decision is correct, but they presumably have some information in this regard. A decision challenged by an uploader or by a right holder is then more likely to be erroneous than the average decision.

Of course, uploaders or right holders can challenge automated decisions even if they believe that the decisions are correct. However, the probability of benefitting

[48] For YouTube, it has been estimated that 16,000 (Liebowitz, 2018, n. 25), 70,000 (M. Lambrecht, 2019), or 150,000 (French Ministry of Culture, 2021, p. 16) full-time equivalents would be needed to manually review all upload attempts. The first estimate is based on a back-of-the-envelope calculation; For the latter two, the calculations are not spelled out. While the estimates may thus deviate significantly from actually needed full-time equivalents and while the workload would be lower for smaller platforms, it is hard to imagine how even small platforms could manually review all upload attempts (cf. Husovec, 2018, p. 65).

from a complaint by having an automated decision overturned increases as the probability of the automated decision being erroneous increases (cf. Shavell, 1995, p. 384). All else equal, uploaders and right holders are thus more likely to be willing to incur the costs of challenging, the higher they estimate the probability of an erroneous automated decision to be.[49] Moreover, platforms may weigh the significance of the observation that an uploader or a right holder has challenged an automated decision based on the trustworthiness of the uploader or the right holder, for example, proxied by the meritoriousness of previous challenges.

To be able to exploit the information that challenges convey regarding the probability of an erroneous automated decision, platforms should establish time-saving mechanisms through which uploaders and right holders can dispute automated decisions. Moreover, informing uploaders about the parts of their upload attempts that triggered the blockings not only helps to identify deficiencies of the reference database but also decreases uploaders' costs of assessing the lawfulness of their blocked upload attempts.[50] To save right holders the costs associated with searching for potentially infringing uploads, platforms should further inform them about uploads that exhibit similarity to their works but were not blocked (Bechtel, 2020, pp. 261–265; Gocha, 2018, pp. 164–165; Nathenson, 2010, pp. 943–944).[51] In addition, platforms should include general relevant and intelligible information on copyright law in their notifications to uploaders and right holders to facilitate assessments of the lawfulness of concerned upload attempts (see Solomon, 2015, pp. 262–263).[52] The direct costs associated with informing concerned uploaders and right holders are negligible because the filtering technology collects the relevant information anyway and because the transmission of the information can be automated.

The results of the automated analysis are a second source of information regarding the probability of an erroneous automated decision. With respect to blocking, platforms use results of the automated analysis only for the binary decision between blocking and allowing an upload attempt. To estimate the probability of an erroneous decision, information on how 'close' the automated decision was can be used. Platforms should thus subject decisions with a higher probability to a manual review, the lower the deviation of the values observed regarding the relevant variables or of the estimated probability of lawfulness from the applicable thresholds.

---

[49] For uploaders, see Kaesling and Knapp (2020, p. 820).

[50] For example, YouTube e-mails uploaders the name of the right holder of the allegedly infringed work and a link to YouTube Studio, where uploaders can see the concerned segment of their upload attempt and find further information on the allegedly infringed work (see TunePocket, 2021).

[51] For example, as part of its Copyright Match Tool, YouTube informs right holders about the view count and the percentage of the video that is made up of their content (Google, 2024, pt. Introduction).

[52] In an empirical study of automated takedown notices, Penney (2019, p. 471) finds that uploaders with greater legal knowledge were more willing to challenge incorrect legal notices.

Selection Based on Net Social Costs of Error

Besides the probability of an erroneous automated decision, the net social costs of an error are informative about whether an automated decision deserves to be manually reviewed. Higher net social costs of an error increase the costs and the benefits of a manual review (see Table 4.2): The costs increase as errors caused by the manual review become more costly, and the benefits increase as error correction becomes more beneficial.

It appears plausible to presume that the probability of an overturned correct decision (i.e., the product of the probability of a correct automated decision and the probability of overturning a correct automated decision) falls below the probability of a corrected error (i.e., the product of the probability of an erroneous automated decision and the probability of correcting an erroneous automated decision). For one thing, a reasonably accurate manual review can be presumed to achieve a small probability of overturning a correct automated decision and a high probability of correcting an erroneous automated decision. For another, by considering the above-mentioned criteria, it can be ensured that only automated decisions with a reasonably high probability of being erroneous are reviewed.

The costs of a manual review are then more likely to fall below the benefits the higher the net social costs of an error are. But how can net social costs of errors be estimated?

The observation that an uploader or a right holder has challenged a decision is not only informative about the probability of an error but also about net social costs. The fact that right holders or uploaders have incurred the costs of complaining speaks against very low net social costs of errors (cf. Schellekens, 2011, p. 172). Moreover, uploaders or right holders may indicate that they consider net social costs of errors to be high.[53] Again, the weight given to such indications may be based on the trustworthiness of the uploader or the right holder, for example, proxied by the meritoriousness of previous indications.

Furthermore, a presumably positive correlation between net social costs of errors and the number of views an upload attempt attracts or would attract over time can be exploited (cf. Eakman, 2015, pp. 660–661). For an upload attempt that has been allowed by the filter, the number of views it already attracted and their development over time provide a basis for predicting the number of views the upload attempt is going to attract. For a blocked upload attempt, the number of followers of the uploader and the number of views earlier uploads by the same uploader attracted are starting points for estimating the views the upload attempt would attract. Moreover, the recency and popularity of the copied-from work, which may be identified through indications in the reference database, and the size of the platform to which an upload attempt is made (measured by the viewing activity) are relevant

[53] For example, in its guidance on Article 17 of the Copyright in the DSM Directive (2019), the European Commission (2021, p. 22) recommends a possibility to earmark works that would produce particularly high harm if uploaded unlawfully (e.g., 'pre-released music or films or highlights of recent broadcasts of sports events') and to apply 'a rapid *ex ante* human review […] of the uploads containing such earmarked content identified'.

for the number of views an upload is going to attract or an upload attempt would attract.

Platforms can use the criteria described in this section to select decisions for the manual review. Considering several criteria presumably achieves the best prediction of probabilities and net social costs of errors. Note that a manual review can then be triggered even if a decision has not been challenged. Alternatively, even if a decision has been challenged, a platform may refrain from reviewing it.

4.4.3.3 Additional Ways to Discriminate Between Automated Decisions

The above-described considerations are not only relevant for deciding whether to perform a manual review but also for how rigorously to review an automated decision. Decreasing the rigour of a review, that is, allocating less time to the review or employing less skilled reviewers decreases direct costs. At the same time, a less rigorous review increases the probability of an incorrect manual decision. In other words, it increases the probability of overturning a correct automated decision and decreases the probability of correcting an erroneous automated decision. These changes in probabilities have a stronger effect the higher the net costs of an error are. Higher net social costs of an error therefore justify a more rigorous review.

In addition to applying the indicators for net social costs of an error outlined in the previous section, platforms can introduce two-tiered processes, in which the first step is a rough review of not only the lawfulness of the upload attempt but also of the net social costs if the upload attempt is blocked or allowed erroneously. If these net social costs are estimated to be high, the upload attempt can then be forwarded to a more rigorous manual review.

Besides selecting upload attempts and adapting the rigour of the review, prioritising upload attempts offers an opportunity for efficiency gains. A quicker manual review reduces the net social costs of an erroneous automated decision that arise between the automated and the manual decision. Efficiency requires automated decisions with a high probability of being erroneous and high net social costs of error to receive priority. Platforms can estimate the probabilities of errors and the net social costs of errors as described above. Prioritisation is particularly important for upload attempts for which the majority of net social costs arises immediately after the upload[54] or immediately after the blocking.[55] Such urgency may again be indicated by uploaders or right holders. The weight given to the indications may be based on the meritoriousness of previous indications.

[54]This may, for instance, be the case for freshly released movies (see Braverman & Southwick, 2008, p. 473).

[55]This may, for example, be the case for reactions to news, to music releases, and to movie releases (see Senftleben, 2020, p. 326) as well as for political speech (see F. Reda et al., 2020, p. 41).

4.4.3.4 Case for Experimentation

Like for the automated analysis, beyond these general considerations, a lack of experience makes it impossible to specify in which cases a manual review is desirable, how rigorous the review should be, and how reviews should be prioritised. Platforms should thus experiment with different approaches.

Platforms can integrate the evaluation of approaches into the manual review. They can track how the share of erroneous automated decisions in the selected decisions develops. Moreover, in addition to deciding on the lawfulness of an upload attempt, reviewers can roughly estimate expected net social costs of errors and the urgency of the review. Platforms can use the resulting information to improve the processes for selecting decisions and for deciding on the rigour of the review and the priority of decisions to be reviewed.

Again, to make experimentation useful for policymakers, researchers, and other platforms, platforms should disclose their design of the manual review and metrics informative about the accuracy of predictions in terms of probabilities of erroneous automated decisions, net social costs of errors, and urgency.

4.5 Multi-Jurisdictional Platform Operation

Up until now, the analysis assumed that a platform only operates in one jurisdiction. This assumption served to focus on challenges related to the automation of an analysis of whether an upload attempt infringes copyright law. Expanding the scope of inquiry to multi-jurisdictional platform operation raises the question to what extent a fragmented automated analysis based on national copyright laws contributes to efficient error avoidance. Before addressing this question in Sect. 4.5.2, it is useful to explain how multi-jurisdictional platform operation affects the legal analysis of the lawfulness of upload attempts (Sect. 4.5.1).

4.5.1 Implications for Legal Analysis of Upload Attempts

Copyright law only affords protection in a specific country (Goldstein & Hugenholtz, 2013, pp. 99–101), resulting in a patchwork of territorially restricted copyright laws. A right holder thus owns a bundle of national rights (Peukert, 2012, p. 189). Section 4.5.1.1 explains why currently used and proposed choice of law principles require an application of different national copyright laws to different upload attempts or even of several national copyright laws per upload attempt.

The necessity to apply different copyright laws only becomes relevant insofar as the laws differ and the differences are decisive for the lawfulness of an upload attempt. Section 4.5.1.2 explains how the harmonisation of copyright laws has made the patches of territorially restricted copyright laws look more and more alike, thereby reducing the risk that a failure to base the analysis on the applicable copyright law leads to a false decision.

4.5.1.1 Necessity to Apply Different National Copyright Laws

Answers to the questions relevant to analysing whether an upload attempt is lawful may vary depending on the copyright law consulted. An assessment of the lawfulness of upload attempts thus requires an upfront determination of the applicable law.

The predominant choice of law rule in the field of intellectual property is the *lex loci protectionis* principle (see Dinwoodie, 2009, p. 729).[56] According to this principle, the applicable substantive law is the law of the country for which protection is sought, for example, Article 8(1) of the Rome II Regulation (2007, EU);[57] Article 3:102 of the CLIP Principles (2011).[58] If an upload to a platform operating in multiple jurisdictions becomes available in several countries, a right holder can seek protection in all of these countries. The *lex loci protectionis* principle thus requires an assessment of the lawfulness of an upload attempt based on the laws of all countries in which it would become available (see Matulionyte, 2011, para. 4; Trimble, 2015, pp. 356–357).

The *lex loci protectionis* principle does not apply to all relevant legal questions. In terms of relevant contracts (e.g., licensing agreements), generally the law governing the contract applies.[59]

Moreover, some countries apply the *lex originis* principle instead of the *lex loci protectionis* principle, notably to questions of authorship or ownership (Dinwoodie, 2009, p. 731; van Eechoud, 2003, pp. 123–124). The *lex originis* principle identifies the applicable law based on the country of origin of the potentially infringed work (e.g., determined by the country of creation or first publication) or based on the country of origin of the author of the potentially infringed work, for example, determined by the author's nationality or habitual residence (Drexl, 2013, para. 3:201.N15). For questions to which it applies, the *lex originis* principle renders one copyright law applicable to a specific work. However, it still requires an application of different copyright laws to different works (see Matulionyte, 2015, para. 35).

Acknowledging the challenges related to the global dissemination of copyright-protected content through online platforms, proposed frameworks on conflicts of

[56] Notably Article 5(2), second sentence of the Berne Convention (1886) may even be interpreted as mandating the *lex loci protectionis* principle, but this reading is controversial (Basedow, 2013, para. 3:102.C05).

[57] With slightly different wording, speaking of 'claimed' rather than 'sought'.

[58] The CLIP Principles (2011) have been developed by the European Max Planck Group on Conflict of Laws in Intellectual Property (CLIP).

[59] The law governing the contract is typically the law the parties have chosen, for example, Article 3(1), first sentence of the Rome I Regulation (2008, EU), or—in the absence of choice—the law with the closest connection to the contract, for example, Article 4(4) of the Rome I Regulation (2008, EU).

laws in intellectual property provide rules for ubiquitous infringements. For instance, Article 3:603(1), first sentence of the CLIP Principles (2011) stipulates that in disputes concerned with the online dissemination of content, 'the law of the State having the closest connection with the infringement' may under certain conditions be applied.[60] § 321(1) of the ALI Principles (2008)[61] proposes a similar rule but requires an application of the 'law or *laws* of the State or *States* with close connections' (emphasis added).[62] Using these principles, for any upload attempt, a platform would only need to apply one (CLIP Principles, 2011) or possibly a few (ALI Principles, 2008) copyright law(s). However, it would still need to apply different copyright laws to different upload attempts.

To limit the number of applicable copyright laws to one, the law of a platform's country of establishment could be declared applicable. EU law applies a comparable approach in the context of communications to the public by satellite (Article 1(2)(b) of the Satellite and Cable Directive, 1993).[63] However, such an approach is currently neither applied to nor seriously considered for online platforms.[64]

4.5.1.2 Harmonisation of Copyright Laws

The previous section has shown that currently employed or proposed choice of law principles require an application of different national copyright laws, at least to different upload attempts. The high degree of harmonisation of copyright laws reduces the risk that national differences become decisive (see Peukert, 2022, p. 53). This section outlines the main driving forces of harmonisation.

A first driving force are multilateral conventions. Despite leaving appreciable room for manoeuvre, mostly only providing minimum standards, and not addressing all relevant questions, multilateral conventions reduce possible divergences of national copyright laws. They inter alia:

- require protection of certain economic rights (e.g., Article 8 of the WIPO Copyright Treaty, 1996; Article 10 of the WIPO Performances and Phonograms

[60] All relevant factors shall be taken into account when determining the state with the closest connection, notably 'the infringer's habitual residence', 'the infringer's principal place of business', 'the place where substantial activities in furtherance of the infringement in its entirety have been carried out', and 'the place where the harm caused by the infringement is substantial in relation to the infringement in its entirety' (Article 3:603(2) of the CLIP Principles, 2011).

[61] The ALI Principles (2008) have been developed by the American Law Institute.

[62] Factors to be considered include 'where the parties reside', 'where the parties' relationship, if any, is centered', 'the extent of the activities and the investment of the parties', and 'the principal markets toward which the parties directed their activities' (§ 321(1) of the ALI Principles, 2008).

[63] Unlike the other discussed principles, this is not a choice of law rule but a substantive provision declaring the act of communication to the public by satellite to only occur in the Member State from which the signals are emitted.

[64] The European Commission (2016, pt. 1/3, p. 27) considered but discarded the idea of introducing such a rule during the impact assessment on the modernisation of EU copyright rules.

Treaty, 1996; Article 14 of the WIPO Performances and Phonograms Treaty, 1996; Article 10 of the Beijing Treaty on Audiovisual Performances, 2012),
- establish minimum terms of protection (e.g., Article 7 of the Berne Convention, 1886; Article 17 of the WIPO Performances and Phonograms Treaty, 1996; Article 14 of the Beijing Treaty on Audiovisual Performances, 2012),
- codify the principle that ideas are not eligible for protection (Article 9(2) of the TRIPS Agreement, 1994; Article 2 of the WIPO Copyright Treaty, 1996),
- limit the ability of states to enact copyright exceptions by the three-step test[65] (e.g., Article 10(1) of the WIPO Copyright Treaty, 1996; Article 16(2) of the WIPO Performances and Phonograms Treaty, 1996; Article 13(2) of the Beijing Treaty on Audiovisual Performances, 2012), and
- render the quotation exception mandatory (Article 10(1) of the Berne Convention, 1886).

Requirements for protection, authorship, and initial ownership are largely left untouched. Moreover, apart from the mandatory quotation exception, there are no minimum standards for exceptions.

Besides multilateral conventions, bi- and plurilateral preferential trade agreements contribute to the harmonisation of copyright laws. Provisions on copyright in preferential trade agreements often extend the geographical scope of multilateral conventions by requiring countries to accede to the conventions or by replicating the conventions' provisions (Morin & Thériault, 2019, p. 3). Other provisions require countries to go beyond multilateral conventions, for example, by stipulating longer terms of protection (Morin & Thériault, 2019, p. 3).

Unilateral measures are another driving force of harmonisation. In this regard, the 'special 301 report' published by the US Trade Representative (USTR) deserves mention. The USTR inter alia identifies countries that 'deny adequate and effective protection of intellectual property rights', 19 U.S.C. § 2242(a)(1)(A). Upon investigation, the USTR may impose trade sanctions, 19 U.S.C. § 2411. Investigations typically lead to new legislation in or a bilateral agreement with the concerned country (Monten, 2005, p. 407).

Finally, regional copyright systems contribute to the harmonisation of copyright laws. EU copyright law is an example of such a system.[66] While copyright protection

---

[65] According to the three-step test, exceptions must be limited to 'certain special cases', 'not conflict with a normal exploitation of the work', and 'not unreasonably prejudice the legitimate interests of the author' (Article 10(1) of the WIPO Copyright Treaty, 1996). For performers and phonogram producers, Article 16(2) of the WIPO Performances and Phonograms Treaty (1996) and Article 13(2) of the Beijing Treaty on Audiovisual Performances (2012) contain comparable provisions.

[66] The *Organisation Africaine de la Propriété Intellectuelle* (OAPI) set up another regional copyright system based on the Revised Bangui Agreement (1999). While mostly seeking to ensure compliance of its members with the TRIPS Agreement (1994), in some respects the agreement results in a higher degree of harmonisation (e.g., by stipulating mandatory exceptions, Articles 11–21 of Annex VII to the Revised Bangui Agreement, 1999) and requires more extensive protection (e.g., a longer term of protection, Article 22, first subparagraph of Annex VII to the Revised Bangui Agreement, 1999).

remains territorial, various acts of EU secondary law and a substantial body of case law leave significantly less room for national divergences than harmonisation on the international level.[67] EU copyright law reduces or even nullifies Member States' room for manoeuvre with respect to the definition of originality, the duration of protection, the treatment of fragmented and non-literal copying, and copyright exceptions.[68] Nevertheless, variations between Member States' copyright laws remain. As a result, an upload attempt may be lawful in some Member States but unlawful in others (*Netlog*, 2012, para. 50; *Poland v. Parliament and Council*, 2022, para. 86; *Scarlet Extended*, 2011, para. 52).

4.5.2 Desirability of Fragmentation Based on National Copyright Laws

The previous section explained that while national copyright laws diverge, due to a high degree of harmonisation, the risk that differences become decisive for the lawfulness of upload attempts should not be overstated. This observation begs the question to what extent a fragmented approach to automated filtering can contribute to efficient error avoidance. To address this question, this section considers the choice between uniformity and fragmentation with respect to the reference database (Sect. 4.5.2.1) and the analysis of upload attempts (Sect. 4.5.2.2).

Both sections consider efficiency from a global perspective, that is, from the perspective of a hypothetical global policymaker who takes repercussions in all concerned countries into account (cf. Elkin-Koren & Salzberger, 2004, pp. 138–139; Guzman, 2002, p. 898). This approach is not meant to imply that individual countries evaluate efficiency in this way. It rather serves to establish an understanding of the level of fragmentation that would approach efficiency from a global perspective.

4.5.2.1 Reference Database

In terms of the reference database, the choice between uniformity and fragmentation concerns questions related to the protectability of content, the term of protection, copyright ownership, and licensing arrangements. It is useful to distinguish between an application of several national copyright laws per work ('within-work

[67] For an overview of the relevant acquis, see European Commission (n.d.).

[68] For an outline of the rules on originality and duration of protection, see Sect. 4.3.1.1; on fragmented copying, Sect. 4.4.1.2; on non-literal copying, Sect. 4.4.1.3; on copyright exceptions, Sect. 4.4.1.4.

fragmentation') and an application of different national copyright laws to different works ('between-work fragmentation').

Within-work fragmentation can only be desirable if a platform can discriminate between viewers from different countries ('geoblock').[69] For explanation, suppose that protection for a work has expired in country A but not in country B. An indication of this difference in the reference database only has an effect if platforms can enable viewers from country A to view upload attempts copying from that work and prevent viewers from country B from doing so.

It appears plausible that platforms can geoblock effectively (see Trimble, 2019, p. 496). Many viewers may not be aware of possibilities of circumvention.[70] And even if they are, they may not care enough about viewing content to make the necessary effort. Moreover, viewers may shy away from using circumvention technology, for example, due to risks in terms of data protection or prohibitions in platforms' terms of service. Finally, platforms can take measures to complicate circumvention (Trimble, 2012, p. 604). Based on these considerations, the remainder of this section presumes that platforms can geoblock effectively.

When discussing the desirability of within-work fragmentation, the question arises whether the social costs resulting from investments in technologies used to locate viewers, circumvent geoblocking, and complicate circumvention must be considered. This would be the case if the investments were (partially) specific to within-work fragmentation. However, as these technologies have various further applications,[71] it appears reasonable to presume that the associated social costs are not specific to within-work fragmentation. These costs can thus be ignored when considering the desirability of within-work fragmentation.

What are the benefits and costs of within-work fragmentation? The benefits are closer reflections of national copyright laws. Thereby, within-work fragmentation enables more accurate considerations of the differences between countries that are reflected in diverging copyright laws, such as differences in the relevance and structure of domestic cultural and creative industries (see Elkin-Koren & Salzberger, 2013, pp. 244–245), economic characteristics (see Watt, 2009, p. 89), and

[69] Geoblocking can, for instance, be performed based on IP addresses. For an overview of different geolocation techniques, see Trimble (2012, pp. 592–597).

[70] Circumvention techniques include using proxy servers or virtual private networks (VPNs). For an overview, see Roberts et al. (2010, pp. 3–5).

[71] Geoblocking is used for various other purposes, for example, price discrimination, enforcement of geographical restrictions in licensing agreements by other actors than user-uploaded content platforms, and reflection of divergences in national rules on issues like online gambling or hate speech (Trimble, 2016, pp. 49–51). Moreover, geolocation technology is used for several other purposes, for example, customisation of online services, targeted advertising, market research, and prevention of credit card fraud (Goldsmith & Wu, 2008, p. 61; Trimble, 2012, pp. 587–591). Likewise, the technology used for circumvention has various other applications, for example, anonymised internet usage or remote access to company networks.

preferences and values.[72] On the costs side, keeping the completeness and accuracy of indications in the reference database constant,[73] within-work fragmentation duplicates the costs of assessing the relevant legal questions.

The benefits and costs of within-work fragmentation differ between the relevant legal questions. With respect to the term of protection, despite only moderate benefits,[74] a high degree of within-work fragmentation appears justified. The reason is that automation can reduce the costs of calculating the different terms of protection to the costs of translating the national rules on copyright terms into algorithms. Such algorithms already exist for many countries[75] and the effort of creating the remaining algorithms is likely to be cost-justified for most countries.

Likewise, regarding the transfer of copyright ownership and licensing arrangements, within-work fragmentation appears desirable to reflect geographical restrictions stipulated in the underlying contracts. A failure to consider these restrictions would weaken the effectiveness of such provisions. The costs of identifying restrictions are low as right holders can derive the restrictions from the contracts.

For the other relevant questions, within-work fragmentation does not appear cost-justified. Applying the rules of several countries generates significant costs for right holders, which can be expected to exceed the benefits of a closer reflection of national copyright laws.

In such cases, between-work fragmentation can contribute to a closer reflection of national copyright laws, notably if right holders apply the law of the country in which upload attempts copying from their works are most popular. Moreover, compared to the application of a uniform copyright law to all works, between-work fragmentation can decrease right holders' costs of assessing the relevant questions if they apply a copyright law with which they are more familiar. A right holder should apply the copyright law that yields the lowest sum of costs resulting from the inaccurate reflection of national copyright laws and costs of assessing the relevant questions.

---

[72] Copyright law is an instrument of cultural and information policy (Austin, 2000, pp. 610–613; Dinwoodie, 2000, p. 471; Ginsburg, 2000, p. 267). Differences in national copyright laws may thus be the result of a pursuit of different policy objectives.

[73] For a justification that applies *mutatis mutandis* to keeping the completeness and accuracy of indications constant, see Sect. 4.3.2.1.

[74] The benefits of within-work fragmentation are moderate as terms of protection are harmonised to a considerable extent. Moreover, given the long duration of protection, the period between the creation of a work and the point in time at which the differences between countries' terms of protection become relevant is long. Since protection in earlier years has a stronger influence on incentives to create than protection in later years, national differences are less important than they may seem. A first reason is that the decision on whether to invest in creation is based on the present, that is, discounted, value of revenues. Revenues earned in earlier years thus have a larger impact on incentives to create than revenues earned in later years (Akerlof et al., 2002, pp. 5–6). A second reason is that the economic value of creative content presumably diminishes over time (Akerlof et al., 2002, p. 7).

[75] For flowcharts for all EU Members States except Croatia (plus Iceland, Norway, Switzerland, and UK), see IP Squared (n.d.).

4.5.2.2 Analysis of Upload Attempts

Having examined the desirability of fragmentation with respect to the reference database, this section explores the same issue for the automated analysis and the manual review. In both cases, it is useful to distinguish between an application of several differently designed analyses per upload attempt ('within-upload attempt fragmentation') and an application of differently designed analyses to different upload attempts ('between-upload attempt fragmentation').

Automated Analysis

Adapting the automated analysis to the copyright laws of different countries promises the benefits of closer reflections of national copyright laws. However, if the automated analysis is performed on the basis of automatable rules, the nuances of existing legal standards are necessarily abandoned. While differences between national copyright laws are manifold, they mostly relate to legal subtleties: Supported by the high degree of harmonisation of copyright laws, a '"rough" global consensus' on what is unlawful can be presumed (Peukert, 2022, p. 73). Automatable rules may approach the 'rough consensus', but it is hard to conceive how they can reflect the differences between national copyright laws. As an alternative to automatable rules, blocking decisions can be made by estimating the probabilities of lawfulness of upload attempts (Sect. 4.4.2.1). If this approach is adopted, differences between national copyright laws can be taken into account when coding the sample of upload attempts.

On the costs side, the social costs resulting from investments in technologies used to locate viewers, circumvent geoblocking, and complicate circumvention can be ignored when examining the desirability of fragmentation (Sect. 4.5.2.1). Moreover, the application of differently designed automated analyses per upload attempt or to different upload attempts is not associated with costs. However, keeping the accuracy of the automated analysis constant (see Peukert, 2022, p. 55),[76] the costs at the preliminary stage of developing automatable rules or of compiling a data set of upload attempts are duplicated.

Balanced against the benefits, the duplication of costs speaks in favour of—if at all—a low level of fragmentation, namely, fragmentation that is at most based on a few large groups of countries.[77] For automatable rules, this is the case as the benefits in terms of a closer reflection of national interests are at best moderate. For the alternative approach of estimating probabilities of lawfulness of upload attempts, these benefits may be higher. Yet, the costs of coding upload attempts based on the

[76] For a justification that applies *mutatis mutandis* to holding the accuracy of the automated analysis constant, see Sect. 4.3.2.1.

[77] Groups of countries can, for instance, be formed based on the 'legal distance' of countries' copyright laws. The term is adopted from Carbonara and& Parisi (2007, p. 372).

laws of several countries are also significant, notably if the coding is sophisticated enough to reflect legal subtleties.[78]

These considerations lead to a situation in which platforms apply the same automatable rules or the same estimates to all countries or groups of countries. This begs the question how rules or estimates for several countries can be determined in such a way that the 'average' of national copyright laws weighted according to countries' relevance in terms of viewing activity is reflected.

For automatable rules, stakeholders from several countries can be involved in the development of the rules. In selecting stakeholders and devising decision-making rules, countries' relevance in terms of viewing activity can be taken into consideration.

For the alternative approach of estimating probabilities of lawfulness of upload attempts, it is conceivable to code upload attempts in the data set based on different copyright laws. Estimates can be steered towards the weighted average of national copyright laws by applying the copyright law of the country in which an upload attempt has received or is predicted to receive the highest number of views.[79] Platforms can predict the country in which an upload attempt that has been blocked would receive the highest number of views inter alia based on the uploader's country of origin, previous upload attempts by the uploader, or the language used in the upload attempt.[80]

Finally, if automatable rules or estimates are determined for several groups of countries, the question arises whether such rules or estimates should be used for within- or between-upload attempt fragmentation. Presuming that platforms can geoblock effectively (Sect. 4.5.2.1), within-upload attempt fragmentation is preferable as it achieves a closer reflection of differences in national copyright laws.[81]

---

[78] Note that the reasons leading to this conclusion are similar to the rationale underlying the proposal to adopt choice of law principles for ubiquitous infringements, namely, that it is appropriate to 'deviate from *lex protectionis* in favour of efficiency and equity in certain cases' (Kur, 2013, para. 3:603.C08).

[79] A conceivable alternative is to select the copyright law that best reflects the weighted average of countries' approaches. However, given the variety of differences and the infeasibility of measuring differences cardinally, it is hard to imagine how an average can be formed.

[80] Note that this approach of selecting the copyright laws applied to upload attempts bears resemblance to the ubiquitous infringement choice of law principles outlined in Sect. 4.5.1.1. However, determining the country (countries) with the closest (a close) connection based on the factors relevant for such principles requires assessments that cannot be automated and would thus increase the costs of coding by adding a manual upfront assessment of the applicable law (laws).

[81] If geoblocking were ineffective, within-upload attempt fragmentation would enable viewers to view content as soon as the rules or estimates for one group of countries allow it. Between-upload attempt fragmentation could then achieve a closer reflection of differences in copyright laws. In selecting applicable rules or estimates, it would then be sensible to rely on the predicted number of views. This would ensure that platforms apply the best suited rules or estimates for the group of countries in which an upload attempt is particularly popular.

Manual Review

Having discussed the desirability of a fragmented automated analysis, this section considers the same issue for the manual review. Once again, the benefits of fragmentation are closer reflections of differences in national copyright laws. Unlike the automated analysis, the manual review can reflect even subtle legal differences. Particularly great benefits in terms of close reflections of national copyright laws are achieved if each upload attempt is reviewed based on the copyright law of the country in which it received or is predicted to receive the highest number of views.[82]

On the costs side, note that some of the fixed costs of manual reviews may be specific to national copyright laws, for example, costs of training reviewers or transaction costs involved in commissioning external reviewers. Between-upload attempt fragmentation thus limits platforms' abilities to exploit economies of scale in terms of addressing the legal questions relevant for manual reviews.

For countries in which a non-negligible number of upload attempts are most popular, these costs are likely to be outweighed by the benefits of closer reflections of national copyright laws. Between-work fragmentation based on the copyright laws of several sufficiently large countries in terms of viewing activity thus appears desirable.[83]

Presuming that platforms can geoblock effectively (Sect. 4.5.2.1), within-upload attempt fragmentation can contribute to an even closer reflection of national copyright laws. However, keeping the rigour of the manual review constant,[84] within-upload attempt fragmentation duplicates the costs of the manual review per upload attempt. Within-upload attempt fragmentation is only justified if the additional costs fall below the additional benefits of closer reflections of differences in copyright laws.[85] Given the high costs of manual reviews—if at all—a low level of within-upload attempt fragmentation appears desirable.[86]

Platforms can make different decisions on whether and how much within-upload attempt fragmentation they apply for each upload attempt. While the costs of a manual review based on an additional copyright law are similar for all upload attempts, the benefits differ. All else equal, benefits are higher, the more views an

---

[82] Again, note that this approach of selecting the applied copyright law bears resemblance to the ubiquitous infringement choice of law principles outlined in Sect. 4.5.1.1.

[83] Note that if an upload attempt is expected to be most popular in a country for which offering manual reviews is not worthwhile, between-upload attempt fragmentation can still contribute to a closer reflection of national copyright laws, namely, if out of the copyright laws for which manual reviews are offered, the copyright law of the country is selected in which the upload attempt is expected to be most popular.

[84] For a justification that applies *mutatis mutandis* to keeping the rigor of the manual review constant, see Sect. 4.3.2.1.

[85] If geoblocking were ineffective, within-upload attempt fragmentation would enable viewers to view content as soon as one reviewer allows it. A closer reflection of differences in copyright laws could then be achieved through between-upload attempt fragmentation in the above-described way.

[86] Again, note that the reasons leading to this conclusion are similar to the rationale underlying the proposal to adopt specific choice of law principles for ubiquitous infringements (Sect. 4.5.1.1).

upload attempt is expected to attract, justifying more within-upload attempt fragmentation.

Moreover, all else equal, benefits are higher if a manual review is more likely to produce different outcomes based on different copyright laws. Several observations can be used to estimate this likelihood. If platforms apply within-upload attempt fragmentation in the automated analysis and the automated analyses yield different outcomes, this suggests that a manual analysis may produce different results based on different copyright laws. In addition, close results of the automated analysis are indicative of questions answered heterogeneously in different countries as most differences in copyright laws relate to legal subtleties. Finally, if platforms conduct a two-tiered manual review (Sect. 4.4.3.3), at the first stage, reviewers can assess whether the second-stage review is likely to yield different outcomes based on different copyright laws.

4.6 Summary and Discussion of Main Findings

This section summarises and discusses the main findings of the above analysis, namely, findings regarding the establishment of a central reference database (Sect. 4.6.1), right holders' role in error avoidance (Sect. 4.6.2), uncertainty in terms of the efficient design of the analysis of upload attempts (Sect. 4.6.3), additional uses of information collected by automated filters (Sect. 4.6.4), and the relevance of multi-jurisdictional platform operation (Sect. 4.6.5).

4.6.1 Central Reference Database

The analysis shows that to approach efficient error avoidance, a central reference database that can be accessed by all platforms and external providers of filtering technology should be established. Moreover, measures to reduce right holders' costs of making the relevant indications should be put in place. Such measures include automated calculations of end dates of protection for different countries, automated screening for overlapping entries, and a time-saving communication channel for uploaders and right holders.

However, neither in the US nor in the EU a central reference database has been established. The US Copyright Office operates a copyright registry (US Copyright Office, n.d.), but—as far as apparent—this registry has not yet played a role for automated filtering.

In the EU, Article 17(4)(b) of the Copyright in the DSM Directive (2019) appears to assume separate reference databases for each platform as it only requires Member States to stipulate a duty of care for platforms regarding works 'for which the rightholders have provided the service providers with the relevant and necessary information'. The extent to which this provision interferes with using a central reference database depends on how the term 'provided' is construed: If notices by right holders to platforms of entries in a central reference database suffice (see Volkmann, 2019, para. 28), a central reference database can still be used. In any case, no private central reference database has yet been built.[87]

Right holders must therefore enter the relevant information into several databases. Keeping the completeness and accuracy of reference databases constant,[88] the lack of a central reference database leads to socially wasteful duplications of direct costs.

In addition, the absence of a publicly established reference database means that potentially inefficient incentives of private database operators, namely, platforms or filtering technology providers, become relevant. As noted in the introduction to Chap. 5, this book does not examine these incentive problems. It should nevertheless be noted that neither US nor EU law imposes obligations on database operators to adopt the above-described measures to reduce right holders' direct costs. If database operators do not have sufficient incentives to take these measures, inefficiently high direct costs for right holders can be expected.

4.6.2 Right Holders' Role in Error Avoidance

The analysis further demonstrates that the reference database may cause errors as it is necessarily incomplete, may contain unprotected content, or may comprise incorrect metadata on who may upload a work. When considering measures to prevent errors, it is therefore important to not only focus on the analysis of upload attempts but to also consider ways in which the accuracy of the reference database can be improved.

Right holders are cheapest cost avoiders when it comes to preventing deficiencies and should therefore be responsible for preventing deficiencies of the reference database. The upshot is that right holders play a key role in preventing errors by automated filters. Nevertheless, measures to improve their incentives have received little attention in the literature and the policy debate (Sect. 5.1). Based on these considerations, Chap. 5 not only discusses how platforms' but also how right holders' incentives in terms of error avoidance can best be improved.

Right holders should only prevent deficiencies if doing so yields a net reduction in aggregate expected net social costs of errors that outweighs the associated direct costs. As a result, not all works are worthy of being entered and not all external elements in works are worthy of being excluded. In other words, some errors caused by deficiencies of the reference database are acceptable. This result must be considered when discussing how right holders' incentives can best be improved.

[87] To facilitate licensing, a 'Global Repertoire Database' for the music sector has been contemplated but the project failed due to a lack of support by collecting societies (Mazziotti, 2021, p. 224).

[88] For a justification for keeping the completeness and accuracy of the reference database constant, see Sect. 4.3.2.1.

4.6.3 Uncertainty Regarding Efficient Design of Analysis of Upload Attempts

With respect to the automated analysis of upload attempts, the analysis shows that errors may be caused as questions related to parallel independent creation, fragmented copying, non-literal copying, and relevant copyright exceptions require a context-specific application of vague legal doctrines that a state-of-the-art automated analysis cannot perform. To nevertheless make blocking decisions, automatable rules may be established or the probability of lawfulness may be estimated based on observable variables.

A manual review of selected automated decisions further contributes to efficiency. Requests and indications on the stakes and urgency by uploaders and right holders, the closeness of automated decisions, the predicted number of views, and results from first instance rough reviews are relevant factors to decide whether, how rigorously, and how urgently to review upload attempts.

For now, it is unclear which approach to take automated decisions and which design per approach is most efficient. Moreover, it is unclear how the mentioned factors can best be combined to design the manual review. It is therefore crucial to try out different approaches, track and disclose probabilities of errors and metrics informative of the accuracy of predictions relevant for the manual review, and disclose the applied design of the filter and the automated analysis.

The observation that for many important aspects conclusions in terms of an efficient design cannot yet be drawn highlights the importance of focussing on right holders' and platforms' incentives rather than prescribing a specific design. This finding is an important basis for the analysis in Chap. 5.

4.6.4 Additional Usage of Information Collected by Filters

The analysis indicates that the benefits of using automated filters go beyond the blocking of unlawful upload attempts. The information collected by filters can be used to notify right holders of potentially infringing uploads that have not been blocked. Doing so reduces right holders' costs of using notice-and-takedown systems as they would otherwise have to screen platforms themselves. Moreover, the information collected can be used to decrease uploaders' and right holders' costs of disputing automated decisions and to improve the selection of upload attempts for the manual review. These additional benefits must be considered when discussing whether filtering is socially desirable.

4.6.5 *Relevance of Multi-Jurisdictional Platform Operation*

Finally, the analysis shows that multi-jurisdictional platform operation leads to additional errors as national copyright laws diverge. If platforms can geoblock effectively, automated calculations of end dates of protection for different countries, indications of geographical restrictions stipulated in copyright transfer or licensing agreements, and between-work fragmentation for the other questions relevant for the reference database contribute to efficiency.

Regarding the automated analysis—if at all—fragmentation based on a few large groups of countries is desirable. For the manual review, the law of the country in which an upload attempt is predicted to receive most views should be applied. Manual reviews of the same upload attempt based on the copyright laws of different countries may be desirable for upload attempts that are expected to attract a high number of views and for which different outcomes based on different national copyright laws are likely.

To approach the desirable level of fragmentation based on national copyright laws, cooperation between states is needed. One reason why, without cooperation, fragmentation creates inefficiencies is that states fully internalise the benefits of fragmentation caused by their approaches, while they only partially internalise the costs. The benefits are closer considerations of national specificities reflected in copyright laws. Costs may arise for right holders, who may have to consult several copyright laws, or platforms, who may have to set several filtering policies, conduct several manual reviews, or invest in geoblocking. In addition, platform participants and third parties are indirectly affected. As right holders' costs increase, less content is created. Moreover, platforms may pass costs on to platform participants, for example, by showing more advertisements, paying uploaders less, or charging advertisers more. Platforms may even cease to operate in some countries (Curto, 2020, pp. 86–87) or globally. Countries internalise some—but not all—of these costs as they arise for domestic and foreign right holders, platforms, platform participants, and third parties.

Another reason why cooperation between states is needed to approach efficient fragmentation is that uncertainties on the best possible design of automated filtering, right holders' and platforms' incentives, and the costs and benefits of measures to improve their incentives may cause diverging views on how to best regulate automated filtering. Put differently, even states that are identical in all relevant aspects would not regulate automated filtering in the same way if their assessments of these matters diverge. Fragmentation caused by uncertainties is inefficient as it produces the above-described costs but does not contribute to closer reflections of national differences.

While approaching efficiency in terms of fragmentation requires cooperation between states, the prospect of achieving encompassing cooperation appears dim because the complexity of the questions involved and divergences of interests within and between countries lead to tremendous transaction costs (see Leistner, 2019,

p. 505).[89] The observation that, to date, international cooperation on the relevant questions is lacking supports this conclusion.[90] On the regional, bilateral, and plurilateral level, some cooperation can be observed.[91] Further cooperation on these levels is conceivable but countries are likely to retain substantial leeway to assert their interests.

Without encompassing cooperation, inefficiencies caused by fragmentation resulting from the pursuit of national interests appear inevitable. By contrast, fragmentation caused by uncertainties can be reduced through a better understanding of the effects of automated filtering and the trade-offs involved in designing and regulating it, to which this book contributes.

References

17 U.S.C. § 101 et seq. (US). https://www.law.cornell.edu/uscode/text/17

19 U.S.C. § 2101 et seq. (US). https://www.law.cornell.edu/uscode/text/19/chapter-12

Access Now, ACLU Foundation of Northern California, ACLU Foundation of Southern California, ARTICLE 19, Brennan Center for Justice, Center for Democracy & Technology, Electronic Frontier Foundation, Global Partners Digital, InternetLab, National Coalition Against

[89] By contrast, Curto (2020, pp. 108–109) takes the view that '[o]nce the representatives of the States fully understand the benefits and advantages' of the treaty she suggests, 'they will […] decide to join the invitation to negotiate the Treaty.' She argues that '[t]he following steps […] will not be easy, but these complicated procedures are an intrinsic part of the "game" played by sovereign nations in the international arena.' While better understanding of the relevant costs and benefits would indeed decrease transaction costs and contribute to more convergence, such understanding is not as easily achieved as Curto (2020) assumes but requires extensive research. Moreover, even with improved understanding, immense transaction costs remain. Declaring them to be 'part of the "game"' does not alter the consideration that they may inhibit cooperation. In any case, while the treaty Curto (2020, pp. 101–103) proposes would have some harmonising force, it would (deliberately) leave substantial leeway for states.

[90] International copyright law is largely silent on intermediary liability. An Agreed Statement concerning Article 8 of the WIPO Copyright Treaty (1996) is the main exception. It clarifies that the 'mere provision of physical facilities for enabling or making a communication does not in itself amount to communication within the meaning of this Treaty or the Berne Convention' (Diplomatic Conference on Certain Copyright and Neighboring Rights Questions, 1996, Concerning Article 8). The relevance of this statement for platforms depends on how broadly the 'mere provision of physical facilities' is construed. In any case, Article 8 of the WIPO Copyright Treaty (1996) neither prescribes nor prohibits liability of platforms. Excluding platforms from the scope of the Agreed Statement does not imply that they perform an act of communication to the public within the meaning of Article 8 of the WIPO Copyright Treaty (1996). If one takes the view that platforms merely provide physical facilities, states can still introduce a broader right of communication to the public or an additional exclusive right as well as secondary liability.

[91] Existing cooperation centres around immunity for platforms that remove content upon notification. Examples include preferential trade agreements between the US and various countries (see Samuelson, 2021, pp. 307–308; Seng, 2014, pp. 373–374) and the EU pre-Copyright in the DSM Directive (2019) legal framework. Article 17 of the Copyright in the DSM Directive (2019) is an example of cooperation on preventive duties, but it leaves room for manoeuvre for Member States.

Censorship, New America's Open Technology Institute, Ranking Digital Rights, Red en Defensa de los Derechos Digitales, & WITNESS. (2021, December 8). *The Santa Clara Principles on Transparency and Accountability in Content Moderation 2.0.* https://santaclaraprinciples.org/

ACI Adam and others (EU). ACI Adam BV and others v. Stichting de Thuiskopie and Stichting Onderhandelingen Thuiskopie vergoeding, C-435/12, ECLI:EU:C:2014:254 (CJEU 2014). https://curia.europa.eu/juris/document/document.jsf;jsessionid=FA09A54B2808F0B028E6B21BBEB0A79D?text=&docid=146201&pageIndex=0&doclang=EN&mode=lst&dir=&occ=first&part=1&cid=14251259

ACRCloud. (n.d.). *Music recognition: The new standard for music recognition.* Retrieved August 27, 2024, from https://www.acrcloud.com/music-recognition/

Act on Copyright and Related Rights (Germany). Copyright Act of 9 September 1965 (Federal Law Gazette I, p. 1273), as last amended by Article 25 of the Act of 23 June 2021 (Federal Law Gazette I, p. 1858). (1965). https://www.gesetze-im-internet.de/englisch_urhg/englisch_urhg.html#p0013

Act on the Copyright Liability of Online Content Sharing Service Providers (Germany), 31 May 2021, Federal Law Gazette I, p. 1204, 1215. (2021). https://www.gesetze-im-internet.de/englisch_urhdag/index.html

Akerlof, G. A., Arrow, K. J., Bresnahan, T. F., Buchanan, J. M., Coase, R. H., Cohen, L. R., Friedman, M., Green, J. R., Hahn, R. W., Hazlett, T. W., Hemphill, C. S., Litan, R. E., Noll, Roger, Schmalensee, R., Shavell, S., Varian, H. R., & Zeckhauser, R. J. (2002, May 20). *The Copyright Term Extension Act of 1998: An Economic Analysis.* Brief 02-1 of Amici Curiae in Support of Petitioners in Eldred et Al v Ashcroft, Attorney General, 537 U.S. 186 (2003) (US). https://www.brookings.edu/wp-content/uploads/2016/06/05_copyright_litan.pdf

American Law Institute. (2008, January 1). *Intellectual property: Principles governing jurisdiction, choice of law, and judgments in transnational disputes.* https://wipolex.wipo.int/en/legislation/details/7687

Anderson v. Stallone (US), 11 U.S.P.Q.2D (BNA) 1161 (C.D. California 1989). https://law.justia.com/cases/federal/district-courts/california/cacdce/11uspq2d1161/4104269/55/87-0592.html

Arsham, B. E. (2013). Monetizing infringement: A new legal regime for hosts of user-generated content. *Georgetown Law Journal, 101*(3), 775–806.

Audible Magic Corporation. (n.d.). *Our core technology.* Retrieved July 2, 2024, from https://www.audiblemagic.com/technology/

Austin, G. W. (2000). Social policy choices and choice of law for copyright infringement in cyberspace. *Oregon Law Review, 79*(3), 575–618.

Basedow, J. (2013). Article 3:102: Lex Protectionis. In European Max Planck Group on Conflict of Laws in Intellectual Property (Ed.), *Conflict of Laws in Intellectual Property: The CLIP Principles and Commentary* (pp. 229–235). Oxford University Press.

Bechtel, M. (2020). Algorithmic notification and monetization: Using YouTube's content ID system as a model for European Union copyright reform. *Michigan State International Law Review, 28*(2), 237–272.

Beckner, C. F., & Salop, S. C. (1999). Decision theory and antitrust rules. *Antitrust Law Journal, 67*(1), 41–76.

Beijing Treaty on Audiovisual Performances (adopted 24 June 2012, entered into force 28 April 2020) 51 ILM 1214. (2012). https://www.wipo.int/wipolex/en/text/295838

Berne Convention. Berne Convention for the Protection of Literary and Artistic Works 1886, as revised at Paris in 1971 and amended in 1979 (adopted 28 September 1979, entered into force 19 November 1984), WIPO Lex No. TRT/BERNE/001. (1886). https://www.wipo.int/wipolex/en/text/283693

Boroughf, B. (2015). The next great YouTube: Improving content ID to foster creativity, cooperation, and fair compensation. *Albany Law Journal of Science & Technology, 25*(1), 95–128.

Braverman, A. N., & Southwick, T. (2008). The user-generated content principles: The motivation, process, results and lessons learned. *Columbia Journal of Law and the Arts, 32*(4), 471–480.

Bridgeport Music, Inc. v. Dimension Films (US), 410 F.3d 792 (6th Cir. 2005). https://scholar.google.com/scholar_case?case=2589269115679339204&q=410+F.3d+792+&hl=en&as_sdt=2003
Bright Tunes Music Corp. v. Harrisongs Music, Ltd. (US), 420 F. Supp. 177 (S.D. New York 1976). https://scholar.google.com/scholar_case?case=7721050309378220492&q=420+F.+Supp.+177+&hl=en&as_sdt=2003
Brøvig-Hanssen, R., & Jones, E. (2021). Remix's retreat? Content moderation, copyright law and mashup music. *New Media & Society*, 1–19.
Buiten, M. C., De Streel, A., & Peitz, M. (2020). Rethinking liability rules for online hosting platforms. *International Journal of Law and Information Technology, 28*(2), 139–166.
Burk, D. L. (2019). Algorithmic fair use. *University of Chicago Law Review, 86*(2), 283–308.
Calabresi, G. (1970). *The costs of accident: A legal and economic analysis*. Yale University Press.
Campbell (US). Campbell v. Acuff-Rose Music, Inc., 510 U.S. 569. (1994). https://supreme.justia.com/cases/federal/us/510/569/
Carbonara, E., & Parisi, F. (2007). The paradox of legal harmonization. *Public Choice, 132*(3), 367–400.
Chafee, Z. (1945). Reflections on the Law of Copyright: I. *Columbia Law Review, 45*(4), 503–529.
Copyright in the DSM Directive (EU). Directive (EU) 2019/790 of the European Parliament and of the European Council of 17 April 2019 on copyright and related rights in the Digital Single Market and amending Directives 96/9/EC and 2001/29/EC, OJ L 130/92. (2019). https://eur-lex.europa.eu/legal-content/EN/TXT/PDF/?uri=CELEX:32019L0790
Copyright Law of 1936 (Austria). Federal Law on Copyright in Literary and Artistic Works and Related Rights. https://www.ris.bka.gv.at/GeltendeFassung.wxe?Gesetzesnummer=10001848&Abfrage=Bundesnormen
Copyright Term Directive (EU). Directive 2006/116/EC of the European Parliament and of the Council of 12 December 2006 on the term of protection of copyright and certain related rights, OJ L 372/12. (2006). https://eur-lex.europa.eu/legal-content/EN/ALL/?uri=CELEX%3A32006L0116
Creative Commons. (n.d.). *Licenses List*. Retrieved July 3, 2024, from https://creativecommons.org/licenses/?lang=en
Curto, N. E. (2020). EU Directive on Copyright in the Digital Single Market and ISP Liability: What's Next at International Level? *Case Western Reserve Journal of Law, Technology and the Internet, 11*, 84–110.
Danaher, B., Smith, M. D., Telang, R., & Chen, S. (2014). The effect of graduated response anti-piracy laws on music sales: Evidence from an event study in France. *Journal of Industrial Economics, 62*(3), 541–553.
Deckmyn (EU). Johan Deckmyn and Vrijheidsfonds VZW v. Helena Vandersteen and others, C-201/13, ECLI:EU:C:2014:2132 (CJEU 2014). https://curia.europa.eu/juris/document/document.jsf?text=&docid=157281&pageIndex=0&doclang=EN&mode=lst&dir=&occ=first&part=1&cid=14298636
Dinwoodie, G. B. (2000). A new copyright order: Why national courts should create global norms. *University of Pennsylvania Law Review, 149*(2), 469–580.
Dinwoodie, G. B. (2009). Developing a private international intellectual property law: The demise of territoriality? *William & Mary Law Review, 51*(2), 711–800.
Diplomatic Conference on Certain Copyright and Neighboring Rights Questions. (1996, December 23). *Agreed Statements concerning the WIPO Copyright Treaty*. WIPO Document CRNR/DC/96. https://www.wipo.int/edocs/mdocs/diplconf/en/crnr_dc/crnr_dc_96.pdf
Drexl, J. (2013). Article 3:201: Initial Ownership. In European Max Planck Group on Conflict of Laws in Intellectual Property (Ed.), *Conflict of laws in intellectual property: The CLIP principles and commentary*. Oxford University Press.
Eakman, A. (2015). The future of the digital millennium copyright act: How automation and crowdsourcing can protect fair use. *Indiana Law Review, 48*(2), 631–662.
Elkin-Koren, N. (2017). Fair use by design. *UCLA Law Review, 64*(5), 1082–1100.

Elkin-Koren, N., & Perel, M. (2018). Algorithmic governance by online intermediaries. In E. Brousseau, J.-M. Glachant, & J. Sgard (Eds.), *The Oxford handbook of institutions of international economic governance and market regulation*. Oxford University Press.

Elkin-Koren, N., & Salzberger, E. M. (2004). *Law, economics and cyberspace: The effects of cyberspace on the economic analysis of law*. Edward Elgar.

Elkin-Koren, N., & Salzberger, E. M. (2013). *The law and economics of intellectual property in the digital age: The limits of analysis*. Routledge.

Elkin-Koren, N., De Gregorio, G., & Perel, M. (2022). Social media as contractual networks: A bottom up check on content moderation. *Iowa Law Review, 107*(3), 987–1049.

Erickson, K., & Kretschmer, M. (2018). "This Video is Unavailable": Analyzing copyright takedown of user-generated content on Youtube. *Journal of Intellectual Property, Information Technology and Electronic Commerce Law, 9*(1), 75–89.

Erickson, K., & Kretschmer, M. (2020). Empirical approaches to intermediary liability. In G. Frosio (Ed.), *The Oxford handbook of online intermediary liability*. Oxford University Press.

European Commission. (2016, September 14). *Commission staff working document: Impact assessment on the modernisation of EU copyright rules*. SWD(2016) 301 Final. https://digital-strategy.ec.europa.eu/en/library/impact-assessment-modernisation-eu-copyright-rules

European Commission. (2021, June 4). *Communication from the Commission to the European Parliament and the Council: Guidance on Article 17 of Directive 2019/790 on Copyright in the Digital Single Market*. COM(2021) 288 Final. https://eur-lex.europa.eu/legal-content/EN/TXT/?uri=CELEX:52021DC0288

European Commission. (n.d.). *The EU copyright legislation*. Retrieved July 4, 2024, from https://ec.europa.eu/digital-single-market/en/eu-copyright-legislation

European Max Planck Group on Conflict of Laws in Intellectual Property (CLIP). (2011, December 1). *Principles on Conflict of Laws in Intellectual Property*. https://www.ip.mpg.de/fileadmin/ipmpg/content/clip/Final_Text_1_December_2011.pdf

Feist (US). Feist Publications, Inc. v Rural Telephone Service Co., 499 U.S. 340. (1991). https://supreme.justia.com/cases/federal/us/499/340/

Ficsor, M. (2003). *Guide to the copyright and related rights treaties administered by WIPO and glossary of copyright and related rights terms*. WIPO Publication No. 891(E). https://www.wipo.int/edocs/pubdocs/en/copyright/891/wipo_pub_891.pdf

Fisher v. Dees (US), 794 F.2d 432 (9th Cir. 1986). https://scholar.google.com/scholar_case?case=16874877052780018691&q=794+F.2d+432+&hl=en&as_sdt=2003

Folio Impressions, Inc. v. Byer California (US), 937 F.2d 759 (2d Cir. 1991). https://scholar.google.com/scholar_case?case=11975953443969329788&q=937+F.2d+759&hl=en&as_sdt=2003

Folsom v. Marsh (US), 9 F. Cas. 342 (D. Mass. 1841). https://law.justia.com/cases/federal/district-courts/massachusetts/madce/9fcas342/4104271/220/no-4.html

French Ministry of Culture. (2020, January 29). *Towards more effectiveness of copyright law on online content sharing platforms: Overview of content recognition tools and possible ways forward*. https://www.culture.gouv.fr/en/Thematiques/Propriete-litteraire-et-artistique/Conseil-superieur-de-la-propriete-litteraire-et-artistique/Travaux/Missions/Mission-du-CSPLA-sur-les-outils-de-reconnaissance-des-contenus-et-des-oeuvres-sur-les-plateformes-de-

French Ministry of Culture. (2021). *Content recognition tools on digital sharing platforms: Proposals for the implementation of Article 17 of the EU Copyright Directive*. https://www.culture.gouv.fr/content/download/282790/file/CSPLA - Report Content recognition tools _ Courtesy translation _ January 2021.pdf?inLanguage=fre-FR

Gallo, L. G. (2010). The (im)possibility of "Standard Technical Measures" for UGC websites. *Columbia Journal of Law & the Arts, 34*(2), 283–315.

German Federal Government. (2021, March 9). *Entwurf eines Gesetzes zur Anpassung des Urheberrechts an die Erfordernisse des digitalen Binnenmarktes*. BT-Drucksache 19/27426. https://dserver.bundestag.de/btd/19/274/1927426.pdf

German Federal Ministry of Justice and Consumer Protection. (2020, June 24). *Diskussionsentwurf des Bundesministeriums der Justiz und für Verbraucherschutz: Entwurf eines Zweiten Gesetzes zur Anpassung des Urheberrechts an die Erfordernisse des digitalen Binnenmarktes*. https://www.bmjv.de/SharedDocs/Gesetzgebungsverfahren/Dokumente/DiskE_II_Anpassung_Urheberrecht_digitaler_Binnenmarkt.pdf?__blob=publicationFile&v=2

Ginsburg, J. C. (2000). International copyright: From a "Bundle" of national copyright laws to a supranational code? *Journal of the Copyright Society of the U.S.A, 47*, 265–289.

Gocha, A. J. (2018). A modern system for resolving online copyright infringement disputes: Administrative rulemaking and adjudication, a one-stop fix to the Digital Millennium Copyright Act. *IDEA: The Journal of the Franklin Pierce Center for Intellectual Property, 58*(2), 131–172.

Goldsmith, J., & Wu, T. (2008). *Who controls the internet? Illusions of a borderless world*. Oxford University Press.

Goldstein, P., & Hugenholtz, P. B. (2013). *International copyright: Principles, law, and practice* (3rd ed.). Oxford University Press.

Google. (2018). *How Google fights piracy*. https://storage.googleapis.com/gweb-uniblog-publish-prod/documents/How_Google_Fights_Piracy_2018.pdf

Google. (2024). *YouTube copyright transparency report*. https://transparencyreport.google.com/youtube-copyright/intro?hl=en_GB

Google. (2022). *Manage references*. YouTube Help. https://support.google.com/youtube/topic/3013248?hl=en&ref_topic=3011550&sjid=7784574668489471573-EU

Google. (n.d.). *Copyright and rights management*. YouTube Help. Retrieved July 17, 2024, from https://support.google.com/youtube/topic/2676339?hl=en-GB&ref_topic=6151248&sjid=7784574668489471573-EU

Gray, J. E., & Suzor, N. P. (2020). Playing with machines: Using machine learning to understand automated copyright enforcement at scale. *Big Data & Society, 7*(1), 1–15.

Grosse Ruse-Khan, H. (2021). Transition through automation. In N. Bruun, G. B. Dinwoodie, M. Levin, & A. Ohly (Eds.), *Transition and coherence in intellectual property law: Essays in honour of Annette Kur*. Cambridge University Press.

Guzman, A. T. (2002). Choice of law: New foundations. *Georgetown Law Journal, 90*(4), 883–940.

Harper & Row (US). Harper & Row, Publishers, Inc. v Nation Enterprises, 471 U.S. 539. (1985). https://supreme.justia.com/cases/federal/us/471/539/

Hartmann, C., Allan, J. E. M., Hugenholtz, P. B., Quintais, J. P., & Gervais, D. (2020, September 25). *Trends and developments in artificial intelligence: Challenges to the intellectual property rights framework—Final report*. https://digital-strategy.ec.europa.eu/en/library/trends-and-developments-artificial-intelligence-challenges-intellectual-property-rights-framework

Helman, L., & Parchomovsky, G. (2011). The best available technology standard. *Columbia Law Review, 111*(6), 1194–1243.

Hristov, K. (2017). Artificial intelligence and the copyright dilemma. *IDEA: The Journal of the Franklin Pierce Center for Intellectual Property, 57*(3), 431–454.

Husovec, M. (2016, May 2). *Accountable, not liable: Injunctions against intermediaries* (2016–012). TILEC Discussion Paper No. 2016-012. http://www.ssrn.com/abstract=2773768

Husovec, M. (2018). The promises of algorithmic copyright enforcement: Takedown or staydown? Which is superior? And why? *Columbia Journal of Law & the Arts, 42*(1), 53–84.

In re Winship (US), 397 U.S. 358 (1970). https://supreme.justia.com/cases/federal/us/397/358/

Infopaq (EU). Infopaq International A/S v Danske Dagblades Forening, C-5/08, ECLI:EU:C:2009:465 (CJEU 2009). https://curia.europa.eu/juris/document/document.jsf;jsessionid=CDE413247EA740C4C5FC47FA92615587?text=&docid=72482&pageIndex=0&doclang=EN&mode=lst&dir=&occ=first&part=1&cid=14016436

InfoSoc Directive (EU). Directive 2001/29/EC of the European Parliament and of the Council of 22 May 2001 on the harmonisation of certain aspects of copyright and related rights in the information society, OJ L 167/10. (2001). https://eur-lex.europa.eu/legal-content/EN/TXT/PDF/?uri=CELEX:32001L0029

IP Squared. (n.d.). *Public domain calculators*. Retrieved July 3, 2024, from https://lawflow.org/public-domain-calculators/

Jacques, S., Garstka, K., Hviid, M., & Street, J. (2018). An empirical study of the use of automated anti-piracy systems and their consequences for cultural diversity. *SCRIPTed, 15*(2), 277–312.

Joskow, P. L., & Klevorick, A. K. (1979). A framework for analyzing predatory pricing policy. *The Yale Law Journal, 89*(2), 213–270.

Kaesling, K., & Knapp, J. (2020). "Massenkreativität" in sozialen Netzwerken: Überlegungen zur Plattformverantwortlichkeit nach der DSM-RL. *Multimedia Und Recht, 23*(12), 816–821.

Kaplan, J. (1968). Decision theory and the factfinding process. *Stanford Law Review, 20*(6), 1065–1092.

Krofft (US). Sid & Marty Krofft Television Prods., Inc. v. McDonald's Corp., 562 F.2d 1157 (9th Cir. 1977). https://scholar.google.com/scholar_case?case=16740683432222862864&q=562+F.2d+1157+&hl=en&as_sdt=2003

Kur, A. (2013). Article 3:603: Ubiquitous Infringement. In European Max Planck Group on Conflict of Laws in Intellectual Property (Ed.), *Conflict of laws in intellectual property: The CLIP principles and commentary*. Oxford University Press.

Lambert, T. A. (2011). The Roberts Court and the limits of antitrust. *Boston College Law Review, 52*(3), 871–939.

Lambrecht, M. (2019, May 14). *La directive européenne sur le droit d'auteur impose-t-elle le filtrage des contenus?* The Conversation. https://theconversation.com/la-directive-europeenne-sur-le-droit-dauteur-impose-t-elle-le-filtrage-des-contenus-117035

Lambrecht, M. (2020). Free speech by design: Algorithmic protection of exceptions and limitations in the copyright DSM directive. *Journal of Intellectual Property, Information Technology and Electronic Commerce Law, 11*(1), 68–94.

Landes, W. M., & Posner, R. A. (2003). Indefinitely renewable copyright. *The University of Chicago Law Review, 70*(2), 471–518.

Laras Tochter (Germany), I ZR 65/96 (Federal Court of Justice 1999). https://www.juris.de/r3/document/NJRE000087344

Lefouili, Y., & Madio, L. (2022). The economics of platform liability. *European Journal of Law and Economics, 53*, 319–351.

Leistner, M. (2019). Intermediary liability in a global world. In T. E. Synodinou (Ed.), *Pluralism or Universalism in International Copyright Law*. Kluwer Law International.

Leistner, M. (2020). European Copyright Licensing and Infringement Liability Under Art. 17 DSM-Directive: Can we make the new European system a global opportunity instead of a local challenge? *Zeitschrift Für Geistiges Eigentum, 12*(2), 123–214.

Lester, T., & Pachamanova, D. (2017). The dilemma of false positives: Making content ID algorithms more conducive to fostering innovative fair use in music creation. *UCLA Entertainment Law Review, 24*(1), 51–73.

Liebowitz, S. J. (2018, February 27). *Economic analysis of safe harbor provisions*. https://papers.ssrn.com/sol3/papers.cfm?abstract_id=3143811

Magdalenenarie (Germany), I ZR 44/68 (Federal Court of Justice 1970). https://www.juris.de/r3/document/NJRE000682798

Matulionyte, R. (2011). The law applicable to online copyright infringements in the ALI and CLIP proposals: A rebalance of interests needed? *Journal of Intellectual Property, Information Technology and Electronic Commerce Law, 2*(1), 26–36.

Matulionyte, R. (2015). Enforcing copyright infringements online – In search of balanced private international law rules. *Journal of Intellectual Property, Information Technology and Electronic Commerce Law, 6*(2), 132–145.

Mazziotti, G. (2021). A data-driven approach to copyright in the age of online platforms. In D. J. Gervais (Ed.), *The future of intellectual property* (pp. 207–228). Edward Elgar.

McJohn, S., & McJohn, I. (2020). Fair use and machine learning. *Northeastern University Law Review, 12*(1), 99–161.

Meyers, B. G. (2009). Filtering systems or fair use: A comparative analysis of proposed regulations for user-generated content. *Cardozo Arts & Entertainment Law Journal, 26*(3), 935–956.

Miller, J. S. (2014). Error costs & IP law. *University of Illinois Law Review, 2014*(1), 175–204.

Möbelkatalog (Germany). I ZR 177/13 (Federal Court of Justice 2014). https://juris.bundesgerichtshof.de/cgi-bin/rechtsprechung/document.py?Gericht=bgh&Art=en&nr=71060&pos=0&anz=1

Montagnani, M. L. (2020). Virtues and perils of algorithmic enforcement and content regulation in the EU: A toolkit for a balanced algorithmic copyright enforcement. *Journal of Law, Technology & the Internet, 11*(1), 1–49.

Monten, L. M. (2005). The inconsistency between Section 301 and TRIPS: Counterproductive with respect to the future of international protection of intellectual property rights? *Marquette Intellectual Property Law Review, 9*(2), 387–422.

Morin, J.-F., & Thériault, D. (2019, May 23). *Copyright provisions in trade deals: A bird's-eye view*. Centre for International Governance Innovation, Policy Brief No. 149. https://www.cigionline.org/publications/copyright-provisions-trade-deals-birds-eye-view

Morrisey v. Procter & Gamble Company (US), 379 F.2d 675 (1st Cir. 1967). https://scholar.google.com/scholar_case?case=9514720516312141729&q=379+F.2d+675+&hl=en&as_sdt=2003

Nathenson, I. S. (2010). Civil procedures for a world of shared and user-generated content. *University of Louisville Law Review, 48*(4), 911–958.

Netlog (EU). Belgische Vereniging van Auteurs, Componisten en Uitgevers CVBA (SABAM) v. Netlog NV, C-360/10, ECLI:EU:C:2012:85 (CJEU 2012). https://curia.europa.eu/juris/document/document.jsf?text=&docid=119512&pageIndex=0&doclang=EN&mode=lst&dir=&occ=first&part=1&cid=13295281

Nichols (US). Nichols v. Universal Pictures Corp., 45 F.2d 119 (2d Cir. 1930). https://scholar.google.com/scholar_case?case=14991934121439658064&q=45+F.2d+119+&hl=en&as_sdt=2003

Painer (EU). Eva-Maria Painer v. Standard VerlagsGmbH and others, C-145/10, ECLI:EU:C:2011:798 (CJEU 2011). https://curia.europa.eu/juris/document/document.jsf?text=&docid=115785&pageIndex=0&doclang=EN&mode=lst&dir=&occ=first&part=1&cid=14017157

Parchomovsky, G., & Goldman, K. A. (2007). Fair use harbors. *Virginia Law Review, 93*(6), 1483–1532.

Pelham (EU). Pelham GmbH, Moses Pelham, Martin Haas v Ralf Hütter and Florian Schneider-Esleben, C-476/17, ECLI:EU:C:2019:624 (CJEU 2019). https://curia.europa.eu/juris/document/document.jsf?text=&docid=216552&pageIndex=0&doclang=EN&mode=lst&dir=&occ=first&part=1&cid=14071261

Penney, J. W. (2019). Privacy and legal automation: The DMCA as a case study. *Stanford Technology Law Review, 22*(2), 412–486.

Peter Pan Fabrics, Inc. v. Martin Weiner Corp. (EU), 274 F.2d 487 (2d Cir. 1960). https://scholar.google.com/scholar_case?case=7909069540715359056&q=274+F.2d+487&hl=en&as_sdt=2003

Peukert, A. (2012). Territoriality and extra-territoriality in intellectual property law. In G. Handl, J. Zekoll, & P. Zumbansen (Eds.), *Beyond territoriality: Transnational legal authority in an age of globalization*. Martinus Nijhoff.

Peukert, A. (2022). Transnational intellectual property governance on the internet. In M. C. Kettemann, A. Peukert, & I. Spiecker gen. Döhmann (Eds.), *The law of global digitality* (pp. 50–73). Routledge.

Peukert, A., Husovec, M., Kretschmer, M., Mezei, P., & Quintais, J. P. (2022). European copyright society: Comment on copyright and the digital services act proposal. *International Review of Intellectual Property and Competition Law, 53*(3), 358–376.

Pex. (n.d.). *Attribution engine*. Retrieved July 3, 2024, from https://pex.com/products/attribution-engine/#section-0

Pippi-Langstrumpf-Kostüm I (Germany), I ZR 52/12 (Federal Court of Justice 2013). https://juris.bundesgerichtshof.de/cgi-bin/rechtsprechung/document.py?Gericht=bgh&Art=en&nr=66496&pos=0&anz=1

Poland v. Parliament and Council (EU). Republic of Poland v. European Parliament and Council of the European Union, C-401/19, ECLI:EU:C:2022:297 (CJEU 2022). https://curia.europa.eu/

juris/document/document.jsf?text=&docid=258261&pageIndex=0&doclang=EN&mode=req&dir=&occ=first&part=1&cid=13289381

Posner, R. A. (1973). An economic approach to legal procedure and judicial administration. *The Journal of Legal Studies, 2*(2), 399–458.

Raue, B., & Steinebach, M. (2020). Uploadfilter: Funktionsweisen, Einsatzmöglichkeiten und Parametrisierung. *Zeitschrift Für Urheber- Und Medienrecht, 64*(5), 355–364.

Reda, F., Selinger, J., & Servatius, M. (2020, November 16). *Article 17 of the Directive on Copyright in the Digital Single Market: a Fundamental Rights Assessment*. https://papers.ssrn.com/sol3/papers.cfm?abstract_id=3732223

Revised Bangui Agreement. Agreement Revising the Bangui Agreement of March 2, 1977, on the Creation of an African Intellectual Property Organization (Bangui (Central African Republic), February 24, 1999). https://wipolex.wipo.int/en/text/181151

Reyher v. Children's Television Workshop (US), 533 F.2d 87 (2nd Cir. 1976). https://scholar.google.com/scholar_case?case=278412908033774123&q=533+F.2d+87+&hl=en&as_sdt=2003

Roberts, H., Zuckerman, E., York, J., Faris, R., & Palfrey, J. (2010, October). *2010 circumvention tool usage report*. https://cyber.harvard.edu/sites/cyber.harvard.edu/files/2010_Circumvention_Tool_Usage_Report.pdf

Rogers, E. (2013). Substantially unfair: An empirical examination of copyright substantial similarity analysis among the federal circuits. *Michigan State Law Review, 2013*(3), 893–931.

Rome I Regulation (EU). Regulation (EC) No 593/2008 of the European Parliament and of the Council of 17 June 2008 on the law applicable to contractual obligations (Rome I) OJ L 177/6. (2008). https://eur-lex.europa.eu/LexUriServ/LexUriServ.do?uri=OJ:L:2008:177:0006:0016:EN:PDF

Rome II Regulation (EU). Regulation (EC) No 864/2007 of the European Parliament and of the Council of 11 July 2007 on the law applicable to non-contractual obligations (Rome II), OJ L 199/40. (2007). https://eur-lex.europa.eu/legal-content/EN/TXT/PDF/?uri=CELEX:32007R0864

Rubinfeld, D. L., & Sappington, D. E. M. (1987). Efficient awards and standards of proof in judicial proceedings. *The RAND Journal of Economics, 18*(2), 308–315.

Samuelson, P. (2021). Pushing back on stricter copyright ISP liability rules. *Michigan Technology Law Review, 27*(2), 299–343.

Samuelson, P., Baumgarten, J. A., Carroll, M. W., Cohen, J. E., Dow, T., Fitzgerald, B., Gasaway, L., Gervais, D., Ilardi, T., Litman, J., Loren, L. P., Lunney, G., Ochoa, T., Reese, R. A., Sigall, J., Spelman, K., Sprigman, C., Traynor, M., Wheatland, T., & Williams, J. (2010). The copyright principles project: Directions for reform. *Berkeley Technology Law Journal, 25*(3), 1175–1245.

Satellite and Cable Directive (EU). Council Directive 93/83/EEC of 27 September 1993 on the coordination of certain rules concerning copyright and rights related to copyright applicable to satellite broadcasting and cable retransmission, OJ L 248/15. (1993). https://eur-lex.europa.eu/legal-content/EN/TXT/PDF/?uri=CELEX:31993L0083

Scarlet Extended (EU). Scarlet Extended SA v Société belge des auteurs, compositeurs et éditeurs SCRL (SABAM), C-70/10, ECLI:EU:C:2011:771 (CJEU 2011). https://curia.europa.eu/juris/document/document.jsf?text=&docid=115202&pageIndex=0&doclang=EN&mode=lst&dir=&occ=first&part=1&cid=14579025

Schellekens, M. (2011). Liability of internet intermediaries: A slippery slope. *SCRIPTed, 8*(2), 154–174.

Schwartmann, R., & Hentsch, C.-H. (2020). Stufenkonzept gegen Overblocking durch Upload-Filter: Ein erster Vorschlag zur Umsetzung von Art. 17 DSM-RL. *Multimedia Und Recht, 23*(4), 207–213.

Senftleben, M. (2020). Institutionalized algorithmic enforcement: The pros and cons of the EU approach to UGC platform liability. *FIU Law Review, 14*(2), 299–328.

Seng, D. (2014). The state of the discordant union: An empirical analysis of DMCA takedown notices. *Virginia Journal of Law & Technology, 18*(3), 369–473.

Shavell, S. (1995). The appeals process as a means of error correction. *The Journal of Legal Studies, 24*(2), 379–426.

Solomon, L. (2015). Fair users or content abusers? The automatic flagging of non-infringing videos by content ID on YouTube. *Hofstra Law Review, 44*(1), 237–268.

SoundCloud. (n.d.). *Copyright information & policies*. SoundCloud Help Center. Retrieved July 17, 2024, from https://help.soundcloud.com/hc/en-us/sections/4402635879707-Copyright-Information-Policies

Spiegel Online (EU). Spiegel Online GmbH v. Volker Beck, C-516/17, ECLI:EU:C:2019:625 (CJEU 2019). https://curia.europa.eu/juris/document/document.jsf?text=&docid=216543&pageIndex=0&doclang=EN&mode=lst&dir=&occ=first&part=1&cid=14296542

Spindler, G. (2019). The Liability system of Art. 17 DSMD and national implementation: Contravening prohibition of general monitoring duties? *Journal of Intellectual Property, Information Technology and Electronic Commerce Law, 10*(3), 344–374.

Triaille, J.-P., Dusollier, S., Depreeuw, S., Hubin, J.-B., Coppens, F., & de Francquen, A. (2013). *Study on the Application of Directive 2001/29/EC on Copyright and Related Rights in the Information Society (the "InfoSoc Directive")*. http://www.crid.be/pdf/public/7363.pdf

Trimble, M. (2012). The future of cybertravel: Legal implications of the evasion of geolocation. *Fordham Intellectual Property, Media & Entertainment Law Journal, 22*(3), 567–658.

Trimble, M. (2015). The multiplicity of copyright laws on the internet. *Fordham Intellectual Property, Media & Entertainment Law Journal, 25*(2), 339–406.

Trimble, M. (2016). The role of geoblocking in the Internet legal landscape. *Revista de Internet, Derecho y Política, 23*, 45–58.

Trimble, M. (2019). Copyright and geoblocking: The consequences of eliminating geoblocking. *Boston University Journal of Science and Technology Law, 25*(2), 476–502.

TRIPS Agreement. Agreement on Trade-Related Aspects of Intellectual Property Rights, Annex 1C to the Marrakesh Agreement Establishing the World Trade Organization, as amended in 2005 (adopted 15 April 1994, entered into force 1 January 1995) 1869 UNTS 299. (1994). https://www.wipo.int/wipolex/en/text/500864

TunePocket. (2021, October 6). *How to resolve YouTube copyright claims*. https://www.tunepocket.com/resolve-youtube-copyright-claims/

US Copyright Office. (n.d.). *Register your work: Registration portal*. Retrieved August 27, 2024, from https://www.copyright.gov/registration/

van Eechoud, M. (2003). *Choice of law in copyright and related rights: Alternatives to the Lex Protectionis*. Kluwer Law International.

Vimeo. (2022, September 1). *Vimeo copyright policy*. https://vimeo.com/dmca

Vmg Salsoul, LLC v. Ciccone (US), 824 F.3d 871 (9th Cir. 2016). https://scholar.google.com/scholar_case?case=2622425068073736501&q=824+F.3d+871+&hl=en&as_sdt=2003

Volkmann, C. (2019). Art. 17 Urh-RL und die Upload-Filter: Verschärfte Störerhaftung oder das Ende der Freiheit im Internet? Zugleich ein konkreter Lösungsvorschlag zur „Quadratur des Kreises“ bei der nationalen Umsetzung von Art. 17 Urh-RL. *Computer Und Recht, 35*(6), 376–384.

Watt, R. (2009). *An empirical analysis of the economics of copyright: How valid are the results of studies in developed countries for developing countries?* The Economics of Intellectual Property: Suggestions for Further Research in Developing Countries and Countries with Economies in Transition. https://www.wipo.int/publications/en/details.jsp?id=289&plang=EN

Westcott-Baker, A., Pure, R., & Seaman, C. I. (2012). Copyright law and the implications for user-generated content. *University of Baltimore Journal of Media Law and Ethics, 3*(1–2), 171–200.

WIPO - Standing Committee on Copyright and Related Rights. (2005, November 9). *Survey of national legislation on voluntary registration systems for copyright and related rights*. SCCR/13/2. https://www.wipo.int/meetings/en/doc_details.jsp?doc_id=52829

WIPO Copyright Treaty (adopted 20 December 1996, entered into force 6 March 2002) 2186 UNTS 121 (1996). https://www.wipo.int/wipolex/en/text/295157

WIPO Performances and Phonograms Treaty (adopted 20 December 1996, entered into force 20 May 2002) 2186 UNTS 203 (1996). https://www.wipo.int/wipolex/en/text/295477

Yu, P. K. (2020). Artificial intelligence, the law-machine interface, and fair use automation. *Alabama Law Review, 72*(1), 187–238.

Chapter 5
Improving Right Holders' and Platforms' Incentives to Design Automated Filtering

Abstract Various measures to regulate automated filtering have been discussed in recent years. However, only few measures have been evaluated in terms of efficiency. This chapter conducts the first comprehensive analysis of how right holders' and platforms' incentives can best be steered towards efficiency. For this, it identifies inefficiencies of right holders' and platforms' incentives in the absence of regulation and assesses to what extent and at what costs the discussed measures mitigate these inefficiencies. The analysis shows that without regulation, right holders have excessive incentives to prevent copyright-infringing uploads and deficient incentives to prevent false positives. It suggests negligence-based liability of right holders for false positives caused by deficiencies of the reference database. The analysis further demonstrates that without regulation, platforms invest too little into filtering and do not take some desirable accompanying measures. It suggests negligence-based liability of platforms for errors caused by the analysis of upload attempts. Platforms escape liability by complying with minimal requirements, which are adjusted as new learnings are collected. Platforms are further required to involve representatives of stakeholders in the development of filtering policies and to take the desirable accompanying measures. Based on these results, shortcomings of current US and EU law are identified.

Keywords User-uploaded content platforms · User-generated content platforms · Economic analysis of platform regulation · Economic analysis of intermediary liability · Automated filtering · Upload filters · Automated copyright enforcement · Copyright in the Digital Single Market · Digital Services Act · Responsibilities of online platforms

The previous chapter reflected on the second-best efficient design of automated filtering. This chapter turns to the most efficient way to approach this design.

The second-best efficient design of the reference database requires a central database with the characteristics described in Sect. 4.3.2 and an alignment of right

O. Englisch, *Automated Copyright Filters*, International Law and Economics,
https://doi.org/10.1007/978-3-031-83161-4_5

holders'[1] incentives to social efficiency. A central reference database can be directly commissioned by the policymaker. In the interest of a focussed analysis, this chapter therefore leaves the incentives of private database operators aside. Instead, it focusses on right holders' incentives.

To reach the second-best efficient design of the analysis of upload attempts, platforms' incentives must be aligned to social efficiency. While many platforms rely on filtering technology providers (Sect. 2.2), examining not only how platforms' incentives can be improved but also how platforms can align filtering technology providers' incentives to their own incentives would add a layer of complication that is not relevant for all platforms[2] and raise challenges that are not specific to automated filtering. As it appears plausible that platforms can achieve a reasonably high degree of incentive alignment,[3] in the interest of a focussed discussion, it is assumed that platforms perform the analysis.

Note that achieving the second-best efficient design of automated filtering requires a perfect alignment of right holders' and platforms' incentives to social efficiency. Yet, perfect alignment requires accurate information on net social and net private costs of errors, which are not available. This chapter thus examines how right holders' and platforms' incentives can best be steered towards efficiency, leading to the 'third-best efficient' design of automated filtering.

While some measures to influence right holders' and platforms' incentives have been discussed, a review of the related literature shows that it has not been examined comprehensively how their incentives can best be steered towards efficiency (Sect. 5.1). Section 5.2 explains the analytical approach adopted in this chapter to address this research gap. Sections 5.3 and 5.4 then reflect on how right holders' and platforms' incentives can best be improved, respectively. Finally, Sect. 5.5 summarises and discusses the main findings.

---

[1] One type of deficiency of the reference database is that a person enters a work despite not owning the rights (Sect. 4.3.1.2). Technically, in such cases it is incorrect to speak of the right holder. In the interest of readability, alleged right holders are nevertheless included in the term right holders. The term alleged right holders is only used when a distinction to actual right holders is important.

[2] This is the case for platforms that use in-house filters, for example, 'ContentID' used by YouTube (Google, n.d., pt. How Content ID works) and 'Rights Manager' used by Facebook and Instagram (Meta, 2024).

[3] Platforms can reduce information asymmetries that create opportunities for moral hazard by testing the accuracy of the analysis or by requiring documentation. Moreover, incentive-compatible contracts that shift liability for errors to filtering technology providers are conceivable. While little is known about contracts between platforms and filtering technology providers, note that the provider Pex offers platforms insurance for 'copyright-related damages and legal fees under Article 17 the [sic!] European Union Copyright Directive [...] and the Digital Millennium Copyright Act' (Pex, 2024).

5.1 Literature Review and Research Question

Measures to improve right holders' incentives have received little attention so far. Yet, some commentators consider negligence-based liability of right holders (e.g., Leistner, 2020, pp. 179–180) or penalties for wrongful indications in the reference database (Goller, 2019; Kalia, 2015; Sag, 2017, p. 557).

Measures to improve platforms' incentives have been discussed more extensively. The measures considered in the literature include:

- strict liability for unlawful uploads (e.g., European Copyright Society, 2017, p. 7; Helman & Parchomovsky, 2011, p. 1215; Husovec, 2018, p. 77; Rendas, 2017, pp. 43–44; Samuelson, 2021, p. 337; Spoerri, 2019, paras. 31, 54),
- negligence-based liability with a standard of care developed by courts (e.g., Harris, 2015, pp. 851–852; Helman & Parchomovsky, 2011, pp. 1223–1224; Leistner & Ohly, 2019, pp. 184–186),
- negligence-based liability with a standard of care imposed by the regulator (e.g., Buiten et al., 2020, pp. 161–162; Gabison & Buiten, 2020, pp. 262–263; Helman & Parchomovsky, 2011, pp. 1224–1225, 1231–1232),
- negligence-based liability with performance targets (e.g., Gabison & Buiten, 2020, p. 280),
- stakeholder participation (e.g., Grosse Ruse-Khan, 2021, p. 171; Kulk, 2018, pp. 303–304; Leistner, 2019, pp. 507–508; Leistner & Ohly, 2019, p. 186), and
- transparency obligations (e.g., Grosse Ruse-Khan, 2021, pp. 171–172; Lefouili & Madio, 2022, p. 344; Lester & Pachamanova, 2017, pp. 70–71; Montagnani, 2020, pp. 34–35, 39–41).

While the liability of platforms for copyright-infringing uploads has been evaluated from an economic perspective (e.g., Beard et al., 2018; Buiten et al., 2020; Gabison & Buiten, 2020; Helman & Parchomovsky, 2011; Husovec, 2016; Lefouili & Madio, 2022), it has not yet been examined comprehensively how right holders' and platforms' incentives can best be steered towards efficiency, leading to the following research question:

Research Question 3
How can a policymaker best steer right holders' and user-uploaded content platforms' incentives to design automated filtering towards efficiency?

5.2 Analytical Approach

To address research question 3, this chapter conducts a two-step analysis with respect to right holders' (Sect. 5.3) and platforms' (Sect. 5.4) incentives:[4]

1. It examines to what extent their incentives deviate from social efficiency in the absence of regulation.
2. It examines what interventions can most efficiently improve their incentives.

This chapter presumes that platforms only operate in one jurisdiction. Steering right holders' and platforms' incentives in terms of fragmentation towards efficiency from a global perspective requires cooperation between countries in this regard. However, as encompassing cooperation between countries is out of reach (Sect. 4.6.5), there is little value in discussing what such cooperation should look like.

The first step of the analysis serves to understand the necessity of and requirements for legal intervention. To develop this understanding, the social costs and benefits of errors are verbally compared with private costs and benefits. To evaluate the costs and benefits, this chapter draws on economic literature on copyright law, digital copying, and platforms.

Having identified inefficiencies, as a second step, measures that have been discussed in the context of automated filtering and related contexts are assessed by verbally weighing their social costs and benefits. To do so, the analysis relies on law and economics research on regulatory measures and applies the insights to automated filtering.

Despite the many valuable contributions in the mentioned fields of literature, the analysis shows that several important questions have not yet been answered conclusively. Conducting further theoretical and empirical economic research on these questions would be useful to move closer to answering these questions. However, doing so would go beyond the scope of this book. Instead of diving into analyses of these questions, this chapter therefore focusses on the conclusions that can be drawn from the current state of the literature.

The analytical steps to draw these conclusions could be presented in a formalised way. However, in this regard economic modelling would not provide added value compared to a structured and thorough verbal analysis. This chapter therefore relies on the latter approach.

Based on the analysis, an approach on how to regulate automated filtering is recommended. One may argue that automated filtering designed in the best

[4]Note that the distinction between right holders and platforms blurs if platforms hold the rights in content (e.g., because they also produce content) or have vested interests in right holders' success (e.g., because they have invested in right holders). The incentive problems in such cases differ from the incentive problems if right holders and platforms are separate entities. In the interest of a focussed discussion and since for now such cases are the exception, this chapter presumes that right holders and platforms are separate entities. For the same reasons, this chapter also ignores the possibility that competing platforms hold the relevant rights or have vested interests in right holders' success.

attainable way is less efficient than an alternative approach, for example, not using automated filtering at all. To examine this claim, the third-best efficient design must be compared with alternative approaches. However, this comparison can only be made once the best possible regulation of automated filtering has been analysed. The reader is therefore asked to suspend objections related to alternative approaches until the end of this chapter: Section 5.5.1 explains why the third-best efficient design can be expected to outperform alternative approaches.

5.3 Right Holders' Incentives

This section examines how right holders' incentives in terms of the reference database can best be steered towards efficiency. Intervention to improve right holders' incentives is only needed if their incentives are inefficient without it. To start off, Sect. 5.3.1 thus considers right holders' incentives if filters rely on an open-to-all and free-of-charge reference database, and neither the policymaker nor the database operator nor the platform takes measures to deter them from making wrongful indications ('*laissez-faire* regime'). Section 5.3.2 uses the obtained insights to explore measures to improve right holders' incentives.

5.3.1 Inefficiency of Right Holders' Incentives in Laissez-Faire Regime

This section assumes that platforms engage in automated filtering. This assumption is plausible because platforms may have incentives to filter even if they are not liable for unlawful uploads (Sect. 5.4.1.4) and because platforms are likely to filter if the suggested measures to improve their incentives are taken.[5]

Note that if the reference database is used for additional purposes, right holders' incentives are also driven by repercussions in these regards. For instance, if the reference database is used to pay right holders for content consumption, a person may claim ownership to obtain payments. For a focussed analysis, this section concentrates on incentives stemming from the use of the reference database for filtering. In any case, considering additional purposes would likely not change the 'direction' of the effects described in this section but only their magnitude.[6]

[5] The suggested measures are summarised at the end of Sect. 5.4.2.4.

[6] This section argues that without liability, right holders have excessive incentives to enter their works into the reference database and deficient incentives to prevent inaccuracies that result in greater protection than copyright law affords. If the reference database is additionally used for paying right holders for content consumption, right holders obtain further benefits from being indicated as right holders of their works but also from being indicated as right holders of content

The rationale underlying the analysis of right holders' incentives is that their incentives would be efficient if their net costs of errors equalled net social costs.[7] Note that right holders' direct costs of error avoidance, namely, the opportunity costs of the time spent on entering works, excluding unprotected content, and indicating metadata on who may upload as well as the costs of gathering information, correspond to the social direct costs of these activities.

Based on these considerations, Sects. 5.3.1.1 and 5.3.1.2 examine to what extent right holders' net costs of false negatives and false positives in a *laissez-faire* regime deviate from net social costs, respectively. Section 5.3.1.3 uses the obtained insights to discuss how right holders' incentives in a *laissez-faire* regime deviate from social efficiency.

5.3.1.1 Deviation of Right Holders' Net Costs of False Negatives from Net Social Costs

To see how right holders' net costs of false negatives in a *laissez-faire* regime deviate from net social costs, it must first be clarified what the net social costs of false negatives are.

False negatives exert a negative effect on incentives to create by reducing prospective creators' expected net benefits of creating content (Sect. 2.1). Decreased costs for creators who seek to incorporate elements of previous works mitigate this effect (cf. Landes & Posner, 1989, pp. 332–333). Moreover, if a filter is sufficiently lenient, false negatives enable more access to some copied-from works (Sects. 3.4.1.4 and 3.4.3). Even if viewers would access the copied-from work through an alternative channel if the unlawful upload were blocked, a false negative may create social benefits, namely, if the unlawful upload is associated with lower transaction costs than the alternative channel. On balance, the social costs of the negative net effect on incentives to create exceed the social benefits of increased access and of decreased transaction costs.[8]

How do right holders' net costs of false negatives in a *laissez-faire* regime compare to net social costs? The availability of unlawful uploads on a platform decreases right holders' profits by creating competition for views of their works (Sects. 3.4.1.4 and 3.5.1.3). The impact of false negatives on right holders' profits also drives the social costs of false negatives but only to the extent that it reduces

they do not own. This increases right holders' incentives to enter their works and makes it more attractive to overclaim ownership.

[7]Right holders are assumed to seek to maximise profits. In discussing their incentives in a *laissez-faire* regime, it is further assumed that the mere risk of regulation does not have an appreciable effect. As this argument has been made with respect to platforms, its relevance is discussed when exploring platforms' incentives, namely, in Sect. 5.4.1.1. The considerations advanced there *mutatis mutandis* make it likely that the mere risk of regulation does not play a significant role for right holders' incentives.

[8]This is due to the assumption that existing copyright law is efficient (Sect. 2.1).

incentives to create. Moreover, from a social perspective, the benefits of reduced costs of creation and increased or cheaper access to some copied-from works mitigate the costs. Such benefits do not mitigate right holders' costs. In a *laissez-faire* regime, right holders' net costs of false negatives thus exceed net social costs.

5.3.1.2 Deviation of Right Holders' Net Costs of False Positives from Net Social Costs

Having considered false negatives, false positives are next in line. This chapter only considers false positives with respect to upload attempts by lawfully copying uploaders. For the same reasons as advanced in Sect 3.2.3.3, it leaves false positives with respect to upload attempts by right holders aside: Such false positives only represent a minor part of the problem of false positives and the hurdles to error-free blocking that are unsurmountable by state-of-the-art filters (Sect. 4.4.1) relate to upload attempts by lawfully copying uploaders. Considering false positives with respect to upload attempts by right holders would therefore complicate the analysis without generating valuable insights.

If false positives lead lawfully copying uploaders to refrain from uploading,[9] they create social costs due to reduced access to the content that is attempted to be uploaded or—if viewers access the content via alternative channels—higher transaction costs. To nevertheless upload, lawfully copying uploaders may over-comply by obtaining unnecessary licences (see Perel & Elkin-Koren, 2016, p. 516) or by modifying their content to make it less susceptible to blocking (Brøvig-Hanssen & Jones, 2021, pp. 9–10; Trendacosta, 2020, pp. 27–28). Doing so produces social costs, namely, the transaction costs of obtaining licences or the opportunity costs of the time spent on modifying content. Moreover, the risk of not being able to upload content reduces incentives to create lawfully copying uploads (Gabison & Buiten, 2020, p. 278), notably for content for which a platform is the main distribution channel (see Brøvig-Hanssen & Jones, 2021, pp. 7–8). In addition, the non-availability of lawfully copying content may decrease a right holder's profits and thereby incentives to create works, for example, if it favourably reviews a work or enhances its popularity.

On the benefits side, it may be argued that even blockings of lawfully copying upload attempts can increase right holders' profits and therefore incentives to create. Such blockings may decrease the competitive pressure right holders are exposed to. Yet, upload attempts that only contain small fragments of works or are only remotely similar to works would presumably only exert negligible competitive pressure if they were uploaded successfully. But even then, successfully uploaded lawfully copying content may reduce a right holder's profits, for example, if it

[9] In an empirical study of automated takedown notices, Penney (2019, p. 446) finds that 71% of affected uploaders where unlikely to try to upload the content again.

negatively reviews or parodies the right holder's work. Moreover, right holders may lose licensing revenues that would stem from unnecessary licences.

Taken together, it is unclear whether false positives with respect to lawfully copying upload attempts are costly or beneficial for right holders and therefore decrease or increase their incentives to create. In any case, even if false positives produce a positive net effect on incentives to create, the resulting social benefits are outweighed by social costs.[10]

How do right holders' net costs of false positives in a *laissez-faire* regime compare to net social costs? Right holders only partially internalise foregone social benefits that would have resulted from reduced costs of creation, social costs of decreased access by viewers, increased transaction costs for viewers who access the content via an alternative channel, and social costs of over-compliance. This internalisation takes place through negative effects on right holders' reputations, which may arise if overreaching claims resulting in false positives are made public (cf. Fiala & Husovec, 2022, p. 2; Loren, 2011, p. 760) and through the effort of resolving deficiencies. Note that the above-proposed notifications to uploaders about the parts of upload attempts that triggered blockings and about the allegedly infringed works (Sect. 4.3.2.1) increase the likelihood that these costs arise. Still, uploaders can only detect deficiencies that led to blockings and many uploaders may fail to uncover deficiencies. Right holders are thus likely to not fully internalise the net social costs of blocked lawful upload attempts.

Right holders may additionally internalise the negative effects of false positives through contracts with uploaders. If a right holder and an uploader have concluded a licensing agreement, the uploader may be able to hold the right holder liable for breaching the agreement if the right holder fails to indicate the license. Moreover, a reputation of not indicating licences in the reference database is likely to decrease future licensees' willingness to pay. It can thus be presumed that blockings of licensees' lawful upload attempts due to failures to indicate licences create appreciable costs for right holders.

5.3.1.3 Right Holders' Incentives in Laissez-Faire Regime

How do the divergences of right holders' net costs of errors from net social costs influence the efficiency of right holders' incentives? Right holders have excessive incentives to take measures that inhibit upload attempts that unlawfully copy from their works and deficient incentives to ensure that lawfully copying upload attempts pass the filter (cf. Helman & Parchomovsky, 2011, p. 1209; see Sag, 2017, p. 557).

Right holders thus have incentives to add their works to the reference database (Helman & Parchomovsky, 2011, p. 1227). They may, however, add works that from a social perspective are not worthy of being entered. Moreover, apart from indicating licences, right holders have inefficient incentives to limit the scope of

[10] Again, this is due to the assumption that existing copyright law is efficient (Sect. 2.1).

protection that automated filtering provides to the content they enter, for example, by marking external elements or contributing to correct calculations of terms of protection.

Based on the comparison of right holders' net costs of errors to net social costs, it is unclear whether in addition to too little incentives to make the required efforts, right holders also have—as is sometimes suggested (Raymond, 2013, p. 498; Zimmerman, 2014, p. 273)—incentives to seek more extensive protection than they are entitled to.

5.3.2 Improving Right Holders' Incentives

The previous section identified two main incentive problems in a *laissez-faire* regime: Right holders have inefficient incentives to limit the scope of protection that automated filtering provides for the content they enter and right holders have incentives to enter works into the reference database that from a social perspective should not be entered.

This section examines how right holders' incentives can best be improved. For this, it weighs the social benefits of measures to improve right holders' incentives against the social costs. The social benefits encompass the social benefits of improving right holders' incentives and the additional social benefits of the measures.

Two starting points to improve right holders' incentives are conceivable. The first is to target the cause of both incentive problems, namely, right holders' inefficiently low net costs of false positives (Sect. 5.3.2.1). The second is to address the incentive problems directly by setting the level of care that right holders must take to limit the scope of protection that automated filtering provides for the content they enter (Sect. 5.3.2.2) or by charging right holders fees for entering works (Sect. 5.3.2.3). Section 5.3.2.4 summarises the suggested approach.

5.3.2.1 Increasing Right Holders' Net Costs of False Positives

Right holders' net costs of false positives can be increased by enabling uploaders to hold them strictly liable for false positives caused by deficiencies of the reference database. As far as apparent, strict liability has not yet been considered as a measure to improve right holders' incentives. However, it has been suggested to penalise right holders who make wrongful indications, without—at least explicit—mention of a negligence requirement (Goller, 2019; Kalia, 2015; Sag, 2017, p. 557; cf. Husovec, 2018, pp. 81–82).[11]

[11] YouTube states regarding its copyright management tools that '[m]isuse [...], such as submitting false information, may result in the suspension of your account or other legal consequences' (Google, n.d., pt. Overview of copyright management tools).

From a right holder's perspective, the type of sanction is not decisive for the effect on incentives. To address the more interesting question whether right holders should be sanctioned regardless of how carefully they acted, it hence suffices to consider one type of sanction. This section focusses on liability for damages, but the reasoning can be transferred *mutatis mutandis* to other 'strict' penalties.

In theory, strict liability can align right holders' incentives to social efficiency. For this, the sum of expected damages and expected litigation costs[12] must equal the difference between the expected net social costs and the expected net private costs of a false positive. However, it is impossible to specify damages in a way that comes close to fulfilling this equation as apart from litigation costs, all relevant variables are extremely difficult to estimate.

If damages are set too low, strict liability does not exhaust the full potential for improvement; if too high, it deters right holders from entering works that are worthy of being entered and encourages them to spend more than socially desirable on the accuracy of entries. It is therefore doubtful that strict liability can be designed in a way that produces social benefits.

On the costs side, to decide whether right holders are liable, it must be evaluated whether they have made deficient entries. Moreover, the magnitude of damages must be determined. Regardless of whether these decisions are made by courts or in private settings, they are associated with social costs. The magnitude of social costs of decision-making and the extent to which damages can approach efficiency depend on the rigour of the decision-making process in opposite directions. The social costs of decision-making are likely to materialise frequently as right holders can be held liable even if they take the socially efficient level of care.[13] Moreover, every right holder must determine which level of care comes closest to minimising costs, resulting in a duplication of costs (see Schäfer & Müller-Langer, 2009, p. 27).

Overall, as it is unclear whether strict liability can produce social benefits and as the associated social costs are substantial, it can be concluded that strict liability is not cost-justified.

---

[12]Litigation costs are understood to be the costs right holders incur related to the assessments whether they have made deficient entries, regardless of whether such assessments are made by courts or in private settings.

[13]With respect to a rule of gross negligence, Leistner (2020, p. 180) notes that '*user inertia* in actually claiming the right to damages [...] seems probable when taking the experience with the DMCA counter notification system into account.' However, experience with counter notifications does not appear informative in this regard because the costs and benefits of counter notifications are not comparable to the costs and benefits of claiming damages. In any case, under strict liability, more claims can be expected than under a rule of gross negligence as uploaders do not face the risk that right holders escape liability by showing that they took due care.

5.3.2.2 Standard of Care Regarding Accuracy of Indications in Reference Database

As an alternative to strict liability, liability can be negligence-based (e.g., Leistner, 2020, pp. 179–180).[14] Instead of improving right holders' incentives by increasing their net costs of false positives, a negligence rule prescribes the level of care right holders must take. While other sanctions to induce right holders to comply with the standard of care are conceivable, this section focusses on liability for damages.[15]

A negligence rule aligns right holders' incentives to social desirability if damages do not fall too far below the optimal level and the standard of care is optimal.[16] Neither excessive nor modestly deficient damages discourage right holders from taking the socially optimal level of care.[17] A severe misspecification of damages may result in deficient incentives, which would nevertheless constitute an improvement over no liability, but not in excessive incentives.

It is reasonable to presume that damages that are sufficiently high to induce right holders to comply with the standard of care can be specified. Note in this regard that a higher likelihood of uncovering deficiencies, which—as suggested in Sect. 4.3.2.1—can be achieved by informing uploaders about the works their upload attempts allegedly infringe, makes it easier to specify damages in this way.

The crucial factor in terms of aligning right holders' incentives to social desirability is the standard of care. To steer right holders' incentives towards efficiency, the standard of care must encompass requirements on the actions right holders must take and on the required effort. The actions right holders must take can be prescribed precisely using the insights obtained in Sect. 4.3.2.2: Right holders should only enter content that is (still) protected and in which they own the rights, indicate end dates of protection (or information needed for calculations thereof), indicate licensing arrangements, and mark external elements.

[14] In the comparable case of bad faith takedown requests, US law provides for liability for misrepresentation, 17 U.S.C. § 512(f)(1). Likewise, German law provides for negligence-based liability of alleged right holders who request blockings of works they do not own (section 18(2) of the Act on the Copyright Liability of Online Content Sharing Service Providers, 2021).

[15] Like in Sect. 5.3.2.1, considering other types of sanctions would add no value in terms of addressing the question whether a negligence rule is desirable. Again, the reasoning can nevertheless be transferred *mutatis mutandis* to other sanctions.

[16] Right holders' incentives are also socially efficient if damages are optimal and the costs of taking due care exceed the costs of taking the socially optimal level of care by more than the sum of expected damages and expected litigation costs if right holders take the socially optimal level of care (see Schäfer & Müller-Langer, 2009, p. 7). This possibility is ignored as it is impossible to specify damages close to social efficiency (Sect. 5.3.2.1).

[17] If compensation is excessive, it is even more beneficial for right holders to escape liability by complying with the standard of care. Modest deficiencies do not induce right holders to deviate from the standard of care due to the discontinuity of their expected costs functions at the standard of care: If a right holder's actual care reaches the standard of care, the expected costs curve jumps down as the right holder no longer faces expected damages (see Cooter & Ulen, 2016, pp. 218–219).

For the effort, it is hardly possible to pre-define precise requirements. The main alternative is to rely on a standard of care that evolves through repeated assessments by courts of whether right holders' entries were sufficiently accurate. While the volatility of the automated analysis of upload attempts is too high for a standard of care to evolve through case law before the automated analysis underwent radical changes (Sect. 5.4.2.3), the factors decisive for right holders' due care are largely stable over time. Courts' repeated assessments of right holders' care can thus create a predictable standard of care. Until the standard has emerged, uncertainty and hence a tendency for excessive incentives can be expected.[18]

If courts accurately apply the marginal Hand rule, the evolving standard approaches efficiency (see Cooter & Ulen, 2016, p. 215).[19] If courts err or apply another decision rule, the evolving standard deviates from efficiency. However, even then it is reasonable to expect that the standard does not severely obstruct right holders' incentives.

A rule of negligence designed in this way improves right holders' incentives to limit the scope of protection that automated filtering provides for their works. Thereby, it also raises right holders' costs of entering works and reduces their benefits of doing so. As a result, it becomes less attractive for right holders whose works are not worthy of being entered to enter their works. The upshot is that negligence-based liability considerably reduces the number of false positives caused by deficiencies of the reference database.

Like strict liability, a negligence rule is associated with the social costs of decision-making. The costs per claim tend to be higher than under strict liability because right holders' care must additionally be evaluated (see Schäfer & Müller-Langer, 2009, p. 24). However, weighing the benefits and costs of the additional effort right holders could have taken does not appear exceptionally demanding. In particular, unlike for the automated analysis, such assessments do not require technical expertise. Moreover, after an initial phase of settling on the standard of care—if damages are sufficiently high to induce right holders to comply with the standard of care—only few claims can be expected to be brought.

Taken together, it is plausible that the social benefits of considerably reducing the number of false positives outweigh the overall moderate social costs and that negligence-based liability in the above-described way is therefore cost-justified.

---

[18] A right holder who seeks to comply with the standard of care but randomly errs about the effort courts require takes excessive precaution to avoid facing expected damages and thus to benefit from the downwards jump of the expected costs curve (see Cooter & Ulen, 2016, pp. 220–221).

[19] The Hand rule is based on the judgement written by Judge Learned Hand in *United States v. Carroll Towing Co.* (1947, p. 173). In its marginal form, it states that a tortfeasor acts negligently if additional precaution is cost-justified, that is, if the marginal social costs of precaution fall below the marginal social benefits of reduced expected harm.

5.3.2.3 Fee for Entering Works

To directly target right holders' incentives to add more works to the reference database than socially desirable, a fee for entering works can be charged. As far as apparent, such a fee has not yet been discussed in the literature or the policy debate on automated filtering. However, in the comparable case of copyright registration associated with procedural benefits, the US Copyright Office charges a fee (US Copyright Office, n.d.). It has been argued that copyright formalities (including this fee) help to separate commercially more from commercially less valuable works (Sprigman, 2004, pp. 502–514). Along the same lines, the database operator can charge a fee for entering works to separate works that are worthy of being entered from works that are not.

A fee deters right holders whose works are not worthy of being entered from doing so if it reflects the difference between their expected net costs and expected net social costs of entering their works. However, it is hard to conceive how a fee can approach this difference. Expected net social and expected net private costs include elements that are extremely difficult to estimate, notably the probability with which entering a work prevents unlawful upload attempts, the probability with which it leads to false positives, and the net private and net social costs of errors. Moreover, the optimal fee differs between works.

If the fee is too low, it is less effective than desirable; if too high, some right holders whose works are worthy of being entered are prevented from doing so. In addition, the determination of a fee is costly, notably if different fees are calculated for different works.

Recall from Sect. 5.3.2.2 that negligence-based liability already significantly increases right holders' net costs of entering works into the reference database. The benefits of charging a fee for entering works are therefore lower than without such liability in place. At the same time, it is then more likely that a fee which is too high is introduced. Given the difficulties in specifying an appropriate fee and the resulting risk of preventing right holders whose works are worthy of being entered from doing so, charging a fee then overall does not appear desirable.

5.3.2.4 Suggested Approach

To sum up, the suggested approach to improve right holders' incentives is negligence-based liability for false positives caused by deficiencies of the reference database. Courts should apply the marginal Hand rule to assess whether right holders took sufficient care to ensure that they only enter content that is (still) protected and in which they own the rights and that indications in terms of end dates of protection (or information needed for calculations thereof), licensing arrangements, and external elements are correct.

5.4 Platforms' Incentives

This section turns from right holders' incentives in terms of the reference database to platforms' incentives in terms of the analysis of upload attempts. The structure corresponds to the structure of the previous section: Section 5.4.1 examines platforms' incentives in the absence of (non-contractual) liability for errors ('*laissez-faire* regime'). Section 5.4.2 uses the obtained insights to review measures to improve platforms' incentives.

5.4.1 Inefficiency of Platforms' Incentives in Laissez-Faire Regime

Platforms' incentives in a *laissez-faire* regime are shaped by the extent to which platforms internalise platform participants'[20] net costs of errors. Additional factors that may influence platforms' incentives have been considered but can—as Sect. 5.4.1.1 explains—be neglected in the present discussion. Section 5.4.1.2 examines how platforms partially internalise platform participants' net costs of errors. The obtained insights are used to compare platforms' net costs of errors in a *laissez-faire* regime with net social costs of errors (Sect. 5.4.1.3). Finally, Sect. 5.4.1.4 discusses to what extent the observed differences in terms of net costs of errors render platforms' incentives inefficient.

5.4.1.1 Focus on Internalisation of Platform Participants' Net Costs of Errors by Platforms

In analysing platforms' incentives in a *laissez-faire* regime, this section focusses on the internalisation of platform participants' net costs of errors by platforms. Further channels through which errors may affect platforms' profits and further motives of platforms to filter have been considered. This section explains why the following analysis leaves such alternative channels and motives aside.

A first alternative channel through which errors may affect platforms' profits is a risk of regulation (see Buiten et al., 2020, p. 150; Husovec, 2016, pp. 14–15; Sag, 2017, n. 244; Zimmerman, 2014, pp. 268–271; cf. Liebowitz, 2018, para. 92). To avoid regulation, platforms may filter voluntarily. This strategy is sensible if the resulting reduction in a platform's expected costs of regulation exceeds the costs of voluntary filtering. However, to reduce the probability of regulation, voluntary filtering must come close to what a policymaker would require. Moreover, for voluntary filtering to reduce the probability of regulation, other platforms must

[20] As explained in Sect. 1.2, in this book the term platform participants refers to viewers, lawful uploaders, unlawful uploaders, and advertisers.

join in (see Husovec, 2016, p. 15). This requires coordination among platforms, which is difficult to achieve. Based on these considerations, this section presumes that the risk of future regulation does not appreciably affect platforms' incentives.

A second alternative channel is a platform's reputation among employees or investors (see Buiten et al., 2020, p. 150).[21] The attractiveness of a platform to employees or investors is an important consideration, but it is likely to be mostly driven by the platform's profits. To the extent that profits drive the attractiveness of a platform to employees or investors, changes in the attractiveness reinforce the effects of errors on the platform's profits. Insofar as the attractiveness of a platform to employees or investors is affected by its reputation as such, and not by its profits, it is likely that this reputation is highly correlated with the platform's reputation among viewers and thus affects the platform's profits in the same direction. Based on these considerations, taking the attractiveness of platforms to employees and investors into account would not qualitatively change the effects observed by only considering the attractiveness to platform participants. For a focussed analysis, the attractiveness of platforms to employees and investors is thus left aside.

As alternative motives for filtering, it has been suggested that platforms may have non-economic interests, for example, 'nurturing a healthy community', 'encouraging creative or innovative offers […] as a goal by itself', or satisfying 'a sense of public obligation' (Buiten et al., 2020, p. 150). However, it is unclear why 'nurturing a healthy community' represents a non-economic motive as it is strongly correlated with the attractiveness of a platform to platform participants. Moreover, these motives have been advanced in the context of harmful content in general. The goal of a 'healthy community' and the 'sense of public obligation' carry more weight for other types of harmful content (e.g., graphic violence) than for copyright infringements. For copyright infringements, it is reasonable to presume that non-economic motives do not—or at least not considerably—drive platforms' incentives. The following analysis thus evaluates platforms' incentives solely by considering the impact of errors on their profits.

5.4.1.2 Internalisation of Platform Participants' Net Costs of Errors by Platforms

Having explained the focus on the internalisation of platform participants' net costs of errors by platforms, this section analyses how platforms internalise these costs. Two channels are conceivable: The first is a changed level of participation on the platform; the second a contract between a platform and a platform participant.

---

[21] As noted in Sect. 5.4.1.2, errors may generate a bad reputation of a platform among viewers by giving rise to allegations of censorship or by creating the impression of a 'shady' venue for piracy. Similar concerns may generate a bad reputation among employees and investors.

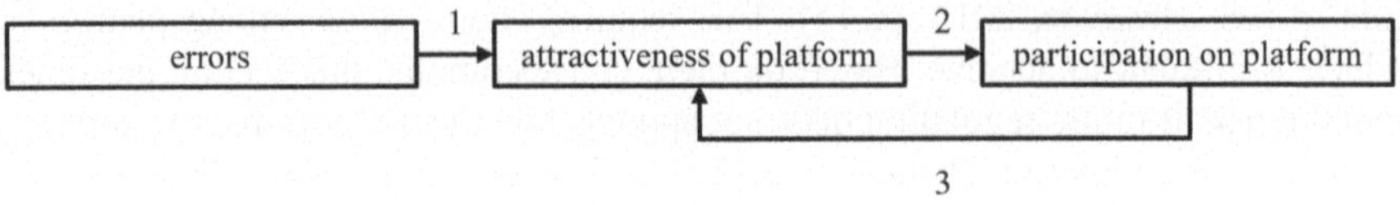

Fig. 5.1 Effects of errors on platform participants' levels of participation on a platform

Internalisation Through Changed Levels of Participation on Platform
Figure 5.1 displays the basic setup of how errors affect platform participants' levels of participation on a platform.

Errors directly influence the attractiveness of a platform to platform participants (arrow 1) and thereby platform participants' levels of participation on the platform (arrow 2). These changed levels of participation, in turn, affect the attractiveness of the platform to other platform participants (arrow 3) and thereby, again, their levels of participation on the platform (arrow 2).

Direct Effects of Errors on Attractiveness of Platform to Platform Participants

Errors directly affect the attractiveness of a platform to viewers, unlawful uploaders, lawfully copying uploaders, right holders, and advertisers. For the reasons advanced in Sect. 5.3.1.2, false positives with respect to right holders' uploads are not considered.

Individual errors directly affect the attractiveness of a platform to viewers if they change the amount of content available on the platform (see Grosse Ruse-Khan, 2021, p. 161; Leistner, 2020, p. 194). However, a false negative does not necessarily imply that viewers have access to more content as the content may already be available on the platform. Likewise, a false positive does not necessarily mean that viewers have access to less content as the lawfully copying uploader may still upload the content, for instance, by obtaining a license or modifying it to circumvent the blocking.

A large number of errors may harm a platform's reputation: False negatives may create the impression of a 'shady' venue for piracy (see Goldman, 2011; Liebowitz, 2018, para. 92). False positives may upset viewers and give rise to allegations of censorship (cf. Fiala & Husovec, 2022, p. 1627; Klonick, 2018, p. 3). The attractiveness of a platform to viewers is presumably affected by its reputation, but there is no systematic empirical evidence of the strength of this effect.[22]

For right holders, Chap. 3 demonstrated that false negatives reduce their profits. False positives with respect to upload attempts that lawfully copy from their works may also affect right holders' profits. However, for the reasons advanced in Sect. 5.3.1.2, the direction of this effect is unclear.

[22] The extent to which errors affect a platform's reputation depends on viewers' beliefs about probabilities of errors. Note that systematic recording and publication of probabilities of errors, which has been recommended in Sect. 4.4.2.3, contributes to an alignment of viewers' conjectured to actual probabilities of errors. The term conjectured probability is adapted from the term 'consumer's *conjectured* care level' used by Daughety and Reinganum (2013, p. 75).

Unlawfully copying uploaders benefit from false negatives as they enable the availability of their uploads on a platform. Regarding false positives with respect to upload attempts that lawfully copy from the same work that they have unlawfully copied, the same costs and—apart from licensing revenues—benefits as advanced in Sect. 5.3.1.2 for right holders apply. It is therefore also unclear how unlawfully copying uploaders are affected by false positives.

Uploaders who lawfully copy from works lose revenues in case of false positives. As noted above, to nevertheless upload successfully, they may over-comply by purchasing unnecessary licences or by modifying content to make it less susceptible to blocking. Modifying content not only requires them to spend time and effort (see Trendacosta, 2020, p. 28). It is also likely to render the content less valuable as the creative expression diverges from the expression initially intended (see Brøvig-Hanssen & Jones, 2021, p. 10; Trendacosta, 2020, pp. 27–28).[23] False positives thus make a platform less attractive to lawfully copying uploaders.[24]

It may be argued that false negatives are costly for lawfully copying uploaders as they create competition for their uploads. Note that a false negative only has this effect if it induces a right holder to upload his work as for the competition exerted on a lawfully copying upload, it is irrelevant how many times a work has been uploaded. And even then, it is unclear how the availability of the copied-from work affects the views attracted by the lawfully copying upload.

Finally, errors negatively affect advertisers if they prefer their advertisements not to be displayed alongside unlawful uploads (Lefouili & Madio, 2022, p. 328) or if errors affect the reputation of a platform among viewers (see French Ministry of Culture, 2020, p. 61; Priest, 2015, pp. 188–190). Advertisements on a platform with a bad reputation may be less effective in changing consumers' preferences,[25] convey less trustworthy information,[26] or create less valuable complements to advertised products.[27]

Influence of Attractiveness of Platform on Levels of Participation

The previous section explained how errors directly affect the attractiveness of a platform to platform participants. Changed levels of attractiveness do not yet affect a

---

[23] Note that while the mashups Brøvig-Hanssen and Jones (2021, p. 10) consider may well be unlawful, their argument that modifications to avoid blockings decrease the value of content applies irrespective of whether the content is lawful.

[24] The extent to which false positives affect the attractiveness of the platform to lawfully copying uploaders depends on their beliefs about probabilities of false positives. As for viewers, systematic recording and publication of probabilities of false positives contributes to an alignment of lawfully copying uploaders' conjectured to actual probabilities of false positives.

[25] This argument is based on the view that advertisements alter consumers' preferences with a view to switching demand from one product to another (see generally Bagwell, 2007, pp. 1710–1716).

[26] This argument is based on the view that advertisements change consumers' behaviour by reducing imperfect consumer information (see generally Bagwell, 2007, pp. 1716–1720).

[27] This argument is based on the view that advertisements and the advertised products are complements. An advertisement creates a sentiment (e.g., social prestige), which complements the advertised product, making it more valuable (see generally Bagwell, 2007, pp. 1720–1723).

platform's profits. For this, they must lead to changed levels of participation on the platform.

With respect to right holders, two decisions are relevant in terms of platform participation. The first is whether their works are made available on the platform. However, if unlawful uploading is possible, this decision is not at the discretion of right holders. The impact of unlawful uploading on the number of works uploaded has been examined in Chap. 3. The obtained results can be transferred to the question how false negatives influence the number of works uploaded to a platform: Stricter filtering in the model created in Chap. 3 is equivalent to fewer false negatives in this chapter. Therefore—leaving an effect on incentives to create aside—if a filter is sufficiently lenient to begin with, a decrease in the number of false negatives leads to a decrease in the number of works uploaded to a platform. Once a certain level of strictness is surpassed, a further decrease in the number of false negatives leaves the number of works uploaded unaffected.

The second relevant decision is whether to create content. This decision rests with right holders. From Chap. 3 we know that a decrease in the number of false negatives leads to an increase in right holders' profits. To the extent that increased profits lead to increased incentives to create, a decrease in the number of false negatives therefore increases the number of works created and therefore uploaded.

Overall, for a platform that employs a sufficiently lenient filter to begin with, it is unclear whether a decrease in the number of false negatives leads to a decrease or an increase in the number of works uploaded. Once a certain level of strictness is surpassed, a further decrease in the number of false negatives overall leads to an increase in the number of works uploaded.

For the other platform participants, the extent to which lower levels of attractiveness of a platform affect levels of participation depends on the costs of changing from the platform to the best alternative, which may be another user-uploaded content platform or an alternative channel, for example, a streaming service that is not open to user uploads.[28] But what are these costs?

Switching costs are one cost component. They may result from a need for specific investments (e.g., in equipment, reputation, or learning how to use a platform or an alternative channel; see Klemperer, 1995, p. 517), from an inner resistance to leaving a trusted platform (see Bamberger & Lobel, 2017, p. 1066; Klemperer, 1995, p. 518), or from long-term contracts (see Klemperer, 1995, pp. 517–518). Switching costs tend to be moderate (Schmalensee, 2011, p. 301) because platform participants and users of streaming services that are not open to user uploads generally do not need specific equipment, the costs of learning how to use platforms and alternative channels are low, platforms usually do not require subscriptions, and uploaders usually grant non-exclusive licences (e.g., Google, 2023; Instagram, 2024; Vimeo, 2024). Higher switching costs can be expected for uploaders who have invested in

[28] For the sake of readability, the following discussion focusses on the effects of a decrease in a platform's attractiveness. The advanced considerations nevertheless apply *mutatis mutandis* to an increase in its attractiveness.

platform-specific reputation and for advertisers who have bought advertising space for a fixed time.

Changing from a platform to another platform or to an alternative channel further generates the costs of using an imperfect substitute instead of the otherwise preferred platform. Network benefits are one reason for preferring a platform to another platform or to an alternative channel. A platform participant who leaves a platform loses the network benefits exerted on the platform. If these network benefits exceed the network benefits available on the platform or through the alternative channel to which the platform participant switches, the platform participant incurs costs in the form of foregone network benefits. Switching then becomes a collective decision, possibly leading to collective inertia (Bamberger & Lobel, 2017, pp. 1068–1069; see also Shapiro & Varian, 1999, pp. 184–186).

The intensity of the resulting lock-in depends on the feasibility of coordination between platform participants (see Farrell & Klemperer, 2007, p. 1975). Multi-homing[29] reduces collective inertia and the need to coordinate: It enables a participant of platform A to try out platform B without losing the network benefits available on platform A (see Evans, 2003, p. 364; Farrell & Klemperer, 2007, p. 2032). The attractiveness of multi-homing inter alia depends on how easily platform participants can transfer data between platforms (see Crémer et al., 2019, p. 59).

Differences in the functioning and design are another reason for preferring a platform to another platform or to an alternative channel (cf. Hamdani, 2002, p. 929). The costs of changing from a platform to another platform or to an alternative channel are higher the larger the differences are. How likely is the existence of a close substitute to a platform?

Positive network effects make it more attractive to use larger than smaller platforms. Such demand-side economies of scale render the co-existence of undifferentiated platforms unlikely (see Jullien & Sand-Zantman, 2021, p. 3).[30] Differentiated platforms (e.g., platforms that offer different features) may nevertheless co-exist (Jullien & Sand-Zantman, 2021, p. 3; see also Parker et al., 2016, p. 88).

Note that even if only differentiated platforms can co-exist, an undifferentiated platform can still enter the market and overthrow the incumbent. The degree of contestability of a market depends on barriers to entry and exit, notably on the sunk costs incurred when entering a market and on an incumbent's advantages vis-à-vis entrants (see Baumol, 1982, pp. 3–4). The sunk costs incurred when entering a

[29] Multi-homing refers to a situation in which platform participants can use several platforms. The term goes back to Rochet and Tirole (2003, pp. 991–993).

[30] Supply-side economies of scale also arise, notably since the costs of building a platform are fixed. Yet, these costs are not overly high because platforms can use existing physical and virtual infrastructure and need little physical equipment (Evans, 2017, pp. 6–7). Supply-side economies of scale thus generally do not preclude competition in the market (see Jullien & Sand-Zantman, 2021, p. 3).

platform market are likely to be low compared to many other industries.[31] An incumbent platform's advantages centre around its base of platform participants,[32] which generates network benefits that an entrant cannot offer. Moreover, the data an incumbent has collected enables it to show more targeted content recommendations and advertisements than an entrant who lacks access to comparable data (Biglaiser et al., 2019, pp. 43–44).[33]

Taken together, notably an absence of another user-uploaded content platform on which comparable network benefits are exerted and which provides similar functions as well as a similar design can be expected to appreciably reduce the extent to which decreased levels of attractiveness of a platform translate into lower levels of participation on the platform. The responsiveness of uploaders to changed levels of attractiveness of a platform is additionally considerably reduced by switching costs resulting from a need to invest in platform-specific reputation.

Indirect Effects of Errors on Attractiveness of Platform to Platform Participants

To the extent that direct effects of errors on the attractiveness of a platform to platform participants trigger changes in those platform participants' levels of participation on the platform, due to within- and cross-group network effects,[34] the attractiveness of the platform to other platform participants is also affected. The relevant network effects for viewers, uploaders, and advertisers are illustrated in Fig. 5.2. Note that uploaders include right holders, lawfully copying uploaders, and unlawfully copying uploaders (Sect. 1.2.1).

The arrows show whether an increase in participation by platform participants who belong to the group from which the arrows originate decreases (−) or increases (+) the attractiveness of the platform to platform participants who belong to the group to which the arrows point. Arrows that originate from the same group of platform participants to which they point represent within-group network effects; arrows between groups show cross-group network effects.

As shown in Fig. 5.2, viewers' usage of a platform generates positive within-group network effects: As more viewers use a platform, more viewers can interact with each other (e.g., by rating content or by commenting on it), making the platform

[31] Again, the fixed costs of entering a platform market are not overly high because platforms can use existing physical and virtual infrastructure and need little physical equipment (Evans, 2017, pp. 6–7). Moreover, only some parts of the fixed costs (e.g., costs of advertisement) are platform-specific and thus sunk.

[32] These advantages only fully materialise vis-à-vis entrants who cannot leverage an overlapping viewer base from another market. The entry of a platform active in another market into a market with an overlapping user base has been referred to as 'platform envelopment' (Eisenmann et al., 2011, pp. 1271–1272).

[33] Note that the presence of an industry that sells big data reduces the significance of this advantage (see A. Lambrecht & Tucker, 2017, pp. 1–2).

[34] The terms are adopted from Belleflamme and Peitz (2018, pp. 287–290). With positive (negative) within-group network effects, a platform participant's utility from using a platform increases (decreases) as more platform participants from the same group use the platform. With positive (negative) cross-group network effects, a platform participant's utility from using a platform increases (decreases) as more platform participants from another group use the platform.

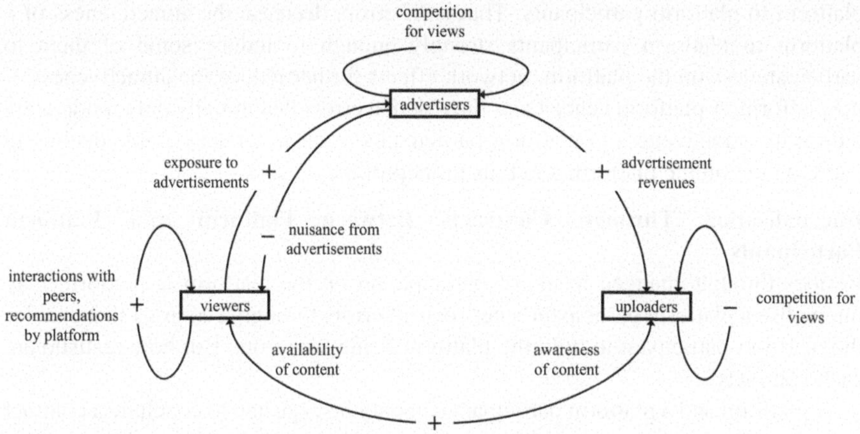

Fig. 5.2 Network effects on a user-uploaded content platform

more attractive to other viewers. Moreover, as more viewers use a platform, the platform can draw conclusions from the behaviour of more viewers, enabling it to provide better content recommendations (see Parker et al., 2016, p. 163). Competition for viewers' attention creates negative within-group network effects between uploaders and between advertisers (cf. Belleflamme & Peitz, 2018, p. 288).

Positive cross-group network effects arise between viewers and uploaders. A platform becomes more attractive to viewers the more content uploaders upload (see Grosse Ruse-Khan, 2021, p. 161; Leistner, 2020, p. 194). It may be argued that viewers dislike unlawful uploads. Yet, viewers often do not know whether uploads are lawful, and even if they do, they often do not care (Sect. 3.2.3.2). At the same time, uploading becomes more attractive as more viewers become aware of the uploads.

Uploaders further benefit from increased participation by advertisers, which enables the platform to pay out higher advertisement revenues to them. Moreover, advertisers benefit from greater or more targeted exposure to their advertisements as more viewers use a platform. Negative cross-group network effects can be expected between advertisers and viewers because for viewers, advertising tends to be nuisance (Belleflamme & Peitz, 2018, p. 305; Evans & Schmalensee, 2016, p. 29).

Note that the described positive network effects can create a feedback loop (Evans & Schmalensee, 2007, p. 159): All else equal, fewer works on a platform result in less usage of the platform by viewers. The platform then becomes less attractive to other viewers, to uploaders, and to advertisers, leading them to view less content, make fewer upload attempts, and spend less on advertising, respectively. As the platform earns less through advertising, it can pay uploaders less, inducing uploaders to make yet fewer upload attempts. Less content on a platform, again, renders the platform less attractive to viewers and so forth.

While negative network effects mitigate these effects, network effects can be expected to overall reinforce the influence of errors on the attractiveness of a platform to platform participants. That is, if errors decrease the attractiveness of a platform to platform participants strongly enough to induce some of them to participate less on the platform, network effects further reduce the attractiveness of the platform. A platform hence faces the risk that errors that initially only moderately reduce its attractiveness to platform participants result in a considerable decline in participation on the platform and thus in its profits.

Internalisation Through Contracts Between Platform and Platform Participants

Besides through changed levels of participation on the platform, a platform may internalise a platform participant's net costs of errors through a contract that enables the platform participant to hold the platform liable for errors. But how realistic are such contracts?

A platform and a platform participant can only be expected to conclude a contract if the contract promises a surplus that is not outweighed by transaction costs. A contractual surplus exists if the benefit in terms of additional error avoidance for the platform participant exceeds the platform's additional costs. A platform participant's benefit of error avoidance is the reduction in net costs of errors, which have been outlined above. The platform's additional costs comprise the costs resulting from additional investments in filtering and the costs associated with deviating from the privately optimal design of automated filtering in the absence of the contract.

Transaction costs not only encompass costs of negotiations but also enforcement costs, which include costs of monitoring a platform's compliance with its contractual obligations. Information asymmetries regarding the platform's filtering effort create opportunities for moral hazard, namely, to filter less diligently than promised. A platform participant can reduce information asymmetries by monitoring the platform's behaviour, but doing so is costly.[35]

The benefits of additional error avoidance to individual viewers and individual advertisers are small relative to the additional costs platforms incur. In any case, even if a contractual surplus existed, it would fall below transaction costs. This problem could be overcome through cooperation among viewers or advertisers. However, due to the high transaction costs associated with such cooperation, it is unlikely to materialise. As a result, it appears unrealistic that contractual relationships between platforms and viewers or advertisers are established.

The situation is different for uploaders with respect to unjustified blockings and for right holders with respect to successful unlawful uploads of their works as they derive considerable benefits from the avoidance of specific errors. Moreover, a

[35] To monitor a platform's behaviour, platform participants can, for instance, require documentation on its filtering efforts. With respect to false negatives, they can further upload copying content for testing purposes or search for unlawfully copying uploads. With respect to false positives, uploaders who are affected by blockings know that their upload attempts have been blocked. Still, they need to ascertain whether their upload attempts were lawful. For platform participants who are not directly affected by the blocking, it is more difficult to find out whether false positives occur. They can perform test uploads or rely on information provided by directly affected uploaders.

platform's costs of avoiding such errors are lower, as it can contain its effort to the avoidance of specific errors, that is, it can filter more leniently with respect to upload attempts by specific uploaders or more strictly with respect to upload attempts that contain elements of works from a specific right holder. In such cases, it is therefore conceivable that a contractual surplus exists.

In most cases, the surplus is likely to be outweighed by the transaction costs described above. However, an increase in the number of upload attempts for which an uploader seeks more lenient filtering and an increase in the number of works for which a right holder seeks stricter filtering can be presumed to lead to a stronger increase in the surplus than in transaction costs as the latter are subject to considerable economies of scale.

Notably a contract between a sufficiently large right holder and a platform is therefore conceivable (see Helman & Parchomovsky, 2011, p. 1210; Husovec, 2016, pp. 13–15). Such a contract may specify that the platform is obliged to prevent false negatives with respect to upload attempts copying from that right holder's work. The notion that a right holder pays a platform for filtering more strictly may seem unintuitive. However, many right holders employ enforcement agents to screen platforms for copyright infringements (Urban et al., 2017, pp. 83–84). There does not appear to be a reason why right holders would not employ platforms as their enforcement agents.

5.4.1.3 Deviation of Platforms' Net Costs of Errors from Net Social Costs

Having explained how platforms partially internalise platform participants' net costs of errors in a *laissez-faire* regime, this section compares platforms' net costs of false negatives and false positives with net social costs.

False Negatives

The net social costs of false negatives, which are outlined in Sect. 5.3.1.1, are likely to exceed a platform's net costs if the platform has not concluded contracts with right holders (see Buiten et al., 2020, p. 151). It is even conceivable that false negatives are overall beneficial for a platform.

A platform does not fully internalise the social costs of false negatives, namely, the costs of reduced content creation. Reduced content creation is costly for a platform as it leads to less content uploaded and thus reduces the platform's attractiveness to viewers. However, the resulting impact on the platform's profits is limited as viewers do not respond perfectly to changes in the attractiveness of the platform (Sect. 5.4.1.2). Moreover, reduced content creation produces costs for society at large (Sect. 2.1), for other platforms, and for alternative channels, which the platform does not internalise. Possible negative effects on the platform's reputation and its attractiveness to advertisers may reduce the difference between social and private costs of false negatives but are unlikely to fully offset it.

It is unclear whether the possible benefit of false negatives in terms of more or cheaper access to some copied-from works is higher from a private or a social perspective. Again, the platform benefits from more content uploaded as it increases its attractiveness to viewers. An argument in favour of lower private benefits is that viewers do not respond perfectly to changes in the attractiveness of the platform (Sect. 5.4.1.2). Moreover, access to content produces social benefits that neither platform participants nor therefore the platform internalises (see also Blevins, 2013, p. 1872; Lemley, 2007, p. 112; Seltzer, 2010, p. 185). On the other hand, if viewers would access the relevant content elsewhere if it were not uploaded unlawfully, the only social benefits are reduced transaction costs. By contrast, the private benefits of increased viewing activity arise irrespective of whether viewers would access the content elsewhere.

In any case, even if social benefits exceed private benefits, it does not appear plausible that the difference between social and private benefits is larger than the difference between social and private costs.

A different picture emerges for uploads that unlawfully copy from works of right holders with whom the platform has concluded a contract. For instance, due to expected contractual damages, it is then conceivable that the platform's net costs of hosting unlawful uploads that copy from works of those right holders exceed net social costs.

False Positives

Having compared platforms' net costs of false negatives with net social costs, this section turns to false positives. False positives create net costs for a platform: They render the platform less attractive to viewers and to lawfully copying uploaders, may harm its reputation, and reduce lawfully copying uploaders' incentives to create. The only conceivable benefits of false positives for the platform are increased incentives for right holders to create. Yet, it is unclear to what extent false positives increase right holders' incentives to create (Sect. 5.3.1.2). In any case, it can be assumed that the resulting benefits for the platform fall below the costs.

False positives thus create net costs from a social and from a platform's perspective. Net social costs of false positives, which are outlined in Sect. 5.3.1.2, are likely to outweigh the platform's net costs.

To be sure, as with false negatives, increased transaction costs are the only social costs if viewers access the content elsewhere, while private costs of reduced viewing activity arise in any case. However, it is likely that many lawfully copying uploaders do not have access to another platform or an alternative channel that enables them to reach a comparable number of viewers (see Brøvig-Hanssen & Jones, 2021, p. 9).[36] Moreover, influenced by the automated decision to block, many lawfully copying uploaders are likely to doubt whether their upload attempts are lawful (see Bechtel,

[36] Note that while the mashups Brøvig-Hanssen and Jones (2021, p. 9) consider may well be unlawful, their argument in terms of the lack of alternative channels with comparable viewership also applies to lawfully copying content.

2020, p. 266; Solomon, 2015, p. 256; cf. Urban et al., 2017, p. 44) and thus to refrain from making the content available elsewhere.

The most plausible reactions of lawfully copying uploaders to blockings are to refrain from making the content available, to distribute it on another platform or via an alternative channel, or to over-comply by purchasing unnecessary licences or modifying the content to make it less susceptible to blocking. As explained above, reduced access to content, which is the result of refraining from making content available or of distributing it elsewhere, creates social costs that the platform does not internalise. If lawfully copying uploaders over-comply, social costs in the form of transaction costs of obtaining unnecessary licences or in the form of the opportunity costs of the time spent on modifying content arise (Sect. 5.3.1.2). The platform does not internalise these costs.

Negative effects of false positives on the platform's reputation mitigate the resulting difference between social and private costs of false positives. However, due to uncertainty about the lawfulness of their upload attempts, many lawfully copying uploaders are likely to avoid drawing attention to their blocked upload attempts (cf. Brøvig-Hanssen & Jones, 2021, p. 6). Moreover, it is unclear how strong the effect of harmed reputation on the platform's attractiveness to platform participants is. Overall, a difference between social and private costs of false positives is likely to remain.

5.4.1.4 Platforms' Incentives in Laissez-Faire Regime

Having compared platforms' net costs of errors with net social costs, this section draws conclusions on the efficiency of platforms' incentives in a *laissez-faire* regime. The starting point is that a platform's incentives would be efficient if its net costs of errors equalled net social costs (see Buiten et al., 2020, p. 148; Gabison & Buiten, 2020, p. 249).[37] Note in this regard that—at least under the assumption that the platform conducts the analysis of upload attempts—the platform's direct costs of error avoidance (e.g., of operating a filter, of defining automatable rules or estimating probabilities of errors, and of manually reviewing automated decisions) largely correspond to social direct costs.

In the following, the efficiency of platforms' incentives regarding the analysis of upload attempts and regarding desirable accompanying measures is discussed.

Analysis of Upload Attempts

It is sometimes claimed that platforms would not filter in a *laissez-faire* regime (e.g., Helman & Parchomovsky, 2011, p. 1201; Hornik & Villa Llera, 2017, p. 14; cf. Lichtman & Posner, 2006, p. 258). This claim is correct if unlawful uploads create net benefits for a platform. By refraining from filtering, the platform then avoids incurring direct costs and ensures that no—privately beneficial—unlawful

[37] Platforms are assumed to seek to maximise profits.

upload attempts are blocked and no—privately costly—false positives are created. The claim is also correct if unlawful uploads do create net costs for platforms, but the net costs are so low that no filtering design can be devised that reduces a platform's aggregate expected net costs of false negatives by more than the sum of the associated aggregate direct costs and aggregate expected net costs of false positives.

If a platform's net costs of false negatives are high enough for a filtering design that fulfils this condition to be devised, the platform would filter in a *laissez-faire* regime (see Gabison & Buiten, 2020, pp. 263–266).[38] This becomes more likely the more right holders have concluded a contract with the platform. Note in this regard that the platform can choose to only filter upload attempts that copy from certain works, for example, from works of right holders with whom it has concluded a contract.[39]

If a platform filters, it cannot be expected to design the analysis of upload attempts in the second-best efficient way, which is discussed in Sect. 4.4. Viewed from a more abstract perspective than above, the platform makes two relevant decisions on the analysis of upload attempts.

The first is how much to spend on the analysis. Since the platform's net costs of false negatives and of false positives fall below net social costs, investments in the analysis are less valuable for the platform than socially. In a *laissez-faire* regime, the platform would thus spend less on the analysis than socially desirable (see Buiten et al., 2020, p. 149; Husovec, 2016, p. 15; Liebowitz, 2018, para. 83). Note, however, that unlike investments in the automated analysis, investments in the manual review can be fine-tuned to specific upload attempts. The platform's investments in the manual review of upload attempts that copy from works of right holders with whom it has concluded a contract are thus likely to come closer to (or even exceed) the socially desirable amount.

The second relevant decision is how to balance probabilities of false negatives and false positives. The platform would strike the socially efficient balance if the ratio of net costs of false negatives to net costs of false positives was identical from its private and from a social perspective. For works of right holders with whom the platform did not conclude a contract, it is unclear how this ratio differs from the platform's and from a social perspective. Note that the platform can apply a different balance depending on the work from which an upload attempt copies. If the platform

[38] Note that Gabison and Buiten (2020, pp. 277–278) assume in their model that filtering does not produce false positives. They discuss the impact of false positives later on, but not for the no liability scenario. False positives make filtering less likely to be efficient for the platform as they increase its costs of filtering.

[39] For example, YouTube limits the eligibility for its Content ID program to right holders who 'own exclusive rights to a substantial body of original material that is frequently uploaded to YouTube' (Google, n.d., pt. How Content ID works). One may argue that such discrimination is not sensible if—as presumed in this chapter—a platform performs the analysis of upload attempts and direct costs of the automated analysis are thus predominantly fixed. However, even then, some costs of filtering are variable: Costs of filtering encompass the aggregate expected net costs of false positives, which increase as the number of works a platform filters for increases, and costs of manual reviews of automated decisions, which are largely variable.

has concluded a contract with a right holder, it becomes more likely that it has incentives to filter upload attempts copying from that right holder's works more strictly than socially desirable.

Accompanying Measures

Besides decisions on the design of the analysis of upload attempts, Chap. 4 identified accompanying measures that platforms should take.

One desirable accompanying measure is that platforms keep track of the probabilities of errors associated with the automated analysis (Sect. 4.4.2.3) and of metrics informative of the accuracy of predictions relevant for the manual review (Sect. 4.4.3.4), hereinafter collectively referred to as 'performance metrics'. A platform benefits from recording performance metrics because doing so enables it to improve the analysis of upload attempts and thus to reduce aggregate expected net costs of errors. As platforms do not fully internalise net social costs of errors, their benefits of improving the analysis fall below the social benefits. Moreover, their benefits of contributing to public knowledge on automated filtering fall below social benefits. Platforms are thus likely to spend less than socially desirable on recording performance metrics, leading to inefficiently low levels of accuracy of the estimations.

Platforms should further disclose the designs of the automated analysis (Sect. 4.4.2.3) and of the manual review (Sect. 4.4.3.4), hereinafter collectively referred to as 'filtering policies', as well as the associated performance metrics. Transparency in these regards enables platforms to counter claims that they use opacity for opportunistic behaviour and creates awareness among platform participants of the challenges involved in designing the analysis of upload attempts. At the same time, it limits platforms' leeway to design the analysis according to their interests, exposes them to criticism, and provides starting points for policymakers to constrain platforms' room for manoeuvre. Overall, it cannot be expected that platforms disclose their filtering policies and performance metrics in the desirable way.[40] Instead, they are likely to

[40] Platforms' existing transparency reports support this conclusion. While they provide information on platforms' copyright enforcement strategies and relevant metrics, they do not detail how filters make decisions and are not informative of performance metrics: Facebook and Instagram report the ratio of the number of proactive removals to the total number of removals (Meta, n.d.); YouTube reports the ratio of the number of automated Content ID claims to the total number of claims (Google, 2024, pt. Our tools are cutting edge). Yet, these metrics do not reflect the share of correct proactive removals/automated claims, as proactive removals/automated claims and the total number of removals/claims comprise removals/claims of lawful content and as not all unlawful uploads are notified. YouTube further reports the ratio of the number of disputed automated claims to the total number of automated claims (Google, 2024, pt. Creating a balanced ecosystem). Yet, this metric is not informative of the share of incorrect automated claims as not all uploaders whose lawful uploads are claimed file a dispute (see Brøvig-Hanssen & Jones, 2021, p. 6; cf. Penney, 2019, pp. 451–453; Urban et al., 2017, pp. 44–45). It is also unclear how many disputes relate to lawful uploads. While YouTube reports the proportion of uploaders and right holders who insist on the lawfulness or unlawfulness of upload attempts throughout the further stages of the process, respectively (Google, 2024, pt. Creating a balanced ecosystem), it is unclear whether uploaders or right holders drop out because they become convinced of the unlawfulness or lawfulness of the upload attempts, respectively, or for other reasons. Note that while these transparency reports have not been published in a

only publish information that promises reputational benefits, resulting in incomplete or biased reports (Perel & Elkin-Koren, 2017, p. 194).

Moreover, platforms should cooperate with the database operator to provide time-saving channels for communication between uploaders and right holders, and platforms should inform the right holders whom uploaders have notified of possible deficiencies of their entries about the parts of their entries that matched with the upload attempts (Sect. 4.3.2.1). A platform benefits from providing such a communication channel and from passing such information to right holders as both measures help to correct and prevent false positives, which produce net costs for the platform. To be sure, platforms do not fully internalise the social benefits of these measures because they only partially internalise net social costs of false positives and because they do not benefit from preventing false positives on other platforms that use the same reference database. Nevertheless, as the costs of building a communication channel and of informing right holders are low, platforms' benefits are likely to be sufficiently high to take these measures.

Desirable accompanying measures further include the provision of time-saving mechanisms for uploaders and right holders to complain about automated decisions (Sect. 4.4.3.2). Platforms benefit from providing a complaint mechanism as it creates positive reputational effects. Moreover, they benefit from correcting false positives and—if unlawful uploads produce net costs for a platform—false negatives. Yet, platforms do not fully internalise the social benefits of correcting errors as they only partially internalise the net social costs of errors. On the costs side, providing a time-saving complaint mechanism induces more uploaders and right holders to submit complaints and to expect reactions from platforms. As handling complaints creates significant costs for platforms, it is overall doubtful whether they have sufficient incentives to offer time-saving complaint mechanisms.

Furthermore, platforms should inform uploaders about the parts of their upload attempts that triggered blockings, about the allegedly infringed works, and about copyright law in general (Sects. 4.3.2.1 and 4.4.3.2). Platforms benefit from doing so as uploaders are likely to be more understanding towards 'explained' blockings, reducing the reputational costs blockings entail. Moreover, the provided information may induce uploaders to refrain from unjustified complaints and may thus reduce platforms' aggregate costs of handling complaints. Platforms further benefit from correcting false positives, even though their benefits in this regard, again, fall below social benefits. The costs of informing uploaders are low, notably as uploaders become aware of blockings even without being informed. It thus appears plausible that the described benefits are sufficiently high for platforms to inform concerned uploaders (Sect. 4.3.2.1).

Finally, platforms should inform right holders about uploads that exhibit similarity to their works but were not blocked and about copyright law in general (Sect. 4.4.3.2). Provided that unlawful uploads produce net costs for platforms, platforms benefit

---

laissez-faire regime, they are nevertheless relevant as there are no obligations to publish reports in this way.

from informing concerned right holders as doing so helps to correct false negatives. However, their benefits of informing concerned right holders fall below social benefits as even if false negatives create net costs for platforms, these net costs fall below net social costs. At the same time, informing concerned right holders creates substantial additional costs for platforms as without the notification, many right holders would not learn about potentially infringing uploads. It is therefore doubtful that platforms have sufficient incentives to inform concerned right holders.[41] A different conclusion must be drawn if and insofar contracts with right holders require platforms to provide such information.

5.4.2 *Improving Platforms' Incentives*

Having explained why platforms' incentives in a *laissez-faire* regime are inefficient, this section examines how they can best be improved. For this, it weighs the social benefits of measures to improve platforms' incentives against the social costs.

As the insufficient internalisation of net social costs of errors is responsible for platforms' inefficient incentives, one starting point is to raise platforms' net costs of errors (Sect. 5.4.2.1). A related approach is to take some decision-making power away from platforms and to place it in the hands of actors who internalise net social costs of errors to a larger degree, namely, representatives of stakeholders (Sect. 5.4.2.2). Finally, the incentive problems can be addressed directly by imposing a standard of care for the analysis of upload attempts (Sect. 5.4.2.3) or by obliging platforms to adopt the desirable accompanying measures (Sect. 5.4.2.4).

5.4.2.1 Increasing Platforms' Net Costs of Errors

This section focusses on strict liability as a measure to increase platforms' net costs of errors.[42] For the same reasons as advanced in Sect. 5.3.2.1, there is no added value in considering other types of 'strict' sanctions.

[41] One may view YouTube's practice of informing right holders about the view count and the percentage of the matching video that is made up of their content via its Copyright Match Tool (Google, 2024, pt. Introduction) as evidence of sufficient private incentives. Yet, YouTube does not operate in a *laissez-faire* regime. While neither US nor EU law obliges platforms to inform concerned right holders, existing notice-and-takedown regimes incentivise right holders to search for and notify possible infringements. Platforms thus bear some of the costs related to right holders' complaints anyway, reducing the additional costs associated with informing concerned right holders.

[42] Regarding strict liability for false negatives, see, for example, European Copyright Society (2017, p. 7); Helman and Parchomovsky (2011, p. 1215); Husovec (2018, p. 77); Rendas (2017, pp. 43–44); Samuelson (2021, p. 337); Spoerri (2019, paras. 31, 54). Strict liability for false positives has not yet been explored. As strict liability for false positives may improve platforms' incentives in the same way, this section considers strict liability for both types of errors.

Note, however, that the discussion of the extent to which platforms internalise net social costs of errors suggests an additional, potentially powerful set of measures to increase platforms' net costs of false positives, namely, measures that intensify the competitive pressure exerted on platforms (see Hamdani, 2002, p. 928). Examples of such measures include a facilitation of data interoperability[43] and a prevention of 'killer acquisitions'.[44] These measures are left aside as platforms' market power is not only relevant for the internalisation of net social costs of errors and these measures thus have numerous implications unrelated to automated filtering. These implications would have to be considered to evaluate the desirability of such measures. Doing so would go beyond the scope of this book as research in these regards is far from conclusive.

For the same reason, this section also leaves measures aside that are intended to counteract an often presumed (e.g., European Copyright Society, 2017, p. 7; Helman & Parchomovsky, 2011, p. 1215; Husovec, 2018, p. 77; Lefouili & Madio, 2022, pp. 341–342; Rendas, 2017, pp. 43–44; Samuelson, 2021, p. 337; Spoerri, 2019, paras. 31, 54), yet questionable[45] side effect of a filtering obligation, namely, an impediment to enter the platform market. Examples of such measures include softened requirements for start-up platforms (Buiten et al., 2020, pp. 153–154; Sartor & Loreggia, 2020, p. 65) and a facilitation of access to filtering technology (Buiten et al., 2020, pp. 163–164; Lefouili & Madio, 2022, p. 346).

The considerations in terms of the benefits and costs of strict liability are comparable to the considerations advanced when discussing measures to improve right holders' incentives (Sect. 5.3.2.1). In theory, strict liability for errors caused by the analysis of upload attempts can align platforms' net costs of errors to net social costs (Gabison & Buiten, 2020, p. 274). However, it is extremely difficult to estimate net social costs of errors, net private costs of errors, and the probabilities with which platforms must pay damages and incur litigation costs.[46] In practice, it is thus hardly

[43] Data interoperability refers to a real-time exchange of data between services (Crémer et al., 2019, p. 84). It renders multi-homing more attractive and thereby reduces collective inertia (Sect. 5.4.1.2).

[44] Killer acquisitions are acquisitions of potential competitors by an incumbent to pre-empt competition (Cunningham et al., 2021). For a discussion in the context of platforms, see Crémer et al. (2019, pp. 110–113).

[45] The plausibility of this effect depends on whether costs of filtering are sunk. It is plausible that platforms cannot fully recover fixed investments in filtering technology upon exiting the market. Yet, it is questionable whether they even need to make fixed investments. A platform needs to make a fixed investment if it builds its own filter (Gabison & Buiten, 2020, p. 270) but not if it reverts to a scalable external solution. While filtering technology providers mostly do not publish their pricing policies, available insights suggest that they offer scalable solutions (European Commission, 2016, pt. 3/3, pp. 167–172; French Ministry of Culture, 2020, pp. 66–67; Leistner, 2020, n. 205; Urban et al., 2017, p. 64). Platforms costs of creating own solutions are further reduced by the existence of open-source services (e.g., AcoustID, n.d.).

[46] Again, litigation costs are understood to be the costs platforms incur related to assessments whether the analysis of upload attempts has produced errors, regardless of whether such assessments are made by courts or in private settings.

possible to specify damages in a way that moves platforms' net costs of errors close to net social costs (see Gabison & Buiten, 2020, p. 272).

Excessive damages would shift platforms' net costs of errors beyond net social costs, inducing them to spend more than socially desirable on automated filtering. They may render platforms unprofitable that could operate profitably if damages were optimal (see Lefouili & Madio, 2022, p. 335). Non-optimal damages may additionally create a new or aggravate the existing disbalance between platforms' net costs of false negatives and false positives. This is particularly likely if probabilities of litigation diverge appreciably between the two types of errors and such divergences are not appropriately taken into account when specifying damages.

Moreover, strict liability leads to frequent claims and the associated costs. Claims would even arise if platforms filter to the socially optimal extent because platforms can be held liable for errors that social efficiency does not require them to prevent. As above, the magnitude of social costs of decision-making and the extent to which damages can approach social efficiency depend on the rigour of the decision-making process in opposite directions. Considering these costs and the practical impossibility of setting damages close to social optimality, it does not appear plausible that strict liability can be designed in a cost-justified way.

5.4.2.2 Regulation of Process of Adopting Filtering Policies

Besides by increasing platforms' net costs of errors, a more desirable design of the analysis of upload attempts can be achieved by imposing requirements on how platforms must proceed to develop filtering policies, notably on who must participate in the process and how participation must take place. It has been suggested to require platforms to involve representatives of stakeholders (e.g., Grosse Ruse-Khan, 2021, p. 171; Kulk, 2018, pp. 303–304; Leistner, 2019, pp. 507–508; Leistner & Ohly, 2019, p. 186; cf. Council of Europe - Committee of Ministers, 2018, section 2.2.2., sentence 2). Compliance with such a requirement can be achieved by fining non-compliant platforms or by making compliance a pre-condition for escaping liability in a negligence-based liability regime.

Involving representatives of stakeholders in the decision-making process reduces platforms' abilities to shape their filtering policies according to their interests. For this, the involvement of representatives must be meaningful and well-balanced. A too lax integration of representatives into decision-making processes would not appreciably constrain platforms' abilities to assert their interests. An imbalanced participation of representatives risks the production of biased filtering policies. The exact requirements for a meaningful and well-balanced involvement of representatives can be developed through case law.

In any case, to keep decision-making processes functional, platforms must retain the final say on questions on which no compromise can be reached. As the relevant actors have widely diverging interests regarding many relevant aspects, this outcome can be expected to occur frequently. Moreover, the involvement of representatives makes it more difficult to adapt filtering policies to learnings or changed circumstances. The involvement must thus be confined to such an extent that it does not prevent platforms from reacting swiftly to learnings and changed circumstances.

Participation of representatives of stakeholders thus only offers limited potential for constraining platforms' opportunities to assert their interests at the expense of social efficiency. On the costs side, the opportunity costs of the time spent by platforms and representatives on negotiating filtering policies must be considered. Taken together, some degree of involvement of representatives of stakeholders appears cost-justified, but this approach cannot be expected to fully solve the incentive problems.

5.4.2.3 Standard of Care Regarding Design of Analysis of Upload Attempts

Besides addressing the cause of platforms' inefficient incentives, the incentive problems can be tackled directly. In terms of platforms' incentives regarding the design of the analysis of upload attempts, it is conceivable to impose a standard of care. To induce platforms to conform to the standard, right holders and uploaders can be enabled to hold negligent platforms liable for damages in case of errors.[47]

To align platforms' incentives to social desirability, damages must not fall too far below the optimal level and the standard of care must be optimal (Sect. 5.3.2.2). It is plausible that damages that are sufficiently high to induce platforms to comply with the standard of care can be awarded.

One approach to develop a standard of care is to rely on courts' evaluations of platforms' care in individual cases (e.g., Harris, 2015, pp. 851–852; Helman & Parchomovsky, 2011, pp. 1223–1224; Leistner & Ohly, 2019, pp. 184–186). It is sometimes claimed that courts do not have the required technical expertise (see e.g. Arsham, 2013, pp. 797–798; Helman & Parchomovsky, 2011, p. 1224). This concern is mitigated by the consideration that courts can consult experts.

Nevertheless, case law does not appear to be a suitable route to develop a standard of care for the analysis of upload attempts. It takes time until a sufficiently large body of case law is established (Maxwell, 2017, pp. 145–146). However, due to the volatility of the automated analysis of upload attempts, the circumstances relevant to previous cases become outdated quickly (see Helman & Parchomovsky, 2011, p. 1224). A reasonably clear standard of care may thus never emerge. This consideration carries over to the manual review as the probability that the automated analysis produced an error is an important factor for determining whether and how quickly automated decisions deserve to be reviewed (Sects. 4.4.3.2 and 4.4.3.3).

The main alternative to developing a standard of care based on case law is to define a standard through regulation. The regulator can stipulate performance targets, for example, maximal probabilities of errors (e.g., Gabison & Buiten, 2020,

[47] For the same reasons as advanced in Sect. 5.3.2.1, there is no added value in considering other types of sanctions.

p. 280; Raue & Steinebach, 2020, p. 362; cf., Garstka, 2020; Husovec, 2016, p. 66). This approach would leave it to platforms to explore the cheapest way to meet the targets.

However, due to a lack of empirical evidence, it is hard to imagine how performance targets can be set in a substantiated way.[48] The observation that a plurality of reasons can explain the absence of unlawful uploads (Sect. 3.8.5) further complicates the definition of performance targets. Moreover, appropriate targets differ between platforms. Hence, there is a risk of setting performance targets that are either unambitious or out of reach. Developing more informed targets requires costly research. The costs arise repeatedly as targets must be adapted to changed circumstances and learnings. Taken together, at least for now, stipulating performance targets does not appear to be a suitable approach.

Instead of setting performance targets, the regulator can prescribe how the analysis of upload attempts must be conducted. For instance, the regulator can stipulate suitable filters (e.g., Arsham, 2013, pp. 797–798; Gabison & Buiten, 2020, pp. 262–263; Helman & Parchomovsky, 2011, pp. 1224–1225), automatable rules, the approach for determining estimates of the probability of lawfulness of upload attempts as well as the critical probability threshold, selection criteria for the manual review, the required qualification of reviewers, or the required speed of reviews.

However, to a large extent, the information needed to set appropriate rules is not yet available[49] and requires costly experimentation to be obtained. The plurality of reasons that can explain the absence of unlawful uploads (Sect. 3.8.5) further complicate the collection of the relevant information. Regulation thus risks stipulating an inefficient approach while providing few incentives to explore more efficient ones. For now, regulation that prescribes how the analysis must be performed thus does not appear advisable.

As an alternative to prescribing how the analysis of upload attempts must be performed, the regulator can impose minimal requirements, for example, a level of similarity that must trigger blockings, a level of similarity below which upload

---

[48] In the context of notice-and-takedown, Husovec (2016, p. 66) supports his proposal to only allow automated submissions of takedown notices 'if algorithms generate a negligible number of false positives, say less than 1 %' by claiming that '[t]his number is informed by empirical evidence of what [...] is currently possible to achieve'. Yet, the empirical evidence cited does not support this proposition: Seng (2014, pp. 457–459) reports takedown rates of up to 99.9% with respect to Google's Trusted Copyright Removal Program. He defines the takedown rate as 'the ratio between a count of the URIs that are successfully removed and the total URIs that are *processed*' (p. 415). By 'number of false positives', Husovec (2016, p. 66) appears to refer to the difference between 100% and the takedown rate. If the takedown rate were the ratio of true positives to all positives, this difference would be the ratio of false positives to all positives. However, not all Uniform Resource Indicators (URIs) successfully removed are true positives as it has not been verified whether they indeed contained copyright infringements (see Seng, 2014, pp. 414–415).

[49] As Sect. 4.4.2.2 explains, it is inter alia unclear whether crafting automatable rules or estimating probabilities of lawfulness is the more efficient approach to make blocking decisions. Moreover, numerous uncertainties regarding the most efficient design of these approaches arise.

attempts must not be blocked, or factors that must lead to manual reviews. Minimal requirements can prevent drastic deviations of platforms' designs of the analysis of upload attempts from social desirability, such as allowing upload attempts that copy substantial portions of other works, blocking upload attempts that are only remotely similar to other works, or offering no manual review at all.

Imposing minimal requirements is beneficial if other measures cannot align platforms' incentives reasonably close to social efficiency. Recall that strict liability is not suitable in this regard and that the potential for improvement resulting from an involvement of representatives of stakeholders in the development of filtering policies is limited. As other measures to move platforms' incentives close to social desirability are not apparent, this condition is met. Minimal requirements do not limit platforms' opportunities to explore different designs of the analysis of upload attempts. Moreover, the effort in terms of expert and stakeholder consultations needed to define suitable minimal requirements is moderate. Taken together, imposing minimal requirements appears cost-justified.

Minimal requirements deliberately leave considerable leeway for platforms to design the analysis of upload attempts. Platforms can be expected to use this leeway to design the analysis according to their interests. This limitation is the result of a lack of knowledge on the best possible design of the analysis of upload attempts.

Note that transparency obligations, which are recommended in the next section, are conducive to generating new learnings. As more insights are obtained, the requirements should be adapted to further constrain platforms' leeway. For this, the regulator must be able to modify rules reasonably swiftly, which can be achieved by delegating the power to adapt rules to a regulatory agency (cf. Buiten et al., 2020, p. 161; Garstka, 2016, pp. 13–14; Gocha, 2018, pp. 162–163; Mazzone, 2009, pp. 434–435).

5.4.2.4 Obligation to Take Accompanying Measures

Like platforms' incentive problems in terms of the design of the analysis of upload attempts, their inefficient incentives regarding accompanying measures can be tackled directly. Specifically, platforms can be obliged to track and report performance metrics in a standardised way, to disclose filtering policies, to establish complaint mechanisms, and to inform right holders of upload attempts that exhibit similarity to their works but were not blocked.[50] To sanction non-compliance, fines for disregarding these obligations can be introduced (see Lester & Pachamanova,

[50] Recall from Sect. 5.4.1.4 that even in a *laissez-faire* regime, platforms have sufficient incentives to take the other desirable accompanying measures, namely, to cooperate with the database operator to provide time-saving channels for communication between uploaders and right holders, to inform the right holders whom uploaders have notified of possible deficiencies of their entries about the parts of their entries that matched with the upload attempts, to inform uploaders about the parts of their upload attempts that triggered blockings and about the allegedly infringed works, and to include general information on copyright law in notifications to right holders and uploaders.

2017, p. 72) or escaping liability for errors can be made conditional on compliance with these obligations.

The desirability of these accompanying measures has been justified in Sects. 4.4.2.3, 4.4.3.2, and 4.4.3.4. Yet, the question arises whether compliance with obligations to take these measures can be monitored in a cost-justified way. The availability of complaint mechanisms can be readily checked. Moreover, sporadic searches by right holders appear to suffice to ascertain whether platforms inform them about uploads that exhibit similarity to their works but were not blocked.

Verifying platforms' assertions on performance metrics and filtering policies is more difficult.[51] To cope with this challenge, performance metrics can be determined or checked by independent auditors, and platforms can be obliged to grant independent auditors or researchers access to interfaces for experimental assessments (cf. Klossa, 2019, p. 71). Verifying platforms' assertions in these ways creates additional costs. However, because of the considerable benefits these transparency requirements bring about, they nevertheless appear cost-justified.

Recall in this regard that transparency helps not only to understand how the analysis of upload attempts can be designed more efficiently but also to adjust minimal requirements. In addition, transparency facilitates assessments and comparisons of platforms' filtering activities by platform participants. It thereby contributes to an internalisation of net social costs of errors (see Elkin-Koren & Perel, 2018, p. 6).

Based on these considerations, it appears desirable to impose obligations to take the mentioned accompanying measures.

5.4.2.5 Suggested Approach

To sum up, the suggested approach to improve platforms' incentives centres around negligence-based liability of platforms for errors produced by the analysis of upload attempts. Platforms are liable for errors in case of gross negligence, that is, if they did not meet minimal requirements imposed by regulation. In the remaining room for manoeuvre, platforms can devise their filtering policies, but representatives of stakeholders must be involved in a well-balanced and meaningful way.

The liability regime should be accompanied by obligations to track and report performance metrics in a standardised way, disclose filtering policies, establish complaint mechanisms, and inform right holders of upload attempts that exhibit similarity to their works but were not blocked. A regulatory agency should review the transparency reports to adjust the minimal requirements.

[51] Lester and Pachamanova (2017, p. 72) claim that '[t]he U.S. Copyright Office is well suited to review and verify the data in question on an annual basis', without, however, substantiating this claim.

5.5 Summary and Discussion of Main Findings

This section summarises and discusses the main findings. Section 5.5.1 discusses whether the third-best efficient design of automated filtering, that is, the design that can be expected to emerge if the suggested measures to improve right holders' and platforms' incentives are adopted, is more efficient than alternative approaches. Using the suggested approach as a benchmark, Sect. 5.5.2 then identifies shortcomings of the current legal situations in the US and the EU and discusses their consequences.

5.5.1 Comparative Efficiency of Third-Best Efficient Design of Automated Filtering

In Sect. 5.2, the reader has been asked to suspend the possible objection that automated filtering designed in the third-best efficient way may be less efficient than alternative approaches. Having explored how to best regulate automated filtering, this objection can now be addressed.

Broadly speaking, the alternatives to automated filtering are to shut a platform down[52] or to operate it without automated filtering. Sections 5.5.1.1 and 5.5.1.2 discuss under what conditions automated filtering is more efficient than these approaches, respectively. Section 5.5.1.3 then examines whether automated filtering designed in the third-best efficient way can be expected to fulfil these conditions.

5.5.1.1 Conditions Under Which Automated Filtering Outperforms Shutdown of Platform

Compared to operating a platform with automated filtering, shutting it down saves the aggregate direct costs of filtering and the aggregate expected net social costs of false negatives. The latter comparative benefits of a shutdown are significantly reduced if automated filtering blocks unlawful upload attempts that copy large parts of other works. Since these upload attempts are most likely to serve as substitutes for right holders' works (Helman & Parchomovsky, 2011, pp. 1229–1230), automated filtering then also avoids the most expensive false negatives.

[52]Unlike for websites dedicated to copyright infringements, which countries frequently block (Cory, 2016, pp. 12–13), a shutdown of user-uploaded content platforms is neither seriously considered in the policy debate nor in the literature. Note that Article 51(3)(b) of the Digital Services Act (2022) includes a possibility of temporary access restrictions to services. However, one condition is that an 'infringement entails a criminal offence involving a threat to the life or safety of persons'. Copyright infringements cannot fulfil this condition. Regarding the somewhat confusing wording of recital 119 of the Digital Services Act (2022) in this respect, see Peukert et al. (2022, p. 374).

At the same time, with a shutdown, the net social benefits of all lawful uploads are lost (see Gabison & Buiten, 2020, p. 262). The resulting costs relative to operating a platform with automated filtering are substantial if a filter at least allows upload attempts that only contain small traces of other works. Such upload attempts produce particularly high net social benefits as they contain high degrees of new creative expression and do not substitute right holders' works.

Taken together, it is plausible that operating a platform with automated filtering outperforms a shutdown if automated filtering blocks upload attempts that copy large parts of other works, allows upload attempts that only contain small traces of other works, and is associated with sufficiently low aggregate direct costs (cf. AG Opinion in *YouTube/Cyando*, 2020, para. 184; Peukert et al., 2022, p. 374).

5.5.1.2 Conditions Under Which Platform Operation with Automated Filtering Outperforms Platform Operation Without

To compare the operation of a platform with and without automated filtering, one may be tempted to compare an automated analysis with a manual analysis, with notice-and-takedown, or with measures that make unlawful uploads less attractive, for example, using digital rights management (DRM) technologies, instituting or threatening legal proceedings against unlawful uploaders, informing users about copyright law,[53] or running campaigns to stigmatise infringements (Hill, 2007, p. 23). However, these are not the relevant comparisons, because automated decisions can still be manually reviewed, upload attempts that pass the automated analysis can be removed upon notification, and measures to deter unlawful uploaders can complement automated filtering.

Instead, the difference between operating a platform with and without automated filtering is how decisions on treating upload attempts that have not (yet) been manually reviewed are made. An automated analysis can make these decisions based on variables related to the overlap between an upload attempt and a work in the reference database, to the upload attempt, to the uploader, and to the copied-from work (Sect. 4.4.2.1). Without an automated analysis, only variables related to the upload attempt and to the uploader can be exploited. Alternatively, all upload attempts can be treated in the same way.

Automated filtering can ensure that prior to or without a manual review, upload attempts that copy large parts of other works are blocked and upload attempts that only contain small traces of other works become available. Without automated filtering, these outcomes cannot be realised simultaneously. Because variables related to the overlap between an upload attempt and a work in the reference database cannot be considered, a differentiation of upload attempts without an automated analysis would allow a substantial number of upload attempts that copy

[53] Informing users about copyright law may reduce unlawful uploads because not being aware of what copyright law prohibits is one reason to upload unlawful content.

large parts of other works and block a substantial number of upload attempts that only contain small traces of other works. Treating all upload attempts in the same way either blocks no upload attempts that copy large parts of other works or allows no upload attempts that only contain small traces of other works.[54]

Furthermore, automated filtering can ensure that upload attempts that have been manually removed are not re-uploaded. Without automated filtering, re-uploads cannot be prevented,[55] unless all upload attempts are blocked until manually reviewed.

Allowing upload attempts that copy large parts of other works and blocking upload attempts that carry only small traces of other works creates high aggregate net social costs. Automated filtering that blocks the former and allows the latter thus produces considerable costs savings compared to operating a platform without it. Moreover, an automated analysis contributes to efficiently selecting upload attempts into the manual review as it allows the closeness of automated decisions to be considered and concerned right holders and uploaders to be informed, who can then challenge automated decisions (Sect. 4.4.3.2). If the increase in aggregate direct costs resulting from the automated analysis is sufficiently low, platforms can operate more efficiently with automated filtering than without it.

Note in this regard that investments in compiling the reference database and in advancing and using content recognition technology are not specific to the automated analysis: In a notice-and-takedown system, without content recognition technology, it is difficult for right holders to detect potential infringements (see Sag, 2017, p. 554). Likewise, if a platform only manually analyses certain upload attempts, it is hard to imagine how it can select upload attempts for the analysis without the aid of content recognition technology (see Sag, 2017, p. 554).[56]

---

[54]One may argue that the outcomes would be simultaneously realised by allowing all upload attempts if highly effective measures to deter unlawful uploaders were in place. However, even though these measures would not lead to blockings of lawful upload attempts, they would still deter lawful uploaders. For example, DRM technologies may inhibit lawful copying and suing or threatening to sue uploaders may chill incentives to upload lawfully. In any case, no sufficiently effective measures are in sight. DRM technologies can only complicate copying but not forestall it. Even if DRM technologies inhibit digital copying, copies can be created by capturing and digitising analogue signals (Sicker et al., 2007, p. 574). Legal proceedings against unlawful uploaders have been shown to reduce unlawful file sharing (e.g., Bhattacharjee et al., 2006). Yet, such suits are likely to only have a small influence on unlawful uploaders who believe that they are beyond right holders' and platforms' reach, for example, because they upload anonymously. Moreover, right holders and platforms may be reluctant to sue uploaders to avoid detrimental effects on their reputations (see Devlin, 2015, p. 296). Furthermore, information and public relations campaigns are unlikely to have a major impact on the number of unlawful upload attempts.

[55]This 'whack-a-mole' problem is frequently pointed to in the context of notice-and-takedown (e.g., Beard et al., 2018, p. 314; Zimmerman, 2014, p. 264).

[56]And even if the selection were conducted without content recognition technology, manual reviewers would need a reference database to assess the lawfulness of upload attempts.

5.5.1.3 Fulfilment of Conditions by Third-Best Efficient Design of Automated Filtering

The previous two sections explained why operating a platform with automated filtering can be expected to be more efficient than shutting it down or operating it without automated filtering if at least upload attempts that copy large parts of other works are blocked until manually approved, upload attempts that only contain small traces of copyright-protected works are allowed until manually removed, and the additional aggregate direct costs are sufficiently low.

Do the suggested approaches to improve right holders' and platforms' incentives lead to a design of automated filtering that fulfils these conditions? This is likely to be the case.

The minimal requirements platforms must meet to escape liability induce them to block upload attempts that copy large parts of works that are contained in the reference database. Since all right holders can enter their works, automated filtering can be expected to block most upload attempts that copy large parts of other works. Moreover, the minimal requirements induce platforms to ensure that no upload attempts that only contain small traces of other works are blocked. In addition, negligence-based liability of right holders for errors caused by deficiencies of the reference database decreases the probability of blocking such upload attempts due to false indications.

The minimal requirements can be modified if platforms' transparency reports show that excessively many false negatives or false positives are produced. Moreover, representatives of stakeholders can weigh in during the development of filtering policies, ensuring that their insights on what unlawful uploads are most costly for right holders and what lawful uploads are most precious to users are taken into account.

At the same time, by only imposing minimal requirements, it is ensured that aggregate direct costs of conforming to the standard of care in terms of the analysis of upload attempts are sufficiently low.[57] The requirements can be met by using state-of-the-art filters and by applying automatable rules that are defined based on rough estimations. Aggregate direct costs are further reduced through the establishment of a central reference database and measures to reduce right holders' direct costs of preventing deficiencies.

Moreover, courts consider right holders' costs of assuring the accuracy of entries in the reference database when deciding whether they acted negligently, thus ensuring that these costs are kept in check. The involvement of representatives of

[57] Of course, platforms can do more than is necessary to meet minimal requirements. Yet, platforms can only be expected to do so if the associated increase in aggregate direct costs falls below the reduction in aggregate expected net private costs of errors. Since platforms' net costs of errors fall below net social costs, such investments are also cost-justified from a social perspective. As a result, not only aggregate direct costs but also the efficiency gains vis-à-vis alternative approaches increase. Aggregate direct costs can thus be expected to remain sufficiently low to justify the use of automated filtering.

stakeholders in the development of filtering policies produces additional costs, but, again, courts take these costs into account when assessing whether the involvement was sufficiently meaningful and can thus ensure that these costs do not become overly high.

When it comes to accompanying measures, only recording and verifying performance metrics is associated with noteworthy costs, but it appears possible to ensure that these costs are sufficiently low when designing transparency requirements and monitoring activities.

Overall, the suggested approaches to improve right holders' and platforms' incentives can be expected to lead to a design of automated filtering that prevents the availability of content that copies large parts of other works and ensures that content that only contains small traces of other works is not blocked. The resulting efficiency gains vis-à-vis alternative approaches are likely to outweigh the additional aggregate direct costs that automated filtering brings about. Operating a platform with automated filtering designed in the third-best efficient way can thus be expected to outperform the alternative approaches.

5.5.2 *Shortcomings of Current Legal Situations in the US and the EU*

This section identifies shortcomings of the current legal situations in the US and the EU and discusses their consequences. The relevant legal frameworks have been explained in Sect. 2.3. Section 5.5.2.1 reflects on shortcomings with respect to measures to improve right holders' incentives; Section 5.5.2.2 on shortcomings regarding measures to improve platforms' incentives.

5.5.2.1 Measures to Improve Right Holders' Incentives

The analysis shows that without regulation, right holders have excessive incentives to prevent unlawful upload attempts and deficient incentives to prevent false positives. Right holders can thus be expected to enter works that are not worthy of being entered and to do too little to limit the scope of protection that automated filtering provides to the content they enter.

The best way to improve right holders' incentives is to introduce a liability rule under which they must pay damages for false positives caused by deficiencies of the reference database if they behaved negligently. Courts should apply the marginal Hand rule to assess whether right holders took sufficient care to ensure that they only enter content that is (still) protected and in which they own the rights and that indications in terms of end dates of protection (or information needed for calculations thereof), licensing arrangements, and external elements are correct.

Neither US nor EU law provides such liability. As false positives are costly for platforms, platforms benefit from sanctioning right holders for wrongful indications or from inducing filtering technology providers to do so. However, as platforms' net costs of false positives fall below net social costs, platforms can be expected to invest less than socially desirable in sanctioning right holders. In any case, it is hard to conceive how a negligence-based system in the above-described way could be implemented on a private basis. Measures that platforms or filtering technology providers adopt on their own initiative thus at most partially make up for the lack of liability.

As a consequence, not introducing liability of right holders for false positives caused by deficiencies of the reference database misses the opportunity of preventing false positives that are worthy of being prevented.

5.5.2.2 Measures to Improve Platforms' Incentives

The analysis further demonstrates that platforms' incentives in the absence of regulation are inefficient. It is questionable whether platforms would filter in a *laissez-faire* regime. And even if they do, they invest too little in the analysis of upload attempts. The policymaker is thus confronted with the challenge of leaving sufficient leeway for platforms to try out different approaches, while at the same time steering their incentives towards efficiency. In addition, platforms have inefficient incentives to take some of the desirable accompanying measures.

The best measure to tackle these challenges is negligence-based liability for errors caused by the analysis of upload attempts. Platforms should be liable in case of gross negligence, that is, if they did not comply with minimal requirements, which should be imposed by regulation. Initially, minimal requirements should leave considerable leeway for platforms, which can be reduced as new learnings are collected. To improve platforms' decisions in this leeway, they should be required to involve representatives of stakeholders in the development of filtering policies in a meaningful and well-balanced way. In addition, platforms should be obliged to track and report performance metrics in a standardised way, disclose filtering policies, set up complaint mechanisms, and inform right holders about upload attempts that exhibit similarity to their works but have not been blocked.

In the following, it is discussed to what extent US and EU law are in line with this suggested approach to improve platforms' incentives.

Comparison of US Law with Suggested Approach

US law does not address the analysis of upload attempts. Yet, it does raise platforms' net costs of unlawful uploads. Specifically, notice-and-takedown establishes liability if platforms do not (timely) remove notified unlawful uploads and creates the costs of reviewing a potentially high number of uploads. Moreover, uncertainties on whether compliance with notice-and-takedown suffices to escape liability exist (Sect. 2.3.1.1).[58]

[58] Note that uncertainties on liability have indeed been reported as a driver for using automated filtering (Urban et al., 2017, p. 58).

US law thus affects platforms' incentives regarding the analysis of upload attempts (see Gabison & Buiten, 2020, p. 267).

However, these effects are not shaped by targeted policies but emerge as side effects of policies that have other ends in view. A striking manifestation thereof is the lack of responsibilities to prevent false positives, which can be expected to lead platforms to invest too little in establishing a design that reconciles the interests of all affected parties. Instead, platforms are likely to avoid unlawful uploads by sacrificing more lawful upload attempts than socially desirable. Such a one-sided approach is therefore not up to the task of steering platforms' incentives towards efficiency. For this, a purposeful policy to shape platforms' incentives that considers the risk of both types of errors is needed (see Senftleben, 2020, pp. 327–328).

Comparison of EU Law with Suggested Approach

Unlike US law, EU law contains a provision that targets automated filtering: Article 17 of the Copyright in the DSM Directive (2019). Nevertheless, it lags behind the suggested approach in terms of steering platforms' incentives towards efficiency.

Liability for False Positives

One difference between Article 17 of the Copyright in the DSM Directive (2019) and the suggested approach is that the former does not balance the liability for unlawful uploads with liability for false positives. It can thus be expected to lead to a tendency to sacrifice desirable preventions of false positives in favour of the prevention of false negatives (M. Lambrecht, 2020, paras. 32–33; F. Reda et al., 2020, pp. 24–30; Senftleben, 2020, p. 326; Stedman, 2019, pp. 32–33).

Note, however, that on the Member State level, the German implementation of Article 17 of the Copyright in the DSM Directive (2019) mitigates this concern by enabling user rights organisations to claim injunctive relief if a platform repeatedly blocks lawful uses (section 18(6) of the Act on the Copyright Liability of Online Content Sharing Service Providers, 2021).

Standard of Care

Another difference relates to the standard of care platforms must comply with to escape liability. Article 17 of the Copyright in the DSM Directive (2019) introduces vague standards, for example, 'high industry standards of professional diligence' and 'best efforts to ensure the unavailability of specific works and other subject matter'. The standards remain vague even if interpreted according to the guidance issued by the European Commission (2021, pp. 13, 15) and must hence be fleshed out by courts.

This approach has been rejected in Sect. 5.4.2.3 as it cannot create predictable requirements. Platforms thus face uncertainties about what designs of the analysis of upload attempts comply with Article 17 of the Copyright in the DSM Directive (2019). Combined with the consideration that the provision renders false negatives more expensive for platforms than false positives, these uncertainties are likely to lead platforms to accept more false positives than desirable.

The approach suggested above creates legal certainty by allowing platforms to apply their own filtering policies, provided that the policies meet minimal requirements and that representatives of stakeholders are involved in a meaningful and well-balanced way in their development. These conditions serve to constrain platforms' abilities to deviate from the socially desirable design of the analysis of upload attempts. Over time, as new insights are obtained, the minimal requirements can be modified to further reduce platforms' leeway.

Note that Article 17 of the Copyright in the DSM Directive (2019) contains minimal requirements on what filtering decisions must be manually reviewed.[59] However, it neither sets minimal requirements for the automated analysis nor creates a mechanism to adapt (or introduce) minimal requirements as new insights are obtained. Moreover, Article 17(10) of the Copyright in the DSM Directive (2019) requires the Commission to organise stakeholder dialogues.[60] Yet, it does not stipulate stakeholder involvement in the development of platforms' filtering policies.

On the Member State level, the national implementations of Germany (section 10 of the Act on the Copyright Liability of Online Content Sharing Service Providers, 2021) and Austria (§ 89b(3) of the Copyright Law of 1936) introduce clear-cut thresholds for uses that must in principle not be blocked.

Accompanying Measures

Regarding the desirable accompanying measures, Article 17(8), second subparagraph of the Copyright in the DSM Directive (2019) requires Member States to oblige platforms to provide right holders upon request with 'adequate information on the functioning of their practices'. However, it neither contains an obligation to track and report performance metrics nor to generally disclose filtering policies nor to inform right holders about uploads that exhibit similarity to their works but were not blocked. In its guidance, the European Commission (2021, pp. 23–24) goes further in these regards as it proposes the publication of 'reports on the content blocked' and states that platforms should inform right holders of matching uploads that passed the filter.

While Article 17 of the Copyright in the DSM Directive (2019) and—to a lesser extent—the European Commission's guidance therefore do not exhaust the potential that the suggested accompanying measures offer to gather new insights, the Digital Services Act (2022) addresses this shortcoming. Even though the Copyright in the DSM Directive (2019) prevails as *lex specialis* (Article 2(4)(b) of the Digital Services Act, 2022), it appears convincing to apply the relevant provisions to OCSSPs because Article 17 of the Copyright in the DSM Directive (2019) only

[59] Platforms must manually review filtering decisions when uploaders complain (Article 17(9) of the Copyright in the DSM Directive, 2019) and take action when right holders report unlawful uploads (Article 17(4)(c) of the Copyright in the DSM Directive, 2019), which may be interpreted as a requirement to conduct a manual review (European Commission, 2021, p. 23).

[60] The European Commission held six stakeholder meetings between 15 October 2019 and 10 February 2020 (European Commission, 2023). The results have been used in the preparation of the guidance issued by the European Commission (2021).

partially addresses transparency (Peukert et al., 2022, pp. 363–364; Quintais & Schwemer, 2022, pp. 208, 215).

According to Articles 14(1) and 15(1)(e) of the Digital Services Act (2022), platforms must disclose filtering policies and 'indicators of the accuracy and the possible rate of error of the automated means' used for content moderation. VLOPs are further subject to independent audits (Article 37 of the Digital Services Act, 2022). Audit reports and—if applicable—audit implementation reports must be published (Article 42(4)(c) and (d) of the Digital Services Act, 2022). Article 40(1) of the Digital Services Act (2022) requires VLOPs to provide the Digital Services Coordinator of establishment[61] or the European Commission upon request access to data needed to assess compliance with the regulation. Upon request by the same entities, they must also grant vetted researchers access to data that helps to identify and understand systemic risks (Article 40(4) of the Digital Services Act, 2022).

Moreover, national implementations of Article 17 of the Copyright in the DSM Directive (2019) contain relevant rules. In Germany, platforms must grant research organisations 'access to data on the use of procedures for the automated and non-automated detection and blocking of content' (section 19(3), first sentence of the Act on the Copyright Liability of Online Content Sharing Service Providers, 2021). Austria requires platforms to inform users about content moderation (section 89b(2) of the Copyright Law of 1936).

The lack of an obligation in Article 17 of the Copyright in the DSM Directive (2019) to inform right holders about uploads that exhibit similarity to their works but were not blocked is not compensated by the Digital Services Act (2022). Despite the above-mentioned statement in the European Commission's (non-binding) guidance, EU law therefore does not take advantage of this opportunity to decrease right holders' costs of finding unlawful uploads.

National implementations of Article 17 of the Copyright in the DSM Directive (2019) mitigate this concern. In Germany, platforms must inform right holders if uses of their works 'presumably authorised by law' are uploaded (section 9(3) of the Act on the Copyright Liability of Online Content Sharing Service Providers, 2021). Austria requires platforms to inform right holders if uses of their works that copy only 'small parts' (section 89b(3), second sentence of the Copyright Law of 1936) or have been pre-flagged by uploaders as lawful are uploaded (section 89b(4), first sentence of the Copyright Law of 1936).

Taken together, Article 17 of the Copyright in the DSM Directive (2019) fails to introduce liability of platforms for false positives, a standard of care for the liability

[61] Article 49(2), first sentence of the Digital Services Act (2022) requires Member States to designate an authority as the Digital Services Coordinator. The Digital Services Coordinator of establishment is the Digital Services Coordinator of the Member State in which the 'main establishment of a provider of an intermediary service is located or its legal representative resides or is established' (Article 3(n) of the Digital Services Act, 2022). Legal representatives must be appointed by intermediary services that offer services but do not have an establishment in the EU (Article 13(1) of the Digital Services Act, 2022).

for false negatives that is based on minimal requirements, an obligation to involve stakeholders in the development of filtering policies, and most of the desirable accompanying measures. With the exception of an obligation to inform right holders about uploads that exhibit similarity to their works but were not blocked, the Digital Services Act (2022) contains the remaining accompanying measures. In Germany and Austria, the identified shortcomings are to some extent compensated by measures on the national level.

References

17 U.S.C. § 101 et seq. (US). https://www.law.cornell.edu/uscode/text/17

AcoustID. (n.d.). *Welcome to AcoustID!* Retrieved July 8, 2024, from https://acoustid.org/

Act on the Copyright Liability of Online Content Sharing Service Providers (Germany), 31 May 2021, Federal Law Gazette I, p. 1204, 1215 (2021). https://www.gesetze-im-internet.de/englisch_urhdag/index.html

AG Opinion in YouTube/Cyando (EU). AG Opinion in Frank Peterson v. Google LLC and others and Elsevier Inc. v. Cyando AG, Joined Cases C-682/18 and C-683/18, ECLI:EU:C:2020:586 (CJEU 2020). https://curia.europa.eu/juris/document/document.jsf;jsessionid=F225D083B049B019F7E3C12A692DB276?text=&docid=228712&pageIndex=0&doclang=EN&mode=lst&dir=&occ=first&part=1&cid=13288016

Arsham, B. E. (2013). Monetizing infringement: A new legal regime for hosts of user-generated content. *Georgetown Law Journal, 101*(3), 775–806.

Bagwell, K. (2007). The economic analysis of advertising. In M. Armstrong & R. H. Porter (Eds.), *Handbook of industrial organization* (Vol. 3, pp. 1701–1844). Elsevier.

Bamberger, K. A., & Lobel, O. (2017). Platform market power. *Berkeley Technology Law Journal, 32*(3), 1051–1092.

Baumol, W. J. (1982). Contestable markets: An uprising in the theory of industry structure. *The American Economic Review, 72*(1), 1–15.

Beard, T. R., Ford, G. S., & Stern, M. (2018). Safe harbors and the evolution of online platform markets: An economic analysis. *Cardozo Arts & Entertainment Law Journal, 36*(2), 309–330.

Bechtel, M. (2020). Algorithmic notification and monetization: Using YouTube's content ID system as a model for European Union copyright reform. *Michigan State International Law Review, 28*(2), 237–272.

Belleflamme, P., & Peitz, M. (2018). Platforms and network effects. In L. C. Corchón & M. A. Marini (Eds.), *Handbook of game theory and industrial organization* (Vol. 2, pp. 286–317). Edward Elgar.

Bhattacharjee, S., Gopal, R. D., Lertwachara, K., & Marsden, J. R. (2006). Impact of legal threats on online music sharing activity: An analysis of music industry legal actions. *The Journal of Law & Economics, 49*(1), 91–114.

Biglaiser, G., Calvano, E., & Crémer, J. (2019). Incumbency advantage and its value. *Journal of Economics & Management Strategy, 28*(1), 41–48.

Blevins, J. (2013). Uncertainty as enforcement mechanism: The new expansion of secondary copyright liability to internet platforms. *Cardozo Law Review, 34*, 1821–1888.

Brøvig-Hanssen, R., & Jones, E. (2021). Remix's retreat? Content moderation, copyright law and mashup music. *New Media & Society*, 1–19.

Buiten, M. C., De Streel, A., & Peitz, M. (2020). Rethinking liability rules for online hosting platforms. *International Journal of Law and Information Technology, 28*(2), 139–166.

Cooter, R., & Ulen, T. (2016). *Law and Economics* (6th ed.). Pearson.

Copyright in the DSM Directive (EU). Directive (EU) 2019/790 of the European Parliament and of the European Council of 17 April 2019 on copyright and related rights in the Digital Single Market and amending Directives 96/9/EC and 2001/29/EC, OJ L 130/92 (2019). https://eur-lex.europa.eu/legal-content/EN/TXT/PDF/?uri=CELEX:32019L0790

Copyright Law of 1936 (Austria). Federal Law on Copyright in Literary and Artistic Works and Related Rights. https://www.ris.bka.gv.at/GeltendeFassung.wxe?Gesetzesnummer=10001848&Abfrage=Bundesnormen

Cory, N. (2016, August). *How website blocking is curbing digital piracy without "breaking the internet"*. Information Technology & Innovation Foundation. http://www2.itif.org/2016-website-blocking.pdf

Council of Europe - Committee of Ministers. (2018, March 7). *Recommendation CM/Rec(2018)2 of the Committee of Ministers to member States on the roles and responsibilities of internet intermediaries*. https://search.coe.int/cm/Pages/result_details.aspx?ObjectId=0900001680790e14

Crémer, J., De Montjoye, Y.-A., & Schweitzer, H. (2019). *Competition policy for the digital era: Final report*. http://ec.europa.eu/competition/publications/reports/kd0419345enn.pdf

Cunningham, C., Ederer, F., & Ma, S. (2021). Killer acquisitions. *Journal of Political Economy, 129*(3), 649–702.

Daughety, A. F., & Reinganum, J. F. (2013). Economic analysis of products liability: Theory. In J. H. Arlen (Ed.), *Research handbook on the economics of torts*. Edward Elgar.

Devlin, A. (2015). *Fundamental principles of law and economics*. Routledge.

Digital Services Act (EU). Regulation (EU) 2022/2065 of the European Parliament and of the Council of 19 October 2022 on a Single Market For Digital Services and amending Directive 2000/31/EC, OJ L 277/1 (2022). https://eur-lex.europa.eu/legal-content/EN/TXT/PDF/?uri=CELEX:32022R2065

Eisenmann, T., Parker, G. G., & Van Alstyne, M. W. (2011). Platform envelopment. *Strategic Management Journal, 32*(12), 1270–1285.

Elkin-Koren, N., & Perel, M. (2018). Algorithmic governance by online intermediaries. In E. Brousseau, J.-M. Glachant, & J. Sgard (Eds.), *The Oxford handbook of institutions of international economic governance and market regulation*. Oxford University Press.

European Commission. (2016, September 14). *Commission staff working document: Impact assessment on the modernisation of EU copyright rules*. SWD(2016) 301 Final. https://digital-strategy.ec.europa.eu/en/library/impact-assessment-modernisation-eu-copyright-rules

European Commission. (2021, June 4). *Communication from the Commission to the European Parliament and the Council: Guidance on Article 17 of Directive 2019/790 on Copyright in the Digital Single Market*. COM(2021) 288 Final. https://eur-lex.europa.eu/legal-content/EN/TXT/?uri=CELEX:52021DC0288

European Commission. (2023, January 11). *Stakeholder dialogue on copyright*. https://digital-strategy.ec.europa.eu/en/policies/stakeholder-dialogue-copyright#:~:text=Article%2017%20of%20the%20Directive%20on%20copyright%20and,for%20cooperation%20between%20online%20content-sharing%20service%20providers%20and%C2%A0rightholders

European Copyright Society. (2017, January 24). *General Opinion on the EU Copyright Reform Package*. https://europeancopyrightsocietydotorg.files.wordpress.com/2015/12/ecs-opinion-on-eu-copyright-reform-def.pdf

Evans, D. S. (2003). The antitrust economics of multi-sided platform markets. *Yale Journal on Regulation, 20*(2), 325–381.

Evans, D. S. (2017, August 23). *Why the dynamics of competition for online platforms leads to sleepless nights, but not sleepy monopolies*. https://papers.ssrn.com/sol3/papers.cfm?abstract_id=3009438

Evans, D. S., & Schmalensee, R. (2007). The industrial organization of markets with two-sided platforms. *Competition Policy International, 3*(1), 151–179.

Evans, D. S., & Schmalensee, R. (2016). *Matchmakers: The new economics of multisided platforms*. Harvard Business Review Press.

Farrell, J., & Klemperer, P. (2007). Coordination and lock-in: Competition with switching costs and network effects. In M. Armstrong & R. H. Porter (Eds.), *Handbook of industrial organization* (Vol. 3, pp. 1967–2072). Elsevier.

Fiala, L., & Husovec, M. (2022). Using experimental evidence to improve delegated enforcement. *International Review of Law and Economics, 71*, 1–18.

French Ministry of Culture. (2020, January 29). *Towards more effectiveness of copyright law on online content sharing platforms: Overview of content recognition tools and possible ways forward.* https://www.culture.gouv.fr/en/Thematiques/Propriete-litteraire-et-artistique/Conseil-superieur-de-la-propriete-litteraire-et-artistique/Travaux/Missions/Mission-du-CSPLA-sur-les-outils-de-reconnaissance-des-contenus-et-des-oeuvres-sur-les-plateformes-de-

Gabison, G. A., & Buiten, M. C. (2020). Platform liability in copyright enforcement. *Science & Technology Law Review, 21*(2), 237–281.

Garstka, K. (2016). Looking above and beyond the blunt expectation: Specified request as the recommended approach to intermediary liability in cyberspace. *European Journal of Law and Technology, 7*(3), 1–23.

Garstka, K. (2020). Guiding the blind bloodhounds: How to mitigate the risks Article 17 of Directive 2019/970 Poses to the Freedom of Expression. In P. Torremans (Ed.), *Intellectual property law and human rights*. Kluwer International Law.

Gocha, A. J. (2018). A modern system for resolving online copyright infringement disputes: Administrative rulemaking and adjudication, a one-stop fix to the Digital Millennium Copyright Act. *IDEA: The Journal of the Franklin Pierce Center for Intellectual Property, 58*(2), 131–172.

Goldman, E. (2011, March 8). *Stanford technology law review symposium on secondary IP liability*. Technology & Marketing Law Blog. https://blog.ericgoldman.org/archives/2011/03/stanford_techno.htm

Goller, M. (2019, September 4). *Copyfraud and overclaiming: What to watch out for when implementing the EU copyright directive*. iRights.Info. https://irights.info/artikel/copyfraud-and-overclaiming-what-to-watch-out-for-when-implementing-the-eu-copyright-directive/29654

Google. (2024). *YouTube copyright transparency report*. https://transparencyreport.google.com/youtube-copyright/intro?hl=en_GB

Google. (2023, December 15). *Terms of service*. https://www.youtube.com/static?template=terms&gl=US

Google. (n.d.). *Copyright and rights management*. YouTube Help. Retrieved July 17, 2024, from https://support.google.com/youtube/topic/2676339?hl=en-GB&ref_topic=6151248&sjid=7784574668489471573-EU

Grosse Ruse-Khan, H. (2021). Transition through automation. In N. Bruun, G. B. Dinwoodie, M. Levin, & A. Ohly (Eds.), *Transition and coherence in intellectual property law: Essays in honour of Annette Kur*. Cambridge University Press.

Hamdani, A. (2002). Who's liable for cyberwrongs. *Cornell Law Review, 87*(4), 901–957.

Harris, D. P. (2015). Time to reboot?: DMCA 2.0. *Arizona State Law Journal, 47*(3), 801–855.

Helman, L., & Parchomovsky, G. (2011). The best available technology standard. *Columbia Law Review, 111*(6), 1194–1243.

Hill, C. W. L. (2007). Digital piracy: Causes, consequences, and strategic responses. *Asia Pacific Journal of Management, 24*(1), 9–25.

Hornik, J., & Villa Llera, C. (2017). *An economic analysis of liability of hosting services: Uncertainty and incentives online*. Bruges European Economic Research Papers 37/2017. http://aei.pitt.edu/92487/1/beer37.pdf

Husovec, M. (2016, May 2). *Accountable, not liable: Injunctions against intermediaries* (2016–012). TILEC Discussion Paper No. 2016-012. http://www.ssrn.com/abstract=2773768

Husovec, M. (2018). The promises of algorithmic copyright enforcement: Takedown or staydown? Which is superior? And why? *Columbia Journal of Law & the Arts, 42*(1), 53–84.

Instagram. (2024, March 6). *Terms of use*. https://help.instagram.com/581066165581870/?helpref=hc_fnav&bc[0]=Instagram Help&bc[1]=Privacy and Safety Center

Jullien, B., & Sand-Zantman, W. (2021). The economics of platforms: A theory guide for competition policy. *Information Economics and Policy, 54*.

Kalia, A. (2015, May 1). *Congrats on the 10-year anniversary YouTube, Now please fix Content ID*. https://www.eff.org/de/deeplinks/2015/05/congrats-10-year-anniversary-youtube-now-please-fix-content-id

Klemperer, P. (1995). Competition when consumers have switching costs: An overview with applications to industrial organization, macroeconomics, and international trade. *The Review of Economic Studies, 62*(4), 515–539.

Klonick, K. (2018). The new governors: The people, rules, and processes governing online speech. *Harvard Law Review, 131*(6), 1598–1670.

Klossa, G. (2019, March 28). *Towards European media sovereignty: An industrial media strategy to leverage data, algorithms and artificial intelligence*. https://ec.europa.eu/commission/publications/towards-european-media-sovereignty_en

Kulk, S. (2018). *Internet intermediaries and copyright law: Towards a future-proof EU legal framework*. Ridderprint.

Lambrecht, A., & Tucker, C. E. (2017). Can big data protect a firm from competition? *CPI Antitrust Chronicle, 1*(1), 1–8.

Lambrecht, M. (2020). Free speech by design: Algorithmic protection of exceptions and limitations in the copyright DSM directive. *Journal of Intellectual Property, Information Technology and Electronic Commerce Law, 11*(1), 68–94.

Landes, W. M., & Posner, R. A. (1989). An economic analysis of copyright law. *The Journal of Legal Studies, 18*(2), 325–363.

Lefouili, Y., & Madio, L. (2022). The economics of platform liability. *European Journal of Law and Economics, 53*, 319–351.

Leistner, M. (2019). Intermediary liability in a global world. In T. E. Synodinou (Ed.), *Pluralism or universalism in international copyright law*. Kluwer Law International.

Leistner, M. (2020). European copyright licensing and infringement liability under Art. 17 DSM-Directive: Can we make the new European system a global opportunity instead of a local challenge? *Zeitschrift Für Geistiges Eigentum, 12*(2), 123–214.

Leistner, M., & Ohly, A. (2019). Direct and indirect copyright infringement: Proposal for an amendment of Directive 2001/29/EC (InfoSoc Directive). *Journal of Intellectual Property Law and Practice, 14*(3), 182–186.

Lemley, M. A. (2007). Rationalizing internet safe harbors. *Journal on Telecommunications and High Technology Law, 6*(1), 101–120.

Lester, T., & Pachamanova, D. (2017). The dilemma of false positives: Making content ID algorithms more conducive to fostering innovative fair use in music creation. *UCLA Entertainment Law Review, 24*(1), 51–73.

Lichtman, D., & Posner, E. (2006). Holding internet service providers accountable. *Supreme Court Economic Review, 14*, 221–259.

Liebowitz, S. J. (2018, February 27). *Economic analysis of safe harbor provisions*. https://papers.ssrn.com/sol3/papers.cfm?abstract_id=3143811

Loren, L. P. (2011). Deterring abuse of the copyright takedown regime by taking misrepresentation claims seriously. *Wake Forest Law Review, 46*(4), 745–782.

Maxwell, W. J. (2017). *Smart(er) internet regulation through cost-benefit analysis: Measuring harms to privacy, freedom of expression, and the internet ecosystem*. Presses des Mines.

Mazzone, J. (2009). Administering fair use. *William & Mary Law Review, 51*(2), 395–437.

Meta. (2024). *Rights manager*. https://rightsmanager.fb.com/

Meta. (n.d.). *Proactive enforcement*. Transparency Center. Retrieved August 27, 2024, from https://transparency.fb.com/data/intellectual-property/proactive-enforcement/facebook/

Montagnani, M. L. (2020). Virtues and perils of algorithmic enforcement and content regulation in the EU: A toolkit for a balanced algorithmic copyright enforcement. *Journal of Law, Technology & the Internet, 11*(1), 1–49.

Parker, G. G., Van Alstyne, M. W., & Choudary, S. P. (2016). *Platform revolution: How networked markets are transforming the economy and how to make them work for you*. W. W. Norton.

Penney, J. W. (2019). Privacy and legal automation: The DMCA as a case study. *Stanford Technology Law Review, 22*(2), 412–486.

Perel, M., & Elkin-Koren, N. (2016). Accountability in algorithmic copyright enforcement. *Stanford Technology Law Review, 19*(3), 473–532.

Perel, M., & Elkin-Koren, N. (2017). Black box tinkering: Beyond transparency in algorithmic enforcement. *Florida Law Review, 69*, 181–221.

Peukert, A., Husovec, M., Kretschmer, M., Mezei, P., & Quintais, J. P. (2022). European copyright society: Comment on copyright and the digital services act proposal. *International Review of Intellectual Property and Competition Law, 53*(3), 358–376.

Pex. (2024). *Platforms*. https://pex.com/use-cases/platforms/

Priest, E. (2015). Acupressure: The emerging role of market ordering in global copyright enforcement. *SMU Law Review, 68*(1), 169–242.

Quintais, J. P., & Schwemer, S. F. (2022). The interplay between the digital services act and sector regulation: How special is copyright? *European Journal of Risk Regulation, 13*(2), 191–217.

Raue, B., & Steinebach, M. (2020). Uploadfilter: Funktionsweisen, Einsatzmöglichkeiten und Parametrisierung. *Zeitschrift Für Urheber- Und Medienrecht, 64*(5), 355–364.

Raymond, A. H. (2013). Heavyweight bots in the clouds: The wrong incentives and poorly crafted balances that lead to the blocking of information online. *Northwestern Journal of Technology and Intellectual Property, 11*(6), 473–500.

Reda, F., Selinger, J., & Servatius, M. (2020, November 16). *Article 17 of the Directive on Copyright in the Digital Single Market: A fundamental rights assessment*. https://papers.ssrn.com/sol3/papers.cfm?abstract_id=3732223

Rendas, T. (2017, September 6). *Form and substance in the value gap proposal*. Better Regulation for Copyright: Academics Meet Policy Makers. https://felixreda.eu/wp-content/uploads/2017/09/2017-09-06_Better-Regulation-for-Copyright-Academics-meet-Policy-Makers_Proceedings.pdf

Rochet, J.-C., & Tirole, J. (2003). Platform competition in two-sided markets. *Journal of the European Economic Association, 1*(4), 990–1029.

Sag, M. (2017). Internet safe harbors and the transformation of copyright law. *Notre Dame Law Review, 93*(2), 499–564.

Samuelson, P. (2021). Pushing back on stricter copyright ISP liability rules. *Michigan Technology Law Review, 27*(2), 299–343.

Sartor, G., & Loreggia, A. (2020, September 15). *The impact of algorithms for online content filtering or moderation: "Upload filters"*. https://www.europarl.europa.eu/thinktank/en/document.html?reference=IPOL_STU(2020)657101

Schäfer, H.-B., & Müller-Langer, F. (2009). Strict liability versus negligence. In M. Faure (Ed.), *Tort law and economics* (Vol. 1, pp. 3–45). Edward Elgar.

Schmalensee, R. (2011). Jeffrey Rohlfs' 1974 Model of Facebook: An introduction with a theory of interdependent demand for a communications service by Jeffrey Rohlfs. *Competition Policy International, 7*(1), 301–338.

Seltzer, W. (2010). Free speech unmoored in copyright's safe harbor: Chilling effects of the DMCA on the first amendment. *Harvard Journal of Law & Technology, 24*(1), 171–231.

Senftleben, M. (2020). Institutionalized algorithmic enforcement: The pros and cons of the EU approach to UGC platform liability. *FIU Law Review, 14*(2), 299–328.

Seng, D. (2014). The state of the discordant union: An empirical analysis of DMCA takedown notices. *Virginia Journal of Law & Technology, 18*(3), 369–473.

Shapiro, C., & Varian, H. R. (1999). *Information rules: A strategic guide to the network economy*. Harvard Business School Press.

Sicker, D. C., Ohm, P., & Gunaji, S. (2007). The analog hole and the price of music: An empirical study. *Journal on Telecommunications & High Technology Law, 5*(3), 573–588.

Solomon, L. (2015). Fair users or content abusers? The automatic flagging of non-infringing videos by content ID on YouTube. *Hofstra Law Review, 44*(1), 237–268.
Spoerri, T. (2019). On upload-filters and other competitive advantages for big tech companies under Article 17 of the Directive on Copyright in the Digital Single Market. *Journal of Intellectual Property, Information Technology and Electronic Commerce Law, 10*(2), 173–186.
Sprigman, C. (2004). Reform(aliz)ing copyright. *Stanford Law Review, 57*(2), 485–567.
Stedman, M. (2019, September 1). *Mind the value gap: Article 17 of the Directive on Copyright in the Digital Single Market*. https://papers.ssrn.com/sol3/papers.cfm?abstract_id=3810144
Trendacosta, K. (2020, December). *Unfiltered: How YouTube's content ID discourages fair use and dictates what we see online*. https://www.eff.org/files/2020/12/10/unfiltered.pdf
United States v. Carroll Towing Co. (US), 159 F.2d 169 (2d Cir. 1947). https://law.justia.com/cases/federal/appellate-courts/F2/159/169/1565896/
Urban, J. M., Joe, K., & Schofield, B. L. (2017, March). *Notice and takedown in everyday practice, version 2*. UC Berkeley Public Law Research Paper No. 2755628. https://papers.ssrn.com/sol3/papers.cfm?abstract_id=2755628
US Copyright Office. (n.d.). *Register your work: Registration portal*. Retrieved August 27, 2024, from https://www.copyright.gov/registration/
Vimeo. (2024, July 8). *Vimeo terms of service*. https://vimeo.com/terms
Zimmerman, D. L. (2014). Copyright and social media: A tale of legislative abdication. *Pace Law Review, 35*(1), 260–284.

Chapter 6
Conclusion

Abstract In the preceding chapters, automated copyright filtering has been examined from a law and economics perspective. This conclusion summarises the main contributions to the literature pertaining to the implications of automated filtering for the objectives of copyright policy, the design of automated filtering, and regulatory approaches. It also identifies relevant open questions to provide starting points for future research.

Applauded by some as the rescuer of the content industries, dreaded by others as an attacker on the free participative web culture, automated filtering clearly is a controversial issue. Despite an intense debate on the topic, economic analyses of the effects of automated filtering and the trade-offs involved in designing and regulating it are rare.

To contribute to filling this gap, this book addressed three pressing yet open research questions. This chapter summarises the main contributions to the literature (Sect. 6.1) and identifies starting points for future research (Sect. 6.2).

6.1 Main Contributions to Literature

This section outlines the main contributions to the literature with respect to the first (Sect. 6.1.1), second (Sect. 6.1.2), and third (Sect. 6.1.3) research question.

6.1.1 Impact of Automated Filtering on Goals of Copyright Policy

The first research question focusses on the effect of automated filtering on the key goals pursued by copyright law from an economic perspective, namely, to

O. Englisch, *Automated Copyright Filters*, International Law and Economics,
https://doi.org/10.1007/978-3-031-83161-4_6

incentivise content creation by increasing right holders' profits and to increase the availability of works.

> **Research Question 1**
> How does automated filtering affect right holders' profits and the number of works uploaded to a user-uploaded content platform when right holders compete with unlawful copiers for views?

To answer this question, Chap. 3 constructed a novel economic model of the interaction between right holders and unlawful uploaders through a platform. It thereby provides a new perspective on how automated filtering influences the goals of copyright policy.

The model draws attention to an unexplored mechanism through which automated filtering increases right holders' profits and thereby their incentives to create content: the competition between right holders and unlawful uploaders for views. Unlike the mechanism considered so far, namely, an improvement of right holders' bargaining position vis-à-vis platforms, this mechanism does not require the blocking of all unlawful upload attempts to increase right holders' profits. It is thus possible to further the goal of incentivising content creation with more cautiously designed filters, which are less likely to block lawful content. This insight is important for discussions on how automated filtering should be designed and on whether its use is socially desirable.

Moreover, the analysis uncovers an unexplored effect of automated filtering on the availability of works on a platform. It shows that automated filtering induces right holders to refrain from uploading certain types of works that they would upload if the platform did not filter. This effect counteracts the effect that by increasing right holders' profits and thereby incentives to create, automated filtering leads to more works being produced and thus uploaded. The identified effect must be considered in analyses dealing with the desirability of automated filtering. Likewise, it must be taken into account in discussions on platforms' private costs of filtering because the variety of works a platform offers influences its attractiveness to viewers.

The model further demonstrates the relevance of the concentration of the market for uploading unlawful copies in terms of right holders' competitive behaviour and profits. Counterintuitively, in certain circumstances, a higher concentration can induce right holders to make less effort to pre-empt unlawful uploads. Right holders then earn higher profits than if the market were less concentrated. The upshot is that other measures to disincentivise unlawful uploading, for example, sanctioning unlawful uploaders or awareness campaigns, can increase right holders' profits even if they cannot ensure that no unlawful uploads of a work appear on a platform. This result is important for evaluations of such measures.

Furthermore, the analysis explores a design choice of platforms that has not yet been examined. It demonstrates that the average strictness of a filter needed to maximise right holders' profits is lower (and thus fewer false positives are produced) if a platform varies the strictness of the filter based on the popularity of the potentially infringed work than if it filters homogenously. This result carries relevance for the design of liability regimes. Specifically, policies that discourage platforms from differentiating between upload attempts, for example, exact rules on the strictness of filters or statutory damages in case of liability, would limit their leeway to design automated filtering in ways that reduce the risk of false positives.

Finally, the analysis shows that conclusions from the availability of unlawful uploads on a platform on the effectiveness of a filter cannot readily be drawn: The absence of unlawful uploads may not only be the result of successful filtering but also of right holders' activities to pre-empt unlawful uploading. This insight must be considered when designing empirical studies on automated filtering and when interpreting their results. It adds to other challenges in terms of answering important questions regarding the most efficient design of automated filtering and thus further dampens the hope that clear answers to these questions will become available in the near future. The upshot in terms of regulation is that instead of stipulating performance targets or a specific design, it is more promising to rely on the distributed knowledge of the relevant actors.

6.1.2 Design of Automated Filtering

The second research question is based on the observation that state-of-the-art filters cannot distinguish copyright-infringing from non-infringing upload attempts with perfect accuracy. It focusses on efficient error avoidance.

Research Question 2
What design of automated filtering best approaches efficient error avoidance?

To address this question, Chap. 4 conducted the first comprehensive and in-depth analysis of why automated filters produce errors and what conclusions in terms of efficient error avoidance can be drawn. It thereby helps to better understand the strengths and weaknesses of possible design choices.

The analysis lends support to the proposition by some commentators that a central reference database that can be accessed by all platforms and external providers of filtering technology should be established. It further identifies unexplored features of such a reference database that help to reduce right holders' costs of providing the relevant information, for example, automated calculations of end dates of protection for different countries, automated screening for overlapping entries, and a time-saving communication channel for uploaders and right holders. These findings point to shortcomings of the current legal situation in the US and the EU.

Moreover, the analysis stresses the importance of two sources of errors that have received little to no attention so far. Existing discussions on how to avoid errors mostly focus on the analysis of upload attempts as such. This focus is too narrow as the accuracy of the reference database and multi-jurisdictional platform operation are also crucial. Regarding the reference database, the analysis shows that the responsibility for preventing deficiencies should rest with right holders. When striving for efficient error avoidance, it is thus important to also reflect on measures to improve right holders' incentives.

Regarding multi-jurisdictional platform operation, it is argued that cooperation between countries can only be expected to a limited extent and that therefore inefficiencies in terms of fragmentation are inevitable. However, not all inefficiencies result from a reflection of national differences. Uncertainties about the effects of automated filtering and the trade-offs involved in designing and regulating it also cause inefficiencies. This consideration provides an additional motivation for future research.

The analysis further highlights that for key questions regarding the most efficient design of automated filtering, conclusive answers cannot yet be given. It is thus important for platforms to experiment with different approaches, track and disclose probabilities of errors, and disclose filtering designs. As a consequence, to maintain sufficient leeway for experimentation, a policymaker, again, should not prescribe a specific design but instead focus on right holders' and platforms' incentives.

Finally, the analysis points to benefits of automated filtering that received little attention so far. Besides for blocking upload attempts, the information collected by filters can also be used to notify right holders of potentially infringing uploads that have not been blocked (thereby reducing their costs of using notice-and-takedown systems) and to improve the selection of upload attempts that are submitted to a manual review. These additional benefits must be considered in discussions on whether automated filtering is socially desirable.

6.1.3 Regulatory Approaches to Automated Filtering

The third research question focusses on the incentives of actors who make decisions that are crucial for the design of automated filtering, namely, right holders and platforms.

Research Question 3
How can a policymaker best steer right holders' and user-uploaded content platforms' incentives to design automated filtering towards efficiency?

To answer this question, Chap. 5 conducted the first comprehensive and in-depth analysis of how right holders' and platforms' incentives in terms of error avoidance in the absence of regulation deviate from social desirability and what policy responses most efficiently improve their incentives. It thereby provides a new perspective on the suitability and side effects of various proposals on how to govern automated filtering.

The analysis demonstrates that in the absence of regulation, right holders have excessive incentives to prevent unlawful upload attempts and deficient incentives to prevent false positives. It suggests that right holders' incentives can most efficiently be improved by introducing a liability rule under which they must pay damages for false positives caused by deficiencies of the reference database if they behaved negligently. However, neither US nor EU law currently provides such liability.

Moreover, the analysis shows that platforms' incentives without regulation are inefficient. It is unclear whether platforms even have sufficient incentives to filter. If they do, they invest too little. Moreover, platforms have inefficient incentives to take some desirable measures accompanying automated filtering, namely, to track and report performance metrics, disclose filtering policies, set up complaint mechanisms, and inform right holders about upload attempts that exhibit similarity to their works but have not been blocked.

The suggested approach to improve platforms' incentives is to impose minimal requirements that filtering policies must meet for platforms to escape liability for errors caused by the analysis of upload attempts. Such minimal requirements grant platforms considerable leeway on how to design automated filtering. As new learnings are collected, the minimal requirements can be adjusted, thereby reducing platforms' room for manoeuvre. To bring platforms' decisions within the leeway closer to social desirability, they should be obliged to involve representatives of stakeholders in the development of filtering policies. Moreover, platforms should be required to adopt the accompanying measures listed in the previous paragraph. Currently, neither US nor EU law makes sufficient use of these measures to improve platforms' incentives.

6.2 Starting Points for Future Research

The analysis reveals starting points for future research, which can be divided into four categories.

The first category is economic research on copyright protection. A key assumption in this book is the efficiency of existing copyright law. The plausibility of this assumption is doubtful (Sect. 2.1). Indeed, to some extent, the opposition to automated filtering voiced in the literature and the policy debate can be traced back to discontent with substantive copyright law. Future research may help to reduce inefficiencies of substantive copyright law. Moreover, despite existing research, uncertainties in terms of the impact of the on-platform availability of a work on the right holder's off-platform profits (Sect. 3.2.3.1) and in terms of the strength of the effect of right holders' profits on incentives to create remain. Further insights in these regards would contribute to a better understanding of the effects of automated filtering.

Second, several alterations of the model constructed in Chap. 3 are conceivable. In the interest of a focussed analysis, the model treats the per-view price the platform charges to viewers and the per-view reward it pays to uploaders as given. Endogenising the price and the reward promises to generate insights on the impact of an obligation to employ a (stricter) filter on a platform's incentives. In addition, again to keep the analysis focussed, the model assumes that the number of people who view works on a platform is fixed. Incorporating effects of automated filtering on the number of viewers who use the platform into the model would help to understand the long-term strategies right holders and platforms pursue.

Third, little is known about the probabilities of errors associated with different approaches to make automated blocking decisions based on observable variables. Research in this regard would be insightful in terms of determining the most efficient design of automated filtering.

Finally, the discussion of measures to improve right holders' and platforms' incentives can be continued. For the reasons advanced in Sect. 5.4.2.1, this book leaves measures to increase the competitive pressure exerted on platforms aside. Nevertheless, the competitive pressure platforms are exposed to is a promising channel to influence the extent to which they internalise net social costs of false positives. Furthermore, this book does not consider the incentives of private reference database operators. If no public reference database is established, research on how the incentives of private database operators can best be steered towards efficiency would contribute to a more comprehensive understanding of how efficient error avoidance can best be approached.

By providing valuable insights on the effects of automated filtering and on the trade-offs associated with its design and regulation, exploring the aforementioned aspects would further advance the fascinating field of research to which this book contributes.